About the edif ...

Tim Allen is professor of development anthropology at the
London School of Economics and Political Science. He has
carried out long-term field research in Sudan and Uganda,
and has also researched in several other African countries,
including Ghana, Zimbabwe, Kenya, Tanzania and Bots-
wana. His books include *Trial Justice: The International
Criminal Court and the Lord's Resistance Army*, *Complex
Emergencies and Humanitarian Responses* (with Mareike
Schomerus) and *Poverty and Development* (edited with Alan
Thomas). In addition to academic work, he has worked as a
consultant with UNDP, UNICEF, UNRISD, MSF, LWF, Save
the Children, World Vision, DfID and many others, and has
presented or contributed to numerous radio programmes
for the Open University and the BBC.

Koen Vlassenroot is a professor of political science at the
University of Ghent, where he also coordinates the Conflict
Research Group. He is also the director of the Central Africa
Programme of Egmont, the Royal Institute for International
Relations in Brussels. He has carried out research in the
Great Lakes region for more than ten years, with a particular focus on militia formation, land issues, trans-border
dynamics and rebel governance in eastern DR Congo and
northern Uganda. He has published widely in international
peer-reviewed journals and has written numerous book
chapters.

1 Joseph Kony and one of his surviving senior commanders, Okot Odhiambo, posing for photographs in Ri-Kwangba. This picture was taken on 12 June 2006, shortly after Kony finished his sit-down television interview (see Chapter 6). Seated below are Ben Achellam (left) and Santo Alit. Achellam was reportedly killed as an ally of Vincent Otti in the LRA leadership struggle in autumn 2008. Alit was reportedly killed in autumn 2009 in the Central African Republic, where he had been part of Kony's protection group. Alit had briefly been in Juba as part of the official LRA delegation to the Juba peace talks (Mareike Schomerus).

The Lord's Resistance Army
myth and reality

edited by Tim Allen and
Koen Vlassenroot

Zed Books
LONDON | NEW YORK

The Lord's Resistance Army: Myth and Reality was first published in 2010 by Zed Books Ltd, 7 Cynthia Street, London N1 9JF, UK and Room 400, 175 Fifth Avenue, New York, NY 10010, USA

www.zedbooks.co.uk

Editorial copyright © Tim Allen and Koen Vlassenroot 2010
Copyright in this collection © Zed Books 2010

The rights of Tim Allen and Koen Vlassenroot to be identified as the editors of this work have been asserted by them in accordance with the Copyright, Designs and Patents Act, 1988

Set in OurType Arnhem and Futura Bold by Ewan Smith, London
Index ed.emery@thefreeuniversity.net
Cover design www.alice-marwick.co.uk
Printed and bound in Great Britain by CPI Antony Rowe, Chippenham and Eastbourne

MIX
Paper from
responsible sources
FSC
www.fsc.org   FSC® C013604

Distributed in the USA exclusively by Palgrave Macmillan, a division of St Martin's Press, LLC, 175 Fifth Avenue, New York, NY 10010, USA

A catalogue record for this book is available from the British Library
Library of Congress Cataloging in Publication Data available

ISBN 978 1 84813 562 8 hb
ISBN 978 1 84813 563 5 pb
ISBN 978 1 84813 564 2 eb

Contents

Table and figures

Table

Figures

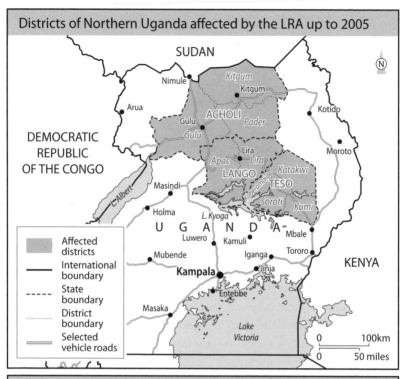

Districts of Northern Uganda affected by the LRA up to 2005

| Affected districts |
| International boundary |
| State boundary |
| District boundary |
| Selected vehicle roads |

Internally displaced persons (IDPs) receiving relief assistance

DISTRICT	DATES	IDP POPULATION	NUMBER OF IDP CAMPS
with predominantly Acholi population			
GULU	July 2005	460,226	53
KITGUM	July 2005	310,111	22
PADER	April 2005	283,781	26
with predominantly Langi population			
APAC	July 2005	98,193	15
LIRA	July 2005	350,828	40
with predominantly Teso population			
KATAKWI	April 2005	approx 140,000	82
SOROTI, KUMI & KABERAMAIDO	July 2005	18,000	22
TOTAL IDPs	**April–July 2005**	**approx 1.5m** (excluding unregistered IDPs)	**250**

Source: OCHA estimates, 2005

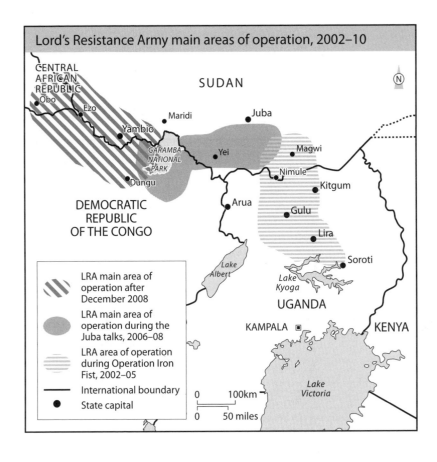

Lord's Resistance Army main areas of operation, 2002–10

CENTRAL AFRICAN REPUBLIC
Obo
Ezo
Yambio
Maridi
SUDAN
Juba
Yei
Magwi
GARAMBA NATIONAL PARK
Nimule
Dungu
Kitgum
DEMOCRATIC REPUBLIC OF THE CONGO
Arua
Gulu
Lira
Soroti
Lake Albert
Lake Kyoga
UGANDA
KAMPALA
KENYA
Lake Victoria

LRA main area of operation after December 2008

LRA main area of operation during the Juba talks, 2006–08

LRA area of operation during Operation Iron Fist, 2002–05

International boundary

State capital

0   100km
0   50 miles

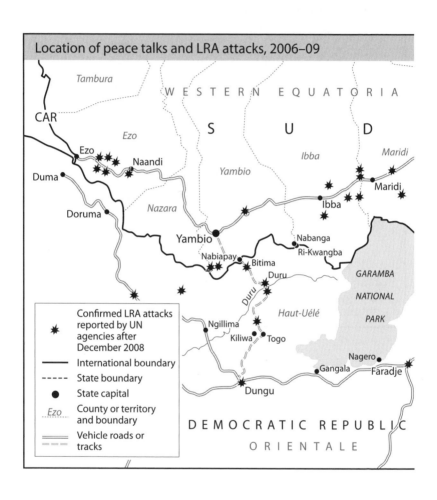

Location of peace talks and LRA attacks, 2006–09

Tambura

W E S T E R N   E Q U A T O R I A

CAR

S   U   D

Ezo

Ezo
Naandi

Ibba

Maridi

Duma

Yambio

Maridi

Ibba

Doruma

Nazara

Yambio

Nabanga
Ri-Kwangba

Nabiapay
Bitima
Duru

GARAMBA

Duru

NATIONAL

Haut-Uélé

PARK

Confirmed LRA attacks
reported by UN
agencies after
December 2008

Ngillima

Kiliwa
Togo

International boundary

Nagero
Gangala
Faradje

State boundary

State capital

Dungu

Ezo   County or territory
        and boundary

D E M O C R A T I C   R E P U B L I C

Vehicle roads or
tracks

O R I E N T A L E

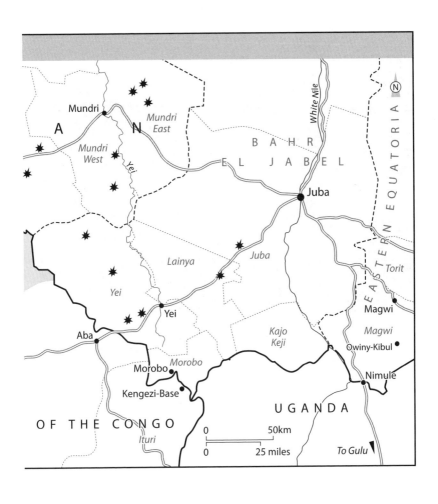

2 Two young LRA guerrillas take basic commodities and utensils back
to their hideout in the DRC's Garamba jungle. Although the goods carry
the UNICEF logo they were supplied on a second-hand basis through the
Government of Southern Sudan, 30 July 2006 (Adam Pletts).

Introduction

TIM ALLEN AND KOEN VLASSENROOT

Towards the end of 2008 rumours were circulating in northern Uganda and southern Sudan that a high-quality military strike against the Lord's Resistance Army (LRA) was imminent. The United States African Command (AFRICOM) was providing intelligence, fuel and equipment to the Ugandan army, and more than a dozen US military advisers and analysts were on the ground. They could be found in bars boasting that a surgical strike against Joseph Kony and his senior commanders was straightforward. Everything was ready to go. It was just a question of 'pushing the button'. Keeping preparations secret was clearly not part of the plan.

The button was pushed on 14 December 2008. Collaborating with the armies of the Democratic Republic of Congo (DRC) and southern Sudan, and assisted by the USA, the Ugandan People's Defence Force (UPDF) launched Operation Lightning Thunder. This was an attack on the LRA in Garamba National Park of the DRC, just across the border from Sudan. Here Kony was known to have a base, a few days' walk from Ri-Kwangba, where he had occasionally turned up to meet with various peace negotiators since 2006. Surgical air strikes were the precursor of a land offensive. This would surely be the end of the LRA once and for all.

Almost immediately after the initial aerial onslaught, Uganda's president, Yoweri Museveni, proclaimed a military success. But it was not the first time he had suggested that the LRA problem had been resolved, and others were less convinced. In typically combative style, Andrew Mwenda, the well-known Ugandan journalist, observed that the attack 'was certainly the right thing to do' but it was 'was ill-timed, poorly planned and incompetently executed'.[1] When the land forces arrived on the scene, Kony and his senior commanders had already escaped. In another article based on interviews with seven Ugandan generals, Mwenda went on to suggest that the UPDF and its allies were not adequately resourced to be able to hunt for Kony in the dense forests, where his forces were so adept at guerrilla tactics. Already the LRA had managed to move behind the UPDF front line, and was attacking the

1

local population around Mundri, deep in southern Sudan. As one of the generals interviewed by Mwenda observed:

> Remember that LRA has 20 years' experience in this kind of warfare [...] They have learnt how to survive under such conditions. Thus, regardless of our moral assessment of Kony, we need to recognise that he is an excellent strategist and tactician. Otherwise we would have defeated him long ago like we did with other rebellions.[2]

More than a year later, Kony remains at large. There are reports that the LRA have been resupplied by air drops from their allies in Khartoum, that they have become engaged in the Darfur conflict, and that they are key players in schemes aimed at undermining the Comprehensive Peace Agreement between north and south Sudan. Hard evidence for such assertions is absent, but there are no doubts about the abductions and killings. Accounts of lips being cut off or padlocked among the Azande people of the most affected region are the stuff of nightmares. Kony may no longer be terrorizing his own Acholi neighbours in northern Uganda, but he has reasserted his capacity to spread fear and skilfully wage a guerrilla campaign. No one knows how many veteran combatants are still with him – perhaps just a couple of hundred. But he understands very well how to punch above his weight.

Andrew Mwenda and the other authors of this book met each other before these recent events. In March 2007 a workshop was convened in London to which were invited almost all the main analysts of the LRA. The prosecutor of the International Criminal Court, Luis Mareno-Ocampo, was also present. It was not a homogeneous group, and participants came at issues from very diverse perspectives, leading to some vigorous exchanges. Over the past three years, we have remained engaged with what has been happening, following closely the negotiations that took place in southern Sudan, and carrying out further fieldwork. Since the London meeting, several of us have collaborated in research, and we have all been in regular contact. It would be fair to say that a greater degree of consensus has emerged between us than might have been anticipated. We have learned to listen to each other, and to an extent we have moved on as a group. Our collective aim in the chapters that follow has been to dig beneath the surface of the LRA war, to pool our understandings of specific places and incidents and glean a better understanding of what has occurred. This has seemed especially important given the far-reaching implications of events in both northern Uganda and southern Sudan. It has also been an appropriate endeavour given the emphasis on underlying causes of conflict in the peace agreement that Kony has refused to sign. All of us have felt too an urgent need to counter prevalent myths.

With a few notable exceptions, international news reporters have been interested in telling adventure stories about their attempts to interview Kony; or have tended to concentrate on the more bizarre aspects of both the war and the peace negotiations; or focus on specific issues – such as the hundreds of children who used to migrate into Gulu (the biggest town in the war zone) in the evenings, where they could be easily filmed and interviewed. Few have seriously investigated how and why events have occurred. Often their news stories have been collected from talks with aid workers and local activists, some of whom may have been insightful, but who have had their own agendas associated with fund-raising for particular projects. Such problems with information-gathering in war zones are hardly unique to northern Uganda, but they have been compounded by attitudes in the Kampala-based Ugandan media, which have tended to reflect prevalent attitudes in the south towards an allegedly barbaric north, and by the political uses made of the LRA war by President Museveni and his government officials. By the end of the 1990s one of the worst humanitarian disasters in the world was occurring, but information about it was partial, superficial and intermittent. Subsequently, international awareness and concern increased, but a great deal of what was reported remained misleading. It was just too easy to represent the horror of it all in terms of 'heart of darkness' stereotypes. More thoughtful analyses were overlooked, while ignorance of the classic earlier studies of the region has been the norm.

Although several of our chapter authors provide information on the history of the LRA and the war in northern Uganda, they assume a degree of familiarity with events. For that reason, in the subsections below, we provide a general introductory outline mainly aimed at readers unfamiliar with the region. Obviously there are different ways of telling this story. Here we keep interpretations to a minimum and try to present an uncontroversial narrative of what has happened. When appropriate, we highlight where themes and events are discussed in more detail later in the book.

Historical background on the Uganda/Sudan border

To begin with, it is important to note that war and mass forced displacements on the Uganda/Sudan border have a history that goes back well before the establishment of the LRA. The lands on both banks of the Nile were devastated from the 1850s by armed traders and adventurers arriving from the north. Their incursions were financed by the ivory trade, and there was a need for large-scale abductions of young men as porters and soldiers, and young women as cooks and concubines. By the 1870s, the devastation was on a huge scale in local terms. The situation was then complicated further by the arrival of hundreds of 'Nubi' soldiers, who were sent to the region to secure it for the Khedive of Egypt. Towards the end of the century the region was also affected by newly introduced bovine and human diseases, leading to further migrations and changes in livelihood patterns. Upheavals continued after the turn of the twentieth century, until a degree of stability was imposed by the Ugandan Protectorate and Anglo-Egyptian Condominium of the Sudan before and during the First World War.

On both sides of the border, local chiefs were appointed as agents, and where they did not exist, chiefs were created to fulfil this purpose. The British officers also used sleeping sickness control programmes to move populations and concentrate them for administrative convenience. It was in this way that the Acholi, the 'tribe' of Joseph Kony, and other 'tribes' of the borderlands, were divided into separate groups. The name Acholi may have been derived by British officials from the word for 'black' in the Lwo language (a language, or rather a cluster of languages, also spoken by other Ugandan groups which came to be classified as belonging to different 'tribes', such as the Langi and Alur). This does not mean that ethnic identities were absent before the establishment of British administration. One of the authors of this book, Ron Atkinson, has used oral histories to trace events back into the past and has sought to show that the population groups 'gazetted' as tribes by the British had existed in some form for a long time (see Atkinson 1999). That may be the case, but there is no doubt that the institutionalizing of indirect rule helped forge identities that became much less fluid than hitherto. These points are important, because interpreting the Acholi past, and making assertions about the nature of Acholi society, has been an important aspect of LRA ideology and also of the responses to the war among influential religious, cultural and political leaders. The debates are taken up by several chapter authors, including Allen, Branch and Finnström.

Under British rule, there were fifty years of relative peace on both sides of the border, but systems of indirect rule using gazetted local languages tended to institutionalize divisions, and give them an ethnic/tribal character. In Sudan this was compounded by the Southern Policy, effectively introduced in the 1920s and formalized in 1930, which meant that the predominantly non-Muslim southern Sudan had a separate administration from that of the largely Muslim north. Up until the late

1940s, British officials had not been fully committed to the long-term administration of the south as part of Sudan. When it became clear that independence was going to be rushed through in the mid-1950s, sudden efforts were made to promote 'Sudanization', but caused considerable resentment, especially among the Christian educated elite. In 1955, a few months before formal independence in 1956, some army garrisons in the south mutinied. This is generally taken to be the start of Sudan's first civil war, although the fighting intensified only in the mid-1960s. It is sometimes referred to as the Anyanya war, after the colloquial name given to the southern rebel forces. The fighting dragged on until the Addis Ababa Agreement of 1972 brought a decade of uneasy peace in most of the country.

War in the south broke out again, however, in 1983. This was partly due to a decision by the northern government to set aside the arrangements that had been put in place for southern regional autonomy. Other factors were concerns in the south about a proposed imposition of Islamic law from Khartoum, and also the bitter political divisions that had arisen between southern political factions. The social upheavals of the second war proved to be extreme, with much of the fighting being waged by militia groups. A difference from the first war was that the main southern military force, the Sudan People's Liberation Army (SPLA), led by John Garang, formed alliances with groups in northern Sudan and claimed not to be campaigning for secession. The war continued until January 2005, when a Comprehensive Peace Agreement (CPA) was signed between the SPLA and the Khartoum government. John Garang then became the vice-president of Sudan. His death in a helicopter crash in July 2005 at first raised fears that the CPA would collapse, but there was a relatively smooth transition to his second-in-command, Salva Kiir.[3]

A specific consequence of Garang's death which should also be noted is that Riek Machar became vice-president of southern Sudan. He had broken with John Garang in 1991 and collaborated with the Khartoum government for a period before returning to Garang's faction of the SPLA in 2002. While acting effectively as a militia commander of Khartoum, he had made contact with the LRA, and had helped recruit them to fight against the SPLA. This subsequently proved significant in the efforts to secure a peace arrangement between the LRA and the Ugandan government between 2005 and 2008, because he was able to position himself as the chief mediator. A full discussion of those peace negotiations can be found in Part Three of this book.

In early 2010, the CPA remains in place, despite numerous violations and continuing insecurity in some areas. A major complicating factor has been the warrant issued by the International Criminal Court (ICC) for President Omar Hassan al-Bashir, Sudan's head of state. The possibility of that happening was made public in mid-2008 by the office of the ICC prosecutor, on the basis of evidence that Bashir may be personally responsible for genocide, war crimes and/or crimes against humanity in Darfur. In the event, judges in a pre-trial chamber of the court found that evidence of genocide was not strong enough to issue a warrant; there was, however, sufficient evidence to issue a warrant for war crimes and crimes against humanity. A warrant citing these crimes was issued by the ICC on 4 March 2009. Assuming the CPA survives, there is supposed to be a referendum in 2011, which will decide if southern Sudan formally secedes from Sudan and becomes an independent country. As noted, that was not what John Garang said that he wanted, but research in southern Sudan carried out in 2009 indicated that a demand for secession will indeed be the result if there is a free vote.[4]

Uganda after independence

Events in Uganda, during and after independence, are analysed in the chapter by Adam Branch, so only a brief outline is given here. In Uganda, an important effect of the indirect protectorate administration was a division of the territory between the Bantu-speaking kingdoms of the south and the Nilotic- and Sudanic-speaking peoples of the north. It is a legacy that remains an impediment to the development of an integrated Ugandan nation. After independence, the first head of state was Milton Obote, who was a Lango, one of the 'tribes' that speaks a Lwo language. In 1971, Obote was overthrown in a coup, led by his army commander, Idi Amin. Amin was a Muslim who came from the northwest part of the country. One of his first acts was to murder Langi and Acholi soldiers in the army. Initially he received considerable popular support in the south as well as from his home region, but this evaporated as the incompetence and brutality of his regime became increasingly apparent.

Amin was overthrown in 1979 following an invasion from Tanzania and, as a result of what are generally agreed to have been flawed elections, Obote was returned to power. Some of those who had opposed Amin were unwilling to accept this outcome, including Yuweri Museveni. During the early 1980s, Museveni waged a guerrilla campaign against the government with support from his own region in the south-west and from the central south of the country, where there was widespread antipathy to what was perceived as northern domination. Much of the fighting between Museveni's National Resistance Army (NRA) and the government's Uganda National Liberation Army (UNLA) was concentrated in the territory around the town of Luwero, north of Kampala. Obote also faced armed opposition in Amin's home area in the north-west.

The UNLA response to these insurgencies differed. In the north-west, a large part of the population was effectively forced out of the country and became refugees. Many ended up in discrete refugee settlements in southern Sudan and Zaire (now DRC). In Luwero, however, there was no border near by. Caught between the warring factions, local people were forced into camps, and found themselves at the receiving end of the UNLA soldiers' frustrations. An estimated 300,000 were killed, supposedly for collaboration with the NRA. The UNLA was nominally the national army, but northerners made up a large part of it, predominantly (although by no means exclusively) from the Langi and Acholi 'tribes'.

Eventually tensions opened up between the Acholi and Langi troops. The former complained they were usually the ones deployed to dangerous locations. In 1985, Acholi soldiers seized power, and Tito Okello became president. He immediately started negotiations with Museveni and a peace agreement was signed in Nairobi. But the NRA proceeded to ignore it, and marched on Kampala – a source of deep-seated grievance among some Acholi, who claim that it shows President Museveni cannot be trusted, and has never really wanted peaceful reconciliation.[5]

The Holy Spirit Movement

After their defeat in the south, many of the Acholi soldiers in the UNLA chose to move into Sudan to regroup. They were able to do this partly because there was an Acholi population in Sudan and their arrival was not altogether unwelcome. Many Sudanese Acholi were opposed to the SPLA, perceiving it to be dominated by Dinka and other groups living to the north of their home area, so they joined or supported the Equatorian Defence Force (EDF), a militia resourced by the Sudan government. Acholi veterans from Uganda were a useful source of reinforcement. Meanwhile, Museveni's forces asserted control over the Acholi areas of Uganda, but just as in Luwero, experiences of persecution by the new government's soldiers helped create a fertile base for guerrilla activity. Initially the most important group resisting the NRA was the Uganda People's Democratic Army (UPDA). This was an entirely secular force, largely made up of former UNLA soldiers. It was also at this point, however, that spirit mediums began to play a significant role in the violence.

As in other parts of Africa, possession of individuals by ghosts or other metaphysical forces had become common. Partly as a consequence of dramatic social changes, local understandings about communication with the spirit world had expanded in ways that helped make sense of what was happening. They had also been profoundly affected by the introduction of Pentecostal Christianity. Numerous healers would mix Christian and local ideas in their seances, and some had considerable influence in their neighbourhoods. Among the Acholi people they were called *ajwaki*, or sometimes *nebi* – the Swahili word for prophet. One such figure was a young woman called Alice Auma. She had become possessed by various spirits, including one known as Lakwena – the Messenger.

In the upheavals that followed the victory for Museveni's forces in 1986, Alice's cult rapidly grew in importance. She performed healing rituals for UNLA soldiers after their retreat from the south, and her spirits offered an interpretation of their defeat by the NRA that seemed compelling to many. She was able to remove *cen* – the dangerous and polluting emanations of those who had been killed. She also explained that war is a form of healing through which people could be purified. The healing is on both sides, as those that die are like the rotten flesh cut out by a surgeon. The pure, on the other hand, could not be killed.

According to Alice herself, her direct involvement in war started on 20 August 1986. She claimed that the NRA soldiers kidnapped many young people of her age in the neighbourhood and imprisoned them at the barracks in Gulu town. Their relatives begged her for help, and her spirits told her to recruit soldiers. With the support of 150 former UNLA veterans and forty guns, she is said to have liberated the prisoners without killing or wounding anyone. This was the start of her campaign against President Museveni's government, witches, other *nebi* and *ajwaki* and 'bad people', such as impure soldiers or individuals who did not obey certain rules. Her movement came to be known as the Holy Spirit Movement or the Holy Spirit Mobile Forces (HSMF), but to what extent this was originally her own term is unclear. In the Acholi Bible, the term used for the Third Person of the Trinity is *Tipu Maleng*, but in other contexts this term can mean 'clean spirit' or 'clean spirits'. It could be that it was journalists reporting on the movement who introduced the explicit association with Christianity. Alice herself does not seem to have asserted that the Lakwena or any of her other spirits were the Holy Ghost. She nevertheless embraced the idea, perhaps because she and her commanders were eager listeners to the BBC World Service, which during periods of 1986 and 1987 was reporting daily on the HSMF's activities.

Alice's movement proved to be surprisingly effective. At the end of 1986 she claimed to have had 18,000 'soldiers'. She prayed with her followers at special sites called 'yards', and anointed them in oil, promising that if they lived their lives according to rules, bullets would not penetrate them. Among many other things, 'purity' included abstaining from sexual intercourse and alcohol. Soldiers in the NRA were confronted by scores of partly naked, glistening men and women marching towards them, some holding Bibles, others throwing magical objects, and a few wielding guns. In several encounters they seem to have been terrified or just did not know what to do. Initially, most ran away. Such early successes brought more and more recruits, with many former UNLA and UPDA soldiers joining her. In October 1987, she left Acholiland with several thousand followers, and led them south in a marauding crusade, overwhelming opposition on the way. They were finally defeated in the swamps to the east of Iganga, some eighty miles from Kampala. Alice escaped on a bicycle, and lived in a refugee camp in Kenya until her death in 2007. She claimed that she abandoned her followers when they revealed impure tendencies during the march south.[6]

Joseph Kony and the Lord's Resistance Army

Back in the Acholi homeland, the UPDA continued its campaign from bases across the border in Sudan until it was drawn into negotiations. Most of its members surrendered to the Ugandan government in 1988, but not all were prepared to accept the terms on offer. They joined a number of other groups, all of which were associated with men who were inspired by Alice Lakwena's example, including a group led by Alice's father, Severino Lokoya, until his capture in 1989, and another led by a young man called Joseph Kony.[7]

It is often claimed that Kony is Alice's 'cousin', or that they are from the same clan (*kaka*). Alice's father was a Madi migrant, however, so the patrilineal connection is not as close as has sometimes been suggested. According to some informants from his home village, they shared a grandfather on their mothers' side. Born in the early 1960s, Kony dropped out of school after six years of primary education and trained as an *ajwaka*. At the time the Holy Spirit Movement was active, Kony was possessed by several ghosts. In some accounts he claimed to have also been seized by 'the Lakwena' as well as by the spirit of Juma Oris, a former minister in Idi Amin's regime (whom Kony subsequently met in Sudan). Alice was mainly operating near Kitgum so Kony began recruiting soldiers and other followers near Gulu. He is said to have tried to form an alliance with Alice, but she rejected him. Kony was apparently humiliated and his followers attacked and killed some of hers.

Kony's early campaign was limited to the vicinity of his home. This changed, however, in 1988. In May, when President Museveni's government signed a peace agreement with the UPDA, many of those who were unwilling to surrender turned to Kony, including one of the UPDA's most ruthless and effective commanders, Odong Latek. From this point, Kony largely specialized in healing and divining, while Latek organized the forces. For a while, the group called itself the Uganda People's Democratic Liberation Army. Latek's influence on the movement was considerable, and Kony seems to have learned a great deal about guerrilla tactics. His ally was killed in battle, but by 1990 Kony's force was the only significant armed unit still fighting in the Acholi homelands. It was after Latek's death that Kony renamed the movement again, calling it the Lord's Resistance Army (LRA).

Continuing to work with a fairly small group, Kony's forces maintained a guerrilla campaign against the government and, increasingly, against anyone who collaborated with it. The size of the LRA is a matter of speculation. One estimate from 1997 suggests as many as three to four thousand combatants. Others were much lower. The confusion arose partly because the size of the LRA fluctuated and also because its main bases were located in Sudan. The number of guerrillas actually operating in northern Uganda at any one time was rarely more than a few hundred. Large numbers were not necessary, because they rarely engaged in pitched battles with government forces, but used terror tactics to maximum effect.

Like Alice, Kony claimed that Acholi society had to be purified by violence, but he has been much more prone to specifically targeting non-combatants, and his forces have specialized in performing shocking atrocities on a few individuals, spreading fear in the population as a whole. The LRA also became associated with forced recruitment or abductions, often of children. Over the years thousands of people have been incorporated into the movement in this way, mainly from Acholi areas, but also from Langi, Madi and Teso, and more recently from areas in Sudan, Congo and the Central African Republic. Some have been forced to perform atrocious acts, such as killing relatives, as part of their initiation. The spiritual aspects of the LRA, the group's political agenda and its military strategies are discussed in several chapters of this book, notably those by Titeca, Branch, Finnström, and Blattman and Annan. In addition, Joseph Kony comments on them himself in his conversation with Mareike Schomerus, presented and discussed in Chapter 6.

Anti-insurgency and talks 1988–96

The Ugandan government's response to the LRA has shifted back and forth between negotiation and military offensives. From the time of the peace agreement with the UPDA in 1988, President Museveni, in particular, has persistently tried to downplay what has been happening. It seems to have been hard to accept that a spirit cult without a clearly articulated political agenda – or at least a very strange one – could sustain resistance against the well-organized and well-trained NRA. From the late 1980s, the war should have been over, and indeed the government frequently claimed that it was. President Museveni's confidence that the northern problem was basically solved is reflected in the appointment in 1988 of Betty Bigombe as Minister of State for Pacification of Northern Uganda, resident in Gulu.

In 1991, irritated by the continuing insurgency, an intensive four-month military operation was mounted called Operation North, the main effect of which seems to have been to antagonize and alienate non-combatants. Betty Bigombe attempted to walk a middle path, trying to keep the door open for negotiation and restrict the NRA's depredations, but also introducing some vigorous anti-insurgency measures – such as arming community defence groups called 'arrow brigades'. The LRA's response was ever more violent. Hundreds of people thought to be government collaborators were maimed or killed. LRA 'punishments' included the amputation of limbs and the cutting of lips, noses and ears. The NRA seemed reluctant to provide protection, and Bigombe's lightly armed 'arrow brigades' were especially vulnerable. Thousands of people sought refuge in the towns.

Nevertheless, in 1994 Bigombe's strategy of keeping a certain distance from all interest groups but being willing to talk to anyone seemed to pay off, and she managed to engage the LRA in discussions about peace. These seemed promising. She went out into the bush without any protection for negotiations. Most of those who went with her on the first occasion were so terrified by the experience that they refused to go again. In the course of four more meetings with Kony, she arranged an uneasy ceasefire, and LRA soldiers were even able to visit and stay at some of the trading centres. It looked as if there was a real prospect of a peace agreement. President Museveni's attitude to the talks was not very enthusiastic, however, and at a political rally in February 1994 he issued an ultimatum to the rebels. The LRA were given seven days to put down their weapons and turn themselves over to government forces. Within three days of the announcement, the killing resumed.

President Museveni has claimed that he had received military intelligence showing that the LRA were involved in peace negotiations only in order to build up their military capacity, and that they had secured assistance from the government of Sudan. Maybe this is true, but there were additional factors. Although expensive, the war in the north had certain political advantages for his government. The upheavals were contained in a part of the country in which he had no power base. In addition, the horrific violence and weird spirituality of the LRA allowed his government to present the north as a kind of barbaric periphery. He used this to present himself to people in the south as the guarantee that the oppressions of Amin, Obote and Okello would not return. President Museveni himself is from the south-west, and some people in Buganda were eager to replace him with someone else. But who else would protect them from the Acholi and other wild northerners? So it was not necessarily in President Museveni's interests to resolve the war by negotiation, and the much-publicized barbarism of the LRA had its political uses. Also the war in the north kept the army occupied, and benefited many soldiers economically. Certain senior officers are well known to have become relatively wealthy from the situation. These points are discussed in the chapters of this book from different perspectives by Mwenda, Branch and Finnström.

Although there was little enthusiasm for the LRA among the Ugandan Acholi population, it had never depended on mass support, and from the period of the failed peace negotiations, a generous line of assistance was indeed offered from Sudan. The Sudan government had decided to assist the LRA in retaliation for the Ugandan government's barely disguised support for the SPLA. In effect, the LRA became one of the many Sudan government militia through which it waged war in the south by proxy, and from the mid-1990s the LRA became directly engaged in fighting the SPLA on behalf of President Omar Bashir's regime in Khartoum, as well as launching attacks into Uganda against the NRA and unsupportive civilians.[8] For this, a much larger armed force was necessary, and this is one of the reasons why the LRA expanded its policy of abduction. With Sudanese support, the LRA was able to launch some of its most ferocious attacks. One of the worst single incidents occurred in May 1995, when the LRA burned scores of homes and killed almost three hundred people in Atiak, a trading centre just south of a large Ugandan army barracks. As on other occasions, Museveni's soldiers failed to respond until the rebels had already withdrawn

A year after that massacre, the LRA announced a brief ceasefire during the Ugandan presidential elections. They even offered to stop fighting completely if President Museveni lost. In the event he won with a huge majority, although he received few votes in the north. Betty Bigombe had continued to maintain contact with the LRA after the collapse in the peace negotiations in 1994, and there were attempts made by a group of Acholi elders to negotiate at the time of the elections ceasefire, but these failed hopelessly (two elders were murdered by the LRA). Always a controversial figure, Bigombe was dropped from President Museveni's cabinet in June 1996 and promptly withdrew from a bruising by-election campaign with Norbert Mao – who was elected MP and is currently the very influential mayor of Gulu (one of the Acholi districts of Uganda, and the location of the biggest town in the region).

Amnesty and 'Iron Fist'

Bigombe left Gulu and was replaced as minister by Owiny Dollo. Meanwhile Mao, together with a group of other Acholi opposition MPs, campaigned for the Ugandan parliament to formally investigate the situation in the north. There was also lobbying for a blanket amnesty that would cover all Uganda's rebel groups, including the LRA. Overcoming opposition from President Museveni, an Amnesty Act was enacted in January 2000. After prolonged discussion, however, the inquiry into the situation in the north ended up accepting the view that the military option should continue to be pursued. In addition, the Anti-Terrorism Act of 2002 appeared to set limits to the amnesty. Anti-insurgency operations continued, culminating with the 'Iron Fist' offensives.

During the later 1990s, international pressure had increased on President Bashir's government in Sudan. The Clinton administration declared Sudan to be a terrorist state because of the government's alleged role in an assassination attempt on President Mubarak of Egypt, and for providing a base to Osama bin Laden – who was believed to be responsible for the bombings of US embassies in Kenya and Tanzania in 1998. By the end of the decade, President Bashir was trying to build bridges with his neighbours, and was doubtless alarmed by the US missile attack in August 1998 on what was asserted to be a chemical weapons factory in a suburb of Khartoum. In 1999, his government decided to ask former US president Carter to become involved in the hope of normalizing external relations. At this time there had been media coverage of abductions in northern Uganda by the LRA, notably of the 'Aboke girls' – a group of schoolgirls abducted by the LRA from their dormitory at St Mary's College in Lira District in October 1996. The Carter Center set about trying to persuade the Sudanese government to stop supporting the LRA, and managed to broker a deal between

Presidents Bashir and Museveni whereby they agreed to stop supporting cross-border rebel groups (although in practice they continued to do so). International pressure on Sudan was further intensified following the terrorist attacks in the USA on 11 September 2001 and by the inclusion of the LRA in the 'USA Patriot Act Terrorist Exclusion List'. As a consequence the Sudan government was persuaded to give permission for the so-called 'Iron Fist' incursions from Uganda in 2002, and the Ugandan army (now called the Uganda People's Defence Force – UPDF) has had a presence in southern Sudan ever since.

President Museveni himself directed the first Iron Fist campaign from a base in the north. With US logistical support, and using helicopter gunships, an estimated ten thousand Ugandan troops were involved. LRA bases in Sudan were destroyed and hundreds of people killed. Understandably, the Ugandan government called those who died 'rebels', but many were abducted people, including children. Whatever military objectives were attained in Sudan, for northern Uganda Operation Iron Fist proved to be a disaster. Kony and almost all of his senior commanders evaded capture, and as fast as abducted people were killed, captured, freed or escaped, others were taken. The LRA was also able to outflank the UPDF and SPLA forces and expanded their campaign in new territories, including the Lira, Soroti, Apac and Katakwi districts of Uganda.

Forced displacement

One of the Ugandan government's strategies for dealing with the LRA insurgency was to remove the people from rural areas where they might assist the rebels, either out of choice or owing to fear of what would happen to them if they did not. In some cases such removals were violently enforced. By the turn of the 1990s, much of the Acholi population was concentrated near the big towns. From mid-decade, after the collapse of Bigombe's negotiations, a more systematic policy was adopted of moving people into internal displacement (IDP) camps.

Scores of these IDP camps were set up. They were supposed to be protected by small groups of UPDF soldiers and 'local defence units' under UPDF command. Cultivation was almost impossible and movement outside of the camps strictly limited. Food and other commodities were provided by aid agencies, such as the World Food Programme. In effect, by the late 1990s, most of the population in the Acholi parts of Uganda were being kept in rural prisons, often in appalling conditions. Following the expansion of the LRA's activities into neighbouring regions from 2002, the numbers forced to move into such IDP camps rose to extraordinary levels – more than one and a half million people by early 2003. An idea of how dreadful these camps could be can be gleaned from the shocking crude mortality rates (CMRs) recorded in some of them by Médecins Sans Frontières (MSF) and the World Health Organization (WHO). These were of an order that might be anticipated in an extreme emergency.

A consequence of these developments – and also of a rise in international awareness and concern about LRA abductions of children – was growing support for those who had been promoting amnesty as the best way of ending the fighting. Efforts were made to contact the LRA in the bush and to convince them that, if they surrendered, they would not be punished for anything they had done. FM radio programmes broadcast from Gulu were one of the methods used. Not surprisingly the offer was treated with scepticism by LRA commanders, but a system was put in place with aid agency funding for those returning from the LRA to be reintegrated into their communities. By mid-2004, around five thousand adults had passed through this system and had been given amnesty certificates. An increase in the numbers accepting the amnesty was partly the result of the Sudan government agreeing to a second Iron Fist offensive from March 2004. This campaign proved more effective than the first one in terms of forcing the LRA commanders to abandon or release many of their recruits – as well as their own families in some cases.

Towards the end of 2004, most of the central north of Uganda remained insecure, and there continued to be small-scale attacks by LRA groups moving across the Sudan border. Nevertheless, the atrocity in Pagak in May 2004, when a group of women with their babies on their backs were taken out into the nearby bush and had their skulls smashed, was the last major LRA atrocity inside Uganda's borders. The chapter by Christopher Blattman and Jeannie Annan discusses aspects of this period, based on interviews with formerly abducted people.

Referral to the International Criminal Court

One reason for the decline in LRA violence inside Uganda was that a new actor had become involved. At the end of 2003, President Museveni was persuaded to refer the situation in the north of his country to the new International Criminal Court (ICC). This was made public by the ICC prosecutor and President Museveni at a press conference in London. It was going to be the ICC's first big case. In the event, the referral has been very controversial. Some analysts argued that the ICC had been drawn into an error of judgement. President Museveni, they suggested,

15

was using the court to deflect attention away from the illegal activities of the Ugandan army in Congo. It was also pointed out that there have been many allegations of serious crimes carried out by Ugandan government forces in northern Uganda: what was the ICC going to do about those? The ICC prosecutor subsequently tried to assert his independence, stating that all actors in the conflict would be investigated. Nevertheless, an implication of bias has remained, and for many was confirmed by the fact that warrants have been issued only for the LRA commanders.

Another line of criticism related to events on the ground in northern Uganda. Aid agencies expressed concerns that the LRA would be unwilling to release abducted people because they might be used as witnesses. In addition, the ICC referral set new limits on the amnesty process. Indeed, it implied that a blanket amnesty, which included those most responsible for the worst of crimes, could no longer be viable. To many activists this seemed to undermine hopes for a negotiated settlement. The best way forward, it was suggested, was a combination of amnesty and traditional reconciliation. The latter was especially associated with a ritual known as *mato oput* or 'drinking the bitter root'. The heated debates about local justice in the region are discussed in the chapter by Tim Allen.

Louis Moreno-Ocampo, the ICC prosecutor, was present at the workshop in London in which this book's chapter authors participated. He was given a difficult time by some of them, and did his best to clarify and defend his decisions. Generally the Office of the Prosecutor is reluctant to make its internal process too public. Its role, after all, is to put together prosecution cases in the expectation that they will at some point be presented in court with the objective of securing the conviction of the accused. It is therefore not surprising that information is kept secret. We are grateful to the prosecutor for allowing a key member of his team, Matthew Brubacher, who was also present in London, to write a chapter for this book. It provides a view of the ICC prosecution from the inside.

Whatever views are taken about the merits of the ICC intervention, there is no doubt that the arrival of ICC investigators in northern Uganda and publicity about the ICC's role worried the LRA commanders. Some of those who surrendered in late 2004 and 2005 stated that fear of prosecution affected their decision. At the same time the behaviour of the Ugandan security forces improved now that there was external monitoring. Indeed, far from preventing negotiation as had been anticipated, the ICC involvement lent encouragement to them, and, once they started in earnest, helped keep both sides focused on debates being aired at the table. On the one hand, the LRA commanders were concerned about what would happen if they were taken for trial. On the other, Ugandan officials, perhaps belatedly, came to realize that the LRA would have excellent defence counsel, and that they too might end up in the dock.

There had been various low-key communications between LRA commanders and certain local activists in 2003 and early 2004, suggesting that at least some of the LRA commanders were willing to talk. Betty Bigombe was asked to return to Gulu and help mediate in discussions – this time not as a government minister, but with Museveni's blessing as well as support from the UN, local officials and aid agencies. At various points in late 2004 there were indications that she had made headway. A ceasefire was declared by the Ugandan government and kept being extended in the hope that Kony and his senior commanders would accept the amnesty. The main negotiator on the LRA side was Sam Kolo. Vincent Otti, the LRA's second-in-command, was also directly involved, occasionally ringing officials and others concerned about the peace process, both in Uganda and abroad. Kony's involvement in these discussions was always ambiguous, however, and in February 2005 Kolo was rescued by Ugandan armed forces, apparently because he realized Kony had turned against him. Otti continued to talk to people from time to time, including Mareike Schomerus – asking her to visit him and Kony, eventually leading to the meetings she describes in her chapters. But the Bigombe negotiations had reached an impasse and the LRA commanders were exploring other options. Riek Machar, the SPLA commander who had worked with the Sudan government for a time, was now vice-president of southern Sudan. He offered himself as a mediator with the LRA, leading to negotiations in Juba, the capital city of southern Sudan from 2006. These are described from very different perspectives in chapters by Sandrine Perrot, Ronald Atkinson, Simon Simonse et al., and Ronald Iya.

The current situation

In many respects the Juba negotiations were remarkably successful. Overcoming numerous obstacles, a wide range of issues were aired, and the two delegations managed to work out an agreement that recognized the grievances of the people of northern Uganda, and proposed ways forward. What was effectively left to one side was the position of the LRA senior commanders for whom warrants had been issued by the ICC. There was lots of talk about setting the warrants aside, but it became clear that to do so would by no means be straightforward. Kony was also expecting rather more than immunity from prosecution. He expected to be accorded status – just as Riek Machar himself had been, following his period as a militia commander for the Khartoum government. The ICC, for its part, kept a low profile. The prosecutor raised concerns that the LRA was regrouping and possibly rearming in the dense forests of the DRC/Sudan/CAR (Central African Republic) borderlands. Privately there was also the hope within the ICC that the LRA commanders would fall out with each other, and become separated from the LRA rank and file. In October 2007 there seemed to be a prospect of that happening. Kony decided that Otti, his second-in-command, had been making a deal on the side and had him killed. Overall, however, the LRA command structure has proved to be extraordinarily resilient.

Attempts to persuade Kony to sign the Juba agreement continued throughout the following year, and on several occasions there were reports that he was about to do so. But he never did. At the time of writing the last face-to-face meeting with him by peace negotiators was that by the Acholi paramount chief, Rwot Acana, and a group of elders in late November 2008. According to Acana, Kony stated that he would not sign the agreement because he had not been properly informed about it and he had not been made an adequate offer. He wanted the ICC warrants dropped, but also other things, including money and a position in government. He asked for President Museveni's phone number, so that he could negotiate with him directly. An account of this last meeting with Kony can be found in the chapter by Ronald Iya, who was also present.

Throughout most of 2008 the Ugandan army (UPDF) remained in southern Sudan but, although there were reported violations, a cessation of hostilities was just about sustained between the UPDF and the LRA. The LRA attacked the SPLA more than once, however, and started to forcibly recruit in the eastern DRC, the CAR and occasionally in southern Sudan. Following the last meeting with Rwot Acana, the ceasefire was set aside. As noted above, on 14 December a declaration was released to the media that a joint military operation against the LRA – called Operation Lightning Thunder – had commenced.

Although relatively minor incidents had been frequently reported while the peace process in Juba was going on, the LRA had kept a relatively low profile in eastern DRC. But this had changed a few weeks before Rwot Acana's last meeting with Kony. The turning point was a raid against the parish of Duru on 17 September. This resulted in the abduction of 161 pupils, the killing of more than one hundred people and the destruction of local infrastructure.[9] Subsequently, the number of attacks and abductions increased considerably, leading to the displacement of large parts of the population. Neither the Congolese army nor MONUC (Mission de l'Organisation des Nations Unies en RD Congo) were capable of offering much protection. Congolese troops had been deployed to the area around Dungu in July, and in October Operation Rudia was launched, with the aim of isolating the LRA from the Congolese population, but it largely failed. Following an LRA assault on Dungu in November, the Congolese army withdrew and closed their bases. The MONUC base remained, but was no more effective at containing the violence, adding to widespread popular discontent and eventually to the formation of self-defence units.[10]

Operation Lightning Thunder was based on a new security agreement between Uganda, southern Sudan and the DRC. This had actually been negotiated back in June 2008. At the end of August 2008 an agreement had also been concluded between the members of the 'Tripartite-plus-One' Mechanism (including DRC, Rwanda, Uganda and Burundi) to neutralize the LRA. On 15 December 2008, one day after the declaration that a joint regional military operation against the LRA was under way, Ugandan (UPDF) troops entered the DRC and were deployed at the Dungu MONUC camp.[11] It was agreed that the Congolese army would support the UPDF. The southern Sudanese (SPLA) troops would not enter the DRC, but would monitor the Sudanese border closely to prevent the LRA from crossing.

At the start of the operation, LRA camps in Garamba were bombed. Ground troops were meant to arrive soon afterwards, but failed to do so for several days, owing apparently to coordination problems. As a result, the LRA was able to withdraw to safer areas and to split into smaller groups to avoid detection. It also seems to be the case that the UPDF and the SPLA relationship became so strained that the latter turned a blind eye to groups of LRA moving around in places they were supposed to be securing.[12] The LRA's response to the offensive was a futher increase in attacks on the local populations. In DRC, Haut and Bas Uélé were the most severely affected. At Christmas 2008, Faradje, Doruma and Gurba were simultaneously attacked, killing several hundred people. The attacks also spread to other parts of north-eastern DRC, and into the Central African Republic. In southern Sudan, the Office of the United Nations High Commissioner for Refugees declared that some 56,000 civilians were being trapped in a war zone. At the end of January 2009, recorded deaths in the DRC/Sudan border region during the previous six weeks had reached almost one thousand. An estimated seven hundred had been abducted, including five hundred children, and more than 130,000 had been displaced. Initially Operation Lightning Thunder was intended to last for one month, but in January 2009 the UPDF mandate to deploy on both sides of the DRC/Sudan border was extended for a further year. In addition, on 26 March 2009 a joint directive was signed between the Congolese army and MONUC, initiating 'Rudia II'. Like its predecessor, it was aimed at containing the LRA threat. Nevertheless, the LRA attacks have continued.

At the time of writing, in early 2010, Kony's precise location remained unknown. At a UN security briefing in Juba in October 2009, red arrows indicating LRA-related incidents littered the left side of the map of southern Sudan. Some sections of the LRA continue to operate from DRC, repeatedly launching raids across the border. Among the Azande population of southern Sudan's Western Equatoria region, there have been scores of abductions, including the kidnapping of girls to take as wives. In one audacious act, a group of girls was taken from the church in Ezo town and a satellite telephone from the administrative headquarters, while UPDF and SPLA troops were stationed in the vicinity. Zande men, it is reported, are not being recruited as fighters, but are forced to carry food and equipment – and made to follow orders in the Acholi language. LRA terror tactics, including mutilations, are also very much back on the agenda. Kony himself, the UN security officials in Juba claimed, was now in the CAR, and was again receiving assistance from somewhere, probably Khartoum. Details, however, were vague. This was also the case with respect to stories about the LRA's allegedly lucrative trading activities. Probably the most reliable are those relating to the smuggling of gold from the Congolese town of Dungu to Juba.[13] Southern Sudan's booming capital is awash with cash dollars, and there are certainly plenty of willing buyers. What was supposed to be the end game for the LRA shows no sign of actually ending. Perhaps Ugandan forces still deployed in southern Sudan and the DRC will have a lucky break and capture or kill Kony in a skirmish. Or maybe French troops in the CAR will do it. If not, and if Sudan drifts back to war, or to multiple wars, as many predict, Kony is likely to remain a player for some time to come.

Meanwhile, northern Uganda has enjoyed a period of relative peace and stability, and there is a growing sense that the LRA will probably not return to wreak havoc. In many places, the population has been slow to shift out of the IDPs after so long, but it is happening. In some locations, notably in Lira District, the camps are now empty. Even where they have remained heavily populated, there is now cultivation and people are moving along the roads and to remote fields. Visiting in 2009, there was a potent sense of things moving on, and a surge in investment in infrastructure. The army has come under closer scrutiny, partly as a result of the ICC intervention, and the behaviour of soldiers has markedly improved. Service provision remains very poor, but here too there are signs of improvement – something that is hardly surprising give the dreadful situation prevailing a few years ago. Uganda, it seems, has exported its war, and Kony's people are reaping the benefits. Discussion of the current situation is presented at the end of the book in the Postscript.

Achnowledgements

Financial support for the workshop held at the London School of Economics (LSE), on which this book is based, as well as for distribution in Africa, has been provided by the Alistair Berkley Memorial Fund. Alistair Berkley was a young law lecturer and graduate of LSE who was killed in the terrorist attack on Pan Am Flight 103 over Lockerbie, Scotland, in 1988. Generous financial support has also been provided by the Crisis Research Group of the University of Ghent. Additional support for the London workshop was provided by the Royal Africa Society, the Development Studies Institute at LSE, and the Crisis Research Centre at LSE (which is funded by the UK's Department for International Development). The editors would also like to thank photo-journalist Adam Pletts for kindly allowing use of his pictures, Karen Büscher for her assistance to the editing process, and Kristof Titeca for first suggesting the project. Thanks too to Ewan Smith for taking such care in preparing the manuscript and to Zed Books for their enthusiasm and encouragement.

3 Amuru internally displaced persons' camp, housing almost 40,000 people, near Kitgum, northern Uganda, 26 August 2006 (Adam Pletts).

PART ONE

Interpretations of Uganda's war in the north

4 LRA guerrilla soldiers stand guard during a meeting between their second-in-command, Vincent Otti, and the Sudanese vice-president Dr-Riek Machar, who was the chief mediator in the peace process between the LRA and the Ugandan government. The meeting took place on the Congo/Sudan border on 29 July 2006 (Adam Pletts).

1 · Exploring the roots of LRA violence: political crisis and ethnic politics in Acholiland

ADAM BRANCH

Introduction

Recent academic work has made important progress in rendering LRA violence comprehensible, despite the moral and political opprobrium such efforts tend to attract. The existence of a political agenda on the part of the LRA and the strategic rationality informing its anti-civilian violence have been well covered (e.g. Dolan 2009; Finnström 2008b; Branch 2005), but less attention has been given to how LRA violence became, at least in the eyes of some, morally and politically justified. To this end, this chapter shows how the LRA insurgency and its use of violence are embedded within two political crises that afflict Acholi society, and how these crises are themselves embedded in the political history of Uganda, specifically the history of ethnic politics.

The argument is as follows. After the NRA takeover in 1986, Acholi society was rent by two simultaneous, and related, political crises: an *internal* crisis stemming from the breakdown of authority within Acholi society, authority that had been legitimized through a discourse of Acholi ethnicity; and a *national* crisis brought about by the destruction of the political links that had tied the Acholi in the district to the national state. Each post-1986 rebel movement in Acholiland – the Uganda People's Democratic Army (UPDA), the Holy Spirit Movement (HSM) and the LRA – were responding to both crises at once, as each attempted to impose internal order upon Acholi society by building a constituency against the National Resistance Army/Movement (NRA/M) based on a particular conception of Acholi political identity. In short, each rebel group endeavoured to resolve the internal crisis through the violent resolution of the national crisis, to create internal order through military struggle against a common enemy, all cast in ethnic terms. The chapter concludes by considering how these crises might be resolved today through the development of an inclusive internal political order and a genuinely representative national leadership as an alternative to the experimental, violent attempts to resolve the crises that have predominated up to now.

Background to crisis

This section explores the historical origins of these two crises. The internal crisis of the Acholi had its roots in the destruction of the dominant internal social-political order, an order that had been anchored, on the one hand, by male Acholi elders and other lineage-based authorities and, on the other, by an Acholi political middle class, both of which justified their authority through a discourse of Acholi ethnicity. Although the destabilization of that order began under Idi Amin, crisis did not erupt until 1986 with the return home of thousands of Acholi troops following their defeat by the NRA, causing a disruption unmanageable by the weakened internal authority structure. The national political crisis similarly had its roots in the destruction under Amin of the national Acholi political middle class and elite, the group that had provided a link between the Acholi peasantry and the central state. This crisis, similarly, did not erupt until the NRA seized power in 1986, proceeded to exclude Acholi political leaders from the new government, and launched a vicious counter-insurgency in Acholiland, leaving the Acholi without effective national leadership or representation in the face of extreme state violence.

Both crises, I argue, took shape in the context of ethnic politics, specifically the intertwining of two types of ethnic political identity. The literature on the current war often fails to account for the historical processes by which ethnic identities were constructed and politicized, instead naturalizing them and not questioning how they came to be bases for communal political identification and action. To help remedy this, I argue that ethnic political identities predominantly took two forms in post-colonial Uganda, which I will term 'tribal' and 'regional'. 'Tribal' ethnic identity arose out of the 'tribes' demarcated by the British during colonialism as the administrative units of indirect rule – that is, the five 'treaty kingdoms' of southern Uganda and the 'districts' of northern Uganda. As each 'tribe' changed from a category of colonial administration to a category of political identity and action, each came to have an internal aspect – for it was in the name of tribal custom that British-appointed chiefs claimed their power and that lineage-based authorities contested that power – and an external aspect, for it was in the name of each tribe that the political elite demanded a place in national politics. The second form of ethnic political identity, 'regional' identity, had a more recent origin. It derived not from the units of indirect rule, but from the north–south divide in Ugandan society and politics that was introduced during British colonialism, consolidated under the post-colonial regimes, in particular the first presidency of

Milton Obote, and became a basis for collective political identification and action in parts of the south during the NRA rebellion. This regional divide between north and south from the beginning has had an ethnic dimension in the putative distinction between the 'Nilotic' groups living north of the Nile river and the 'Bantu' groups living to the south. This chapter does not investigate the specific history in Uganda of the categories 'Nilotic' and 'Bantu' as they came to pertain to north and south, an important subject in its own right given the very different way in which these categories have been constructed and deployed elsewhere in the Great Lakes region. Instead, I simply note that the regional divide between north and south in Uganda has at times been ethnicized as a distinction between Nilotic and Bantu in the service of certain political agendas and often continues to carry these ethnic connotations today.

The dominant internal political order within Acholi society had its origins in the 1950s, specifically in the political alliance between lineage-based authorities and the emerging petty bourgeoisie. The former, who had held significant, but highly counterbalanced, authority within a decentralized pre-colonial socio-political structure, had seen that authority challenged as the British colonizers proceeded to select and impose their own administrative chiefs.[1] For its part, the Acholi petty bourgeoisie, given the lack of a large landholding class and a significant private sector, was based mostly upon state employment, and so was dependent upon state resources for its position.[2] Both groups, resenting the discretionary power of the British-appointed chiefs and seeking economic and political concessions from the colonial government, posed a significant threat to the British administration.

The British introduced district councils to deal with just this threat (Gertzel 1974: 15–23).[3] While this attempt at co-optation kept these groups within institutionalized politics, however, it also provided the lineage-based authorities and petty bourgeoisie a stage upon which to come together and articulate a common political position. This became increasingly important as political parties began organizing in Acholiland in the mid-1950s and found a ready-made vehicle for their activities in these councils (ibid.: 60–62; Leys 1967). The petty bourgeoisie became the key link between the Acholi peasantry and the national government, as the parties offered the national organization needed to effect local reform but proceeded by building a base at the local level first. The political parties catalysed a community of interest between the petty bourgeoisie, the lineage-based authorities and the rural Acholi, effecting a new political order within Acholiland and bringing the Acholi into national politics (Gertzel 1974: 66–7). It was also within this context – a petty bourgeoisie organized around the district council demanding consideration on the national stage, and the lineage-based authorities, also organized on an Acholi-wide basis in the council, demanding a moderation of the despotic powers of the appointed chiefs – that claims to Acholi identity became a mode of legitimizing political authority (Finnström 2003: 83; Sathyamurthy 1986: 344). The articulation of an Acholi political identity and the assertion of Acholi unity by the petty bourgeoisie in national politics had made ethnicity a viable discourse through which Acholi lineage-based authorities could assert the legitimacy of their own claim to internal authority over the Acholi as a group. Acholi ethnicity has remained the dominant discourse of internal authority until today, its precise content contested but not its basic legitimacy.

At independence, the political parties, especially the Uganda People's Congress (UPC), had presented members of the Acholi petty bourgeoisie with significant access to government positions at the national level, and personal ties and the political parties' dependence upon local political mobilization meant that the Acholi political stratum remained a coherent group (Leys 1967). Thus, the emerging politicized middle class, growing out of the petty bourgeoisie, had one foot in the national government, through elected positions in parliament, appointed positions in the civil service and officer positions in the military, and one foot in rural Acholiland, among those who formed their base of support. A dominant internal order was stabilized around the discourse of Acholi ethnic identity, as was the place of the Acholi within national politics.

During Obote's first period of power (referred to in Uganda as Obote I), this petty bourgeoisie expanded and its political role intensified, as Obote brought significant numbers of northerners into the central state, both through the civil service and the military, and created a patronage machine in northern Uganda (Kasfir 1976: 212). By the end of the 1960s, the stakes of government patronage had increased significantly, and an Acholi and Langi 'economic bureaucracy' appeared at the national level, increasingly differentiated from the local leadership, encompassing the local middle class, the lineage-based authorities and UPC-appointed administrative chiefs, which was incorporated through patronage (Mamdani 1976). In addition to the expansive UPC organization, Obote also depended heavily upon the security services. During the colonial period, those Acholi who were without the education needed to join the civil service, but did not want to farm, generally entered the security forces, so they were over-represented in the military and police both pre- and post-independence (Kasfir 1976: 183, 185). As Obote expanded the army in the 1960s, he also entrenched the northern dominance of the armed forces; the army grew from 700 troops at independence to 9,000 at the time of the Amin coup, of which over one third were Acholi (Omara-Otunnu 1987: 51, 81–5; see also Mudoola 1996: 97). The consequence of Obote's strategy was to introduce a new regional north–south cleavage into national politics. Although this cleavage would not provide the basis for a northern political identity, it would eventually provide an ideological basis for the southern political identity that proved to be central to the NRA rebellion.

In this sense, Idi Amin's coup demonstrated the continued importance of *tribal* ethnic political identity in Ugandan politics (Mudoola 1996: 103; Mutibwa 1992: 71–2; Omara-Otunnu 1987: 87–91). The 1970s saw the destabilization of the dominant internal Acholi political order and the destruction of the link between the Acholi and the national government. Amin declared an end to ethnic favouritism towards the Langi and Acholi and took steps to eradicate their hold on state power. He filled the army ranks with West Nile and Sudanese troops and purged it of Acholi and Langi (Omara-Otunnu 1987: 104, 133–6; Mamdani 1976; Sathyamurthy 1986: 615), and then used the military and other security forces to purge the national civil service of the Acholi and Langi political elite (Mutibwa 1992: 108; Sathyamurthy 1986: 613, 644–5 nn. 22, 23). At the district level, by 1973 local government had become an extension of the security services, as military and police officials displaced the appointed chiefs who had enjoyed significant power under Obote during the 1960s (Omara-Otunnu 1987: 104, 133–6). The local Acholi political leadership and lineage-based authorities suffered significant losses as Amin launched a series of violent political purges in Acholi and Lango districts, leading to tens of thousands of civilian deaths (Kasozi 1994: 121; Mutibwa 1992: 88). Many of the national and local Acholi elite, especially the middle class, who were not killed were driven into exile, giving birth to the large diaspora that persists today. The lineage-based authorities who remained in Acholiland generally withdrew from political life.

The Acholi middle class and political elite, lacking a base independent of the state, were easily eliminated by that state, and without these groups there was no independent economic foundation to build a new mediating class between the peasantry and the government. The order that had pertained inside Acholiland was destabilized, and the link between the Acholi in the district and the national state was destroyed. When Obote returned to power in the early 1980s, it did not ameliorate the situation: although certain prominent Acholi were incorporated into the new government, there was no return to the massive patronage machine of Obote I, and there was no wide-scale political rehabilitation of the Acholi middle class (Mutibwa 1992: 153). Instead, Acholi were brought into the state principally through the military, and the officer corps of the Uganda National Liberation Army (UNLA, i.e. the new national army) again became heavily weighted towards the Acholi and Langi (Omara-Otunnu 1987: 149–51). Thus was the stage set for the internal and national political crises that would grip the Acholi in the wake of National Resistance Army (NRA) victory in 1986.

The NRA rebellion was the crucible in which the north–south divide was ethnicized and took a central place in national politics. A. G. G. Gingyera-Pinycwa has argued that a 'Northern Question' emerged in the late 1970s and early 1980s among a group of southerners, many of whom were in exile, who saw it as necessary to remove northerners from national power in order to establish a new national equalization and end northern military dictatorship (Gingyera-Pinycwa 1989: 53).[4] Anti-northern sentiment would perhaps have remained an elite bias, however, if it had not served a key role in building support for the NRA in Luwero.[5] Museveni and most of his comrades were Banyankole, from Ankole in south-western Uganda, but many Banyarwanda refugees (i.e. mainly Tutsi refugees from Rwanda) were also part of the NRA, eventually comprising 3,000 of the 14,000 troops (Kuperman 2004: 66). The Luwero Triangle, however, had a heterogeneous population, among which the two most populous groups were Baganda peasants and Banyarwanda migrant workers. Therefore, the NRA's decision to base themselves in the densely populated Luwero Triangle region presented the incipient rebel movement with a problem: they were unable to appeal to *tribal* ethnic commonality in building the peasant support essential for their anticipated protracted struggle, both because of the heterogeneity of the Luwero population and because of their own lack of tribal ethnic commonality with those living there. In the face of this challenge, it appears that the NRA built support in Luwero, and then throughout the south of Uganda, in part by framing their revolution in *regional* terms, as a struggle to throw out the north in favour of the south, which carried with it the ethnic connotation of Nilotic and Bantu.

This designation of a northern ethnic enemy resonated with the experience of those living in Luwero and beyond, who suffered greatly under the UNLA's counter-insurgency. Because of the war, the peasantry experienced the power and violence of the central state directly without mediation by the local state. The Acholi ended up bearing the brunt of this anti-northern sentiment as a result of their disproportionately large presence in the armed forces, especially among the rank-and-file troops sent to fight in Luwero, and of the colonial stereotype of their being a 'martial tribe'. This was further reinforced with the Acholi-led coup in 1985, and subsequently, in many parts of the south, the most common appellation for UNLA soldiers was simply 'Acholi' (Finnström 2003: 108).

By positing their armed rebellion in north–south terms, and thanks to the UNLA's violent counter-insurgency, the NRA managed to overcome the challenge posed by Uganda's tribalized political heritage and thus find an ethnic commonality between themselves, the Baganda peasantry and the other southern tribes, through a regional ethnic commonality as members of the Bantu south that transcended the tribal ethnic lines which divided them. Furthermore, the deployment of a north–south division may have helped to resolve two other potential antagonisms within the political bloc the NRA was trying to construct: first, the contested division in Luwero between Banyarwanda 'foreigners' and Ugandan 'natives', and second, the division between the Tutsi, who mostly comprised the Banyarwanda contingent of the NRA, and the Hutu, who comprised the Banyarwanda population in Luwero. Thus, the north–south framework provided by the NRA was popularized among the southern peasantry, and by the end of the bush war, within significant sectors of the NRA/M command and their support base, the war against the Obote II regime had been reinterpreted as a war of south against north, often distilled into a war against the Acholi as the embodiment of northern political-military power.

As the NRA's military struggle gained ground, the Langi–Acholi alliance within the UNLA broke down (Mutibwa 1992: 161), and by July 1985 Acholi troops, led by Bazilio Okello and Tito Okello, had carried out a coup against Obote. But, lacking popular support and the skill and resources needed to rehabilitate the Acholi political elite, the Okello regime soon fell. The NRA took Kampala and sent the last remaining Acholi UNLA troops fleeing north. As a result, when these two military forces – the routed Acholi UNLA remnants with the NRA on their tail – arrived in Acholiland, they faced a population divested of local and national political leadership. In this context, the UNLA's arrival sparked an internal crisis, as the surviving Acholi authority structure tried to deal with this new influx of armed young men. The southern-based NRA, which saw the Acholi as its ethnic enemy, compounded this internal crisis by proceeding to repress responsible local leadership. At the same time, the NRA's occupation sparked a national political crisis, as Acholi leaders were excluded from the new government and the NRA launched a violent counter-insurgency.

NRA occupation and the rise of the UPDA

When the fleeing UNLA and the victorious NRA arrived in Acholiland, of the social-political groups that had taken form under colonial rule and during Obote I – lineage-based authorities and the middle class and national political elite – only the first was left with any internal authority. It is not a surprise, then, that the arrival of the UNLA proved an event so disruptive that the fragile internal order presided over by the remaining elders was thrown into crisis. Indeed, the fleeing troops were not the political-military elite who had previously provided a link between the rural Acholi and the central state, and except for a few top figures they had little legitimacy among the Acholi. Consequently, they failed to rally the Acholi behind them and could only hunker down in Gulu and Kitgum towns to await the NRA,[6] and when the NRA arrived, the UNLA forces withdrew and evacuated Gulu and Kitgum towns without a fight. Many UNLA soldiers went back to their villages, and the rest accompanied their commanders to Sudan.[7] By the end of March, the last pockets of the UNLA had disappeared from Acholiland and the NRA had effectively occupied the subregion.[8]

This flood of thousands of undisciplined, armed young Acholi men was seen by male elders as a significant threat. Perhaps if an Acholi middle class had remained, they could have together managed the new influx. But, with the internal Acholi political structure weakened as it was, the new arrivals threw the internal order into crisis. In response, many lineage-based authorities mobilized the discourse they had employed since the 1950s, and tried to secure their position through an appeal to 'Acholi tradition'. Acholi ethnicity was reconfirmed as the dominant legitimate discourse of internal political order, which aspirants to internal political authority continue to invoke and work within.

In a process similar to what is seen today, lineage-based authorities claimed that Acholi tradition demanded that the UNLA returnees go through cleansing rituals, which they were to preside over. Many lineage-based authorities, as anthropologist Heike Behrend explains, claimed that 'the returnees were the cause of all evil. They had become alien to those who had remained at home. During the civil war, they had plundered, tortured, and murdered, primarily in Luwero, and had become "of impure heart". Because they had killed, they brought *cen*, the spirits of the killed, to Acholi, thus threatening the lives of those who had stayed at home' (Behrend 1999a: 24, 28). The lineage-based authorities lay claim to the exclusive capacity to ritually cleanse the returning soldiers, a power they claimed in the name of saving the Acholi community from the powers of *cen*, thus putting themselves forth as the principal arbiters of internal authority. The returnees, however, in large part refused to conform to elders' authority and thus introduced explosive tensions into the already fragile internal social-political order.

When the NRA arrived, they fundamentally misinterpreted the situation. They did not understand the political bankruptcy of the Acholi ex-UNLA, nor the alienation of the returning soldiers from significant sectors of Acholi society. The NRA had cast its enemy in ethnic terms – the Acholi as the consummate northern tribe – and so presumed that there would be an automatic, natural bond between the Acholi troops and the rural Acholi population. This presumed identity gave rise to the spectre of a substantial political-military force in Acholiland, so the NRA prepared for a long, difficult fight to win Gulu and Kitgum (Amaza 1998: 62; Behrend 1998: 109; Pain 1997: 48).[9] Even once it had occupied Acholiland, notwithstanding the ease with which it had accomplished the task, the NRA continued to act as if it faced a situation characterized by ethnic political solidarity, not internal conflict. The NRA, it appears, could not escape the ethnic terms in which it had framed its rebellion, and the north–south articulation that the NRA/M had given the question of national power determined its political-military approach to the Acholi: it proceeded as if it were occupying enemy territory and tried to solve the Northern Question for good by destroying the putative ethnically based power of the ex-UNLA (Gingyera-Pinycwa 1992, 1989).

Politically, the consequence was that the NRA/M excluded the Acholi from national power and so reflected its southern base: the cabinet, for example, was made up of less than 6 per cent Lwo speakers, and their appointment to other government positions was similarly disproportionately low (Omara-Otunnu 1987: 177). The NRA was composed of over 90 per cent Bantu speakers, and the police force saw over three-quarters of its members summarily dismissed (ibid.: 178). At the local level, the new government refused to deal with respected Acholi politicians and elders and instead picked out marginal figures who would cooperate with the new regime.[10] Instead of working to re-establish legitimate state authority, the NRA/M undermined its possibility in Acholiland.

Militarily, the NRA launched a counter-insurgency without an insurgency. Although Museveni claims in his autobiography that 'there was total peace in the North between March and August 1986' (Museveni 1997: 177), newspapers and human rights reports present a starkly different picture. Stories of harassment and abuse of civilians by the NRA began circulating in mid-April 1986.[11] NRA orders for general disarmament went largely unheeded, evoking as they did memories of Amin's order to the same effect, which had turned out to be a plot to disarm and kill Acholi soliders (Behrend 1999a: 25; Doom and Vlassenroot 1999: 13–14). Reports of looting and rape by NRA soldiers while on 'their frequent operations for hidden guns' made their way into the national press.[12] Acholi civilians expressed a willingness to assist in ending the insecurity – indeed, the returnees had brought only disturbance – but complained that it was hard even for them to know who had guns and about losing property to the NRA.[13] When the security situation degenerated in June and armed men began to rob civilians and attack government vehicles, the NRA, blaming the escalated violence on the Acholi as a group for refusing to cooperate in collecting guns, stepped up their use of force.[14] Again, the NRA/M's ethnic lens prevented it from distinguishing between Acholi civilians and the ex-UNLA.

By mid-August, the situation had deteriorated further, and the NRA began broad 'security swoops' or 'screens', detaining hundreds. Open violence escalated: the most infamous incident was the massacre of over forty civilians from Namu-Okora by the NRA and FEDEMU in late 1986, news of which spread rapidly throughout Acholiland (Amnesty International 1989, 1991; Gersony 1997: 21–3). Museveni consistently dismissed allegations of abuse, blaming it on the indiscipline of a few, stating that allegations of NRA human rights abuses were 'absolutely rubbish and contemptible'.[15] The national political crisis was by that point fully in evidence: the Acholi, divested of political leadership, were subjects of a violent military occupation by their own state, which exercised power over them devoid of accountability or restraint.

The paradoxical result would be that the NRA/M's wrong-headed strategy, in particular its violence against Acholi civilians, would give birth to the very rebellion the NRA/M had expected. It created the conditions for the temporary resolution of the internal crisis through a mutually convenient alliance between the ex-UNLA and Acholi elders oriented towards military struggle against the NRA. Thus, when several thousand ex-UNLA, reorganized as the UPDA, entered Uganda from southern Sudan, they turned to lineage-based authorities as the only group that still held any legitimacy in Acholiland, who in turn gave support to the UPDA. Faced with a common external enemy, one that identified all Acholi as its ethnic enemy,[16] the UPDA and Acholi elders were able to tenuously come together and stabilize internal order around a discourse of Acholi identity. The returned Acholi youths who threatened internal order were to be disciplined by the UPDA, either through recruitment or coercion, and the elders were to give the UPDA the mantle of 'traditional Acholi' authority.

The UPDA was soon able to gain significant support among the civilian population through this alliance and by responding to the Acholi population's need for security against the NRA. This led to a number of changes in the rebels' approach. They forbade looting, promised compensation for requisitioned property, and conducted meetings in occupied areas to explain their struggle.[17] Furthermore, the UPDA tailored their demands to gain popular support. When they attacked Gulu in August 1986, their intention had been to capture and use it as a base for retaking Kampala[18] – a demand derived certainly from the mindset of the ex-UNLA. But, it appears, they found little support for these claims to national power among Acholi elders and civilians generally. Rather, the UPDA found support by responding to the demands of Acholi civilians and promising to stem NRA violence. Consequently, by early 1987 the UPDA had come to phrase their national project in a language of human rights, democracy and political inclusion.[19] They called for the fulfilment of NRA/M promises of democracy and security in the north as well as the south, proposing a political resolution to the national crisis of the Acholi that would have resonance with the elders and the population at large.

The insurgency that the NRA only imagined it had been fighting since April became real, the counter-insurgency was escalated, and opposition newspapers were reporting NRA atrocities by September 1986.[20] By December, these accusations had reached the national and international media.[21] Rumours of genocide began circulating (Gersony 1997: 12),[22] and the NRA allowed Karamojong cattle raiders to loot with impunity as far west as Gulu town, sometimes participating in the looting themselves, thus destroying one of the bases of Acholi livelihood (Dolan 2000b; Finnström 2003: 106–7).[23] As in Luwero, where the national state had made itself known to the peasantry through its military, in Acholiland the new NRM government made itself known through the NRA. As a result, the NRA's ethnic interpretation of the insurgency led the Acholi to see the occupying army, and the government, in similarly ethnic terms. These terms are predominantly regional – the NRA/M as representing the south – but have also been tribal – the NRA/M as a tool of a Banyankole or Bahima-Tutsi conspiracy.

The NRA counter-insurgency proved so brutal that the UPDA was unable to provide adequate protection to the population, and it appears that the elders' authority was too attenuated to serve to keep the population aligned with the UPDA in the face of government violence. The UPDA held together until the beginning of 1987, when it began to factionalize.[24] In a climate of escalating violence, the UPDA had to step up coercion to ensure supplies of food and recruits,[25] and as a result, the provisional alliance between Acholi elders and the UPDA began to break down. The internal social crisis again began to make itself felt as the unclean young men, the ex-UNLA and the UPDA, once more challenged the elders' fragile authority.

The UPDA's failure to score significant military victories and the NRA/M's military approach would ensure that the Acholi political crises would end up being further entrenched. The NRA/M's counter-insurgency prevented the development of responsible, experienced leadership at the local and national levels, instead opening the way for politically inexperienced and experimental armed groups to take the stage. Thus, as the UPDA failed to resolve the national crisis, the internal crisis erupted again, and a new rebel group emerged to try to assert legitimate authority over the population.

The Holy Spirit Movement (HSM)

The new rebel movement that attempted to mediate these crises was led by a female Acholi spirit medium, Alice Auma, known as Lakwena, or 'Messenger'. Lakwena attempted, like the UPDA, to resolve the internal crisis by asserting her legitimate authority over Acholi society against a common external enemy, the NRA. She began by mobilizing a discourse of spiritual cleansing within Acholiland, drawing upon a long-standing alternative tradition of Acholi spirituality that contested the claims to authority made by male Acholi elders and 'chiefs' and which allowed her to assert authority over the UPDA, the ex-UNLA and Acholi civilians generally. Lakwena presented herself as being able to cleanse the swelling ranks of impure Acholi, re-establish order within Acholiland, and combat the NRA, thus addressing the internal and national crises at once. As Tim Allen argues, Lakwena's spiritual discourse of cleansing presented a challenge to the elders' claim to exclusively possess the power to cleanse; thus, through appealing to aspects of Christian imagery that were outside the authority of the elders, Lakwena trumped the elders' authority and their claim to represent the Acholi, while offering a route to cleansing and social inclusion for those ex-UNLA and ex-UPDA who did not want to submit to the elders' authority (Allen 1991b: 378). To that end, once her movement was established in Acholiland by late April 1987, she tried to co-opt remnants of the UPDA. The UPDA's leadership refused, and subsequently turned on the HSM (Behrend 1999a: 85). Lakwena's forces counterattacked, and she overran a number of UPDA brigades, collecting guns and absorbing troops (Allen 1991b: 372–3).[26] Lakwena's movement reconfirmed Acholi identity as a dominant discourse in which legitimate claims to internal authority were made, proving that Acholi 'tradition' or 'custom', which is typically assumed to be the exclusive preserve of male elders and 'traditional chiefs' (an assumption promoted especially by Western donors in Acholiland), has in fact always been a contested terrain of inter-generational, inter-gender and intra-Acholi struggle.

Lakwena's claim to spiritual authority, however, took on a national and then universal aspect, going beyond the exclusive concern with Acholi identity. Her assertion of spiritual authority through a discourse of cleansing became focused on purging not just Acholiland but Uganda of the corruption and violence of the NRA/M. At several points, she presented her movement in even more universal terms, claiming her next target after Kampala would be South Africa. With this expansive discourse of spiritual cleansing, in July 1987 Lakwena's HSM began moving east and south, following the course of the Nile through Lango and Teso. They recruited heavily in the areas they moved through, and as a result the ethnic make-up of the HSM was constantly shifting – for example, while in Teso, the Iteso made up the largest contingent of soldiers – testament to the appeal her movement had throughout the north and east of Uganda (Behrend 1999a: 67–8). Indeed, the HSM found support in precisely those places where the NRA's arrival had been interpreted as an occupation instead of a liberation (ibid.: 70).[27] The HSM was thus able to find regional, not only tribal, appeal and was able to temporarily unite non-Bantu groups – Acholi, Langi, Iteso and Jo-Padhola. The response on the part of the population was positive enough to provide the HSM with a significant amount of popular support (Omara-Otunnu 1992: 443–63),[28] and Lakwena eventually assembled an army of 7,000–10,000 troops (Behrend 1999a: 67–71).[29]

Lakwena managed to find success beyond Acholiland, something the UPDA and later the LRA failed to do despite their often more coherent political messages and orthodox leadership. By proposing first a thorough cleansing of the Acholi, and then by invoking a broadly applicable language of spiritual redemption, Lakwena trumped the UPDA's (and elders') claim to legitimacy internally and, outside of Acholiland, distanced herself from the intra-northern tribal animosities that the UPDA had inherited from the UNLA. The limit to this alliance was precisely the border between north and south.[30] As the rebels made it to within a few dozen miles of Kampala, they crossed into a Bantu area where the HSM was no longer a liberator but rather was an invading northern army, frightening enough to motivate the peasantry to cooperate with the Resistance Councils (RCs) and Local Defence Units (LDUs). Within a couple of weeks, the HSM had disintegrated in the face of the combined NRA–LDU–civilian defence (ibid.: 92–3; Mamdani 1995a: 50–2).[31]

At the same time, Lakwena was not above employing secular institutions in her pursuit of spiritual redemption. In its early days, the HSM appears to have forged a tenuous alliance with some Acholi elders, who might have seen Lakwena, despite the challenge to patriarchal authority she represented, as a useful tool for disciplining the ex-UNLA and UPDA and calming the general insecurity in the region, thus setting the stage for a future reassertion of their own power. There are reports that in places where the NRM had established RCs, Lakwena ordered the people not to cooperate with them, and in places where elders and chiefs remained, Lakwena instructed the HSM not to interfere with their work (Behrend 1999a: 70).[32] Lakwena also developed 'War Mobilization Committees' (WMCs) in some of the areas the HSM moved through as a direct challenge to the NRM's RCs. These WMCs, organized at the sub-county and village levels, were to help fulfil supply, information and recruitment functions (ibid.: 67–71).[33] But these more secular strategies were ultimately subjugated to her spiritual project, whose military defeat wiped out any institutional developments the movement might have catalysed. Acholiland was left even more devoid of leadership, responsible organization and basic security.

The Lord's Resistance Army and anti-civilian political violence

After Lakwena left Acholiland, violence there between the remaining rebel factions intensified as the fragmented UPDA and the splinters of the HSM terrorized each other's suspected civilian supporters. Additionally, once Lakwena had exhausted the supply of volunteers, those factions remaining had to step up forced recruitment. It was from this environment that Joseph Kony emerged. Although at first Kony may have gained some support, albeit limited relative to Lakwena's, from lineage-based authorities,[34] he was generally confronted with a deficit of volunteers, a population unwilling to support continued violence, and a number of different enemies, many from within Acholiland itself. As a result, Kony had to rely on increased violence against civilians for his group's material and social survival.

Lakwena had demonstrated to the NRA/M the dangerous potential for popular mobilization in Acholiland and throughout the north. Ever since, the Ugandan government has worked to tribalize the conflict and frame it as an exclusively Acholi problem, one that threatens, rather than appeals to, other northern tribes. Within Acholiland, resolved to not let this level of support develop again, the NRA has generally abandoned the population to rebel violence, letting it continue as a kind of collective punishment by proxy, ensuring that the rebels did not gain significant support but also doing nothing to build support itself.[35] Acholi civilians were left without any clear leadership or agent of political change: none of the rebel factions had achieved dominance, and the government had only displayed its incapacity and unwillingness to provide protection. The Acholi were alienated from the rebels at the same time as they realized that they could not actively support the NRA.

Two developments took place in late 1987 and early 1988 that would significantly change the character of violence in Acholiland. First, the UPDA dissolved for good, as those who had not joined Alice Lakwena accepted the government's offer of amnesty, joined the faction of the UPDA that concluded the Pece Peace Agreement with the NRM in June 1988, or joined Joseph Kony's forces – which by the end of the decade had become known as the Lord's Resistance Army (LRA).[36] The Ugandan government entered into negotiations with Kony in early 1988, but these came to nothing (Lamwaka 2002: 31).[37] The result was threefold: Kony's force was strengthened and became the sole viable rebel group in Acholiland; the incipient LRA appears to have come to see the ex-UPDA who had accepted amnesty and been incorporated into the NRA as having betrayed them (Behrend 1999a: 173–4); and, judging from later statements by the LRA leadership, Kony and other commanders seem to have become intensely suspicious of government peace initiatives. The Ugandan government, meanwhile, stepped up its violence against civilians, launching a wave of forced displacement in October 1988 (Lamwaka 2002: 32–3).

The second development was the consolidation of the RC system and the creation of Local Defence Units (LDUs) in Acholiland. RCs had first been introduced into parts of Acholiland immediately following the NRA's occupation, but violence prevented their consolidation until late 1987. In the interim, a significant national debate had transpired over the RC system as it had been set up in the south, specifically around the question of whom the RCs effectively served: the state, the NRM or the people (Ddungu 1994: 367–9; Mamdani 1995b; Oloka-Onyango 2000). In Acholiland, however, there was little question as to the function of the RCs: as one critic declared, they 'are more or less extraneous to the immediate popular interest and are almost entirely organs of the NRM's/state's local expression and not of the people'.[38] Instead of fulfilling their mandated role of providing a check upon the NRA, they facilitated the NRA's counter-insurgency through surveillance and control. To ensure their cooperation, the NRA/M frequently purged the RCs of those it believed to be sympathetic to the rebels, and accused RCs that opposed the NRA's violence of being rebel supporters.[39] Furthermore, as the NRA/M began organizing LDUs in Gulu in February 1988, mostly from ex-UNLA or ex-UPDA chosen by the RCs, the RC system became an integral part of the state's military apparatus.[40] The result was that, in Acholiland, the NRA/M's reform of local government created an undemocratic local administration embodied in a hierarchy of agents serving an ethnically exclusive central state. The RCs and LDUs effectively localized the state down to the village level, and this diffuse security apparatus became, in the eyes of some, the tool of the state, the NRM, the NRA and the south all at once, thus localizing the ongoing national crisis as well.

These developments – the switch by many UPDA to the NRA, and more importantly the apparent insertion of the foreign occupier into the heart of Acholi society through RCs – provided Joseph Kony with the opportunity to propose a new and violent resolution to the twofold political crisis. The LRA came into existence in a context where both the previous modes of asserting legitimacy – the UPDA's alliance with elders, and the redemptive, inclusive spiritual discourse of the HSM – had been exhausted. The UPDA had posited an alliance between themselves (that is, the very social faction whose presence had precipitated the internal crisis), the elders and the peasantry in order to combat the NRA, while Lakwena had founded her authority upon the claim to resolve what she framed as the key internal cleavage – between the UPDA/ex-UNLA and the Acholi community – through cleansing, and to lead that new purified community against the external enemy, the NRA.

Kony, however, posited a new, more fundamental internal cleavage, one between the genuine Acholi whom he would lead against the NRA/M, and the corrupt, false Acholi who had gone over to the NRA/M. Like Lakwena, Kony proposed the cleansing of an internal enemy (Allen 1991b: 378); but in Kony's conception, it was not the spiritual corruption of the ex-UNLA to be cleansed, but rather the political corruption of the administrative and security apparatus of the NRA/M, embodied in its Acholi agents. Equally importantly, whereas Lakwena had proposed a discourse of cleansing that went beyond the boundaries of Acholi identity, Kony's discourse was limited to the Acholi, as the UPDA's had been. For Kony, the internal crisis merged with the national crisis, as the first was rephrased in terms of the second and the external enemy, the NRA/M, was transposed to the inside of Acholi society in the form of NRA collaborators, the new internal enemy. To this end, Kony invoked a language of Acholi identity as a way of asserting authority over a new potential constituency by framing the division between NRA collaborators and LRA supporters as a difference between false and genuine Acholi. Kony dismissed the power of elders or any other Acholi leadership to determine the bounds of Acholi identity; it was the LRA alone which would decide who would be relegated to the category of the impure, corrupt Acholi, needing to be cleansed from Acholi society.

This new conceptualization had highly destructive consequences. Because the north–south divide had been imported within Acholi society, to fight the south, according to Kony, part of Acholi society would have to be fought as well, and so anti-civilian violence would be the privileged tool for carrying out this political programme. Kony turned his violence upon the internal enemy as the manifestation of the external enemy, upon the local state as the representative of the central state. Because that local state used Acholi agents, LRA violence would, from then on, take on an intra-Acholi visage; at the same time, since violence was being used against supposed foreigners, it could take on a relatively unrestrained character. The spiritual discourse of cleansing became one of violently expurgating the internal enemy from Acholi society.

For the LRA, the question became who was included in the genuine Acholi and who was part of the internalized enemy. At times, the LRA would frame this discourse of cleansing in millenarian terms – for example, when an LRA commander declared that they were going to kill all Acholi, leaving only 10,000 who would be the basis for a new, purified tribe.[41] The Ugandan government and international media have made much out of these types of statements; in practice, however, they did not appear to inform the LRA's use of violence, since the LRA never explicitly tried to follow through on threats to eradicate the Acholi en masse. Moreover, the LRA has often framed its goals exclusively in a secular political language (Finnström 2008b),[42] conducted information campaigns in the villages,[43] and issued political statements and manifestos. The LRA even declared a ceasefire for the 1996 presidential elections,[44] conducted political rallies, and encouraged the Acholi to vote for Museveni's opponent, Paul Ssemogerere, a supporter of peace negotiations.[45]

Instead of attempting to eradicate all Acholi who do not join them, the LRA's approach has instead generally been to use its worst violence against those it suspects of overt government collaboration, while dealing with the rest of the Acholi population through a series of rules with violent sanctions, including maiming and death.[46] The enforcement of some of these rules – such as no bicycle riding or no working on certain days – had certain direct benefits for the LRA by keeping people out of the way of their operations or preventing people from reporting on LRA movements, while also demonstrating to the population that the government was uninterested in protecting them. Other rules that lacked obvious strategic benefit for the LRA may have been intended to assert the LRA's more general authority over the population, part of a project of purifying the Acholi population from the internalized influence of the NRA by subjecting them to LRA authority and dismantling government authority and institutions – purification not through death, but through conforming to the authority of the LRA.

The problem was that what perhaps appeared from the LRA's perspective to be a reasonable strategy for purifying the Acholi and eradicating the internal enemy looked from the Acholi civilians' perspective to be an unpredictable, vicious reign of violence. For one thing, the LRA's ideas about who represented the impure, corrupt Acholi were constantly in flux and had little to do with who the civilians understood to be government collaborators. For example, the LRA incorporated the RC system into its pro-government versus anti-government dichotomy, arguing that it represented a tool of the NRM government. While many Acholi do see the RC/LC system as being manipulated by the government, however, many also see the system as having the potential to serve their own interests. Thus, LRA violence against the RC/LC system sometimes targeted those who were seen by Acholi civilians as legitimate, independent leaders. Another issue was that the LRA often blamed Acholi civilians for going along with policies that those civilians felt the government had forced upon them; for example, when the Acholi were forcibly displaced into camps, the LRA stepped up their violence against the displaced people, accusing them of being government supporters, burning camps down, and calling on people to go back to their villages. From the perspective of the Acholi population, however, the LRA was blaming them for what the government had forced them to do.

In short, the LRA represents another attempt, following in the footsteps of the UPDA and the HSM, to assert what they saw as legitimate authority over the Acholi, and thus resolve the internal political crisis by mobilizing a constituency around a particular conception of Acholi identity and against the NRA/M. The Manichaean political framework within which the LRA was operating, however, and according to which it sought to establish its legitimacy, led its use of violence to be subject to imperatives alien to the population's own interests or needs. The result has been a regime of violence that might make sense from the LRA's perspective but has failed to resonate with the Acholi population, serving only to further entrench the political crises.

Conclusion: resolving the crises, ending the war

Over the two decades of war, the national political crisis and the state's lack of accountability to the Acholi have remained more or less constant, deriving from the lack of a national political elite, the exclusion of legitimate Acholi representatives from the government, the repression of Acholi opposition leadership, and the failure of the Acholi diaspora to engage meaningfully in Ugandan politics. The internal crisis has taken on new dimensions, however, which have made its resolution all the more complicated. Each of the elements of the internal crisis in 1986 – the returning soldiers, the missing local political elite, and threatened Acholi lineage-based authorities – has undergone change. First, the UNLA has been replaced by a new group of 'returnees', the ex-LRA. Second, the Acholi political middle class, which would serve as the link between the rural population and the national government, remains missing. What has replaced it is a donor-supported, NGO-oriented, unrepresentative, non-political Acholi 'civil society'. Finally, the status of the lineage-based authorities is still a matter of controversy: they have seen their authority slip further, but some have also managed to tap into foreign donor support within the 'traditional justice' agenda.

At the same time, new social and political forces have emerged in the intervening years to complicate the internal political crisis. Indeed, lineage-based authority has waned not only as a result of continued war and displacement, but also as a result of a new upsurge of authority among women and youth. Women and youth have profited from foreign-sponsored humanitarian and peace-building initiatives in the camps, while older men have seen their role as providers stripped away as foreign relief agencies take over the function of providing food and other material resources. Male youth have also come into new authority through their participation in the various military and paramilitary forces, either the UPDF, LRA or LDUs. This has presented a challenge to the older male authority structure, a challenge that these older men tend to frame as a simple breakdown of 'traditional' order. In fact, however, these new political forces represent the potential for the inclusion of previously excluded groups and for a degree of local democratization that must not be overlooked.

As of yet, neither military modes of organization – the UPDF, HSM and LRA – nor institutionalized political modes of organization – the RC/LC system and multiparty elections – nor non-institutionalized political modes of organization – 'traditional' authority, a new political middle class or the emergent youth – has managed to establish legitimate local political authority or leadership among the Acholi. This failure has rebounded upon the failure of a viable national political leadership to emerge that could represent the Acholi in the national government. In this context, a resolution of the internal crisis would necessarily involve a negotiation between at least five social-political forces: first, lineage-based authorities; second, the newly empowered youth and women; third, pro-government Acholi; fourth, the LRA and its supporters; and fifth, a rehabilitated Acholi political middle class, a group that is currently divided between the diaspora and a local non-political NGO-based 'civil society'. This would be combined with the actualization of the promise of popular participation embodied in the RC/LC system. If these can occur, then perhaps a popularly legitimate internal political order may emerge in Acholiland, contributing to local democratization. This would also promote the emergence of a significant national-level leadership that could help resolve the national crisis of the Acholi. The resolution of the national crisis, however, also requires the rehabilitation of the national Acholi political elite, both through the promotion of certain members of the local political elite and also through the responsible political engagement of members of the Acholi diaspora.

The major social and political upheaval caused by the ongoing conflict should not prompt conservative calls for re-establishing an idealized pre-war order. Indeed, too many factors are at play now to pretend that, for example, the revival of 'traditional authority' through external support would do anything more than consolidate the power of one particular faction – older men – at the expense of women and youth, thus increasing tensions within Acholi society. Rather, the ongoing armed conflict should be seen as offering the opportunity for new, more inclusive and more democratic political configurations to come about through the rehabilitation of previously existing political groups, the empowerment of emerging social forces, and the institutionalization of genuine political participation and representation. Otherwise, legitimate and inclusive internal order will continue to be elusive, the Acholi will remain incapacitated in national politics, and violence will persist as a viable – and even apparently reasonable – political option.

2 · Uganda's politics of foreign aid and violent conflict: the political uses of the LRA rebellion

ANDREW MWENDA

Uganda under President Yoweri Museveni has been presented as a successful case study of 'post conflict reconstruction' (World Bank 1998, 2000). But it is an assessment that reflects only a part of the reality. Over the last two decades, the north has been mired in a brutal rebellion. Nearly one third of the country has been directly affected by the fighting. This presents a dilemma. Although most of Uganda has economically recovered from years of Idi Amin's mismanagement, followed by an international war with Tanzania and later a five-year civil war, the northern region has experienced only despair. Although the national average for poverty in the country is now at 31 per cent, down from 56 per cent in 1992, the average for the northern region is 65 per cent (Republic of Uganda 2007). Almost two million people have been living in internal displacement (IDP) camps, many of them in conditions of extreme deprivation. To a large extent, charity from non-governmental organizations (NGOs) has substituted for the state.

While many observers have presented the tragedy in northern Uganda as a residual challenge in the government's otherwise commendable efforts, this chapter suggests that the conflict has been an integral part of Uganda's foreign-aid-driven reconstruction process. It is argued that the interaction between the National Resistance Movement's efforts to consolidate its position under the twin pressures of donor-driven economic/institutional reforms on the one hand and electoral competition on the other transformed the conflict in northern Uganda from a threat to political consolidation into an instrument of it. Indeed, many of the achievements Uganda has realized under the NRM were *partly* possible at the price of escalating that conflict. The threat from the north was transformed into an opportunity.

First, a caveat! I am not advancing a conspiracy theory that the government has had a 'master plan' to deliberately sustain the war as an instrument of rule. The end of the conflict would most probably have come as a welcome relief to the government, President Museveni and some in the military. My argument rather is that, over the years, the conflict has continuously presented opportunities which Museveni and his military have exploited to their advantage. This has reduced their incentive to rigorously pursue a military victory or seek a negotiated settlement.

Economic reform and political consolidation

When it captured power in January 1986, NRA/M inherited a collapsed state and economy. State collapse was manifested in widespread violence and impunity, and institutional weakness – police, civil service and the judiciary could hardly perform basic state functions. Economic collapse was manifested in acute scarcities of basic necessities like salt, sugar, soap and kerosene and in the collapse of physical and social infrastructure – railways, telecommunications and roads were in a state of disrepair, while schools went without books and teachers and hospitals without drugs, doctors and nurses. Rather than engage with the state, many Ugandans fought or simply avoided it.

For the National Resistance Army/Movement (NRA/M), therefore, restoring law and order was the first step to legitimizing its rule. Ensuring basic security of person and property had an economic dividend too: it would create incentives for peasants to return from subsistence to commercial production and business from speculation to investment. The NRM found it easy to re-establish security only in those areas where it enjoyed popular support. In the north, it looked on the entire population as enemies and therefore generated resistance – both violent and pacific.

Second, in the context of collapsed industry, the NRM needed foreign exchange to import spare parts to rehabilitate industries and also to import essential goods in order to ease acute scarcities. Government also needed funds to deliver basic social services such as supplying drugs to hospitals, paying civil servants, reopening schools, etc. But most important for this chapter, the NRA/M desperately needed funds to buy arms, ammunition and fuel to prosecute counter-insurgency operations in northern Uganda. Its legitimacy in the south was tenuous while its military control over the state was strained by the rebellion.

Third, the NRA/M was a left-wing organization hostile to international financial institution (IFI) economic policy recommendations. Between January 1986 and May 1987 the NRA/M government pursued a development strategy involving barter trade, price and foreign exchange controls, reliance on state marketing boards to distribute basic goods, and high fiscal deficits to finance a huge military budget. The results were disastrous as the economy shrank and inflation skyrocketed (Ochieng 1991). The government needed foreign aid but this was a period of reforms in the Soviet Union and its satellites, and the NRM could not get aid from its ideological allies.

The only source of foreign financial support were the Western powers. Members of the Organisation for Economic Co-operation and Development (OECD) refused to provide the necessary funding, however, insisting that the government first reach an agreement with the International Monetary Fund (IMF). The government was therefore forced to reach accommodation with the IFIs. In May 1987, when its delegation arrived in Washington, DC, to negotiate for aid with the IMF, the country had foreign exchange worth only two weeks' fuel imports.[1]

The IMF made its usual case for demand contraction austerity measures, while the World Bank pushed for its standard Structural Adjustment Programmes (SAPs). Desperate, the government could only sign up to the demands of these institutions, and as one member of the delegation told me, 'Under such circumstances, how could I return to my president and tell him I had rejected IMF/World Bank money because of conditionality.'[2]

Upon its signing up to the reform agenda, the international donors responded by opening their cash taps. Between 1987 and 1990, the government received an average US$650 million per annum as foreign aid and economic growth averaged 7 per cent. Beyond helping put the economy back on the growth path, foreign aid bolstered the state's capacity to prosecute counter-insurgency operations. Between 1990 and 2005, aid averaged US$738 million per year. The NRM's strategy of political consolidation came to rely increasingly on its ability to trade economic reform for foreign aid.

The transformation of the army

The outbreak of the war in northern Uganda took place when the NRA, a former guerrilla army built around personalized and informal structures, was beginning its own process of transformation into an institutionalized national army, but in the context of the outbreak of yet another threat, the HIV/AIDS pandemic. The scale of the devastation wrought by HIV/AIDS on the NRA was reflected in the fact that 40 per cent of its officer corps was infected with the disease.[3]

Because AIDS was killing the best of the NRA officers, it was difficult to professionalize the army. The twin threats of insurgency and AIDS transformed the NRA. With the outbreak of the rebellion before formal structures in the army could be put in place, the prosecution of the war took precedence over institutionalization. Commanders in the field with control over financial and other resources to prosecute the war found, in the context of weak institutional mechanisms for accountability, an opportunity to enrich themselves.

Thus supply of logistics to the fighting troops soon became the quickest route to riches. Commanders allied with civilian business people to inflate prices of supplies (if they supplied any logistics at all) and make huge profits. Other officers did not report the dead and missing in their units, and instead continued to receive salaries of these 'ghost soldiers' for their personal enrichment.[4] Initially imposed on them by circumstances, both the war and the weak and incoherent army structures were transformed into an opportunity.

The NRA/M had argued that previous armies in Uganda were a continuation of the colonial legacy, i.e. anti-people and parasitic. The NRA promised to be a disciplined and productive force. Upon taking power, it established the National Enterprises Corporation (NEC) to be its productive arm. The NEC owned ranches, pharmaceutical plants, bakeries, arms factories, and so on, and army officers were put in management positions in these businesses.

In the late 1980s and early 1990s, when the AIDS pandemic was beginning to decimate the NRA officer corps, official salaries for the military were meagre; IMF demand-management austerity measures had forced the state to withdraw from the provision of free basic healthcare as well as primary and secondary education; and there was no scheme to cater for the families of deceased army officers.

The above factors, coupled with poorly developed institutional structures of accountability, created pressure on army officers and opportunities for those in command positions in war areas, or in management positions in army enterprises, to appropriate resources to treat themselves and their families, pay their children's fees, build houses or set up businesses for them in case they died.[5]

As tends to happen in such situations, these developments, initially on a small scale, later spread through the ranks, especially as the commander-in-chief was not strict with his officers. Over the years, military corruption and plunder were to grow into a cancer and permeate almost the entire military command (Tangri and Mwenda 2004). While initially a temporary side effect of the conflict and weak army structures, war and military plunder were over time transformed into a strategy of political consolidation.

The transformation of rebellion

Over the years, the rebellion has gone through different phases of intensity, under different organizations. The defeat of one group – such as the Uganda People's Defence Army (UPDA) – led only to the birth of another, the Holy Spirit Movement (HSM). From the ashes of the defeat of the HSM emerged the LRA. In 1991, the government launched a vicious counter-insurgency campaign – Operation North – which almost crushed the rebellion in 1992. This coincided, however, with changing regional politics.

The Cold War ended in 1990, and this shifted US geostrategic concerns from the threat of communism to the spread of Islamic extremism. In 1989, the army, under General El Bashir, had seized power in Sudan and immediately allied itself with the National Islamic Front (NIF) to form a government in Khartoum. The USA responded by labelling the regime in Khartoum a threat, and thus began to finance the rebel Sudan People's Liberation Army (SPLA). Uganda became the conduit of this assistance.

In retaliation, Sudan began to support the LRA with money, arms and bases. This gave the LRA a new lease of life and altered its incentives. While previously the LRA had sought to win popular support in Acholi to prosecute its war, support from Khartoum rendered this strategy unnecessary. This insulated the rebels from the population. It also transformed their political and military strategy. Instead of employing selective violence against its enemies in its areas of operation, the LRA increasingly became a criminal/terrorist organization unleashing indiscriminate violence and terror on the civilian population.

While Sudanese support transformed the LRA, the US alliance altered the Ugandan government's incentives, especially with regard to Museveni. By crafting his own agenda in line with the US agenda to fight the spread of 'Islamic extremism' in the region, the Ugandan president brought the diplomatic, financial, logistical, technological and moral resources of the world's sole superpower to his side.[6] Museveni realized that the war brought Uganda right into the heart of US geostrategic interests in the region.

Rebellion and the politics of economic reform

After 1992, Uganda fully embraced the IMF and World Bank liberal reforms. This gave international donors control of policy and the budget-making process. The civil service and the cabinet were reduced in size, state enterprises were sold and the economy liberalized. All these measures reduced the amount of patronage the NRM could leverage to build its political base.

Museveni found himself in a favourable position not only to access large inflows of foreign aid, but also with a free hand to pursue his preferred political and military objectives. Politically, he was able to consolidate a one-party system in the post-Cold War Africa when donors were forcing multiparty politics down the throat of other governments. Militarily, the donors allowed Museveni a free hand (sometimes even gave him a helping hand) to pursue his preferred security agendas in the country (especially northern Uganda) and in the region, such as invading Rwanda, Sudan and later DRC.

Donor control of the budget-making limited his ability to use the formal budget process to finance political patronage. Museveni was increasingly forced to rely on defence and security budgets because of their very large 'classified funds' for political finance. Procurement of heavy and therefore expensive military equipment created the best opportunity to cream off large funds through inflated costs. By the late 1990s, some of the most extreme forms of corruption in Uganda were in military procurement. A government investigation found that key military tenders were being awarded by the president personally.[7]

This way, the war became increasingly influential for Museveni's politics, especially in his relations with an increasingly intrusive donor community. It provided him with an important justification for increasing the defence budget. As a result, the battles between Museveni and the donors during this period zeroed in on defence spending. Donors pushed for reduced defence spending and Museveni argued for increasing it.

Three things shaped this debate. First, the donors framed their argument poorly: instead of questioning and therefore discussing the policy of war as an instrument of resolving the conflict in the north, they pitched their argument on the budgetary aspects of the war, i.e. that military spending should not exceed 2 per cent of GDP. Museveni was able to outwit them on this point because the violence against civilians by the rebels made the donors' argument sound unreasonable. Second, Museveni could increase defence spending in a growing economy. Third, the Ugandan government had consented to virtually all the donors' economic and institutional reform recommendations. Often, the donors found it difficult to refuse this single request from the government – 'allow us some degree of independence to shape our defence and security requirements'. Thus, in allowing donors to take control of the policy and budget-making process, Museveni found that he had bought himself independence and discretion to pursue his preferred military and political agendas.

It is also the case that Museveni's ceaseless yet fruitless pursuit of a military solution was shaped by his personal ideological predisposition to militarism and a rejection of the option of negotiating with 'irrational' insurgents. This approach has prevented a rapprochement between the regime and the population of affected areas, particularly the Acholi, despite their increasing rejection of the rebellion.

The bilateral donors were divided between those countries with a geostrategic interest in the region (the USA, the UK and France) and those whose main concern was poverty reduction (the Nordic countries, Japan, Belgium, Ireland and the Netherlands). With Uganda acting as a front-line state in their war against the spread of 'Islamic extremism', which later became a 'war on terror', the US and UK governments began to use their influence in the IMF, the World Bank and the wider donor community to bolster Museveni's demands for increased defence spending.[8]

Thus, Museveni's national and regional military orientation policy grew stronger. In 1990 he had helped Tutsi refugees in Uganda to return home by a military invasion of the neighbouring state of Rwanda. In 1996, the Clinton administration began to give Uganda, Ethiopia and Eritrea annual 'non lethal weapons military aid' in their role as front-line states containing the spread of 'Islamic extremism' by the Khartoum regime. In 1997 the USA supported them in a secret invasion of the Sudan.[9]

Uganda's economic and institutional success compounded problems generated by the conflict in the north. Donors began to refer to it as an African success story. Thus, the World Bank published reports referring to Uganda's experience as post-conflict reconstruction (World Bank 1998, 2000, 2004). This claim made the different parties to Uganda's 'success' seek to obscure key realities about the country: the everlasting dependence on foreign aid, which was creating incentives for the escalation of the rebellion in the north, and how this in turn was helping the regime in its other projects, such as the closure of political space and the continued central role of the military and security services in the country's politics.

Thus, the more donors gained control of the policy and budget process, the more Museveni called for increased defence spending. From 1992 onwards, donors and Museveni fought ferocious battles over defence spending. Museveni always won; the donors lost. In 1992, defence spending had been US\$42 million. By 1996, it had increased to US\$88 million. In 2001, it reached US\$110 million. By the beginning of 2004, it had reached US\$200 million. Today, it is at US\$260 million. Because donors focus on inputs, not outputs, they were unable to link increasing defence spending to increased efficiency or effectiveness of the military in countering insurgents. Without this key input, the donors became accomplices in the process that nurtured the growing corruption in the army.

As defence spending grew, so did procurement of military supplies become ever more riddled with inflated purchases of junk equipment – tanks, jet fighters, helicopter gunships and anti-tank guns, expired-food rations and undersize uniforms. Ghost soldiers became so endemic in the military that by 2003 between one third and two-thirds of the army were actually dead or missing. In 1998, Uganda had invaded Congo, and soldiers there began to plunder the resources of their mineral-rich neighbour.[10]

From this point, military corruption and plunder became a key strategy through which Museveni rewarded army officers. An army investigation into the existence of ghost soldiers estimated that, in the best-case scenario, ghost soldiers cost the army up to US$40 million per annum. For example, in February 2002 the army was poised to launch Operation Iron Fist under an agreement with the Khartoum government to enter southern Sudan to rout the rebels there. Before the invasion, it carried out an audit of the strength of the 4th Division based in northern Uganda. Out of the expected 7,200 troops in the division, there were only 2,400. If you subtracted the sick and administrative staff, the actual combat effectiveness of the division was about 1,500 soldiers.[11] At this time, the army estimated the rebels to have about two thousand troops.

In spite of huge increases in the defence budget, the money was not going into the army. The size of the army deployed to fight rebels and protect the population compares badly with that of the president's personal escort unit – the Presidential Guard Brigade – which is 12,000 troops strong. This further demonstrates that the president had limited interest in seeking a military victory.

By 2003, many units in the north were going into battle with insufficient ammunition, running out of bullets and being massacred by the rebels. Soldiers would have no pouches for magazines, no boots and uniforms, and would go without dry rations. The army would give them dry beans and maize flour, yet there was no time for cooking during operations as they were chasing a highly mobile enemy on foot. The rebels would look better than the UPDF soldiers.[12]

At the beginning of Operation Iron Fist, there were 350,000 civilians in IDP camps. By August, the number had hit a record 1.8 million, and the government was asking donors to 'increase defence spending' in a context where there were anything between 18,000 and 36,000 ghost soldiers on the army register.[13] By August 2003, Operation Iron Fist had delivered the opposite of its objective, as the war spread from the three districts of Acholi region into Lango, West Nile and Teso regions, covering eleven districts. With a disaster on this scale, it was increasingly morally difficult for donors to refuse the government an increase in the defence budget to 'protect its people' from the 'terrorist LRA'.

These were not residual weaknesses within the military. These dysfunctions became increasingly instrumental in Museveni's strategy of rewarding loyal officers and controlling the population in the north. The forceful removal of civilians from their homes into camps was a strategy employed to separate rebels from the population that – on the basis of ethnic identity – the government suspected of collaborating with rebels. This is a long-used colonial policy – by the British during the Boer War in South Africa and against the Mau Mau in Kenya. The government of Museveni rules the north as if it were a colonial territory.

The donors were learning, however, that increased defence spending did not reduce the theatres of conflict or its intensity; rather that it was increasing military corruption through defence procurement and ghost soldiers. Donors could no longer ignore press reports of endemic corruption in the army and therefore insisted that the regime tackle the issue of 'ghosts' on the army register and punish offenders as a precondition of increasing the defence budget. President Museveni appointed a high-powered commission. Its report led to the sacking of 127 officers and the establishment of a military court martial to try offenders.

Over the years, however, the regime has learnt how best to play mouse to the international community cat. A trial started in October 2003, but, after a series of highly publicized hearings, the government insisted it would hold subsequent hearings *in camera*. Shortly afterwards, well knowing that the donors have a limited attention span, the president sent the chairman of the court martial, a former army commander and a virtually retired lieutenant general, on a military course, thus bringing an end to the circus.

The war and electoral competition

Museveni's strategy of political consolidation was built on two pillars: on the one hand, political stability and economic reconstruction in the south; on the other, the military capacity to defeat or cripple armed insurgents to the north. Both of these came to increasingly rely on an alliance with international donors. While the war raged, destroying most economic activity in the north and north-east, economic activity proceeded apace in the central and western regions of Uganda – the ethno-regional political core of the regime, the nation's administrative centre and the heart of the country's economic activity.

This dichotomy in economic fortunes came to reinforce the ethno-regional political differences in the country. As beneficiaries of foreign-aid-driven reconstruction, populations in the south increasingly became content with a growing economy in a stable and secure political environment. The war in the north now became a constant reminder of the prospect of 'northerners coming back to power'. This reminder and threat now became an important factor in rallying southerners around the regime, especially during times of electoral competition.

The first visible and blatant exploitation of this ethno-regional divide was the 1996 presidential elections. President Museveni's election task force designed radio campaign ads using the voice of someone with a northern accent holding civilians to ransom at a roadblock. The unruly soldier would threaten, rob and kill his hapless victims. Then the ad would remind its listeners that if they elected Paul Ssemogerere (who was himself from the south), northerners and their murderous ways would come back to power. Newspaper ads superimposed Obote's head on Ssemogerere's face to enhance the effect.

From then on, the war became an important political instrument to literally blackmail people in the south to support the NRM – simply by equating a change in government with a return of violence and northern domination. The war also became an effective tool to delegitimize voices of opposition from northern Uganda. Many senior politicians from the north were labelled rebel collaborators by the regime. Being associated with a murderous cult greatly weakened their national appeal, especially among populations in central and western Uganda. This strategy shifted from being a temporary expedient during elections to being a permanent fixture of the NRM's political narrative in the south.

Over the years, the war provided the justification for the broader assaults on individual freedoms. Newspapers and radio stations would be illegally closed and journalists detained and harassed. The justification in all these cases was 'security'. Opposition politicians who threatened the president were emasculated, harassed and sent into exile, and their supporters incarcerated for months on grounds that they were supporting the LRA rebellion. The detention and trial of former presidential candidate Kizza Besigye, on charges of treason and allegations of colluding with the LRA, are the most visible expression of this aspect of the political utility of the LRA war. The use of former LRA commanders as state witnesses was possibly the most blatant reflection of this perversion.

Dynamics of the rebellion

On top of threatening populations in the south to rally around Museveni, the brutalities the LRA unleashed on the civilian population in the north cast the Ugandan government in the image of a victim of fanatical aggression in the eyes of major constituencies in the Western world. This 'victim' image brought international sympathy for the government. With this sympathy, the NRM government received increased foreign assistance, especially given its economic, institutional and political record in the south. This assistance came in the form of diplomatic, financial and humanitarian help. Second, rebel atrocities blinded observers to the government's human rights abuses, which were alienating the population in the north.

The real victims, the people of northern Uganda, especially the Acholi, were caught between the fire and the frying pan: a hostile army of occupation and a 'terrorist' rebel group. Forcefully moved out of their homes, they were herded into 'protected villages' – officially called internal displacement (IDP) camps, where life reflects Thomas Hobbes's words – 'solitary, poor, nasty, brutish and short'.

Many people ran away from their homes, fearing rebel atrocities. Many more were forcefully evacuated from their homes in order for the vast territory to be left 'free' for the two warlords to tussle it out. Yet it is a basic tenet of warfare that wars are about people – defending their homes, their lives, their property, their livelihoods and their way of life. In northern Uganda, especially the Acholi region, however, neither side recognized this responsibility. The civilian population was a mere statistic that could be moved into what are politely called IDP camps but which in fact are concentration camps.

There were few soldiers deployed to defend these camps – a camp of 15,000 thousand people would be defended by about fourteen soldiers, mainly drawn from a state-organized local militia rather than from the mainstream army. Often, the soldiers lived inside the camps, where the civilian population provided them with a human shield against rebel attacks.[14] Meanwhile, the rebels continued to attack the camps, killing and abducting children at will, as the cases of Barlonyo and Acholi Pii, where rebels attacked and in each case killed over three hundred people, so effectively demonstrate.

Regardless of how people got into the camps (whether by running away from rebels or by forceful eviction by the army), the government simply dumped them there and abandoned them. International humanitarian organizations provided people with food, blankets, sanitation and water. Yet, in spite of millions of dollars invested by these organizations in the camps, life remained extremely miserable. Deaths from camp-induced conditions such as overcrowding and poor sanitation are estimated to be 1,000 people per week. The camps thus produced an outcome worse than the solution they were intended to provide: they turned out to be a death trap for the civilian population. The rebels did not have the capacity let alone the will to kill 1,000 civilians a week.

But this is how international humanitarian assistance produces outcomes at odds with the otherwise good intentions of its promoters. By providing food, shelter, water and other basic needs to the people in the camps, international humanitarian organizations achieved limited short-term humanitarian objectives. This was at the expense, however, of helping the government sustain a policy of keeping its citizens in concentration camps akin to those of the Nazis during the Second World War. It also inadvertently allowed the government to avoid its responsibility to defend its people.

More critically, it shielded government from the consequences of its failure to provide such basic security. What would have happened if people had gone into these camps without access to water, shelter and food? Is it not likely that they would forcefully go back to their homes? In which case, the choice would be between helping the government defeat the rebels or joining the rebellion itself. In the latter case, the rebellion would likely have become a threat to state power in Kampala, thus forcing the government to seek a military victory or a political settlement.

Conclusion

In July 2006, the government of Uganda began peace negotiations with the LRA in Juba under the mediation of the Government of Southern Sudan (GoSS). This has allowed the current uneasy peace. It is not clear, however, whether the agreement is genuine, and if so whether the two parties are willing to abide by it. The optimism surrounding the Juba process is based on false hope because there seems to be no strong incentive on the part of Museveni to secure a lasting solution to his country's north–south divide.

Notwithstanding their posturing, there is strong evidence that the rebels have a stronger interest in peace than the government. This may sound confusing, since one would expect the government to be more reasonable than the rebels. People do not negotiate for peace out of altruism, however, but from self-interest. It is therefore by understanding the incentive structures of the actors that we can explain who has a stronger stake in the peace and is therefore committed to the Juba talks.

For a start, the peace agreement between the Sudanese government in Khartoum and the SPLA has denied the LRA a core military asset – a territorial sanctuary. Southern Sudan is where the LRA could train its troops, keep its supply routes open or withdraw to, to reorganize and re-group whenever the military going got tough inside Uganda. The Sudan/SPLA peace deal has also reduced the incentives for the LRA's major financial and logistical benefactor, the regime in Khartoum, to invest in the rebel group. The crisis in Darfur has shifted the geographical atten-tion of the regime in Khartoum from the south to its western region, politically from the LRA to the Janjaweed.

These developments in Sudan have therefore left the LRA highly vul-nerable – militarily and financially. Without money, arms and sanctuary, the LRA has limited capacity to survive. The SPLA government in Juba does not want Kony there because he is a destabilizing factor – both for them locally and in their relations with their main ally, Museveni. With international arrest warrants issued for him and his top commanders, Kony's only hope lies in reaching an agreement with Museveni; hence he has a strong stake in the talks in Juba.

For his part, Museveni has said that he accepted negotiations as a gesture of goodwill to the GoSS. He said that Kony was killing southern Sudanese. For the GoSS to consolidate its position, it needed Kony out of its territory. Since the SPLA was not interested in fighting the LRA, and given that Museveni had failed to defeat the insurgent army in twenty years, a peace settlement was what the GoSS believed would end the war. Journalist Charles Onyango-Obbo has added an important dimension to this: the SPLA has close ethnic ties with the LRA, and was willing to use this to broker a peace.[15]

Museveni therefore entered the talks because he did not want to antagonize his political allies in Juba. This is a weak incentive, however. That is why the Ugandan army has tended to exploit every mistake the LRA makes in its political posturing to claim the rebel group is not committed to peace, thereby justifying a resumption of hostilities.

Given his psychological frame of mind, Museveni would like to defeat Kony militarily, a clear boost to his ego, as he is likely to want to leave a legacy as the undisputed champion of warfare in Uganda. This incen-tive interacts, however, with the influence of the war outlined above to undermine his commitment to end the war – even militarily. At the very best, Museveni's incentive is to maintain the LRA as a crippled marginal inconvenience in a remote region of the country, along international borders, where it is incapable of threatening his power base in the central and western regions.

Two factors can fundamentally alter Museveni's incentives in the war. First, if the USA removed the LRA from the list of terrorist organizations so that Washington could openly support the peace negotiations. It could then follow this by tacitly showing Museveni that if he does not seek an early end to the conflict, it would support investigations into war crimes committed by the UPDF in both Congo and northern Uganda, a factor that could lead to his own indictment – as happened to Charles Taylor.

Second, Western donors need to shock Museveni with a threat of total withdrawal of both financial and humanitarian aid. This would have serious implications for his ability to sustain patronage in southern Uganda, and finance a corrupt military to contain rebellion in the north. A withdrawal of humanitarian assistance, especially to IDP camps in the north, would transform the nature of the conflict. Without food, people would choose between joining Museveni to fight the rebels – which is unlikely – or joining the rebels to fight the government – which is also unlikely. The likely outcome is that a new rebellion independent of Kony would be born with greater political legitimacy to represent the interests of the region's downtrodden citizens.

3 · The spiritual order of the LRA

KRISTOF TITECA

Introduction

In April 2007, I arrived in Kampala for another period of fieldwork in
northern Uganda. Before leaving for the field, I was invited by a friend
for an informal dinner in Kololo (the posh Kampala neighbourhood
where many expatriates and wealthy Ugandans reside). My friend, a
diplomat, was leaving the country, and had invited several diplomats
and expatriates working for international organizations. At one point
the discussion at the table turned to the conflict in northern Uganda
and the Lord's Resistance Army (LRA). A senior diplomat, from a key
donor country, who was involved in the peace negotiations, summarized
his views in a particularly blunt manner: 'The Lord's Resistance Army
is just a group of lunatics led by Joseph Kony who want to install the
Ten Commandments in Uganda.'[1] Everyone at the table agreed: the LRA
were simply a bunch of 'religious lunatics'.

This view is not exceptional, but has become commonplace, even
among highly educated people whose work concerns northern Uganda.
The spiritual and religious aspects of the Lord's Resistance Army have
been sensationalized through reports about the 'sinister former priest'[2]
Joseph Kony, bizarre rituals, the participation of spirits on the battlefield
or Joseph Kony's Ten Commandments. An emphasis on these characteristics, fundamentally unfamiliar practices to Western observers,
has often been used in portraying the LRA's actions as primitive and
irrational madness, and as such in line with other 'irrational' rebellions
such as those of the Revolutionary United Front (RUF) in Sierra Leone
or the LURD in Liberia. No newspaper article about the LRA can be
written without emphasizing these aspects. These often ethnocentric
descriptions of religion and spirituality give exoticizing and isolated
reports which do not take into account the wider political, social and
economic context, representing the LRA's activities as radically irrational
and as such neglecting, for example, how a spiritual discourse can act
as a medium through which other grievances can be framed.

Analyses from the wider field of African studies have demonstrated
the importance of religion and spirituality in Africa as both a 'cultural

practice and as a determinant of social action' (Green 2006: 635). In this sense, religious and spiritual practices do not signify irrationality or a 'retraditionalization of society' but rather a rational and important element of contemporary social and political life. Ellis and Ter Haar convincingly analyse religion as a determining element of the social and political worlds in Africa, in which political practice is clearly situated within a religious universe (Ellis and Ter Haar 2004). Religion also is an important factor in civil war and conflict, as demonstrated by the collection of articles in Kastfelt (2005).[3] A central theme in Kastfelt's book is the rationality of religion in war, analysing the logic of apparently irrational religious beliefs in war and the use of violence. One of the contributors is Paul Richards, who in his earlier book *Fighting for the Rain Forest* formulates a critique of what he calls the 'New Barbarism' thesis. He argues that the acts of terror against civilians are not the actions of mindless savages, but rather are 'rational ways of achieving intended strategic outcomes' (Richards 1996: xx). In his contribution to the book *Religion and African Civil Wars*, Richards (2005a) analyses the RUF in terms of a neo-Durkheimian functional sociology, seeking 'answers to questions about what has been created by social intelligence in specific, and in this case highly adverse, circumstances' (ibid.: 125). In the specific circumstances of the RUF (forest incarceration, civilian hostility, state and movement violence, etc.), a social organization char-acterized by meritocracy, egalitarian distribution, a specific leadership style and resocialization proved to be the most functional. Although it is pointed out how functional values such as rituals, music and worship emerged in the making of a forest camp, the chapter principally focuses on non-religious issues in the making of the RUF as a 'circumstantial sect'. A question that is therefore left partly unanswered is that of a deeper exploration of the functional character of religious practices. On this specific issue, Wlordarczyk argues how witchcraft practices can serve strategic functions in contemporary African warfare. She argues that 'traditional beliefs and practices serve distinctive strategic func-tions. They can therefore be understood as (instrumentally) rational elements of strategic behaviour, serving the same ends as means em-ployed in other strategic settings' (Wlodarczyk 2004: 2). By elaborating on Alice Lakwena's Holy Spirit Mobile Forces, the LRA and additional examples from Liberia, Mozambique and Zimbabwe, she argues that traditional beliefs are significant for the legitimacy, mobilization and discipline of the armed force, as well as intimidating the enemy and the civilian population.

This chapter seeks to build further on these findings. It seeks to analyse how the LRA's beliefs and practices are constructed into a spiritual order which serves rational and functional purposes in the operations of the rebel movement. Concretely, it is shown how the spiritual order serves both internal functions in guaranteeing internal cohesion and controlling and motivating the combatants; and external functions, in intimidating the outside world. The chapter does not aim to analyse whether the beliefs of this spiritual order are 'true' or not, but instead examines the functional effects of this spiritual order on the intended aims, i.e. the military struggle of the movement. The military struggle and spiritual order can therefore not be seen as separate, but rather as intimately connected. As will be analysed, the spiritual order performs clear pragmatic functions for the military organization, for example, and helps to structure the lives of the new abductees in the movement, making the military organization more effective.

This does not mean that the role of the spiritual order is limited to pure functionalism, as an instrumental force by a few elite members of the LRA. As has already been demonstrated for ethnicity or nationalism, this would be as misleading as portraying spirituality and religion as the main motive of the movement's actions. The religious and spiritual creed of the movement (both ordinary soldiers and commanders) is therefore not questioned. Before the current conflict, these religious practices were already playing important roles (Girling 1960; Ocan Odoki 1997), and throughout the conflict they continued to play an important role for the rebel groups and the population (Finnström 2003). This has already been explained in detail by Heike Behrend (1999a, 1999b) for Alice Lakwena's Holy Spirit Mobile Forces (HSMF), the LRA's predecessor. Also, the LRA is firmly embedded in these local belief systems, even though they have been reshaped into a new spiritual order. On the other hand, drawing on these real beliefs serves a strategic rationality, as they are locally embedded realities which can guide armed struggle and serve certain rational ends. They are therefore a means or 'strategic imperative' (Vinci 2005: 362) to bring about these ends, which can provide a (rational) solution for military and organizational challenges such as internal cohesion or battle tactics.[4]

It is difficult to gather primary sources about this subject. Hardly any written documents are available, and contacting the LRA is too difficult and dangerous, raising immediate suspicion from the Ugandan authorities. Information on the LRA's spiritual order was therefore pieced together through interviews with ex-rebels: primarily ex-commanders and former religious functionaries called controllers and technicians, with whom long in-depth interviews were conducted, some lasting several days[5] (none of whom wanted their names to appear in this text), as well as three prominent former LRA commanders, who wrote a document entitled 'LRA religious practices' (Anonymous 2005). These three commanders were prominent eyewitnesses to and participants in the struggle of the LRA. This primary source therefore proved a useful mine of information for a 'thick description' (Geertz 1983) of the various spiritual and religious practices within the LRA.

Strategic functions of the spiritual order in the LRA

Internal strategic functions This section argues that the spiritual order is serving strategic functions in ensuring internal cohesion, through motivating, legitimizing and intimidating the individual fighter. First, the spiritual order of the LRA has led to a complex system of control over its members, wherein the transcendental character of the rules is an authoritative incentive for compliance. Central to the LRA is the fact that its leader, Joseph Kony, claims to be possesed by a number of spirits.[6] These spirits introduce the rules into the organization, which have to be strictly respected: if they are adhered to closely, the fighters are rendered immune on the battlefield; if not, the fighter will be punished (i.e. killed) on the battlefield. In this situation, punishment is not only carried out by the LRA commanders, but primarily by the spirits, who always know who has been breaking which rules, in which case the ultimate punishment, i.e. death because of impurity, becomes operative. Because of the great number of spiritual rules, as well as the fact that they are continuously changing, there is almost unavoidable violation of them, developing a sense of guilt which enhances the process of culpabilization (Behrend 1999a: 48). Absolute obedience to the many, and frequently changing, spiritual rules is in this case the only way to survive life in the bush.

It is therefore not surprising that there are many reports of abductees who did not escape at the first opportunity, or even refused to be released during peace negotiations,[7] out of fear of spiritual revenge. This power is strongly linked to the rituals and ceremonies. Fighters are, for example, told that the 'Moo ya' (shea nut oil) with which they were smeared in initiation rituals will make it easier to find them (Human Rights Watch 2003); or that Joseph Kony can read their minds (Allen and Schomerus 2006: 27). Moreover, rituals performed by the movement's religious functionaries (so-called 'controllers' or 'technicians') are not only used for fighting the enemy, they are also performed for 'internal' control: it prevents the 'confusedness'[8] and escape of the fighters. Testimonies to this effect were given by ex-rebels who had previously tried to escape, but who claimed they were suddenly no longer able to move, which they attributed to the power of the spirit. On top of this, the fighters have to monitor each other to prevent their escape.

Second, whereas abductees might initially not be keen on fighting for a movement that has abducted them or even killed their families, they necessarily adjust to their new situation. In this context, the many spiritual rules and practices play a crucial role for the fighters to 'grow into' the LRA.[9] The many different rules and regulations, from military regulations to spiritual orders, are crucial in structuring the individual's life in the LRA. As a former commander from the 'Trinkle Brigade' illustrates:

> There were rules for everything in the bush. For example, an important rule of the spirit was that everything must be done at speed 99! You must do it very quickly, so the enemy cannot get you. Also walking must be on 99. They tell you, for example: you go to Lacor, we give you one hour. You must do anything as fast as possible, and keep the time they tell you! Cooking must be done in thirty minutes and going for washing as well. Because if you delay with cooking, you are going to meet your enemy. So you need the speed![10]

This strict order to some extent replaces the sense of uncertainty which is felt upon being abducted and entering the LRA. From the moment abductees enter the LRA, they go through initiation rituals and have to abide by strict rules on, for example, food, sexual intercourse and their relation with elements of nature.[11] These rules and rituals help individual fighters to find their way in this 'new world' and again give them a certain sense of control over their lives, a process enhanced by the fact that many rules and rituals are rooted in local belief systems and therefore are an accepted local point of reference. In this sense, rites help the fighters in their 'particular anxieties and difficulties' and help to maintain 'the confidence of the whole community and its sense of cohesion' (Richards 1939, in Finnström 2003: 41). The abductees realize that by abiding by the rules of this spiritual order, they do not have to fear too much, as the spirits kill only if the regulations are ignored.[12] In this aspect, the LRA bears similarities to the RUF in Liberia, in which the fighter's world was 'pulled apart by social exclusion and capture and then put together again through initiation and social control' (Richards 2005a: 125). The different rituals and rules are therefore important in integrating the abductees into the spiritual order of the LRA, in which this order becomes an important legitimizing frame of reference, giving meaning to their activities. Adhering to this order therefore becomes a source of reassurance and a motivational force for the members. The following extract from J., a former commander, about the anointing rituals before going into battle, is illustrative in this context:

> The holy spirit reported to the chairman [Kony], who selected the soldiers who could be on 'stand-by'. He picked the controllers. He ordered them to mix this type of herbs, mixed them in powder form, put them in a basin together with water and Moo ya. The controllers stand near the basin and splash the soldier, one by one. When the soldiers are near the basin, they put their gun three times in the basin, and women four times. You put the gun up and you say 'God, you are stronger than anything in the world, therefore the power belongs to you'. We also sing songs like 'Polo Polo' ['Heaven should come to rescue us in our lives, and we shall never leave the way to heaven'], because when we sing, we do not even hear gunshots! When you finish, you cannot believe what you have done. You say: what has happened, how did I do all this? It is as if you are not the one who did it! It is a force which you have in you: it gives you courage and strength! [...] All the spirits are with Kony, but if you are going to the battle, you feel that something is with you. In the battlefield, they will be doing their duty and take care of you: everyone will feel very strong.[13]

In this way, the spiritual order constructs a perception of 'fearlessness and omnipotence' (Vinci 2005: 371) for the combatants. As this quote exemplifies, (anointing) rituals play an important role in constructing this image, as well as the different spirits and their rules. The most visible manifestations of this 'fearlessness' are the battlefield rituals: controllers often walk unarmed in front of the troops to clear the battlefield by sprinkling water or other rituals,[14] while as a general rule combatants cannot take cover on the battlefield: they cannot hide or sit down but instead have to walk forward.[15]

Third, the spiritual rules serve certain pragmatic functions for the movement. Certain spiritual orders, such as 'Don't be ambitious, i.e. don't want to be a commander', or 'The LRA should not bring too many women among them as they will impair operations', can be seen as clearly pragmatic and enhancing the proper functioning of the organization.[16] The spiritually informed centralized leadership – only Joseph Kony is possessed by the spirits – can be seen as another form of organizational pragmatics with clear organizational benefits for the movement, and in particular for leader Joseph Kony, who has a strong degree of control over the movement. This pragmatic nature of the spiritual rules also points to their transformative character. For example, whereas initially neither Moo ya nor water from civilians' homes could not be drunk, this changed after Operation Iron Fist. As conditions became much harder, both Moo ya and civilians' water could be drunk. (Before anyone could drink civilians' water, however, he first had to drink Moo ya.)

Fourth, on a more general level, the LRA's belief system can be considered a radically 'new order' (Van Acker 2003) which provides members with a renewed identity, values and beliefs. After initiation, abductees live in a completely new environment, which sets them apart from the society in which they originate and strengthens internal cohesion and social boundaries.[17] Yet it is important to note the strong reference to local Acholi belief systems: various Acholi traditions are respected, such as rituals with regard to birth; and many references are made to Acholi traditions, for example by the frequent use of 'Moo ya'.[18] The members of this newly constructed belief system are referred to as the 'Acholi Manyen' or 'new Acholi', which in turn refer to a mythologized and pure 'Old' Acholi, cleansed of 'impure' influences such as witchcraft, Westernization and corruption (Dolan 2005: 89). It illustrates how the LRA wants to make a new Acholi society purified of all these impure elements. This new Acholi society is also open to non-Acholi and refers to different traditions: other references are also made to existing Christian (e.g. the many biblical references) and Islamic (e.g. Friday as a holy day) traditions. On top of these existing traditions, certain LRA-specific elements (such as Juma Oris Day on 7 April) are added. As Kastfelt argues, in the process of constructing this belief system, local religious traditions are 'renewed through the eclectic and dynamic use of prophetism, healing and spirits' (Kastfelt 2005: 13). A good example of this is the use of the Ten Commandments by the LRA, referring not only to the biblical Ten Commandments, but also to the Acholi tradition of conveying a list of proscriptions in times of crisis, which should heal a crisis situation and its disturbed moral order.[19] The belief system therefore offers a recognizable yet alternative model of identification, playing an important role in integrating individual members in the movement, certainly in the historical context of a society in crisis, which produced a deep sense of disorientation (Adam et al. 2007). The LRA therefore constructs a belief system that is clearly identifiable for insiders (i.e. the rebels), as well as for outsiders (i.e. the general population in northern Uganda); yet at the same time strengthening boundaries between these in- and out-groups. In other words, a 'new order' (Van Acker 2003) is established which sets the movement apart from the wider society (by combining elements from different traditions), yet at the same time refers to existing and recognizable traditions.

External strategic functions Not only does this spiritual order serve important internal functions, it also defines the relationship with the outside world. The all-encompassing spiritual order systematically and ritually establishes boundaries between the in- and out-group, wherein members are separated from the out-group through a strict system of beliefs (Green 2006). Ritual purity is achieved through initiation and the acceptance of the many spiritual rules. It is therefore important to accept that rituals are not a simple reflection of these beliefs, but that 'it is rituals that create beliefs and not the other way round' (Diken and Lausten 2003: 5). As Allen and Schomerus point out, 'As religious practice demonstrates everywhere, regular collective performance of rites affects what people come to think is true, and this is particularly so for children' (Allen and Schomerus 2006: 27). In this way, the rituals and rules establish a set of shared values which serve to emphasize these boundaries between the (ritually) 'pure' insiders and 'impure' outsiders. This spiritual order entails strict guidelines for interaction with this outside world: as it does not abide by the spiritual rules, it is seen as 'impure', immoral and corrupt. From the beginning, the LRA has been fighting a war against witchcraft and unbelief, and has been targeting what it considers 'impure' traditional Acholi elements such as 'ajwakas',[20] ancestor shrines and clan elders. This is nothing new: in this firm targeting of Acholi 'witchcraft' practices, the LRA is a radical heir of Alice Lakwena's HSMF (Behrend 1999b). In this situation, the LRA is fighting a wider spiritual struggle (of the 'new/pure order') against the external 'impure order'.

A good illustration of this is the fact that former rebels consistently claim that the UPDF is using powerful witch doctors to combat them. Whenever battle tactics were discussed with former rebels, the issue of witch doctors would always come up: whenever the battle had proved to be very difficult, they would always find a witch doctor with the UPDF. As an ex-commander argues:

> According to Kony, the whole UPDF is controlled by Satan, and all their witch doctors belong to the devil. These witch doctors are very powerful! They can use the nature and animals. Often goats, birds or dogs are used by the UPDF, and even rain! These witch doctors can also instruct the UPDF to use local herbs. [...] Kony is always aware of what these witch doctors are using, and he would instruct us what to do to defeat it.[21]

Many narratives about powerful UPDF witch doctors (with names such as 'Firepower' or 'Black Lion') circulate within the LRA and northern Uganda in general. The most well-known story is about the witch doctor Ali. Slightly different versions of the story were circulating, but the main narrative was always the same: the LRA was experiencing more and more difficulties in the battle and even the supernatural powers of the LRA were starting to fail. Soon, it was discovered that this was because the UPDF was using a powerful witch doctor, Ali from Zanzibar (according to other accounts, from Nigeria). He could not be hit by bullets or bombs; and was using horns of hippos or cows, leopard claws and even clouds and rain to battle the LRA.

Because of his extraordinary power, the Holy Spirit soon instructed his troops to kill Ali in Alero. The responsible commander did not strictly follow the instructions, however, and left too late. As a result, Ali escaped and went up to Paraa with the UPDF. Paraa is a traditional spiritual centre, which was very important in the spiritual struggle of Alice Lakwena's Holy Spirit Mobile Forces (Behrend 1999a: 30–3). Before the commander had even come back, the spirits had informed Kony about the commander's failure, because anything you write in a security report on a mission, Kony will know before through the spirits. Thereafter, Kony gathered his combatants, and told them about Ali's escape. As the spirits were not happy about Ali's escape, they threatened to bring Ali to the LRA combatants – something they feared very much, as Ali had killed many. Finally, the combatants were instructed to kill Ali in Paraa.

Upon reaching Paraa, they started fighting in the early morning (6 a.m.), but at midday they still had not advanced the slightest bit: according to the narrative, bullets were not hitting the enemy and bombs were not exploding – instead, small birds would come out of the bombs. The combatants therefore sent a message for help to Joseph Kony. He ordered the controllers to get water from Amuru spring.[22] Upon receiving the water, Kony and some controllers reached Ali's hut (Kony had told his troops that Ali was staying in a hut with a green roof), where they started pouring water into a calabash. After this, they started throwing water at Ali's hut, saying 'The power of the world is in the hands of God'; and 'Satan, Jesus defeats you'. Ali also started pouring water over them, however. As he had the power from Satan to control the water, he said, 'Jesus, Satan defeats you!' In this fierce spiritual battle, Ali soon died. The moment he was killed, many birds flew from his house, and the battle with the UPDF was easily won. When Ali was found, he had two long green teeth and woman's breasts.

It does not really matter whether these stories are actually 'true' or not. What does matter is the effects they produce. Testimonies, from both within and outside the LRA, gave the impression that they were believed completely. For the LRA combatants, it therefore became a strongly spiritual battle: it was no longer a war led by the holy spirits against conventional government troops, but a battle embedded in a wider spiritual context, in which both sides are making use of spiritual elements. From a functionalist perspective, this serves two purposes for the LRA leadership: it further enforces strict adherence to the spiritual rules, and it explains possible defeats and failures. As LRA combatants are operating in a strongly spiritual environment – with powerful witch doctors who are able to kill them – strict respect for the spiritual rules is needed in order to survive this great danger. Moreover, the LRA is fighting a spiritual struggle in a very hostile environment, in which governmental actors are making use of 'satanic' actors (the witch doctors), who in turn make use of animals or other elements of nature. The story of G., a former 'controller' (religious functionary), is typical in this respect:

> Kony told us the government is sending goats, cows or dogs to battle the LRA. When these animals come to us, they are the first enemy. Also birds can attack the troops, they are very dangerous. About four or five hundred birds are sent at once. If the birds come and they touch you, the bullet will hit you there. So we try to shoot the birds. But this is very difficult! Because after ten minutes you have birds, then after ten minutes you have rabbits, and so on. All these were sent by the UPDF to check on us. Or it often happened that when we were going to attack, it was raining heavily or a rainbow was there. This was because of the UPDF witch doctor, therefore we would not attack. Or even when rain was coming, we would not attack, because it was sent by the UPDF's witch doctor.[23]

In order to survive this spiritual minefield, in which elements of nature are actively participating in the struggle, the only person with the power to guide the troops is Joseph Kony. Salvation can therefore only take place through strict obedience to Kony, and strict adherence to the internal rules, because of the general impurity of the outside world. In this context, a further polarization between the 'pure' internal order and the 'impure' outer world is taking place. This is illustrated, for example, by the 1994 peace negotiations, in which the government delegation was sprinkled by the chief controller and technician in order to 'purify' them. A former LRA representative at these peace negotiations argued that these rituals were necessary for protection in this 'impure' context:

> The ones coming out of the bush were given certain things to protect them: oil of mudfish would be in your hand. This is because if anybody

from the government has a strong charm to bewitch you, you are protected. If you suspect someone has put poison in your food, you put mudfish
oil on your food, and you will detect it. You especially do it if you are eating food of the government troops.[24]

Also, the Catholic Church is very much part of this impure environment, as it has diverted too much from the 'pure' Catholic religion[25]
and has become too much involved with witch doctors ('ajwakas'). As
former LRA chief catechist Abonga Papa summarizes:

The LRA does not have much interest in the Catholic Church, because
it is full of sin. Because it allows witch doctors. Jesus cannot stay with
Beelzebub! Because some witch doctors, they put on a rosary and they
are called Lay Apostle, and then they say they are holy. But at home, they
are an ajwaka! The Catholic Church, they even sprinkle water with a tree
which is used by the ajwaka. The Catholic Church is no longer a church.
The Catholic religion is too mixed up![26]

In this 'structure of rejection' (Foucault 1973, in Behrend 1999a: 32),
the spiritual order acquires a (supernatural) logic of its own, which acts
as a legitimizing framework for the individual fighters to act in the impure outside world. They therefore do not hesitate to follow orders and
commit brutal acts of violence. In particular, the 'impure' traditional
Acholi elements such as witch doctors, ancestor shrines and clan elders
are targeted. As Finnström indicates, this new order gives the rebels the
legitimacy to abduct children (which are more easily integrated into this
spiritual order), as well as to mutilate and kill people (Finnström 2003:
7–8). Abduction is not only a strategy of forced recruitment, but also a
way to rescue children from the impure outside world.[27] Although this
spiritual order should save the Acholi, on a worldly level it only leads to
their destruction: the 'outsiders' (including the non-LRA Acholi) are seen
as non-believers, who can be killed by the 'insiders', the LRA – similar to
the biblical prophets who could save the sinful people, 'bringing curse
upon curse on them, in order to save a small minority considered to
be the pure at heart' (Doom and Vlassenroot 1999: 25).

Not only does the spiritual order inform the rebels' relationship with
the external order, it also has an intimidating effect on this external
world. Whereas the stories about the use of witch doctors by the UPDF
are hard to verify – the UPDF naturally denies their use – individual UPDF
soldiers were encountered who were using local herbs from an 'ajwaka'.
These soldiers claim the herbs not only give them the ability to protect
themselves from the LRA's spiritual powers, they also enable them to
counter these powers and effectively shoot them. As a UPDF soldier

commented, 'When we detect the enemy [the LRA] here, unlike other wars, it takes between ten and thirty bullets to kill them! Whenever they start fighting, they are not themselves – they become something else.'[28] (Similar reports were encountered about individual SPLA soldiers who, after consultation with local witch doctors, were putting wire around their guns for similar reasons.) In other words, the spiritually informed image of 'fearlessness and omnipotence' definitely has an intimidating effect on the enemy, who is puzzled by this invincibility. This is not only the case for the UPDF (and SPLA) soldiers, but also for the population of northern Uganda.

Violence embedded in local belief systems has added to the intimidating character of the LRA's actions: not only is the LRA violent and ruthless, but it also has spiritual powers that amplify its strength. In northern Uganda, there seems to be a general consensus that Kony has 'some spiritual powers', not only among (former) rebels but also among the general population and governmental representatives. These actors might not necessarily believe in the legitimacy of Kony's power, but they none the less accept his power. In this way, the spiritually informed practices of the LRA could be seen as a 'fine-tuned' instrument of torture: as has been documented extensively elsewhere, spirits play an important role in Acholi tradition, and the LRA is therefore relying on locally embedded traditions to intimidate the population, making these strategies even more effective. As Wlodarczyk argues, 'As the cosmology of traditional religion centres largely around power – whether used for constructive or destructive purposes – it is eminently suitable as a framework for intimidation of this kind' (Wlodarczyk 2004: 19).

To some extent, this also had some effect on governmental representatives, the most infamous example being the July 2003 intervention of the Minister of State for Defence, Ruth Nankabirwa, who declared in the weekly cabinet press briefing, flanked by Minister for Information James Nsaba Buturon, that '[...] this spirit factor cannot be ignored [...] the people believe in it and we cannot ignore it'. She called on 'everybody, including spiritual leaders' to come forward: 'Anybody who thinks he can be helpful to end this rebellion is welcome.'[29] She later denied having made this statement.[30] Nevertheless, journalists had published her statement, and, responding to her call, the National Council for Traditional Healers and Herbalists Association (Nacotha) announced that they would deploy bees and horrible diseases to confront the LRA. There have also been other statements by government officials describing the conflict as a 'spiritual war'.[31] Also, the many prayer rallies in Kampala and 'prayer journeys' to the north, organized in order to protest against and even stop the war in the north, are examples of this 'spiritual resistance'.[32]

Conclusion: the spiritual order in a dynamic perspective

This chapter has pointed out how relying on a coherent system of beliefs and practices of a spiritual order serves clear strategic and rational advantages: it guarantees the internal cohesion of the rebel group through legitimizing the struggle and motivating and disciplining its combatants, as well as intimidating the outside world. Contrary to the widespread portrayal of the LRA as a chaotic gang of rebels, the combination of military and spiritual-religious arrangements therefore offers strategic advantages and makes it a relatively organized movement, which has a strong control over the lives of its individual members. Rather than 'exoticizing' the spiritual order, it therefore has to be understood in the local context of meaning, in which it can be seen as a functional answer to the specific difficulties created by the (changing) context in which the LRA is acting: at different stages in the history of the LRA, the spiritual order has been supplementing the military structure. This point, however, also draws attention to the limits of the functionalist argument. Just as there has been a 'marked shift in the character of the movement' (Doom and Vlassenroot 1999: 22), so the spiritual order underwent a transformation. Whereas some of these transformations support a functionalist logic, other, more recent, developments contradict this.

In the initial stages of the movement, the spiritual order proved a useful framework for compensating for the (relative) lack of an elaborated military infrastructure. There were many pragmatic spiritual rules concerning the use of machinery, which, for example, limited the use of bullets.[33] It was during these years that stone bombs were used and strict rules were in place regarding, for example, trees and anthills.[34] In this phase, the movement can be seen as the radical heir of Alice Lakwena's HSMF. As a former commander testifies:

> From the beginning till about the early nineties, you had to follow the spiritual rules very strictly! Action was taken immediately. [...] For example, during that time you could not have a wife. Or you had to respect things like trees very much, but afterwards this changed. The reason was that in the beginning, we were all new with the organization. It was central then to [teach] the fighters the rules, to let them know what was going on. We were all seen as students then, who had to learn the rules! Because without any rules you cannot control any organization. All these rules came from the spirit, he was the one ordering.[35]

Although the LRA has always been more a conventional guerrilla army than Alice Lakwena's HSMF, it was the creation of safe havens in Sudan, as well as the general aid from Sudan, which provoked a change from 'a motley group of rebels into a coherent, well-supplied military enterprise' (Van Acker 2003: 25), with training grounds, military bases and sickbays. This transformation also had an impact on the spiritual order. Gradually, certain strict spiritual rules of the initial years disappeared. Many informants argue that the spirits started visiting Kony less in Sudan.

This transformation is in line with a functionalist argument, in which the importance of the spiritual order diminishes after the group becomes better organized and integrated into larger military structures – this was, for example, the case for certain Mayi-Mayi groups in eastern DRC (Vlassenroot, forthcoming). Nevertheless, this is not the full picture, as other spiritual functions gained importance, further supplementing and structuring the 'military enterprise' the LRA had become: during this period, many places for worship (yards) played an important role, as well as structured praying sessions and regular biblical rituals. As explained above, this was serving certain strategic functions for the organization, furthering the internal cohesion.

After Operation Fist in early 2002, the conditions rapidly changed, as the LRA lost its bases and structural aid from the Sudanese government. According to a functionalist perspective, spiritual rituals and functions should gain more importance during this phase: as the infrastructural and organizational circumstances became much more difficult, ritual aspects could be used to supplement the diminishing military structure of the organization, in guaranteeing the internal cohesion and motivating its combatants – as in the initial stages of the movement. This, however, was not the case.

On the one hand, another transformation took place in the spiritual order, adapting to the new, and more difficult, circumstances. For example, whereas before Iron Fist all battalions had their own controllers (religious functionaries), after Iron Fist they were attached only to the high command: there were simply not enough controllers for all battalions, and consequently commanders were allowed to take over some of the functions of the controllers. Moreover, whereas before Iron Fist controllers were strictly forbidden to carry guns, they were allowed to do so post-Iron Fist.

On the other hand, and on a more fundamental level, the spiritual rituals and functions also became less significant. Recent returnees have been much less well informed about the spiritual order, and do not know rituals that were considered central before Iron Fist. Some do not even believe in the spiritual order. Although it could be argued that, as most of the recent returnees have spent only relatively little time in the LRA, they have not really 'grown into' the spiritual order of the organization (see the contribution by Ben Mergelsberg in this volume), there is more to it, suggesting an actual decline in spiritual rituals and functions. Since Iron Fist, the spiritual aspect very much depends on the individual character of the unit: it is up to the individual commander to decide on the spiritual order of his unit. For example, whereas some units are still following the structural prayer routine, other battalions hardly ever pray. Most importantly, most returnees (and large parts of the population in northern Uganda) claim that Kony has lost much of his spiritual power, and that the spirits have stopped visiting him at all. The three ex-commanders' paper argues that the spirits stopped visiting Kony as early as 1999 – at Jebel Lem (Two Rocks) in Sudan (Anonymous 2005: 4). Again, it does not really matter whether this is actually true or not; what is important is whether this produces effects on the ground. And interestingly, many ex-rebels gave Kony's loss of spiritual power as one of the major reasons for their defection. Just as there was a consensus that Kony has certain spiritual powers (not only among ex-combatants, but also among large parts of the population in northern Uganda), this consensus has shifted in recent years to the belief that Kony has lost many or even all of these powers. Also, during the Juba peace negotiations, no references were made to the spiritual aspect,[36] although it is yet unclear whether the movement is downplaying the spiritual aspect, or whether this signifies an actual decline in the spiritual functions.[37]

4 · An African hell of colonial imagination? The Lord's Resistance Army in Uganda, another story[1]

SVERKER FINNSTRÖM

Wars are partly what the media make them (Allen and Seaton 1999: 3). Not surprisingly, in the international media the consensus has been that the Lord's Resistance Army (LRA) in Acholiland, northern Uganda, fights for some bizarre and mysterious reasons. 'I will use the Ten Commandments to liberate Uganda,' a headline from *The Times* declares, quoting Joseph Kony, the LRA leader. 'As we walk into the dark, airless jungle clearing after 12 days of increasingly arduous travel,' the author Sam Farmar writes in the article that follows, 'I understand how Stanley must have felt when he finally tracked down Livingstone.'[2] As many journalists before him have, Farmar refers to nineteenth-century travelogue mythology and other familiar markers to once again reproduce a contemporary version of 'that African hell of colonial imagination', to borrow Whitehead's (2004: 16) fitting description.

Despite Farmar's presence at the interview between Mareike Schomerus and Joseph Kony described in Chapters 5 and 6, his writing mirrors years of repeated (media) truths on Kony and his rebels: 'The LRA combined the fanaticism of a cult with ruthless military efficiency,' Farmar writes, 'and while its apparent aim was to impose the Ten Commandments on Uganda, its means could scarcely have been more evil.' Journalist Matthew Green (2008: 316), for his part, tells the story of his editor at Reuters in London who ordered him to restructure his news piece to get 'the bit about the Ten Commandments up high'. In producing persons like Joseph Kony and Alice Lakwena, opposition in northern Uganda was now at 'its most bizarre', wrote Woodward (1991: 181), an academic, while journalist Catherine Bond concluded that Alice Lakwena was 'a voodoo priestess and a former prostitute' and Catherine Watson, also a journalist, summarized the war as one between Ugandan president Yoweri Museveni and 'the primitive challenge' (both quoted in Omara-Otunnu 1992: 457f.). More recently, De Temmerman (2001: 51) has written of the 'savage world' where Kony is the absolute ruler. And in December 2006, some months after Farmar presented his account in *The Times*, Museveni gave the LRA a new epithet – 'Satan's Resistance Army'.[3]

After more than two decades of war, the LRA's extreme violence against civilians and their notorious mass abduction of minors into the fighting ranks have become dominant issues in the debate. The movement is now world infamous for its war crimes and crimes against humanity, and its leaders are wanted by the International Criminal Court (Allen 2006; Branch 2007b). Still, over the years there has been a rather one-sided focus on the religious and cosmological, even pseudo-cultural, aspects of the war, described by Karlström as 'a tragically suicidal popular uprising in northern Uganda' and 'a mass movement of collective moral expiation and salvation' (2004: 598). Consequently, as most observers, and academics, have dismissed the LRA on moral grounds, they have also disqualified the movement as resolutely non-political (Branch 2005: 7). True, the war has become an end in itself, with violence reinforcing further violence, and numerous actors with various agendas – indeed, as described by Nordstrom (1997: 37), a global 'warscape' that by now has expanded, geopolitically, far beyond the scope of this chapter. This fact may contradict any political rationale for which the LRA claims to be fighting. The challenge is, of course, to see whether any claimed political rationale for fighting has resonance with issues relevant to most people in Acholiland, despite the rebels' violent military tactics on the ground.

Thus, it is a heterogeneous, fragmented and very complex reality of which I will relate only one aspect, complementary to the other contributions to this volume. Some readers may find it provocative that I do not follow the common trend that concludes that the LRA are rebels without a cause, led by Joseph Kony, who is 'possessed by spirits' and who 'seemed to have no other aim than to terrorise his own ... people' (Allen 2007b: 147). Or, according to Prunier in *Le Monde Diplomatique*, a movement with 'bizarre syncretic beliefs'. In *Le Monde Diplomatique* we again read about the biblical theme of rebel leader Joseph Kony. 'His only political programme is observance of the Ten Commandments and opening of a Bank of Uganda in Gulu.'[4] In an interview in the *New Vision*, the Ugandan state-controlled daily, Prunier simply concludes that the LRA rebels are 'mad',[5] and more recently, in an academic analysis, he again describes them as a 'bizarre syncretic and millenarian movement' (Prunier 2004: 359). Chabal and Daloz, for their part, admit that the LRA may have a political dimension to their religiously motivated violence, but still conclude that their 'millenarian agenda places them firmly outside the political and criminal organizations' they find relevant to examine (Chabal and Daloz 1999: 86).

So, when it comes to any political rationale of the LRA, the story very much ends where I will start my assessment. I base my account on more than ten years of anthropological commitment to northern Uganda, with intermittent fieldwork periods starting from 1997, against which I have balanced my reading of the literature on Uganda. Throughout my years of research, I have neither seem the claim about a bank office in any LRA document nor heard of it in any of their statements, but rather than being something we may ridicule, it can be noted that today even Barclays has opened an office in northern Uganda, connecting previously disconnected Ugandans to the outside world and its wider developments. I have encountered intelligible manifestos and documents which outline the LRA's *political* grievances, and my examination of some of these documents will indicate a direction alternative to those more commonly narrated. My story is basically a story of marginalization and exclusion in the context of Uganda's wider development from the colonial days to the present. Here Fithen and Richards's note on the Revolutionary United Front (RUF) in Sierra Leone also says something about the LRA. 'Collapse into fatalistic violence and random killing is a development which might have been foreseen by opponents of the RUF,' they note, 'had they been less busy denying the movement's reasons to exist' (2005: 123).

I first encountered an LRA manifesto in 1997, a tattered one-page ten-point programme. Some ten years later, with peace talks held in Juba (South Sudan) that started in 2006 but ended some two years later, my file with LRA written statements has grown big. This is basically also the time frame that I cover in this chapter. Some LRA documents have been given to me by diaspora contacts in Sweden and the UK, a few I have downloaded from the Internet – often copies of documents circulating on the ground – but most of them have actually been shown to me during fieldwork in Uganda, by people who put their trust in me despite a situation of severe state oppression. There is a clear continuity in claims put forward in the LRA documents that I have gathered over the years, and I will present something of a rarity in the academic literature on the war in northern Uganda. My narrative will also function as an implicit chronology.

I have mainly worked with young adults in their twenties and early thirties, who were internally displaced to squalid camps or towns. Some I have followed in their struggles for education for several years now, others in their small-scale businesses or farming. Some have left or escaped from the rebel side, but the majority of my informants, one could perhaps say, have been semi-urban non-combatants. Given that I am a male anthropologist, my material, I have to admit, has a certain male bias. I have also interviewed rebel supporters, and interacted with former LRA commanders, both in Uganda and in the European diaspora, as well as with LRA representatives to the Juba peace talks. Over the years, I have also followed Ugandan and international media and popular reporting on the war, of which I will give a few examples as well, before I proceed to discuss the political rationale of the LRA in manifestos and Ugandan understandings. To contextualize my argument better, I will start with a brief background.

The debated background

Joseph Kony's group, today known as the LRA, can be said to be a successor to Alice Lakwena's Holy Spirit Movement, but over time it has incorporated elements from other rebel factions as well (Allen 2006; Branch 2005; Doom and Vlassenroot 1999; Finnström 2008a). My informants differentiated between two dimensions of armed resistance in northern Uganda: the initial, politically motivated insurgency groups and the spiritually motivated groups that emerged slightly later, such as Alice Lakwena's Holy Spirit Forces. The first dimension of the resistance they called 'the army of the earth' (*mony me ngom*) and the second 'the army of heaven' (*mony me polo*). It is obvious that the Juba peace talks between the LRA and the Ugandan government opened the space for the rebels' 'earthly' dimension to be better heard than ever before, but I would still prefer to describe the 'earthly' and 'heavenly' aspects of the insurgency campaigns as parallel intertwined aspects of the same fragmented war reality. War evolves over time, and at some moments in history one facet dominates over the other, and of course it all depends on whom you ask, how you ask and when you ask.

Allen (1991b) and Behrend (1999a) have delineated the religious and cosmological aspects of the rebel movements in Acholiland, while Lamwaka (1998, 2000, 2002) has written invaluable accounts of the politically motivated rebel factions of the early years, such as the Uganda People's Democratic Movement/Army (UPDM/A). Nyeko and Lucima have provided brief profiles of the parties to the conflict (Nyeko and Lucima 2002), and Onyango-Odongo has written background to the conflict from a local historian's viewpoint (Onyango-Odonga 1998).

There are basically two strands in the virulent debate about the origin of the conflict. One claims that people from northern Uganda initiated the rebellion in an effort to regain the state power they lost when Museveni captured Kampala in 1986 (Gersony 1997: 14). To recapitulate the argument, two governments led by Ugandans from the north (Milton Obote was from Lango, and Tito Okello was an Acholi) followed in the wake of Idi Amin (of Kakwa origin, from the West Nile region in north-western Uganda). With Museveni's takeover, the presidency was handed over to a Ugandan from the south (Museveni is a Munyankole), and this, it has been suggested, people from the north simply could not accept (e.g. Ottemoeller 1998).

A complementary and more contextual version pinpoints the realities that developed on the ground in northern Uganda. There, rape and other forms of physical abuse aimed at non-combatants became the order of the day after Museveni's and his National Resistance Army's (NRA) military takeover. Torture and maltreatment became common. Thousands of suspected rebels were taken into detention. Amnesty International reports a consistent pattern of army- and government-sponsored executions (Amnesty International 1992; see also Branch 2007a). The main remaining insurgency group, the LRA, has retroactively given their perspective on the situation: 'The NRA did to us what the Turk slave hunters did to us in the 19th century. They both treated us like animals, with contempt and open abuse; devastated our land, social infrastructure, decimated our culture and drove us out of our homes, into the bushes and hills' (Lord's Resistance Army/Movement 1996a). As had been the case already during the colonial days, northern Uganda became effectively excluded from economic and political developments going on in other parts of Uganda, notably the central south (Omara-Otunnu 1995: 230).

Nevertheless, the war has frequently been described as one of those bizarre African wars that really cannot be comprehended, and obviously the LRA, because of their gross violence on the ground, has became a co-author in the process. This is a paradox of life, but again, there is more to the story than that. Well aware of this powerful version of the situation, LRA supporters and others with knowledge of LRA manifestos were often careful when they expressed their views in the public arena, and it took quite some time for me to gain their confidence so that they could freely share their feelings, views and ideological standpoints. Without being able to provide any proper or final statistics, I want to question the conclusion by Gersony that of the Acholi people in the most immediate war zone, 'more than 90% do not respect, welcome, encourage, support or voluntarily assist the LRA' (Gersony 1997: 59). Another consultant concludes that he 'could find no one in Acholi who would admit to having any sympathy for the LRA as such'.[6] But frankly, who would welcome war? And who would openly admit support for the LRA or their predecessors, as it is possible, even likely, that such public support could result in treason charges? With this in mind, I suggest that there is a measure available to assess the above figures.

In the 1996 and 2001 presidential elections, fewer than 10 per cent of the voters in the north supported Museveni and his government; in 2006 some 16 per cent did so. In all three campaigns, state-sponsored intimidation and open violence were rampant. The number of people who have welcomed Museveni's rule, then, is basically as small as the number who welcomed the LRA.

Fragments of non-understanding

A documentary called *The Mission* from 1998, screened in various European countries, is a good illustration of Western visions of wars in Africa. Towards the end of the film, the viewer is presented with low-quality archival video material of the LRA from the peace talks in 1993/94, which eventually failed. The film provides no information about these talks. Joseph Kony at one point addressed invited elders for three hours during the talks. According to one elder who attended, Kony wanted to make sure that the LRA was received well by the community. 'He gave assignments to the elders to make all traditional arrangements for their return home,' the elder told me in 1998. Kony also spoke about previous peace talk failures and raised the sensitive issue of Mike Kilama and other high-ranking rebels who accepted an amnesty in the 1980s, only to die in unclear circumstances, some while imprisoned by the Ugandan government. The untimely deaths of these former rebel commanders have remained a critical issue over the years (Lamwaka 1998: 157–8; Okuku 2002: 34–5), but the viewer of *The Mission* is left in ignorance of all this. Most of Kony's comments are presented without translation. Only parts of his speech to the team of peace negotiators are translated into English, and these parts almost exclusively concern his references to the Bible, but again no context is given to his comments. As with Farmar's story for *The Times*, there is no immediate logic comprehensible to the Western audience, only undirected fragments of *apparently* bizarre statements.

A more recent documentary film, *Invisible Children (Rough Cut)* from 2004, is a gripping documentation of the plight of children who, because of security concerns, including the fear of being abducted by the rebels, but also because humanitarian organizations give them food and shelter, trek from their rural homes to towns at night. With a potent Hollywood horror aesthetic framing the film, this film too falls short when the historical background and socio-political context are considered. Lacking photo material of the LRA, the film-makers use clippings from Kamajo (hunter) militia and child fighters in Sierra Leone. And when the rebel leader is depicted, besides recycling old and low-quality photos, the film-makers use drawings. With its dramatic artistic dimension, the film fully plays with Eurocentric imaginations – not really Uganda, not really Sierra Leone, just imaginings of Africa. In the USA and beyond, just like Save Darfur, the Invisible Children movement has become a standing feature of humanitarianism and popular culture, for example in the Oprah Winfrey and Veronica Mars TV shows where it featured.

Other imaginings of Africa

The Ugandan army promotes itself as the rational and modern party to the conflict. The words of Museveni, who is also commander-in-chief of the army, are significant. With reference to the late Alice Lakwena and her Holy Spirit Mobile Forces, the predecessors of the LRA, Museveni has described the rebels in northern Uganda as nothing but criminals and murderers, or at best victims of primitive and primordial senti-ments and perverted local religious traditions. 'The poor Lakwena girl was being manipulated by criminals who would intoxicate soldiers on marijuana,' and supporters of previous regimes were 'intoxicating poor peasants with mysticism and incredible lies' (Museveni 1997: 115). From his perspective, 'the Lakwena peasants' used 'mysticism instead of sci-ence' in their effort to fight his 'modern army' (ibid.: 116). References to primitive superstition and alleged drug abuse are used in an effort to deny any political dimension to the conflict. Instead 'obscurantism', 'witchcraft' and 'backwardness' are said to block modernization and development in Uganda (ibid.: 173).

Over the years, other influential individuals have tuned in to the propaganda of war. Major General James Kazini, one of the president's closest military associates, blames all military violence upon the Acholi. 'If anything, it is local Acholi soldiers causing the problems,' he claimed in an interview with Human Rights Watch. 'It's the cultural background of the people here: they are very violent. It's genetic' (Human Rights Watch 1997: 59). Thus Kazini takes the argument back to the days of the colonialists. As was the case then, the assumption is that the Acholi are primordially violent.

President Museveni and his associates' language of denigration has taken a symbolic dimension understandable to most Africans. Now and then, Museveni calls his opponents in arms 'hyenas'.[7] The meta-phor of hyenas presents them as wild creatures, which in many African cosmologies means that they have vitality and power, but more, that they represent the uncultured wilderness, danger, depredation, death, sorcery and witchcraft. 'Hegemonic groups are able to define such a vocabulary, an ability that enables them to identify opposition and protest as witchcraft, banditry, and terrorism,' writes Winans (1992: 110) with reference to south-central Tanzania on the eve of independence.

With a focus on the rebels' incomprehensible religious practices and gross abuses of basic human rights, and with the rebels themselves characterized as hyenas, terrorists and agents of Satan, but ignoring the Ugandan army's habitual misconduct, comprehensive peace talks for many years were repeatedly dismissed on moral grounds (e.g. Parliament of Uganda 1997). Ehrenreich, who chaired a Human Rights Watch report on the conflict, was less judgemental than the people quoted above but was still pessimistic. She noted that unlike, for example, the IRA of Northern Ireland, the LRA rebels 'have no "political wing", which make public pronouncements and negotiations difficult'.[8] One report to the United Nations concludes that the LRA 'lacks any clearly formulated political objective',[9] yet another that 'the LRA has no coherent political or other objectives'.[10] Instead it is concluded that the LRA follows a leader who 'has created an aura for himself and his organization of deliberate irrationality and obscurantism'.[11] Indeed, as Adam and colleagues have shown in a recent article (2007; see also Behrend 1999a; Titeca, this volume), the LRA's explicit use of Christian symbols and rituals, combined with testimonies from ex-rebels about the rebels' long praying sessions, have led many to portray the LRA as a Christian fundamentalist organization. Adam et al. present several examples of the LRA's ritual activities with Christian and biblical references, but at the same time they wisely add that one has to be careful with this analysis.

Again, this is only one side of the coin. During the years of evolving war, the political and socio-economic dimensions have developed as increasingly central issues of debate and contest in Uganda, particularly in the north of the country. Kayunga writes that it was only in the process of the evolving war that insurgents in northern Uganda framed their ambitions in terms of a struggle for multiparty politics and democracy, 'if only', as he holds, 'to win international sympathy and support' (Kayunga 2000: 112; see also Lord's Resistance Army/Movement 1997). In their documents, the LRA feeds on an increasing local discontent with neoliberal developments in Uganda, explicitly mentioning structural adjustment and other development measures demanded by the donor community. Today the programmes of structural adjustment and cost sharing have reached almost every sector of Ugandan society, particularly health and education. Young Acholi men and women, especially, often communicated to me their experience of being effectively denied Ugandan citizenship. 'Accountable democracy', or 'participatory democracy', to repeat the commonly heard buzzwords of international development rhetoric, is defined by a government's ability to make certain services available to its citizens, such as clean water, food, healthcare and education. Such everyday democracy is generally not found in Acholiland. In the pre-war situation, livestock was sold now and then to pay school fees for young people, but the war has disrupted this and other foundations of income. In frustration, many young people desperately seek economic assistance. One young man wrote in a letter to me, 'My father who was struggling sponsoring for my fees was killed by the rebel force. That is why I got stuck on the way.'[12] The writer concludes that he can see only one option for the education he was forced to abandon. 'I will be compelled to join the rebel force to fight the Uganda People's Defence Forces [and the] government.' This is an example not of greed but of grievance in the absence of democracy and functioning state services (see Richards 2005b).

My young informants felt especially marginalized in their poverty. In their view, they are denied many of the most mundane and everyday aspects of citizenship, for example security, and, as some of my informants put it, 'freedom from oppression'. They feel disconnected from Uganda's wider developments, even future developments (see Ferguson 1999). One issue often emphasized by young people in Acholiland was the importance of including the northern region in Uganda's national development and national future – indeed, this is a theme frequently invoked in LRA statements and documents over the years. Yet the rebels do little to follow their own written endorsement of respect for democracy and human rights, a paradox pointing towards a rather complex reality on the ground. In the words of a young woman, 'I do not support the rebels, nor am I supporting the government. I am just in a dilemma. I would like to support the rebels, but they are killing my people.'[13] Norbert Mao, a politician from northern Uganda, has stated his opinion: 'We in northern Uganda also have our grievances against the LRA just as we have issues to sort out with the Ugandan government. But we can not denounce a good idea simply because it is coming from the LRA.'[14]

When you can do nothing ...

It is not relevant to analyse such seemingly perplexing questions in terms of logical inconsistency, or as irrational and uninformed, as this would indicate an inability among my informants to grasp the complexity of the war. The young woman's statement is typical of the wartime realities of people in northern Uganda, just as seemingly contradictory standpoints are common in every human setting. People often tried to comprehend the discrepancy between the LRA's stated agenda and their violent military strategies on the ground. Sometimes they put forward very frank conclusions. In 2000, for example, 'David', a twenty-five-year-old unmarried teacher, out of frustration concluded that terrorist attacks, sometimes even against their own people, can be legitimate when no other options are open, when the political climate has stifled any oppositional effort, 'when you can do nothing'. He had never been a rebel himself, nor did he seriously think about joining them on the battlefield, but he still held that in an increasingly hostile political environment, 'the rebels are becoming more meaningful'. In late 1999, the LRA distributed their most developed manifesto so far, and elaborating upon what he saw as a new phase in the war, David continued that 'they are becoming more meaningful in the sense that they have been able to publish a manifesto, which they used not to have'.[15]

During my fieldwork in 2002, the language of young people had changed even more. Now and then I encountered urban young men, especially, who talked about the rebels as freedom fighters. 'These are', as one young man said, 'people called terrorists. The world knows them as terrorists.' With them labelled as terrorists, the man continued, for all these years the Ugandan government, with the silent approval of the outside world, has manhandled any person who has tried to initiate dialogue with the rebels. 'Which means', he further proposed, 'as long as they are terrorists in the bush, the people of Acholiland can continue to suffer. [...] Maybe the world sees them as a terrorist organization, for real, which they do not still see [themselves]. These are freedom fighters!'[16] Another young man added, with reference to the blanket amnesty offered to the rebels in 2000 but later, at least for the rebel leaders, overruled by the International Criminal Court's arrest warrants: 'To me, this amnesty, even if the president accepted it coactively, does not apply to rebels. Amnesty only applies to gangsters, robbers, or those kinds of bandits. But to a rebel who has a constitutional right to liberate his country – because these [rebels] call themselves liberators, they want to liberate the country – they don't see that they have done anything wrong.'[17] The discussion among my student informants went on and a third young man broke in, 'I think they have been very wise to know that the amnesty thing was bogus.'[18]

Senior LRA commanders, for their part, have consistently opposed any amnesty if it is not accompanied by political dialogue. From their perspective, when the amnesty law was introduced, to respond positively to it and ask for pardon was tantamount to a capitulation. 'We are not going to lay down our arms as long as Museveni is still in Uganda as president, because the only language he understands is the one that comes from the barrel of the gun,' they wrote in a response to the amnesty law. 'We are not going to be intimidated or baited into compromise through the amnesty law because we have a clear agenda for fighting.'[19]

In the printed manifesto circulated on the ground in northern Uganda in 1999, a note attributed to the LRA leader Joseph Kony serves as a preamble to the political issues raised. The effort to deny the fundamentalist label is central (see also Schomerus, this volume). 'There have been misinformations about this Movement, its name, objectives, policies and even its entire membership including leadership,' Kony writes. The movement is for all Ugandans, he furthermore claims, and the term 'Lord' is explained as a simple thanks to the 'Heavenly Father' who has made it possible for the movement to resist Museveni's army, which nevertheless 'is always armed from tooth to nail'. The rebel leader continues, 'While a big percentage of the Movement's members are ordinary and Practicing CHRISTIANS, I would like to strongly deny that these members are or in any way have the intention of becoming Christian Fundamentalists' (Lord's Resistance Army/Movement n.d.). An LRA political commissary gave his version of the movement's name. 'The group constantly prayed and thanked God for keeping them alive,' he writes. 'In appreciation for the mercy and protection God had shown on them, these survivors gave the name LORD'S RESISTANCE MOVEMENT/ ARMY (LRM/A) to their liberation movement' (Lord's Resistance Army/ Movement 1997). The movement's spokespersons often try to distance themselves from the issue of the Ten Commandments, and the same argument is put forward in yet another rebel document. 'Serious reflection on moral codes and religion may help us now and in the future,' it is claimed. The document continues by saying, however, that prayers 'are not compulsory' and Uganda needs 'freedom of association and belief' (Lord's Resistance Army/Movement 1996a).

Versions of the reality

Most observers have dismissed rebel documents as inauthentic diaspora creations which bear no relation to Ugandan realities (e.g. Human Rights Watch 1997: 73, n. 85).[20] While ignoring the fact that the LRA's original peace delegation to Juba was actually appointed by the rebel high command itself, an influential think tank still concludes that the delegation is a diaspora creation that 'lacks competency, credibility, and cohesiveness'.[21] But the fact that the war in northern Uganda connects to global realities and the wider world, including the Ugandan diaspora, of course, should neither come as a surprise nor be dismissed. And there can be no question that LRA political documents circulate on the ground in northern Uganda, which is where I encountered them in the first place. For example, when in 2000 I enquired among government officials in Gulu, the response was a solid denial of the existence of any LRA manifestos, past or present. As mentioned, however, in late 1999 the rebels had distributed a printed manifesto to religious and political leaders, and it soon attracted great interest from the public. Even representatives of some international NGOs who I knew had received copies denied this in interviews with me. One of the manifesto's main authors, who eventually left the rebel movement and thereafter told me his version, claimed that 2,000 copies were printed and distributed to several national and international NGOs as well as to foreign missions in Kampala. I have also documented that a number of Acholi who were known critics of the government, and therefore suspected of having copies, have perished in Ugandan prisons.

This fact gives a most real, lived dimension to the manifestos. An official discourse of denial is violently at play: not only is it denied that the LRA has manifestos, but people who dare to voice the contrary run the risk of being imprisoned. As reported by the Uganda Human Rights Commission (2003) and Human Rights Watch, (2004) a growing number of people countering the official line have been arrested on charges of treason or suspected terrorism, but denied court trials. Locked in army prisons or detention centres commonly known as 'safe houses', they have disappeared from public view. It is suspected that some have died in custody, under conditions that most of my informants find mysterious and 'bad', or in any case not natural. As mentioned, this was notably the case with rebel commander Kilama and others who surrendered, only to die. The fates of these individuals have had a profound impact on Acholi people, who remember the violent rule of Idi Amin in the 1970s.

Friends in northern Uganda have told me how they occasionally have been stopped at rural roadblocks manned by the rebels. After hasty political lectures by the roadside, they have been given written manifestos with the order to continue their travels and tell fellow Ugandans about the LRA's claimed agenda. Most often, however, people destroy these documents out of fear of being labelled rebel collaborators, and even arrested, by the state machinery. Yet in 1997, during fieldwork, I was given one such manifesto. The one-page document promotes, first, the immediate restoration of multiparty politics and, second, the introduction of constitutional federalism. Following these opening statements, it expresses support for human rights, stresses the need to develop nationwide socio-economic balance, and promotes restoration of nationwide peace and security and an end to corruption. The next items express the need for free and fair elections, the establishment of good relations with neighbouring countries, improvements in the judicial system, and demands that the military organization be separated from the judiciary and executive. Finally, the document argues for the reform of parliament so that it can become capable of tackling 'critical political and economic issues of the country' (Lord's Resistance Army/ Movement 1996b).[22] A subsequent and much longer manifesto, given to me by a diaspora contact, also promotes human rights, as well as 'national unity' and the restoration of 'political pluralism' (Lord's Resistance Army/Movement 1997). Again it can be noted that at this point in time, informants felt sceptical about the rebels' claim to support any human rights, because of the many abductions and gross atrocities that they continued to commit.

When I came across the printed political manifesto in late 1999, it was shown to me independently, by different rebel supporters. This undated pamphlet repeats many of the issues put forward in the previous manifestos. But at eighteen pages in length, it also includes more detailed criticism of the practices of Museveni's government. Among other things, Uganda's armed involvement in the Congo is questioned, and multiparty politics are promoted. The pamphlet, which is an obvious continuation of previous manifestos, furthermore acknowledges that structural adjustment programmes are necessary but questions how they were being implemented in Uganda. It argues that people at the grassroots level suffer the most, especially in peripheral areas in the north and the east. The manifesto also includes brief descriptions of the LRA's economic programmes and proposes policies on education, agriculture, health, land and natural resources, infrastructure, commerce and industry, and defence. Finally, the printed pamphlet questions the concentration of the executive, legislative and military powers in Uganda in the hands of a single individual, the president (Lord's Resistance Army/Movement n.d.: 5).

Today the Kampala region is booming and expanding rapidly, and Uganda has been widely regarded, among both academics and influential organizations such as the International Monetary Fund, as a success story of reconstruction, structural adjustment and economic liberalization. Peripheral regions are lagging behind, however; and my informants said that they had benefited only partially from the development, privatization and alleged prosperity of the country. These are of course themes taken up by the rebels, as they try to seek local support and air their political ambitions:

LRM/A recognize the importance of the World Bank and IMF Structural Adjustment Programs. However, we also recognize that these programs have concentrated on achieving low inflation and deregulating markets to the exclusion of other considerations. The resulting deflationary pressures have undermined prospects for economic recovery, compounding inequalities, undermining the position of women, and failing to protect poor people's access to health and education services. They have contributed to high levels of unemployment and the erosion of social welfare provisions for the poor. Meanwhile market deregulation [has] brought few benefits for those excluded from markets by virtue of their poverty and lack of productive resources. (Lord's Resistance Army/Movement n.d.: 11)

The Ugandan government is said to be 'selling off' the country and its human and natural resources. The rebels are not alone in their critique. Academics Tangri and Mwenda, for example, have shown that the extensive privatization programmes initiated during the 1990s, more often than not infested with corruption, have 'promoted the creation of a tiny wealthy class' rather than following the objectives of 'broadening the basis of ownership' (Tangri and Mwenda 2001: 132f.). Even more vulnerable to such developments, of course, are people who live with bitter war, when little can be done with private means to improve the prospects for the future.

With such developments in mind, it is notable that virtually all LRA manifestos present a critical stance against 'the New World Order' as described by the sociologist Zygmunt Bauman. He does not refer to Uganda in his book; but interestingly, Bauman quotes Zapatista rebels in Chiapas, Mexico, when he tries to put his finger on the frustrations at the so-called peripheries in today's 'process of a world-wide *restratification*', which benefits only very few (Bauman 1998: 70).

What illustrates the new world order is not, perhaps, the weakening of states, as many have suggested, but rather, at least in the Ugandan case, the militarization of the state and its elites in particular (Finnström 2009a). So even if most government officials as well as external observers have dismissed the rebel manifestos as diaspora creations disconnected from Ugandan realities, it must be noted that these documents pinpoint the issues relevant to most people in Acholiland in particular and in Uganda in general. This does give them a certain degree of authenticity. And this, I argue, is a bitter fact of war, just as the gross rebel violence is. In periods of relative calm, the LRA have tried to establish themselves in the political arena, most recently so in the Juba peace talks in South

Sudan. As the LRA peace delegation argues in their opening statement to the talks:

> Your Excellency, it is not true, as has been suggested, that the LRM/A has no political agenda. To say so is to underrate the problem at hand and to give the false impression that LRM/A has no cause for its armed rebellion. Failure to express its Political Agenda loudly [...] does not mean the lack of it. Until now we have been speaking through action. We now want to use this forum, space and time to express our agenda in words. Let the world and all the stakeholders grasp this opportunity to hear us out and be the final judges. (Lord's Resistance Army/Movement 2006)

Without closure: global politics at the peripheries?

On 26 August 2006, the LRA and the Ugandan government signed a cessation of hostilities agreement. This was something that the rebels had long insisted as necessary for serious peace talks. Listening to some of my informants over the phone, and to those who live in the Swedish diaspora, I could hear them voice their scepticism, based on personal experiences and a history of failed talks. They were apprehensive, but I could also sense hope. I especially remember one political refugee living in Sweden, who had suffered tremendously in Museveni's prisons. From our exile in Sweden, we had both done our best to follow the talks in Juba, and when the agreement was signed, he immediately called me. It was a simple fact, he argued with some excitement, that in signing this initial agreement with the LRA, the government had finally, after so many years, recognized the LRA as a political force in Ugandan politics. So too did the outside world, he argued later on, when Jan Egeland, the United Nations undersecretary-general for humanitarian affairs, visited Sudan and met with Joseph Kony in November 2006.

This may be a provocative parallel to end with, but it is essential if we are to better grasp the kind of lived political milieu that has kept the LRA rebels motivated for two decades (see also Branch 2005). It is not surprising that the logic of war alienates people in the war-torn region from the central government. To put it simply, the more violence the rebels have committed against the non-combatant population, the more the government have been blamed by the same exposed people for its failure to protect and provide for its citizens (Doom and Vlassenroot 1999: 28). After the 11 September attacks on the United States in 2001, world politics became more black-and-white than ever. The global war on terror provided the Ugandan government with international support in its own war on terror, and its unconstitutional counter-insurgency violence increased (Finnström 2009a).

Indeed, the LRA has proved to be one of the most violent rebel groups on the African continent. But as I have tried to show, the story has other aspects to it as well. A growing number of especially young people feel that the war increasingly excludes them from development in Uganda – in other words, that their right to exercise citizenship is denied them. They feel severed from the Ugandan nation and its economic, legal and educational services. To the Ugandan citizenry living in the marginalized north, then, manifestos like those of the LRA may be increasingly attractive.

The manifestos – and the war as such – confirm their experiences of marginality. Here we can recall former US president George W. Bush's stand after the 11 September attacks, 'Either you are with us, or you are with the terrorists.' This black-and-white rhetoric, with only two possible alternatives, narrowed young people's ability to manoeuvre their way in life, in Uganda also. Social hope has been shrinking, resulting in a radicalization of the position of the rebels, but also of people outside the movement, including its victims. The sensationalist exaggerations of Sam Farmar and many other Western journalists have fuelled this radicalization. 'As citizens we shall not accept injustices to continue,' David, the unmarried teacher also quoted above, told me in 2000. 'If we continue to point out the wrongs and yet there is no change, then we shall look for other options. The present rebellion can be used.'[23] A decade later, there is still no peaceful closure. On the contrary, as I indicated at the beginning of this chapter, the conflict continues to expand geopolitically in Africa and beyond, far beyond the facets covered in this chapter. The LRA is indeed a fluid and changing organization, to use Blattman and Annan's apt description (this volume). After the failed peace talks held on Sudanese territory in 2006 and 2007, and subsequent bombings of rebel encampments in the Congo in December 2008, as well as rebel counter-attacks on mainly Congolese and Sudanese civilians, perhaps anything can happen.

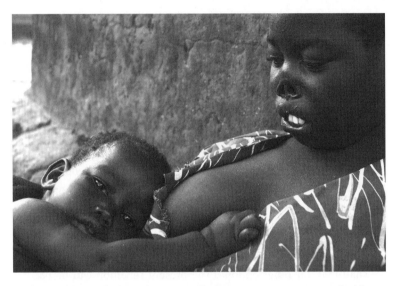

5 Consolata Achelem of Unyama displacement camp was attacked in 2004 by LRA guerrillas while walking alone along a road shortly before sunset. They cut off her lips, ears and nose. In 1994 Kony justified such terror tactics, saying, 'If you lie about us we will cut your lips off, if you run from us we will cut your legs off.' She is seen here with her daughter Aloya in September 2006 (Adam Pletts).

PART TWO

Experiencing the LRA

6 Joseph Kony during peace talks at Ri-Kwangba, 1 August 2006 (Adam Pletts).

5 · Chasing the Kony story

MAREIKE SCHOMERUS

Introduction

On 28 June 2006, *The Times* of London ran a front-page photograph of a rather puzzled-looking Joseph Kony, rebel leader of the Lord's Resistance Army (LRA). The headline for the accompanying article, advertised as the first-ever interview the LRA leader had given, read: 'I will use the Ten Commandments to liberate Uganda'. As Finnström observes in Chapter 4, the author of the article evoked stereotypes to describe his dramatic entry into the world of the LRA: 'As we walk into the dark, airless jungle clearing after 12 days of increasingly arduous travel, I understand how Stanley must have felt when he finally tracked down Livingstone.'[1] The person he had found was of course much more terrifying than the Victorian missionary. At last, a fearless reporter had ventured into the heart of darkness and found the elusive perpetrator of two decades of atrocities, the creator of a community of brainwashed followers, inculcated with his bizarre Bible interpretations. The interview was a great scoop.

In reality, this story by Sam Farmar was a misleading account of what had actually taken place and of what Kony had said. I should know because I was there, in the sunny and breezy jungle clearing. And I conducted the interview. Only marginally less misleading was the representation of the interview on television by BBC's flagship programme *Newsnight*. Both versions made no attempt to interrogate the myths and discourse about the LRA but were content to replicate them. The BBC and *The Times* followed to the letter Binyavanga Wainaina's sarcastic recommendations for those who write about Africa: use the words 'darkness' and 'keep your descriptions romantic and evocative and unparticular' (Wainaina 2005: 92). The key fact, that for the first time Kony had tried to communicate his point of view through the international media, was set aside in favour of a dramatic first-person narrative, deemed to be necessary to communicate with what were presumably taken to be ignorant and uninterested audiences. Thus the story was more about Farmar than it was about Kony. Yet the 'lone journalist in the jungle' was effectively a protagonist invented by himself and his editors.

Having worked for many years as a journalist in various countries, I thought I was not naive about the ways news is manipulated. The determination of reputable media establishments to depict the LRA exclusively in a manner that echoes familiar tales of white adventurers in brutal Africa, however, took me by surprise. Facts were set aside or distorted without any apparent concern for conventional, journalistic ethics, and signed off by senior editors. This is the story of how the interview with Joseph Kony presented in Chapter 6 actually occurred. None of the media professionals in the story comes out well – including myself. The experience rather bruised me.

I did not set out to 'chase the Kony story', although I inevitably became caught up in the endeavour, and took some pride in having won the race to secure the first proper filmed interview with the rebel commander. When the idea was first mooted a year earlier during discussions with former LRA combatants, it did not seem a likely prospect. Yet I came to know several key figures in the rebel movement in the course of my PhD fieldwork. An interview would be invaluable to shine light on the complexities of the situation; maybe it could even help to move beyond superficial stereotypes. I have tried here to give as accurate account as I can of why these stereotypes persist in most Western media. In this chapter, I contrast the events as I saw them with the misleading representation in *The Times*. I attempt to shed light on some of the journalistic conventions that limit our view of particularly African conflicts and to add another perspective to the 'Kony story', partly because the significance of the interview has increased. Instead of being Kony's first effort to explain himself to an international audience, what he said to me may turn out to have been his only attempt to do so.

The chase

The Times article states that 'this is the first interview Kony has given to a journalist', yet this is untrue. Indeed, up until 2006, Western journalistic encounters with the LRA high command had barely occurred. Only these seem to count for *The Times*. Yet several African journalists had spoken to him in the 1990s. Sudanese journalists, for example, recorded Kony when the LRA first moved into Sudan. Most information about Kony's ways, however, had been provided by LRA returnees: stories about prayer days, dozens of wives, breathtaking brutality and spirit possession. Admirers would mention his military foresight and occasionally jolly nature. Both enemies and supporters testified to his powers. But Kony himself had no voice. His deputy, Vincent Otti, was occasionally heard talking on the radio via satellite phone. Kony himself appeared in a few photographs and a low-quality video snippet in the mid-1990s. He looked an unlikely monster with his dreadlocks and 'Born to be wild' T-shirt. Once, in 2002, he was put on air, although it was never clear whether it really had been him. The mystery of the man was perfectly and forcefully upheld.

Scores of journalists writing about the war in Uganda fell for the narrative of a freakish conflict with a crazy figurehead. Western media latched on to a stereotype that had been successfully perpetuated by Ugandan government propaganda and the LRA themselves. The LRA war, in the mind of the Western public, had become the ultimate horror story in which a gang of child soldiers was led towards darkness by a Bible-quoting psychopath. The *New York Times* described the LRA as 'a drugged-out street gang living in the jungle with military-grade weaponry and 13-year-old brides. Its ranks are filled with boys who have been brainwashed to burn down huts and pound newborn babies to death in wooden mortars, as if they were grinding grain.'[2]

Before I first went to Uganda in 2005, I too had heard about Kony's ambition to run the country according to the Ten Commandments. Having read that 20 per cent of the population of northern Uganda had been mutilated by the LRA, I travelled to the region with trepidation.[3] It was a time when yet another peace process had just failed and the International Criminal Court (ICC) had started investigating Uganda at the referral of the Ugandan government. I spent five months interviewing former LRA members, UPDF soldiers, aid workers, families and teachers. What I found was rather different to what I had expected.

There were not thousands of mutilated people, and the 'drugged-out street gang' turned out to be Africa's only rebel force known for its shunning of drugs and alcohol. Some former LRA combatants did talk about the Ten Commandments, but none talked about Kony using them to liberate Uganda in the way that was later reiterated in *The Times*' hyperbolic headline. Perhaps less surprisingly, streets for gangs turned out to be scarce in the bush of northern Uganda and southern Sudan. None of this takes away from the fact that terrible things have happened. Many people I met had appalling physical and mental scars, and more than a million others were living cramped together like animals. I found people who had returned from the LRA who were confused and scared. Some of the former LRA fighters quite openly admitted that they would be prepared to go back to the LRA because they saw no hope at home. People interviewed also spoke about their troubles with the Ugandan army – abuses, threats and the de facto imprisonment in the camps.

One afternoon, Tim Allen and I were taken to meet a group of former

LRA commanders. We asked the usual questions: how long had they been with the LRA, what rank had they acquired, how did they get back, did they have amnesty? The young men were talking openly while some other people listened. Yet when we walked back towards the car, the mood changed. One of the men handed Tim a note, requesting a private meeting. The young men wanted to tell us that life outside the LRA was tough, but they also wanted to know more about what was going on outside Uganda. What exactly was the ICC planning to do?

Over the course of the coming months, as I continued meeting with them, the men's admiration for Kony became obvious. They would casually allude to still having contacts with the LRA leadership, offering to put me in touch with the high command. In August 2005, I received a hand-delivered letter. It was signed by Vincent Otti, the LRA's second-in-command. He wrote that he hoped to tell me one day what the LRA was really all about. Shortly after, one of the young men told me that Otti wanted to talk to me and asked me to use my phone. It did not make any sense. Why would Otti want to talk to me? It seemed like a scam. I heard someone laughing on the other end of the phone line. 'I am Vincent Otti,' the voice said.

It seemed ridiculously easy to get Otti on the phone. He was talkative, telling me how the LRA was doing in their camp and that they were moving around a lot. I asked where he was and why he wanted to talk to me. He knew about me, he said, from his men. His men had told him that I had information. He wanted to talk about the possibilities for peace, and he wanted to know more about the ICC. The ICC had not yet issued warrants for the LRA leadership, but rumours were rife that they existed. Otti did not know what the ICC involvement meant. His understanding was that he would be taken to a foreign location and executed. I suggested that I could meet him to talk in person. He said it could be arranged and, yes, I could interview Kony, too.

Months went by. We spoke regularly. I racked up hundreds of pounds in phone bills. My phone would beep at any given time to signal that I should call back – 3 a.m., in the afternoon, Sunday morning. For a long time I thought I was being taken for a ride. Occasionally, I received frantic midnight text messages from the LRA camp, accusing me of working for the ICC. I never spoke to Kony, but in November 2005 was informed that a meeting would be possible soon. Much later, in the autumn of 2006, I asked a member of the LRA why they allowed me into their camp to speak to the chairman. 'Because you did not belong to an organization,' he said. 'Because you had no agenda.' They had decided that I was no threat. They also expected useful advice on the ICC.

Agreements and delays

About six months after my initial conversation with Otti, Tim Allen received a phone call. A BBC reporter called Sam Farmar was on the line, asking whether Tim saw any possibility of facilitating a contact to the LRA leadership. Having freelanced for the BBC before, I thought it would be helpful to have a reputable news organization behind me and I liked the idea of working in a team. I agreed to meet Sam Farmar in London in December 2005.

Farmar told me that he had contacted Betty Bigombe, the government's former peace negotiator, a few times and was confident that he would be off to the bush soon to conduct an interview with Kony. I thought this unlikely. Bigombe is a remarkable person, but from my conversations with LRA commanders, it had become apparent that they were no longer willing to accept her as a negotiator or peace talks facilitator and that contact with her had ceased. I knew it would be difficult to sustain my LRA connections if I became associated with her. So I told Farmar that, if it became likely that I would be able to meet Kony and film an interview, I would contact him. At that point, conducting the interview was a potentially dangerous and expensive endeavour. The LRA had crossed the River Nile towards the Democratic Republic of Congo (DRC) under military pressure from Ugandan and southern Sudanese troops. Meeting Kony would have likely involved hiring a private plane or even a helicopter and flying to a meeting point under attack. Working with a BBC journalist seemed like a good set-up to get some back-up support – even if, as it turned out, he soon became a freelancer. And I liked Farmar's attitude. We seemed to agree on how this story needed to be reported. He agreed that, if the interview with Kony became possible, we would make sure that it was properly con-textualized, and that we would look behind the façade of LRA myths. I was opposed to a reporter-led approach. Farmar agreed. He said that, like myself, he disliked TV stories that put the reporter in the centre through incessant on-camera presence.

Editors, however, like to see an intrepid reporter on camera. The reasoning goes that the journalist can draw in the viewer by going through an experience for them. That might be true. It might be easier for people in Britain or the United States to connect to the suffering in African refugee camps if a reporter like Sorious Samura sets out to live there, personally experiences the plight of the people, and relates it to the camera.[4] It has been called 'real reality TV', and the fact that Samura is Sierra Leonean gives him credibility to engage in the suffering, although it is not a storytelling device that I particularly like.

And I certainly did not think it was appropriate for me (or Farmar) to adopt this approach towards the LRA. Leaving aside the fact that we are both white and have not suffered anything like what Ugandans and Sudanese have had to go through, there had already been rather too much of that kind of reporting on the region. I was keen that the story should try to communicate the seriousness of what has been happening. The last thing I wanted was for misinformed conceptions of African barbarism to be contrasted with the rational and bemused gaze of the Western commentator.[5] Farmar agreed. At least he said that he did.

Setting up the interview became a series of delays. In early 2006, Otti told me that the LRA was under attack. At times, he was not reachable for days. On 12 February, Otti said that the LRA wanted to talk peace, but not before the Ugandan elections on 23 February because he did not want to boost President Museveni's election campaign. In early April, I received a phone call from someone I did not know. He asked me to join him and two LRA representatives in Nairobi. They would arrange a meeting with Kony, preferably in the Central African Republic. It was impossible to say whether this was going to happen, but travelling to Nairobi seemed vital. The contact stressed again that the meeting was going to be part of the LRA's attempts to initiate peace talks.

I arrived alone in Nairobi on a Wednesday evening in late May 2006, not knowing what to expect. At the immigration queue, I glanced at the news on a massive flat-screen TV. The headline caught my attention: 'First pictures of Africa's most elusive rebel leader'. A man who looked like an older version of the one depicted in the infamous Kony photograph repeated that he was 'not a terrorist'. A meeting with Riek Machar, the vice-president of the Government of Southern Sudan (GoSS), had taken place. Machar had handed Kony US$20,000 and had offered to act as a peace mediator. I was stunned. In the arrivals hall, I was met by four LRA representatives.

Over the next few days, they treated me with courtesy and distrust. At one point, we got in a car, the men locked the doors and we took off for an unknown destination. I was undecided whether this was perfectly normal or utterly stupid of me. On the way, we stopped to buy Ugandan newspapers. The front pages showed Kony and Otti, surrounded by the same men who were now driving me towards the outskirts of Nairobi. I was about to find out that they were taking me to Nairobi's racecourse to watch the horses.

The logistics of the meeting with Kony were only slowly becoming clearer to me. I was told that we would fly to Maridi in Western Equatoria, southern Sudan, and stay a night in an NGO compound. At the time, that seemed a ridiculous idea – how on earth was the LRA going to be allowed in an NGO compound? On 30 May, I was told that after the upcoming meeting, the high command would withdraw entirely to await the outcome of the peace negotiations. The main purpose of this trip was not for me to interview Kony. It was to solidify peace talks arrangements. Delegates seemed to be flying in from everywhere – the UK, the USA – to join those who were living in Kenya or Uganda. The delegation was to be an eclectic mix of Acholi diaspora, LRA commanders and Gulu residents who would travel to meet Kony. Representatives from IKV Pax Christi, who had facilitated the previous Kony/Machar meeting, and members of Sant'Egidio, an Italian organization, would travel as well. I called Farmar in London and told him to get on a plane. Farmar describes this lead-up in his article as having 'made it my mission to track down Kony, putting out feelers wherever I could'. Knowing that I was organizing everything from Nairobi, he could hardly have been that surprised when 'finally, this month, I received a call from Nairobi: Kony would meet me'.[6]

That night, I was bombarded with text messages from Otti's number. He kept asking me who I was and where I was. When I told a member of the LRA delegation about it the next day, he said: 'They are afraid that they might be betrayed.'

The road to Ri-Kwangba

Farmar's article in *The Times* speaks of 'twelve days of increasingly arduous travel' to get to Kony. The truth is that, after leaving London on an overnight flight to Nairobi on 31 May, he took a taxi to the four-star Jacaranda Hotel, had a leisurely tropical breakfast, a relaxing day in Nairobi and dinner by the pool. The next day, the delegation, the peacemakers, Farmar and I flew to Juba in southern Sudan on a commercial flight. In Juba, we were waved through immigration without a travel permit and treated as VIPs, like the rest of the official delegation.

We stayed in Juba until 10 June. The GoSS provided accommodation in a tented camp beside the River Nile, one of the few up-and-running camps at the time and arguably the best accommodation one could have in Juba. A tent usually cost $100 a night, but we stayed for free. When the camp filled with EU delegates, the LRA offered to share their accommodation with us: air-conditioned container rooms, inclusive of three meals a day at a total cost of $160 a day per person. To allow me privacy as the only woman, one LRA soldier moved out of his container. Farmar shared a room with others.

We spent most of our time sitting with cold drinks under a mango tree or playing pool in an air-conditioned tent. The most arduous problem was posed by ants: they kept falling from the tree on to my laptop, which made using the WiFi slightly cumbersome. Evening entertainment came via a satellite flat-screen TV – we watched Germany beat Costa Rica in the opening game of the World Cup. The waiters wore slogan T-shirts: 'World Cup 2006 – We support Sudan'.

Contrary to what the *Times* article conveys, the trip into Sudan did not revolve around 'their' reporter. Although Farmar states that 'we waited for a week as the LRA men checked me out', the waiting was unconnected to his presence. The LRA was relying on Machar to help them – and so were we, for that matter. Machar was providing security, logistics and the communication bridge to the government of Uganda that everyone hoped would facilitate peace talks. Machar was held up on business in Khartoum.

In the absence of 'the big man', the LRA delegation met with local politicians and some aid organizations, being advised and challenged. The general mood was hopeful. The delegation felt that another meeting between Kony and Machar was a real achievement. At one point, they were trying to get Kofi Annan's phone number to try to engage direct UN support. Kony cheered his people on from afar. I was shown a text message that he had sent. 'HEAVEN watches over its TREASURES and you'r one of its FINEST and most PRECIOUS,' Kony had texted. 'Live your life knowing that GOD will never take His eyes off you! Am prayin 4 u al!'

One regular visitor to the LRA delegation was the Honourable Betty Ogwaro, member of the southern Sudan Legislative Assembly for Magwi County. Ogwaro's constituency had borne the brunt of the imported Ugandan conflict. The LRA had been based there for over a decade, establishing a relationship marked by both violence and coexistence with the residents. Three armies – the SPLA, Sudan's armed forces and the Ugandan army – had militarized local life (Schomerus 2007). As a representative of her community, Ogwaro wanted answers from the LRA, but she also had the foresight to see what would turn out to be a great challenge in the peace process: 'The LRA will need a lot of support so that others will accept that they are human beings,' she said. 'We have to remember that the LRA have a reason to fight and that they deserve to be heard.' The main point, she said, was that 'the LRA need to be capacity-built. They need a real tough negotiation team to navigate this. The government has a very well-trained team. Someone needs to teach the LRA how to keep up.'[7]

A few days after we had arrived in Juba, the town was gripped with excitement – a UN Security Council delegation had arrived to discuss

Darfur with Salva Kiir, the president of southern Sudan. Around lunchtime, several members of the UN press corps strolled into our hotel compound and asked around for LRA members. Machar had let slip that the LRA delegation was staying there. It caused a quick debate in the LRA delegation as to whether it would be worthwhile to face the press or not. When asked, I advised against press exposure. It seemed premature, and the delegation was not ready to face a barrage of questions. I was also being self-serving. I did not want anybody to tag along, worried that a commercial media outlet would come up with the idea to offer Kony money for an interview.

At one point, Farmar and I were asked to present 'our mission' to the assembled LRA delegates. I said that we would attempt to represent the meeting with Kony and the peace talks in a fair way, and give the LRA a chance to explain their actions. We also told the delegation that we would not accept restrictions on our reporting, but that we would make sure that our videotapes and information were used responsibly. Ironically, given what was to occur subsequently, Farmar reiterated that we had signed a contract preventing use of the material without both of us agreeing, as a way of ensuring that it was used in an appropriate way. Members of the delegation told us after the discussion that it had been a test. They would have kicked us out if we had agreed to sign a deal with them. It would have shown that we were not responsible reporters.

The entire time, we were guests of the Government of Southern Sudan, although in *The Times* article, the power relations seem to have shifted in favour of the European reporter. It becomes the journalist who paved the way for Machar: 'Mr Machar announced that he would come with me to meet Kony. The next day, accompanied by 40 Sudanese security men, we boarded a charter flight to Maridi, the closest Sudanese airstrip to the Democratic Republic of Congo.' Machar and Farmar did board the plane on 10 June – along with forty Sudanese soldiers, the LRA delegation, three peacemakers, several journalists who had been invited by Machar and Pax Christi, and myself.

Machar usually travels with a cameraman and another Sudanese journalist came along. We were not worried about either of them. We arrogantly noticed that the cameraman's equipment was by far inferior to ours and that he would not know how to feed to international outlets. The Sudanese writer seemed so inconspicuous he almost did not matter. We felt quite superior with our international knowledge and contacts. The presence of two Dutch journalists on the morning of the departure, a writer and a photographer, was more worrying. They could scoop us by feeding both words and pictures within minutes if they had brought satellite equipment. The last thing I wanted was for this to turn into a press conference with everyone rushing to their phones to call in quotes. The Dutch journalists also made the delegation nervous. They did not know them and their presence had not been cleared with the high command.

Some delegation members then argued that it would be better if no journalist at all came on the trip. The prospect of months and months of work and hundreds of pounds in phone bills being utterly wasted flashed through my mind. I spoke privately to delegation members to reassure them that we would be able to deliver a high-quality TV piece and should be allowed still to meet with Kony privately. The LRA's suggestion that everyone would cover the meeting, but that Farmar and I would interview Kony and spend the night at the camp, seemed like a good solution.[8] In retrospect, my protection of the exclusive interview with Kony had further implications. The absence of other observers opened space for the encounter to be elaborated.

Arrival at the LRA camp

Having landed in Maridi we were greeted with tea and food at the compound of the NGO Care, which had offered assistance to the peace mission. Machar's aides went off to organize cars. After four hours' drive on a bumpy road, we arrived in Ibba, where the commissioner had prepared a warm meal and accommodation. A further two hours' drive took us to Nabanga, located about six miles from Ri-Kwangba on the Sudan/DRC border.

What was reported in the *Times* article as '12 days of increasingly arduous travel' had come to an end. We were about to meet with Kony, an encounter that *The Times* made comparable to the famous meeting between Stanley and Livingstone. Given the way the meeting was reported there was an unintended irony in that analogy. Stanley's account, which helped establish the convention of first-person journalism, was fictional (see, for example, Lindqvist 1997; Dugard 2003; Pettitt 2007).

Farmar tells us that after two days of further travel his satellite phone showed that 'we had crossed the border into Congo. We soon stopped and two LRA fighters armed with Kalashnikovs jumped in. Their eyes were blank and bloodshot, their hair in dreadlocks, strings of bullets hung around their necks. We looked at each other and said nothing.'

In reality, the LRA fighters had been waiting with the Sudanese soldiers on Sudanese territory, in the SPLA barracks at Nabanga. Far from it being a chilling encounter with wild African Rastas, we, together with the delegation, were warmly met with cheers and smiles. It was disconcerting and unexpected rather than frightening. We all laughed when one fighter accidentally almost stabbed me with his bayonet when squeezing into the car next to me. It was unintended comic relief.

The meeting between Machar and Kony took place in the afternoon of 11 June. To reach the meeting point, we had to wait in a clearing. SPLA and LRA fighters were lounging about in the grass. Machar was talking to the local county commissioner. It was my first time face to face with active and armed LRA fighters. One of them showed me his black wristband. 'If I take this off, I die,' he said. 'This is our culture in the bush, this is our life. Joseph put it on me eight years ago.' He was wearing a T-shirt of the Ugandan army, probably bounty acquired after a fight. 'Together in arms we shall succeed', it read. His nails were varnished red. I took his hand and asked him why he had painted his nails. He laughed. 'That is life,' he said. All of a sudden, I burst into tears. It came out of nowhere and I walked to the side to hide my emotions.

When Otti appeared, he greeted us courteously, taking my hand in both his hands. After all, we had spoken on the phone a lot. We then all marched into the bush, led by Machar, who had without hesitation agreed to take only minimal security. The meeting was set up on makeshift bamboo benches with Kony and Otti seated on plastic chairs in a clearing. Nobody was allowed to take any pictures or roll a camera. The atmosphere of the meeting was not tense, but direct. The LRA had positioned three rings of security around the site with six soldiers standing directly behind Otti and Kony. Kony, sporting a blue beret and silver tassels, spoke very little. Otti did most of the talking in a hushed voice. None of the LRA soldiers showed any reaction. I caught the gaze of the soldier with the painted nails and he acknowledged me with an almost imperceptible nod.

'Peace talks', said Machar, 'are more difficult than war.'

Otti answered that he had heard on the radio that the LRA had two months to surrender, but that there was no sign of talking.

'Surrender is not my business, I don't work for that,' answered Machar. 'But you know what war does. You know what war did in our country. It is about who will win over the table, not who will defeat the other.'

Then Kony spoke: 'We are committed to talk [...] to see peace in our country and south Sudan. Our people are ready. This time we want to see who is going to spoil this thing. We are waiting what is coming from your side. We are seeing you as our father, our negotiator. From our side, we are ready for everything.'

When Kony asked for time to consult with his delegation, the SPLA left and Farmar and I stayed behind for the night. Some LRA soldiers went to the cars and picked up our luggage, carrying our heavy bags and equipment through the bush. Kony disappeared and in the meantime we were made to feel welcome as guests. The LRA served us food, fresh bread and mashed chickpeas. Everyone chatted around the campfire. I sat down with Otti, who was carrying some papers and a Lwo–English dictionary. 'I need to learn,' he said. 'Learning is always good.' He was reading Sudan's Comprehensive Peace Agreement (CPA). Machar had brought three copies for the LRA to study. Other LRA members were reading as well from an eclectic and for me unexpected collection including *The Complete Idiot's Guide to US Special Ops Forces*, Tom Clancy's *A Guided Tour of US Army Special Forces* and Clausewitz's *On War*. The choice of literature present in the LRA camp was puzzling, a strange mixture of boyish fascination with weapons and iconic writing about European wars.

Otti took my reporter's notepad from me and, using coloured pens and a ruler, meticulously drew the symbol of the LRA in the back of it. He had designed it himself, he said, explaining the meaning of its design elements: Uganda's national bird, the crane, the star and half-moon and a heart with the Ten Commandments, surrounded by two palm branches symbolizing peace. Over Christmas 1985, he said, his nephew was attacked by Museveni's National Resistance Army (NRA) forces in a shop in Kampala. The nephew was killed instantly and Otti packed up the next day to join the rebels in the bush. It was not the story I had heard about how Otti joined the LRA, but it was his story. Later on, the LRA physician took me aside to tell me that he needed drugs for about a hundred patients with malaria or various wounds. He had trained as a doctor thirty years ago in Mbale in Uganda, but had been in the bush since 1986.

The next morning, we were led into the next clearing to meet Kony, while Otti went to see Machar to clarify the peace talks set-up. Incidentally, someone reported live from the Machar/Otti meeting via text messages. It must have been the Sudanese journalist to whom I had paid so little attention. Kony spoke for more than eighty minutes. In the last ten minutes, Farmar asked a few questions while I took some cutaway shots with a second camera. We had agreed that we would both ask questions, yet Farmar had not said anything until I asked him whether he had additional questions. After we finished the interview everyone gathered in another clearing. Kony was joking with the delegation about what he found most remarkable about the unusual interview situation. 'Malaika asked me a lot of questions, she is very tough,' he said. 'She asked me if I had child soldiers.'

Some members of the delegation had never been in the bush to visit the LRA. On this trip, they were getting to know their leaders. By now, Otti had replaced his gumboots with flip-flops and Kony had changed into an ironed shirt instead of his blue T-shirt. He gave a long speech in Lwo, saying that he was ready for peace – but if that was not going to work he was also ready to go to total war and to arm every child in Uganda. I moved to the side and started taking notes. An LRA soldier, a teenage boy, approached me and asked what I was doing. 'I am taking notes,' I said. 'I am thinking.'

'Why are you thinking?'

'It is my job. It is the purpose of my job. What is the purpose of yours?' I asked.

'I forgot,' he said. 'It is too big a question. I am only fifteen.'

Getting the news out

Upon leaving Ri-Kwangba, Farmar tended to business. He called Channel 4 and BBC *Newsnight* in the UK to tell them that the interview had taken place. I did not pay much attention until I overheard him describing the interview on the phone with *Newsnight*'s commissioning editor, during which he gave what I felt was a misleading synopsis of what Kony had actually said. Afterwards I confronted him about this and we started to argue. By the time we arrived back in London the next morning, BBC *Newsnight* had agreed to buy the piece. I was about to learn how British mainstream media work.

At *Newsnight*, the commissioning editor greeted me with the words that she was 'perturbed' that there were no shots of Farmar with Kony. She clearly had not been told by Farmar that we had agreed not to feature ourselves. In the end, I agreed to let Farmar read the script – it did not seem like such a big deal to me. In retrospect I gave in too quickly, not anticipating that the piece would still turn out to be told in the first person – even without pictures of the reporter. We were assigned a producer and Farmar started on the script while I looked at archival footage previously shot in Uganda by the BBC. I had insisted on seeing the script every step of the way. I had also suggested certain parts of the interview that I thought should be included in the final piece.

One line that I did not select was when Kony addressed me to say 'you are the first journalist to come to me in the bush like this'. In the BBC version, this is the first sentence we hear Kony speak in English. Kony seemingly addresses Sam Farmar directly. Editorially, this introduction makes clear who the main protagonist of the piece is. The editorial choice implies that even Kony finds the visit of the journalist the most remarkable aspect of the situation – never mind the two decades of war that needed to be discussed. Although most of Kony's answers in the final *Newsnight* piece were given as direct responses to Farmar's questions, parts of what Kony said to me were edited as if they were still a response to Farmar. At no point is it mentioned or alluded to that any journalist other than Farmar was present at the meeting.

If I was cross about the emphasis on the reporter, words almost failed me when I first saw Farmar's draft script.[9] He described the LRA delegation as 'child-like' with 'no formal schooling', driven by a 'mixture of distorted Christianity and brutality' and 'having manipulated the Bible for their demonic cause'. He called Kony 'messianic'. I insisted on changes, including having 'child-like' deleted: it was an inaccurate and patronizing description of adult delegation members, many of whom had attended or finished school. Despite making some changes, however – including removing 'child-like' and 'having manipulated the Bible for their demonic cause' – Farmar largely stuck to his original script, citing pressure from the producer. I was simply sidelined and the LRA's Christianity remained 'distorted'. The reporter, it was clear from the script, had a superior interpretation of the Christian faith to offer.[10]

In the end, I sent a protest email to the commissioning editor, the producer and Farmar before the broadcast to request changes, listing the parts that were biased and not factual. I also pointed out that Kony did not, as expected, present himself as a messiah sent to fight this war. Instead – despite claiming innocence – he took full responsibility for what he had done, and defended it in a rational way. I also pointed out that the credit given to the reporter of the piece was incorrectly allocated to Farmar, and that if the statistics on abductions mentioned in the commentary were accurate, the LRA would be much larger in numbers than the entire Ugandan army. The *Newsnight* team assured me that the script was being worked on 'point by point'. Somewhat mollified, I took a plane to Nairobi to connect to Juba to follow developments. The BBC report was not going to be the kind I had wanted, but I was sure that the errors and misrepresentations were being corrected. I was naive.

When the *Newsnight* piece was broadcast, it was a personality-driven jungle adventure following the pursuits of lone intrepid journalist Farmar, who even signed off the piece pointing out that 'the fact that [Kony] allowed me to spend time with him may be significant'.[11] The piece bore little resemblance to my experience of the encounter. After the piece, eminent *Newsnight* host Jeremy Paxman welcomed Uganda's high commissioner to the UK to the studio to reply to Kony's accusations against the government. Paxman pushed the high commissioner to say that they should do 'more' against the LRA. It was an easy point for the high commissioner to agree with. None of the complexities – or indeed the common lore that the army quite liked to avoid direct battle with the LRA – was touched upon. *Newsnight* promoted the piece on their website: 'Speaking in the jungle of the Democratic Republic of Congo, surrounded by some of what he estimates as 3,000 heavily-armed fighters, [Kony] insists he is not the monster he is portrayed to be.'[12] One of the big mysteries of the peace talks remained how many LRA there were in the bush. Nobody has ever seen 3,000 fighters. To coincide with the BBC broadcast, it turned out that Farmar had also secretly arranged for an even more misleading account of our journey to meet Kony to appear in *The Times*.[13] I read it in Juba, dismayed that editors of two of the world's major news outlets seemed happy to publish only what conformed to their preconceived notions – although the then head of *Newsnight*, Peter Barron, had written on the *Newsnight* home page that 'our aim [is] always to question the way things are'.[14] Yet contrary to what *Newsnight*, Farmar and most of the press claim to do – investigate objectively and convey the truth – they had actually followed the storyline established over years as propaganda by both the LRA and the Ugandan government.[15] In addition, supposedly level-headed journalism is often infused with Christian value judgements. The same journalists who so readily latch on to the freakishness of Kony's spirit communication see no problem in calling him 'evil'. Invoking spirituality by calling someone 'possessed by the forces of the devil' (the dictionary definition of 'evil') seems acceptable if used by the Western journalist.

Among analysts of Uganda and southern Sudan, the broadcast and article were a source of disappointment and even outrage – for two reasons. One was personal: colleagues felt that I had been treated badly. The other related to the inaccurate news content of the report and to the questionable representation of the material as a heroic journey into darkest cliché-ridden Africa. Without my knowledge at the time, at least four complaints I subsequently became aware of were made to the BBC. The stated policy of the BBC is that 'our commitment to our audiences is to ensure that complaints and enquiries are dealt with quickly, courteously and with respect'.[16] None of the people who have told me that they submitted complaints ever received a direct reply or an acknowledgement. There were some informal, emailed responses from *Newsnight* editors, but these occurred only after the director of the Royal Africa Society had personally pointed out to Jeremy Paxman how problematic this broadcast was. At this point, Jeremy Paxman seems to have expressed concerns about what had happened with the broadcast in graphic terms, and this was probably linked to Barron's defensive reaction. In an internal BBC email Barron wrote that 'I think we need to concede that we could/should have been clearer that this was a joint enterprise, and that "we" would have been better than "I", but that is a stylistic point rather than one of substance of dodgy journalism. (It will help greatly if Mareike's name did appear on the credits – it does on the running order I hope the credits did run, and we can also point out that Farmar himself never appears.)' Following this, in one informal reply to an emailed complaint, Barron asserted he had 'carefully checked the facts of the matter' and was convinced the criticisms of Farmar's reports were 'inaccurate and unfair'. Essentially, the *Newsnight* position was that the two journalists who had brought the piece to them had now had a falling out, and that the BBC did not need to take any responsibility.

Upon my return to Sudan, I found myself in a difficult situation. The LRA felt betrayed. It was partly a question of honour. They had asked to be treated fairly, rather than being portrayed as mindless freaks. The outcome had been just that. I was yelled at and accused of two-facedness. One night, an LRA fighter grabbed me in a dark alley and asked me for the videotapes. Could I assure him that the uncut footage was not going to The Hague to be viewed by the International Criminal Court? Since Farmar at that point was refusing to return the original tapes to me, I said that I could give no guarantees. The LRA commander underscored his threat to my security by choking me.

It was cringeworthy and embarrassing to be asked about the article in Sudan, especially by those who had been part of the 'dangerous journey' into the bush. A few weeks after the publication, just before the opening of the peace talks in Juba in July 2006, Machar travelled back to Ri-Kwangba to convince Otti to join the delegation around the negotiating table in Juba. Otti let him wait for two days. Machar, seated in a forest clearing and reading Stephen Hawking's *A Brief History of Time*, at one point looked up and let his gaze wander over the Reuters correspondent, the camera crew from al-Jazeera, the stringer for AFP and myself and then said: 'Well, at least we can now all be like Stanley about to meet Livingstone.'

A consequence of the BBC and *The Times* representation was that its content became the only accepted narrative, quite simply 'the truth' about Joseph Kony. I learned this after having taken the material to German broadcaster ARD and their flagship foreign affairs programme *Weltspiegel*.[17] When I submitted the manuscript, a version of events a lot less dramatic and adventurous than the BBC script, there were some minor changes requested and the manuscript was signed off with the editor's remark that the piece would 'adorn the programme'.[18] The broadcast was scheduled for 2 July 2006, a few days after the *Newsnight* broadcast.

I was back in Juba when a German colleague called me and told me that the piece was not being broadcast. This was unusual – if there is a problem after signing off, an editor will usually get in touch with the reporter. But I had heard nothing. I tried reaching the editors to find out whether this was an oversight, but to no avail. I asked my colleague to follow up. She was told that after seeing the BBC coverage of the interview, ARD started to have doubts about my version of the story. Eventually I was told that I would have to rework the piece in the style of the *Newsnight* report. I was unwilling to do so, and the piece has never been broadcast.[19]

A few months later, I received a communication from *Newsnight*'s senior editor, Peter Barron. He wanted to enter the Kony piece for the Royal Television Society Awards. He explained that, 'given the controversy at the time it went out I want to make sure you are not unhappy about this and get the credit you deserve. The piece will be included in our general entry, but I would also like to enter Sam Farmar in the young journalist category.'[20] I did not agree to the piece being entered into any awards. The award for international news went to ITV for a story on China.[21]

Journalism and abuse of trust

After the fall-out with the BBC and *The Times* and the humiliating reactions back in Sudan, I tried to dissect why things had gone wrong. Doubtless it was partly because I did not assert my views strongly enough. But I was also uncomfortable about something else. I felt that I had let down people who in the eyes of most do not deserve to be treated with decency. I had told my LRA contacts and their commanders that I wanted to portray them fairly. That was true, but I also said it because it was the obvious thing to say. It is the journalist's (or the researcher's) oldest trick to make someone 'open up'. Malcolm calls this combination of trust-gaining and setting the agenda an inherently 'unhealthy' relationship between journalist and subject. 'The moral ambiguity of journalism lies not in its texts, but in the relationships out of which they arise – relationships that are invariably and inescapably lopsided' (Malcolm 1983: 162). I had managed to get to the LRA and gain their trust by promising them fairness – fairness that critics called bias.[22] And I had not delivered fairness or objectivity.

I had sat down with Kony, shared food from the same plate, and joked with him. Before I left, someone took a picture of myself and Kony. Just before the click of the shutter, Kony put his hand on my shoulder. The picture shows him standing behind me like a well-meaning friend. It is an adequate depiction of his treatment of me – courteous, with some curiosity and bemusement. In the picture, I am clutching my own hands and am barely mustering a tortured smile. I find it hard to show the photograph to anyone.

After the trip, I did not sleep properly for weeks, waking up night after night to imagined phone beeps, signalling text messages and requests to call, as so many times before. In my dreams, I was running away from burning villages, feeling guilty that I had, from the comfort and safety of my London home, tried to comprehend the people involved in the breathtaking brutality of this war. I had touched a world that was not mine, yet I had somehow, minimally and temporarily, become a part of it in order to understand it.[23] Professionally, I found myself in an impossible position. I was angry at myself for not being able to overcome simplistic media stereotypes to shift the news coverage towards an engagement with the real issues of war – the issues of politics, militarization, violence, suffering, justice and human rights. I found the output of my reporting of unbearably low quality. Yet since I had not wanted to make a big deal out of the scoop in the first place, why should I defend it now? Also, did it actually matter to the audience who asked the questions? Not at all. So what really was the achievement that I wanted to defend? That I could claim to be the only interviewer to gain the trust of Kony? I found myself stranded in the grey area of humanity, confused by my own experience as a reporter.

While the attitudes of the reporter and editors I dealt with still puzzle me, it is the fact that the analysis of the story will remain reduced to a dangerous journey to a mad man which still angers me.[24] If the first major Kony interview had been published contextualized, it might have put positive pressure on the peace process. We do not know, but a reassessment of the common discourse might have pushed the international community to support the talks quickly and wholeheartedly, rather than spending months deliberating and in the end never solving its own political ambiguity towards negotiating with a wanted war criminal. Maybe the LRA would not have wasted so much time negotiating for their dignity at the negotiation table.[25] It is impossible to say whether fair publicity and the presentation of the initial journey to Kony in the bush as what it was – the courageous and controversial African led effort to end one of Africa's longest conflicts – would have created an atmosphere that would have encouraged Kony to walk out of the bush in the spring of 2008 to sign the Final Peace Agreement (FPA). Instead, by 2008 he had all but disappeared from the peace process, resulting in a botched military operation with disastrous consequences for civilians (Schomerus and Tumutegyereize 2009). In 2009 and 2010 hundreds of civilians were killed in reported LRA attacks in the DRC.

As a minimum requirement, the standard of reporting ought to have been reasonably accurate without facts being jiggled around to make them fit a preconceived storyline just that little bit better. Significantly, the LRA was not particularly bothered by the ambiguity of numbers about abductions. They wanted to know why it had turned out to be a story that made the attempts at peace look ridiculous. They felt insulted because Farmar portrayed himself as more engaged than he was. They related to the experience in what for me was an unexpectedly personal way, well aware of the value of the prize of the Kony interview. In September 2006, Santo Alit, a senior LRA commander, invited me for a cup of tea in the LRA assembly area in Ri-Kwangba.[26] He explained that my experience was like the biblical story of Jacob and Esau. Jacob deceives his father to receive the blessing that should have been Esau's. Someone you trusted betrayed you and deceived others into receiving praise, Alit said.

I learned through this experience that the LRA's understanding of trust and betrayal, of accountability and culpability, of right and wrong, is complex, but not simply unreasonable. Kony denied the atrocities, but what else would anyone expect? Other things he said give insight into the inner workings of this war, into the intense personalization of the war parties and the damage inflicted by the rhetoric of the 'war on terror' on conflict resolution efforts, the protection of the LRA through the spirit world, the confusing layout of international justice instruments and the ambiguous role of international organizations that have done too little or the wrong things to improve the situation in northern Uganda, even in the eyes of the LRA.[27] These points were simply lost in coverage that aims to avoid complexities, reduced to a headline in *The Times*: 'I will use the Ten Commandments to liberate Uganda'. Significantly, Kony never said this. It was not an actual quote by Kony, and yet it could have been read as such. It is an invented quote, presumably what the reporter had wanted to write or what editors thought the audience would want to hear. The imagination of London-based newsroom staff had outweighed what the person at the centre of the conflict, the interviewee, actually said. Ironically, Kony said in the interview that people were using his Christian beliefs as propaganda.

After years of coverage of this type, it is impossible to attempt to establish anything that resembles 'the truth' about the LRA war – not least because the LRA at times changes its behaviour as a consequence of the coverage. Leaving aside the perpetuation of imagery this creates, even attempts at factual accuracy are not aided by the media's hypocritical hunger for the exotic and by journalists' ruthless practices in advancement of their own careers and ratings. As a result, the LRA war will most likely forever be perceived in terms of the dominant discourse largely created by international news organizations. A complicated conflict with many villains of many skin colours has been reduced to the tale of an imaginary journey, a bite-sized narrative with a white hero and an African scoundrel. The real Kony story, however much we chase it, is elusive.

6 · 'A terrorist is not a person like me': an interview with Joseph Kony

MAREIKE SCHOMERUS

A meeting over breakfast

Joseph Kony was sitting in Ri-Kwangba, a clearing on the Sudan/ Democratic Republic of Congo (DRC) border, and reading the news-papers. It was 12 June 2006, but Kony's copies of *Newsweek*, the *New Vision* and the *Daily Monitor* were a few weeks old. Having foreign visitors around during his breakfast of sweet, slightly earthy-tasting hibiscus tea and freshly made mandazis clearly made for an unusual situation; and Kony seemed a little akward. He apologized profusely about the lacklustre food on offer. 'Life in the bush is very difficult,' he said. 'To stay in the bush. When we are at home [in Uganda] we don't eat this one, we have special food at home, but in the bush we eat because there is [not] anything that you can get apart from this one. At home we eat biscuit, we eat buffalo.'

The interview was conducted in English and only very occasionally did Kony lean over to ask one of his commanders for a clarification.[1] His English, although always understandable, was not perfect. The text reproduced here has been lightly edited and annotated for clarity, but retains his manner of expressing himself as much as possible.

What is a terrorist?

Kony was continuing to skim through the papers as he finished his breakfast. Charles Taylor was on the cover of the copy of *Newsweek*: Taylor was about to be extradited to stand trial in The Hague at the Special Court on Sierra Leone. The extradition seemed puzzling to Kony, and so he was the first to ask questions.

Me, I stay in the bush for almost twenty years, for nineteen years. But I hear many African countries and some other Eastern countries, they are talking the word terrorist. They say Saddam Hussein [is a] terrorist, they said Osama bin Laden [is a] terrorist, they said [that in] Sudan, most of Sudan people, they are terrorist also [...] I hear from some other radio that the government of [Sudan's president] al-Bashir is supporting terrorists [...] And I hear also in Uganda Museveni said, [opposition leader] Kizza Besigye [...] is a terrorist. Joseph Kony, me, that I am a terrorist. Last time, I heard from Sudan government also. They said [the late SPLA/M leader] John Garang, the late John Garang was a terrorist also. So I don't know what kind of [people are] those people. Terrorist. What is the meaning of terrorist? [...] I never knew or I never heard that kind of word [terrorist], but I heard [it] from the words of some African news. Here they are saying such and such is a terrorist, some opposition or most Arabs they are terrorist. Osama bin Laden – terrorist. Saddam [Hussein] is also supporting terrorist. So I did not know. I did not know well. Because I hear in Uganda also they say that I am a terrorist. So terrorist is what? What kind of people? How is terrorist people look like? I don't know [...] I don't know, that is why I ask you. I want to know from you what is terrorist. Because I hear now that most opposition in Uganda, the government now say that they are terrorists, they are terrorists, they are terrorists. I don't know why.

I asked him why he thought Uganda's president Yoweri Museveni had applied the terrorist label to his challenger Kizza Besigye – and accused Besigye of supporting the LRA.[2]

Museveni said Kizza is a terrorist and me is a terrorist. I know that I am not a terrorist, Kizza also is not a terrorist. But people, all African leaders, they are using the word terrorist only to give a big threat to opposition so that they should be afraid. They make it as a propaganda so that people fear [these people called terrorists]. Because if some other Western [countries] hear [the word terrorist] they will support anybody who [does not] want these terrorist people. Because [terrorists] are bad. Even me, I know terrorist is bad [...] but the way some other people is saying is not clear, or is not good. A terrorist is not a person like me. Because [...] we are soldiers. We are international people who [are] fighting.

Kony wanted to emphasize his humanity.

You see, a terrorist can be like me? No. We are now talking with you, we are now staying together, we are eating with many people. A terrorist person [has to] be alone, [has to] die alone also, [has to] fight alone, [has to] die with civilians. [A terrorist does] not confront soldiers as I am thinking, it is like that [...] You are the first journalist to come to me in the bush like this. So with me, I am now here. You have now seen me, I am a human being like you. I have eyes, I have brain [...] I wear clothes also. But [until now] Museveni has been spoiling our name, [saying] that we are animals. We don't talk with people. We are like lion [...] We eat people also. We are killer [...] When we get you, we kill you [...] But now you have seen everything with your eye and [...] you know very well this time people are fighting with propaganda. But for me as a guerrilla, I [have] not yet reached [that level of fighting with propaganda]. I am lacking so many things, that is why you hear all thing from Museveni side [...] I do not have proper propaganda machineries.

Why had he decided to talk to me, when he had so persistently refused to speak to other journalists or researchers.

Museveni [...] did not want other journalists to come to me [...] They don't want people to come to me so that if they did not come to interview me, to talk to me, then he will continue telling the world [lies]. [The government of Uganda] will continue lying [to] the world saying that [Kony] is doing this and this and this, which is not true. It is not true. I am also a human being. I am fighting for the right cause. Our people is now suffering there, in Gulu, you have seen. People are in camp[s]. They went in the camp by Museveni. Museveni forced them. Museveni shoot them with helicopter gunship. They beat them. They torture them [...] And you hear many people also, they are saying that northern Uganda is very bad [...] Even a certain organization, which was called Human Rights Watch. They went also there. They have seen very many things, which was happen there. People are dying daily. People are dying. Their children are dying [...] You see, but Museveni did not want people to come to me because he know that when [...] people, journalist like you come to me, I am going to tell the world. And you are going to confirm that Joseph is there, he is right for his war. Because what is happen there is very bad. It is very, very bad.

But if this is so, why did he not try to communicte using his phone, his contacts, the written word? Manifestos that had circulated in Uganda had always been rather basic and had usually been dismissed by the government as not authentic. I told him that the most common thing said about the LRA was that nobody knew what they were fighting for. Why had they never put out a properly publicized manifesto?

We have done our manifesto [...] It is there in Uganda. Everybody knows that one. We have stated to the world. We have [written] in the paper like this or in a small book our political agenda. Everybody knows what is happen in Uganda, everybody knows. Our wealth, our property was destroyed by Museveni. [Our belongings were] collected, like [our] cows. Our people was killed. Those things [were] known to the world, openly. Everybody in Uganda, they know that one. Even if some of people like you did not read in the book, but the people know. Our political agenda, our manifest[o] is open. Everybody knows what was happen there. Even if we did not explain to the world, but it is already there in Uganda and is being seen by the eye.

So how exactly had Museveni stopped journalists from visiting and speaking to the LRA?

I don't know. But when any person or when any white who want to know what is happen here in the bush [tried to come here], Museveni did not agree. He will stop them. Like Will Ross [long-time BBC correspondent in Kampala]. Last time when we fight in Sudan, [during Operation] Iron Fist, Will Ross was trying to come to see what was taking place and what was happen in southern Sudan. Museveni stop him, in Palotaka. He refuse Will Ross to come and meet us. He refuse Will Ross to come and get us.[3]

'We did not kill'

Kony explained that Museveni killed and destroyed homes in northern Uganda and that the LRA was 'fighting for the right cause [because] what Museveni has done in our place is very, very bad'. I pointed out that people say it is Kony who is doing it, that he is the one who kills people and destroys homes.

[The following paragraph was said later in the interview, but has been moved forward to improve comprehension.] People say like that all right. But they [are] saying without seeing. They just read in the paper like this. They just hear from the radio, but they did not see it with their eye. But we did not kill people. If we kill people, [why are] there [...] so many people now here. We did not kill even one. We went to Congo, we stayed there for almost three months, we did not kill anybody. We stayed in Uganda almost for twenty years, we did not kill any civilians. But civilian is now dying in the camp in the country where Museveni is ruling. But in the bush there is not anybody who is dying. If I kill people, why people is now joining me, why do you meet me if I am a killer? You come to meet me because I am not a killer. I don't kill people. I am a human being. I am a person, also.

I did not kill. But I kill the force, the soldier of Museveni, I did not kill the civilian of Uganda. I kill the soldier of Museveni. Museveni also, he know very well [...] the people of Uganda they know very well that me, I did not kill civilians. But Museveni used that word to spoil our name, to spoil our name so that people did not support us. Some other country don't support us, UN organization did not support us. Just they use that kind of word, as a propaganda so that when people read in the paper like that, they think that we kill people. But we don't kill people. We don't.

Kony also denied committing atrocities in Sudan.

[Museveni] just put propaganda on it that Mr Joseph is selling people in Sudan [...] Mr Joseph is now selling children to Sudan and training with gun. But now we are in Sudan, we are talking with Sudan. If I sold those children in Sudan, do you think Sudan will talk to us? And [now], we are in 2006. The period of slave trade has gone [...] You know if we [sold] those children to Sudan, UNICEF is in Sudan. UN is in Sudan [...] Why did they not come with that kind of work?

I asked him to explain to me what kind of war he was fighting and what kind of military orders he gave.

We, the LRA, we don't fight civilian. We fight the force of Museveni, which come to us in the bush, we fight them. And if we found them also [if we pursued the UPDF ourselves], if we know them also in their barracks we go and fight them there in the barracks. We ambush them also, we ambush their armoured car, like Mamba [military vehicle], but we don't kill civilian.

He gave his explanation for the civilian deaths in Uganda.

The tactic which Museveni [has] done this time [...] he collected the whole civilians together and put them in a camp then he brought his force and deploy around those civilians. So when he want to fight us, he will go and fight us and then they come back to the camp. So if we follow them, we reach the opposition, they will come and they will say that we want to kill the civilians.

In Kony's view, civilians were often dying because they supported the LRA.

When we start to fight [the UPDF], we fight them together with civilians. So when we shoot, the close fire will kill civilian also. That is the tactic, which Museveni now [has] started in Uganda. They mix soldier with civilians so that when we fight [the soldiers] we kill civilian. And then he will say that those people they kill civilian, they kill civilian. This is the tactic, this is what he is doing. But for us, we fight soldiers of Museveni only. We don't fight anybody. And we plan, we collect our soldiers, we give them order to go and shoot the military man. Not civilians.

I wanted to use an example. What about, for instance, the incident in Atiak? The LRA killed about 250 people in 1995. Atiak is Vincent Otti's home town. Why would the then second-in-command of the LRA have given such an order? What had happened?

We are in Sudan in that time, we are not in Uganda. Most of our people [are] in Sudan. And in that period, that month also is the time, which Museveni ordered the people to go to camp. Then some other people they refused [...] Then he said that those who do not want to go to the camp, they are part of LRA. So they shoot them. They start to fight them. And then they say that we are the one who kill them. They say [that the people of LRA is the one who kill them]. But not us. At that time all of my force was in Sudan. We are not in Uganda in that period. But Museveni, he done a certain trick to spoil our name [so he said] that our people is in the force, we kill people in Atiak. But not our force. It is not [...] LRA who fight there. And we are not. Majority of LRA was in Sudan, in southern Sudan, not in Uganda.

'I did not abduct anybody'

I asked Kony about the abductions of children. If it was true, as he claimed, that the LRA was not doing it, why do so many mothers not know where their children are?

We are not abducting anybody in Sudan [...] But the government of Museveni said that we abducted 15,000 soldiers. But now you have seen me, we are now talking together, I don't have even enough gun and money. I don't have acres of maize, of onion, of cabbages. I don't have food. If I abducted children like that, here in the bush, what do they eat? They eat what? I don't have enough food also to feed those people. Then we eat what?

But the people, which was in the bush here [with me], they run from what Museveni is doing inside Uganda there. They run to me, they follow me in the bush. That is why we are now here with them. We are fighting together with them. But I did not abduct anybody there. Some civilian there, they are volunteer themselves to come and join me so that we stay together, to protect their life, to defend theirselves here. Because in Uganda, at home there, they will kill. Museveni will kill them [...] Recently the soldier of Museveni, they kill people in Lira District in Okole. Thirty-six were shot [...] I have seen in the paper. That one also Museveni he said that my force or my soldier is the one who shoot those people [...] But I was here in Sudan, he said that we are the one who killed people there. But on that [accusation]: we are not abducted children. [...] I mean, Museveni is fighting us with gunship, with armoured cars. Do you think that children can afford that condition of war? They will not! That is propaganda which Museveni is playing. I don't have any children here.

I had found that some of the older commanders in Kony's immediate circle were very open when they talked about their history with the LRA. Many of them explained that they had been abducted and had in the early days tried to escape a few times. But when they had failed they had decided to stay and had embraced the cause to fight for the Acholi. So I raised this with Kony. Why do many of those who are with him claim that that they were abducted?

No, no, no, no! [...] That one, that one is not true. Because some of our people which went to Museveni, they were trained, they were forced to say that if the journalist get you or meet you, tell to them that I was abducted by LRA [...] They say that when any white man come to you, tell them that you were abducted by LRA people. [Tell them] we have [been tortured] by LRA. We have [been] raped by LRA. [...] They were all trained like that. But we did not do. They are my people, they are my tribe. Do you think it is good if I, let me say, you think, brother can kill brother? No, it will not happen. I cannot kill them. I cannot abduct them at a young stage like this. If we want soldier, if we we are lacking soldiers, we will go there at home in the village and many youths will come to us because they are seeing what Museveni is doing. But we did not do any abduction by force, no.

I tried to push him further on these issues. I added that, although he claimed that he had not recruited children, I had seen some myself at his camp.

I have my children here in the bush. They are with me in the bush, my children. I have them with me [...] Some of their mother was killed. Some of their mother was shot. They have wound also and they are here with me, my children [of a] younger age.

If that was the case, why had I seen a young boy wearing a uniform and holding a gun?

Maybe they were given guns just to hold it for the time being [...] Maybe that commander or that soldier [who owns the gun] was going for food or was going for what. And they said my friend you help me, I am going for short call or I am going to do this and have the gun, they will come and take it. But they are not soldier, they are not soldier. They are young, they are young. They cannot go to front. They cannot do anythings apart from staying, waiting for food, eating food. They don't fight, they don't do anything. They are my children. They are not soldiers.

At this point, Kony was handed a satellite phone. He listened to his second-in-command, Vincent Otti, who was in a nearby meeting with southern Sudan's vice-president, Riek Machar. Otti was handing

Machar the list of appointed delegates for the peace talks. 'It is good, OK, correct,' Kony said into the phone. He then turned again to me.

I returned to the issue of child abduction. I said that all over the world, people are angry. Everybody says that the LRA are taking children. If the Acholi people were with us here at his camp, they would also ask why their children had been taken. What would he say to them?

To the Acholi people, what I can say [is that] the people [...] in the bush here [i.e. the LRA], they are here because of what was Museveni doing inside Uganda there. They are children, which was suffering in the camp there. It is not because of us. It is because of Museveni who is now punishing their fathers. But not me who is making them suffering there. But the message, which I can tell to them is that they should pray to God to help them. They should work hard to see that what Museveni is doing inside Uganda is stopped, politically. That only thing which I can say to them. Because with Museveni he will not accept anythings. He like fighting [...] when you start to talk, he will not accept, he will not agree. But the children of Uganda, which is suffering now, it is upon Museveni, not me. It is Museveni who is punishing them, who is betraying them. Not me. They should plan [...] another way to let them all be in peace.

'What could the other way be?' I asked

By talking. By talking with international body, by talking with some other country, [with] NGOs so that they give pressure to Museveni to agree peace talk so that everything will stop.

I asked whether I had understood correctly. Despite the fact that people say that he had been taking children, he was only protecting them. Was that correct?

We have force only, there is no any children apart from my children which was born in the bush. But some other civilian if they come to us, yes we protect them. If they follow us in the bush or if they join us, we protect them from what Museveni is doing there at home. We protect them. Because some of men which was there, their wife was taken by Museveni force, by Museveni soldier. They took their wives. They give them AIDS so those husband, they run away. They leave their home. They come to the bush, they run away from the camp. So when they come to us, we don't kill them or send them away. We just keep them together with us.

'They want Acholi to remain poor'

I asked him whether he had any evidence for his accusations against the UPDF. He said the LRA had a lot of evidence. Among other incidents, he referred to one in Soroti. This was the Mukura massacre of 11 July 1989. The then NRA killed dozens of civilians by locking them in a train and lighting a fire underneath.[4]

There are so many things which UPDF have done in Uganda there. Last years, [Museveni] ordered civilian to go to the camps. He give to them twenty-four hours. Failure to do, he shot. He did that one also. He went to the village and found many people were drinking. They were entertaining. [He] killed them just there in celebration, he killed them all. He found the [animals people owned], they killed them all [...] Museveni [was] also in Soroti. He said that some other Teso they support LRA. [He] put them in the train [...] put them, lock all of them, they all died there [...] [Museveni] went to my home, in Odek. He collected people [...] very many [...] children, goats, and together with human being, they collected them there and killed them all. [The UPDF] said that [those collected and killed] are supporting their son, Joseph Kony. And now they are capturing some of our people from the town, they are capturing, they go and put you in the house without thinking about you, you stay there, sometime you die. They went in some other village [to] collect people [forcing them to make] very big graves. They pack people there, they bury them all.

'Why do they do that?' I asked. 'Why does Museveni not like Acholi people?'

They did that because they know that Acholi, they are clever [and] strong also [...] Acholi – people love them. Acholi [are] known worldwide. And the land of Acholi is very good and there are so many minerals in Acholi. So [Museveni] want to destroy in Acholi so that those things will be his own things. He [wants] to destroy all Acholi so that the land of Acholi will be his land. This is what I know.

Our land is now being given to some other people. Some other owner, they are now buying our land. The whole people of Uganda, they know that one. Even the member of parliament they talk about that. And most of [the people who are taking Acholi land are] from Mbara.[5] They are brought to Gulu to occupy the land of Acholi. It is like that. They want Acholi to remain poor. Let me say it, Museveni he did not want Acholi to be in their land there. He want Acholi to be out, to complete, to die all. To be completed, by all means. This is what Museveni is doing.

He said there was proof for this motivation. The proof was that there was a lot of army activity in areas where there was no LRA.

There is no war there, but Museveni is killing people there. Why? There is no war. There is no soldiers. There is no guerrilla in some other places in our country there, in Uganda. Places like Pader, there is no rebel activities in Pader. There is no rebel activities in Pakwach. There is no rebel activities in Lango. But Museveni is killing people there. Because he don't want this tribe called Lwo [i.e. all the Lwo-speaking groups, including the Acholi, Langi and Alur] to be in Uganda, he want all of us to go away.

I said that I was surprised to hear that there was no LRA in Pader. On the contrary, I said, when I had been to Pader I had been told that there was an LRA shrine there, close to Acholibur. And that this was a holy place the LRA always had to visit after entering Uganda from Sudan. This was supposedly one of the reasons why Pader was so insecure. Kony seemed genuinely puzzled and I had to repeat my question several times. Finally he said 'no, no, no' and that the story was not true: 'Pader is no important shrine as you say for us, it is not like that [...] I did not come about that story.' But the story about the shrine and the rituals that were needed when the LRA entered Sudan triggered him to talk about his own belief.

'A clean war is known to God only'

Many people is now talking about [how] we the LRA, they say that we are fighting for Ten Commandments and we are fundamental. [They say] we are Christian fundamental. We are fighting for Ten Commandments.

This was obviously an important point to him as he addressed me directly and assumed that I was of Christian faith:

And now I want you to know, Malaika, as you are first journalist, if we are fighting for Ten Commandments [for you as] a Christian, is it bad? The law of the God is the best one in the world. God, he gives us his law because he know that we can follow. He cannot give us any difficulties. We [are] able to follow that law. But if I am also fighting for Commandment of God, is it bad? Is that bad? It is not against human right. [It does] not give pressure to anybody. But the whole people in the world – I know that they are following the Commandment of God. But Museveni is stating in a wrong way that I am a fundamentalist, but not.

Kony referred to me as Malaika, rather than Mareike. Malaika is Swahili for 'angel' and is the way I am often referred to by members of the LRA because my first name sounds similar.[6] Kony also knew that I am German, so he used my background as an example to make his point. 'If [you] steal something in Germany, they will kill you. If you love somebody's wife in Germany, they will kill you. They will kill you,' he said. I protested to say that neither theft nor adultery was punishable by death in Germany – nor was any crime. Kony took the point.

They will not kill you, but they will arrest you. When you get somebody wife to be yours, you get it, they will talk about it, they will arrest you. In Uganda also, if you get somebody's wife to meet them or to have sex with them, they will arrest you. If you kill somebody purposely they will arrest you. If you tell [lies] to somebody either this man is a thief, he steal money like this, like this, they will take you to the court, you pay. If you do bad things [...] like stabbing somebody with the knife or giving somebody poison in Uganda, they will arrest you. In Sudan, they will arrest you. Even in Germany, they will arrest you. In Britain, they will arrest you.

So the Commandment which people are talking about, for us, we see that it is good. It is good. But [...] we see that everybody in the world, they are following the commandment. And that commandment was not given by Joseph, was not given by LRA to the world. No, that Commandment was given by God.

He said that he believed the Commandments to be true. '[That] does not mean that we are fundamental as Museveni said. [That] we kill people when we get somebody [...] No! We don't do that.' He said that the law of God was 'all over the world [...] German people, they don't want a thief. The Uganda people, they don't want a killer. Sudanese people, they don't want a thief also or a liar.' He then used his example to return to an earlier point made about propaganda, saying that the LRA's Christian belief was now used against them:

But people is now turning this word as a propaganda, so that people do not love us. They do not like us, we are fundamental. But I assure you that we are not fundamental people. We are a Christian. Like you. Like anybody. We are a believer of God. That there is God, there is Spirit which is controlling the whole world [but] which is not seen by the eye.

I wanted to find out more about how he saw the role of the LRA in the conflict, wanted to move away from his own propaganda. I asked him whether he believed that there was such a thing as fighting a fair war. 'Can there ever be a situation where one side fights a clean war and the other side fights a dirty war?'

In a war, it is very difficult to say that this man is fighting [a] clean war. This man is fighting dirty war. It is very difficult to tell. Because one man can say that [the enemy] is a Satan to let people refuse [the enemy's] policy or to let people see him as a bad person. And [the enemy] also, if he refuted this [accusation of being a Satan], he say [the other man] is a Satan also. So to say that this is a clean war or this is a bad war, is very difficult to say. As I am saying, is very, very, very difficult. I cannot say that we are fighting clean war. [I cannot say] Museveni is fighting dirty war [...] Because a clean war is known by God only. Is known by God, not by us. This is what I know.

I wanted to know more about his god, about his beliefs and of course about his communication with spirits. The answer was surprisingly simple.

We don't know where heaven is. And we have not seen any spirit there in heaven [we can say] that is the spirit of Malaika. We have not seen. But we believe that heaven is there and we believe that spirit is there. But for me, as I am saying, to say this is clean war and this is dirty war is very difficult. Because nobody knows what was God planning on earth [...] Only God [knows] what is taking place in the earth.

So he had said that he could not see my spirit – but he had seen other spirits, according to numerous eyewitnesses. Did he have a spirit?

Yes, we have a spirit [...] that one I can tell you. Holy Spirit is with us. Because we [...] pray. Anything we are doing in the bush here, we pray [to] God. And we are following the law of God who give to us here. And God, the Spirit of God, he tell us what to do, he tell us what is coming to us. The Spirit of God also give to us what is needed for us.

For example, you know, we are guerrilla. We are rebel. We don't have medicine. But with the help of spirit they will tell to us, you, Mr Joseph, go and take this thing and that thing [tree bark or herbs] and give to the people. Then they will be treated well. It is true, it has happened with us. So that you see our force here, they are all OK, they were all OK. And then when something is going to happen on us, [the spirits] will tell us, don't do this and this and this. If you do this thing, it is bad. And then when we want to do that thing, we pray to God. And he will come and say that, now, don't do this thing. Do that thing, instead of this, like that. All of our activities [...] all of our live we are being conducted by Holy Spirit.

How exactly do the spirits tell you this? I asked.

They will come to us. They will load through me. They will come through me. Then they talk to the people what to do. They will talk to the people what is going to happen. They will talk to the people what [...] shall we do. They will tell us. If you want to treat people [for illness], [the spirits] will come. Maybe through dreaming, they will come like dreaming. They will tell us everythings. At daytime we will go and do what he told us. And he will come at any time, he will come to us and tell us, please go and do this and this and this. Mostly when we are in this place [in a foreign location in the bush] [...] when we are in a place like this where we don't know the tribe, which was here. Because you see we are Acholi and our country is in Uganda, we are very far from here now. Now we don't know anybody from here.

We don't know the language of the people here, in Sudan here, we don't know the language of Congo people, of Democratic Republic. We don't know their language. But spirit that come and say that now, you go this way. If you go this way, you are going to meet some other people there. Tell them like this, like this, like this. Then they are going to give you this and this [...] Even you, before you come here, [the spirits] told us that there is a lady coming from Germany. [She] is going to meet you, you talk to [her], don't refuse. And we are now talking.

I asked him whether the spirit changed him or whether he stayed the same person. 'No, I will remain like this,' he said.

Only that I will use any language which [...] people can understand. Which can make person understand. [The spirit] can come with English or Kiswahili or Arabic. Any language he can speak when Mujungu with me, we will talk Mujungu [...] Any, any, any, any, tribe with me, he will talk the language of that people. But I remain like this, as we are now talking.

I wondered how exactly this worked. Does it mean that Kony was literally talking in a different language? 'Do you then start speaking Arabic?' I asked. 'He talks through me Kiswahili. Or he talk through me English or he talk through me French. Any language he can talk.' But how was anybody able to understand the spirit? Did Kony himself understand?

When Frenchman come to me, [the spirit] talk in French. He talk French language. When Acholi come to me, he talks Acholi. When Arabs come to me, he talk Arabic. But if he talk Arabic to us, some of us they know Arabic. Or when we are together with Arabic, he talk. He talk Arabic. So that people of Arab understand, Arab people they will understand well.

And French? I asked. Who among the LRA speaks French?

Me? I don't know. But the spirit know. The Holy Spirit know French language. But me, I don't know. I don't know French.

So how, then, does anybody know what the spirit is saying?

For example now, if the spirit come because you are German, he talk English. So you know what the spirit will say. With our people, when the spirit come, he talk our language so our people will know that the spirit say like this. Or he come as a dream to us, showing the whole thing this is what is going to happen. Then I will come and say to the people: You people be aware, this thing is going to happen [...] So we should do like this, like this, to avoid this thing is going to happen. It is like that.

So was the spirit giving orders or recommendations? I wondered. 'Can you refuse to do what the spirit tells you?' I asked. Kony thought this was a funny question. He laughed when he answered.

The spirit cannot talk anything which we cannot do [...] God [knows] that we are going to do that thing [recommended by the spirit] and that thing also we [are] able to do it. That is what the spirits say to us [...] But always, he will not order us to go and do things. He will stop us from what we are going to do if that thing is bad. He will stop us to do bad things [...] He will show to us what is going to happen in the future or before he will tell to us. And he will tell us the stories what will going to happen. But he will not tell us, you go and fight, no. You go and do this, no. You go and kill this person, no. He will not do that [...] He will tell us what is going to happen. And he will tell us how we should win our enemy, that if you want to win your enemy, please, you do like this, like this, like. And then you will be safe.

Or your enemy is coming from this side. You go like this. And they are now planning like this. You, Mr Joseph, tell your people that the enemy is planning to come and attack you. So to avoid that attack you withdraw your people from here, go this way. Or [the enemy is coming] in two directions, maybe [...] they are coming from this side and from this side.

Then the secretary who write what [the spirit] says, he will tell to the people now, the spirit said like this, like this, like this. Then we will go. Sometimes we will stand to [prove] if that thing is going to happen. Now, but he will not give us. I mean [the spirit] will not order the soldier to go and do anything. And if something is going to happen [...] he will come and tell us that when you do that thing, something will happen. You don't do this, you don't kill this. You don't do bad things like this. It is like that. And when people are planning on us, he will tell us.

Many LRA members I had met had talked about prayer ceremonies. Some of them were conducted according to Muslim customs. Five prayers a day, a month of fasting. I asked Kony whom he was praying to – and how.

We are praying [to the] Christian god [...] and we pray as Christianity pray. [The] majority of our people, they are Christianity. Even me, you know my name is Joseph Kony, which means I am a Christian.

'I am not guilty'

I asked him whether he was aware that he was wanted by the International Criminal Court.

That one, I hear. I read in the paper like this. LRA leadership, Joseph Kony is wanted by International Criminal Case. That one, as I see, I am not bad or I am not guilty. I did not. I have not done what Museveni is accusing me of.

I interrupted him. In this case, I said, it was not Museveni accusing him of anything. It was an international court – and did he know what he was accused of? He did not. I offered to show him his warrant, which I had brought with me so he could see what he was wanted for. He was not willing to look at the accusations.

It is not true. Because what they are saying that I have done, this is not true. And that accusation was sent by Museveni to [The Hague] [...] we know very well that Museveni is the one who did that to block us or to spoil our name.

You say you have not done it, I interrupted, but without knowing what was in the document. 'Have you seen the document? Have any of the five wanted commanders seen the document?'

We did not see any, but we hear that the arrest warrant of LRA, the command of LRA, was given to Sudanese, was given to Congo, it is like that [...] But that one I know it is not true. Because as I am seeing you cannot hear the word from one side only. You cannot say that Mr Joseph is guilty without hearing anything from [me], then you say that he is guilty. [...] the reason why I say like that, it is better if those people [the ICC], they hear, they come and talk to me as you are now talking [...] then they hear what I am saying and what Museveni saying. Then [after hearing both sides] they will come with that, that you are bad. But this one, they only hear from Museveni side, from my side they did not hear any things. They did not question me, they did not ask me, they did not interview me about that ICC.

I offered again to show him his warrant, but he was not interested. It was clearly not the right time.

No, because we are not in that task. You have come here not for it. So if you want that one which you are now saying [looking at the warrants], [...]

we will have at least [some other] time to see or to talk about it [...] I hear the things like that. So I see that if I did not see [the warrant] is the same, because I already hear what they say about that ICC [...] As I said, I am not guilty. I am not guilty. I am not guilty. And we did not know that reason why we are accused in The Hague. We don't know. They just hear from what Museveni stated to them only. So if they want peace, they will take that case from us [...] But if they do not want peace, then they will continue with it. Or if they want peace, they will take a proper way to convince Kony or to talk with Kony [and] Museveni. And going to talk, so that they will prove that who did those things. Who did the thing, which people say that we are being accused. Who did that things [that] the international body want to know. If they want peace to be, they will call all of us together then we talk about it. But [it is not enough to say] that I am guilty or I am wanted with the ICC. Then come here to arrest me without knowing [my side of the story]. That is not true. And it will not happen to us.

So if he was keen on establishing his side of the story, did that mean that he would go to court to defend himself?

I cannot call any court to defend myself, because it is difficult. How can I call them? Where are we going to meet?

I explained to him that there would be a defence team ready for him that would defend him against the prosecutions. So knowing that, would he go to The Hague?

At this time, it is very difficult to do. But when we talk this peace talk, when we talk and everything is finished well, we go. We go and talk. We go and judge that case to show that I am not found guilty. Yes. But this time, as I am saying, it is very difficult even to meet those people [of the ICC]. Unless we talk with Museveni and Museveni agrees to meet, agree to talk peace with him. Then everybody would be free and we move one by one by one step until we reach that problem. And through this peace talk, I know that we are going to solve all those things, we are going to solve all those problems.

So how did he envision the peace talks?

There is nothing [bad] which is going to happen. We are all going to be OK. This peace talk is good for me from my side. I see that it is good. There is nothing bad. But I don't know from Museveni side. But from our side there is no problem. We are waiting for our mediator [Riek Machar] to present what we have discussed here to Museveni. If Museveni agree, he is going to send his committee to meet our committee also. Then they will discuss and then they will make agenda which we are going to talk about.

An agenda for the talks had not been outlined or even talked about – after all, it was not clear at that stage whether the Ugandan government was even going to agree to talks. Nevertheless, maybe he could spell out the LRA's most important demands?

Everything which was happen in Uganda, it is very important. Which was happen in my place there, in Gulu, Kitgum and some other district. It is important. All of them is important. Like how the people which was in the camp. We want them to be free. We want them to go back home. So if Museveni, really Museveni want peace as me now, they should let those people go back home. Give freedom for my people and this people to walk free without anything. But we want freedom mostly for the people of Uganda. And we want civilians and some other people also to be free.

I asked him whether he wanted to give a message to Museveni, make a statement of some sort.

I have said so many thing to Museveni, as now you said that I should tell something to Museveni [...] My message to Museveni is if Museveni can agree to talk with me, it is only a very good thing which I know will bring peace to the people of Uganda. My message to Museveni is only to agree the peace accord which we are talking now. It is only that one.

'I am a freedom fighter'

At this point, Sam Farmar, who had been videoing the interview, asked Kony to explain again who he was, and what his objectives were.

I am a military position who is fighting in Uganda. I am a freedom fighter who is fighting for freedom in Uganda. But I am not a terrorist [...] We want the people of Uganda to be free [...] We are fighting for democracy, we want people to be a total democracy. We should be free to elect our leader. We want our leader to be elected [...] but not a movement like the one of Museveni [...] But not to force them by force as it is now happened in Uganda. We want Uganda to be democracy, to be democrat.

But you are the one making trouble in Uganda, Farmar said.

No, I am not the one making trouble in Uganda. That one is not true. If you now seen what was happen in Uganda. Many people are now being arrested, many people are being killed. Like Kizza [Besigye] was arrested, like some other politician was arrested [...] who is arresting them? Not me! [It is the] government of Uganda.

But these arrests happen because of your attacks, Farmar said. People are saying that you bring the violence and Museveni is only defending.

That one is not true. I am not the one who is bringing the problem in Uganda [...] It is Museveni who was bringing problem in Uganda. I did not giving people of Uganda problem as Museveni is now doing. I am not. I am also fighting as some other politician is now fighting politically. But I am military position, which is fighting militarily in Uganda. But the problem, the reason why we are fighting, because Museveni is a dictator. He is not doing good things in Uganda. Not working very well in Uganda there, is not a democratic leader.

When Farmar said that the people of Uganda had voted for their leader, Kony replied:

That is not true. The election which take place in Uganda is not good election. Is not true election. Is not fair. Kizza was arrested. Many people was killed. Some other people [were] beaten. They were doing bad things. So Uganda is not totally democratic. Uganda is not a democratic country. So we want our people of Uganda to be democratics.

So did God tell you to fight this war? Farmar asked. Kony did not understand the question. Farmar had to repeat it.

No, no, no, no, no. It is not like that. God did not tell me to fight this war, no [...] Many people say like that. But God did not tell me to fight the people of Uganda or to fight the government of Museveni. Only the government of Uganda who want to fight us because they said that we are [...] using spirits, or spirit is with us so [Museveni] want to kill all of us [...] But God did not told me to fight Uganda people. He told me to teach the Uganda people how to be a democratic system, how to be in a good leader. How to work together. How to be in God's law. But not to kill the people of Uganda.

Farmar asked Kony how many spirits speak to him: 'I don't know. Very many. I don't know the number but they speak to me. They talk to me.' You have been accused of terrible crimes, Farmar said – he had seen pictures of people with their lips cut off.

That one is not true, that is propaganda which Museveni made [...] Let me tell you clear, that thing was happen in Uganda. Museveni went in village and cut ear of the people, telling the people that that thing was done by LRA [...] it is not LRA. And the people of Gulu and Kitgum also, they know very well that this thing was done by soldier of Museveni, not LRA. And so many people also were tied with the ropes, put up on the trees, fire behind [them] like this. People were drying in the fire, [that] also was done by the people of Museveni in Uganda there. And that one also saying that the LRA is the one who was doing this. Which is not true. So if you want to understand very well from that thing which was in the village, ask the people around which that thing was happen, but some other people which was taken to hospital, which was taken to town, they were [...] forced to say that this thing was done by LRA. Which is not true. I cannot cut the ear of my brother. I cannot kill the eye of my brother. I cannot kill my brother. That is not true. See that is very very wrong. We don't do that thing. That thing was done by Museveni's soldiers, they turn to us because we don't have proper propaganda machines and we don't have many people which can tell those things that this thing was not happened by LRA. That is what you should know very well.

Farmar asked whether that meant that the LRA had never been involved in any abductions, mutilations or rapes.

LRA has never been involved in that one. LRA has never been involved. Because many people many people say that we abducted. We don't pabduct many people, we don't abduct children. If I abduct children here how do they stay? We don't have home here, we don't have food, we don't have medicine. They will die and now you have met some of our people also. There is not children here apart from my children. Apart from my children which was born in the bush. But we did not abducted any people. But some other people from the village, they come to us because they fear this one which was in the camp in Uganda, the condition, that is why they ran to the bush. So when they reach us here, we don't kill them, we don't send them away. We keep them to stay with us. Because they are our brother, our sister. But we don't abduct any children. And there is no any use of children in the bush here. That one Museveni say like that, just to spoil our name. We don't do that one. That is our country, that is our place. So in the bush here, we don't use our elder sister or elder brother to come here. No. Because they are young, they cannot afford to walk in the bush. And they don't know how to fight. They don't know war. But people say like that so that some other people, the world will say that bad, I am bad, that only is the weapon which Museveni is using to the world, that people know that I am bad. I am a killer or I abducted many people. No, it is not like that.

And then Joseph Kony took the microphone off his T-shirt.

7 · On the nature and causes of LRA abduction: what the abductees say

CHRISTOPHER BLATTMAN AND JEANNIE ANNAN

Introduction

Twenty years after its birth, the strategy, organization and motives of the Lord's Resistance Army remain shrouded in mystery and supposition. What little we know is drawn from interviews with former participants, commanders and civilian victims. What emerges is a patchwork of motives, methods and structure, with different accounts sometimes in direct conflict.

The phenomenon of abduction is also poorly understood. While we know that many youths met terrible fates – whether killed, forced to commit unspeakable acts or taken as slaves for combat or sex – we have little sense of what experiences are exceptional and which are the rule. Finally, we can only speculate as to the reasons for mass child abduction – perhaps the same barbarism and irrationality that are said to have characterized the LRA's other activities.

In the absence of a public face and (until very recently) an active political arm, the LRA's activities, motives and structure have been defined by external actors, most of all journalists, human rights groups and the Ugandan military and government. One thus worries that the most sensational rather than the most common experiences have found their way into discourse.

An emerging historical, political and anthropological literature – much of it summarized in this book – has begun to challenge the misconceptions about the LRA, abduction and the war in general. This chapter presents data from Phase I of the Survey of War Affected Youth, or SWAY, a representative survey of hundreds of young men and boys in northern Uganda.[1] Results from SWAY Phase II – a subsequent study of women and girls in the LRA – are detailed in Annan et al. (2009). The collection of systematic quantitative data enriches this understanding, and allows us to obtain a sense of proportion and present a more accurate picture of both the LRA and abduction.

This evidence suggests that the LRA appears to be a much more strategic and conventional military organization than often supposed, however terrible its violence. A different view of abduction also emerges. On the one hand, abduction is seemingly more widespread, more focused on adolescents and (on average) less grotesquely violent than often imagined. On the other hand, what is more common and broad based than previously supposed is the emphasis on political ideology in the group, as well as the level of cooperation and allegiance to the rebel cause reported by abductees – a testament to the LRA's (at least temporary) success at disorienting and indoctrinating their unwilling recruits.

Most importantly, what emerges is an answer to why children (especially adolescents) were so attractive to the LRA. Dozens of hypotheses appear in the large and growing literature on child soldiers, yet virtually none has been tested. While all explanations are undoubtedly influential, which dominate and which are marginal is essentially unknown. New data allow us to discriminate between these competing accounts. In northern Uganda, child (specifically young adolescent) recruitment reveals itself to be a product not of barbarism but of rational calculation. The data suggest that young adolescents were disproportionately targeted for three principal reasons: because they were over-represented in the population; because they were more effective guerrillas than younger children; and, perhaps most importantly, because they were more easily indoctrinated and disoriented than young adults. By understanding the dominant forces influencing child recruitment in this instance, we are in a better position to change the incentives and constraints facing rebel leaders and more effectively minimize the recruitment of children.

Data: the Survey of War Affected Youth

In order to understand the long-term impacts of the war on youth, in 2005 and 2006 the authors and a team of local assistants conducted a representative survey of 1,016 households and 741 male youths in eight sub-counties in the districts of Kitgum and Pader.[2] The survey collected two main forms of data: first, current well-being (economic, physical, psychological and social) and, second, detailed information on abduction and other war experiences.[3] It is the latter which forms the basis of this analysis. Thirty of these youths were followed up for in-depth qualitative interviews.

The population surveyed covered males currently aged fourteen to thirty. Former abductees were over-sampled, and 462 were interviewed in total. In the eight regions surveyed, roughly two in five young males now aged fourteen to thirty had ever experienced an abduction of any length, and roughly one third reported an abduction of at least two weeks.

Females reported abduction with less than half the frequency – fewer than one in six women now aged fourteen to thirty report abduction of any length. At the time of writing, an in-depth survey of females was under way. Their experiences, especially those of women taken to become fighters and 'wives', will be examined in future work.

Had the survey sampled only youth presently in the camps, it would have missed migrants and unreturned abductees, as well as those who perished during the conflict. Instead, the authors sought to develop a representative sample of youth living in the region before the conflict and track them across the country.[4] In-depth qualitative interviews were also conducted with abductees, and community and clan leaders. Among the LRA, interviews focused on foot soldiers and mid-level officers, including junior commanders, catechists, spies, 'wives', bodyguards and even accountants.

Throughout this chapter, 'abduction' refers to any time forcibly spent with the rebels, regardless of length. Abductees thus include those taken for a few hours up to those absent for a decade. One concern with such data is that youths may have misrepresented themselves as abducted in the hope that it would lead to assistance. If this were true, both the numbers and the patterns reported in this analysis might be biased. We took three precautions to minimize this risk. First, all abductions were cross-checked. Household heads (who were typically interviewed months before the individual youth) were asked to report the abduction experiences of all household members. Major inconsistencies between these reports and answers from the youths themselves were investigated.[5] Second, upon being interviewed, all youths were informed repeatedly that the survey was not tied to any assistance. Finally, during the survey, youths who reported an abduction were asked multiple questions on their particular abduction experience, making misrepresentation significantly more challenging. As a consequence, in our opinion abductions are overstated by no more than 5 per cent, and possibly not at all.

The scale and incidence of abduction

These data suggest that the scale and incidence of abduction are different than what has been presumed in the past. First, it appears that the scale of abduction has been underestimated, in part because the percentage of abductees who passed through reception centres has been overestimated. Moreover, the LRA's focus has been largely upon adolescent males aged twelve to sixteen. Younger children were often deliberately avoided and were more likely to be released. Other than by age, however, there is little pattern to abduction by the LRA.

Scale The total number of abductees is difficult to ascertain, and any figure is at best an educated guess. Widely quoted is a UNICEF figure of 20,000 to 25,000 children passing through reception centres. The total number of abductees, including those who do not return through the official system, may be three times this amount, however. Survey responses from our eight sub-counties suggest that only half of male returnees passed through a reception centre. Based on the retrospective household rosters, one fifth of male abductees never returned. Finally, at least one fifth of abducted youth are not children but aged between eighteen and thirty at the time of abduction. These figures suggest that for every three children in the official reception centre count, ten youths were actually abducted – suggesting a figure of at least 66,000 abductions in total.

Could 66,000 abductions be an overestimate? Such a large figure is consistent with the high level of abduction reported in the sample, and is likewise consistent with the results of a recent assessment of abduction's incidence based on reception centre records (Pham et al. 2007). One concern, however, is falsely reported abductions, which (as discussed above) may lead to at most a 5 or 10 per cent overstatement of abduction. A more significant concern, however, is that not all those taken by the LRA are arguably 'abducted' as many of them are released or escape almost immediately.[6]

Indeed, a third of young men in our sample escaped, were rescued or were released within two weeks (see Table 7.1).

These short abductions are especially important to capture, however, for at least two reasons. First, they often included a great deal of violence, and are significant and grave experiences in the lives of most respondents. Second, in most cases it seems that the intent of the rebels was to keep the youth for as long as possible. Fewer than 5 per cent of male youths reported they were released – in almost all cases because they were either 'too young' (under eleven), 'too old' (over about twenty-three) or too injured to walk. Thus if male adolescents and young adults remain with the LRA for only a matter of days, it is probably because they escaped rather than were released. Accordingly, for the purposes of this report we consider any time with the LRA – regardless of length – as an 'abduction'.

Incidence Popular wisdom has it that 80 per cent of the LRA is made up of abducted children. As for many of the numbers in the north, the factual basis for the claim is unclear.[7] Survey data suggest that 80 per cent is only a mild overstatement, however. Of those males abducted

TABLE 7.1 Self-reported abduction experiences from returned former abductees (N = 462 abducted males aged fourteen to thirty) (percentages)

	Abducted					Never abducted
	<2 weeks	2 weeks to 3 months	3 months to 1 year	>1 year	All*	
Proportion of abductees	32	23	21	23	100	
Violence experienced						
Severely beaten	36	57	75	71	57	23
Attacked by someone with a weapon	20	13	36	30	24	3
Tied up or imprisoned	43	65	76	70	61	6
Forced to carry heavy loads	68	96	93	91	85	12
Violence committed						
Forced to abuse dead bodies	8	19	39	29	22	0
Forced to beat/cut a family member or friend	3	16	15	18	12	0
Forced to beat/cut another civilian	10	15	29	34	20	0
Forced to kill a family member or friend	3	11	7	12	8	0
Forced to kill another civilian	8	15	20	32	17	0
Forced to kill a soldier	3	14	16	25	13	1
Ever killed at all	9	20	27	42	23	1
Abduction experiences*						
Received an initiation ceremony	10	48	73	88	50	
Ever rewarded for a job well done		1	8	9	6	

Ever given a gun	13	54	85	50
Allowed to sleep with a gun	8	39	75	40
Minimum no. of months before receiving a gun	0.6	2.3	4.5	3.4
Ever received a rank	1	7	17	9
Mindset*				
Ever felt loyal to Kony	32	45	56	44
Ever felt like an important member of the group	20	49	49	39
Ever felt that the commanders could depend on you	3	28	48	26
Ever felt they wanted to stay in armed group	5	22	29	19
Ever felt safer inside than outside the LRA	1	4	14	6
Ever felt you wanted to be a commander	3	8	15	9
Return				
Escaped				80
Released				15
Rescued				5

Note: * Some abduction experiences and mindsets were not recorded for youth abducted less than 2 weeks in total. In these instances, the 'Abducted: All' column averages over those abducted 2 weeks or more alone.

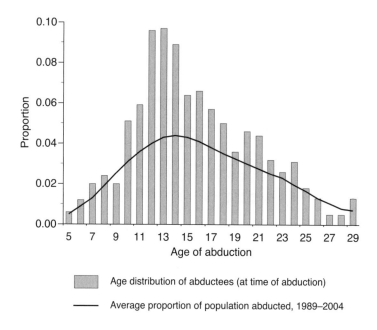

Age distribution of abductees (at time of abduction)

—— Average proportion of population abducted, 1989–2004

Figure 7.1 Distribution of LRA abductions of males by age of abduction[8]

before age thirty, over two-thirds were under eighteen (and over three-quarters were under twenty-one).

Figure 7.1 displays the distribution of age at the time of abduction. By far the most heavily targeted group appears to be adolescent boys, and the rebels seem to have been especially focused on boys aged twelve to sixteen. In fact, as demonstrated in Blattman and Annan (forthcoming), age seems to have been the sole criterion for abduction – neither poverty nor orphaning nor any other observable characteristics other than age seems to be associated with abduction at all. In fact, the LRA's manner of abduction is indistinguishable from a random draw of the population, stratified by age.

Age, however, was of critical influence. The distribution of abduction age in the sample indicates that four times as many males aged fourteen were abducted as those aged nine or twenty-three (Figure 7.1, vertical bars). The preference for adolescent boys holds true even after adjusting for the disproportionate number of young people in the population. From 1989 to 2004 a fourteen-year-old youth in the study population had an average of a 5 per cent chance of abduction – twice the level of risk faced by one aged either nine or twenty-three (Figure 7.1, connected line).

The focus on adolescents is even more pronounced once we account for youth released by the LRA. According to interviews with former commanders and abductees, rebel raiding parties commonly abducted all able-bodied members of a household to carry looted goods, but were usually under instruction from the senior leadership to release children under eleven and adults older than their mid-twenties after loot was delivered to a safe location. Eight per cent of male abductees were released in the first month of abduction (not counting those left behind because of injuries). The probability of release is close to 17 per cent for children under eleven, dips to 8 per cent for adolescents, and is rising in age thereafter.

While these figures suggest that the bulk of abductees were indeed under the age of eigheen, this does not necessarily mean that at any given point in time the LRA itself contained so many young people. First, the core leadership was for the most part adult volunteers, drawn from the initial LRA fighters from the late 1980s and early 1990s. Second, child soldiers that remain with the group inevitably grow to become adults. Even so, it seems likely that abducted children under the age of eighteen made up the majority of LRA ranks.

Command and control within the LRA

The data also reveal the LRA's means of command and control. Media accounts of the LRA often focus on the use of violence as a tool of control. Commonly reported are accounts of ritual killings of new members, of abductees being forced to kill a parent or brother, or of the massacre of children who attempt to escape. How common are such experiences? What other tools of control are employed? How effective are they? The survey data provide some unexpected answers. The LRA's use of disorientation and misinformation was not only common but also seems to have been effective. In the end, a near-majority of youth abductees explained that there was a time when they felt loyal to (and important members of) the rebel force. While the experience of some form of violence is nearly universal, a minority of youth report being forced to commit the most terrible acts.

Methods of motivating forced recruits The LRA's almost total reliance on forced recruitment distinguishes it from the majority of rebel movements in Africa and elsewhere. Nevertheless, the LRA, like any other rebel force, has had to motivate its recruits not only to participate (i.e. not run away) but also to carry out their dangerous duties well. Interviews with rebel commanders and abductees reveal the methods employed by the LRA to motivate participation and performance. Table 7.1 lists summary statistics from the survey, based on males abducted for less than two weeks (30 per cent of abductees), two weeks to three months (22 per cent), three months to one year (24 per cent) and more than one year (24 per cent).

The provision of material incentives was relatively rare. Only 7 per cent of all youth abducted report ever being 'rewarded for a job well done', reaching a high of 12 per cent among those abducted more than a year (Table 7.1). Among these, moreover, the most commonly cited reward was food. Remuneration with money or loot was exceedingly rare. Even commanders seldom received loot, as there was little to give. Material rewards were promised upon victory, however. According to one long-term abductee interviewed, 'they used to tell us that if we fight and overthrow the government then we shall get wealth and even the young soldiers would get high ranks in the army'. Many long-term abductees appear to have been convinced, at least for a time, of these future gains. As we will discuss below, the gradual realization that no gains would come would lead many to abandon the group at a later date.

Violence and the threat of punishment were principal instruments of control in the LRA, and even short abductions involved exposure to significant brutality. Real and threatened death and injury were among the primary means of discouraging escape and motivating performance. 'In the bush,' explained one youth abducted for two years, 'you do things out of fear.' From Table 7.1, 61 per cent of abductees report having ever been severely beaten (compared to 23 per cent of non-abducted youth) and 26 per cent report being attacked with a weapon (compared to 3 per cent of non-abductees). Beatings rise to three-quarters and attacks to one third of the youth abducted for three months or more. Severe beatings or death are reportedly the most common fate of any abductee caught trying to escape, a sentence other abductees were often forced to carry out with sticks or machetes – 55 per cent of abducted youth report that abductees were 'often' or 'sometimes' forced to beat or kill new arrivals.

Previous studies of forced recruitment in Uganda and elsewhere have presented the forcible commission of violence (typically killing or the desecration of dead bodies) as a key feature of initiation into the group, one that serves several purposes: terrorizing the youth to break down his psychological defences, raising the spectre of punishment by his community if he were to return, and desensitizing the recruit to violence (Honwana 2006; Singer 2005). The survey suggests such horrible tactics are all too common but fortunately not pervasive. From Table 7.1, a minority of abductees report ever being forced to kill (24 per cent) with a larger proportion of long-term abductees reporting being forced to kill a soldier or civilian (49 per cent). The most sensational of reported practices – being forced to kill a friend or family member – occurs more rarely. Fourteen per cent of abductees report being forced to beat someone close to them, and 8 per cent report being forced to kill a family member or friend – figures that rise slightly among long-term abductees.[9] While even one such act is too many, it is important to note that our worst fears are not confirmed.

The LRA also sought to limit escape opportunities by quickly moving the abductee as far as possible from home. Sixty-three per cent of abductees report being tied, usually for the first one to two weeks of capture (Table 7.1). The first day's march would often deliberately backtrack, move in circles and disorient the abductee. Within the first week or two of capture abductees would be taken as far as possible from their place of abduction, preferably to the bases in Sudan (where escape was nearly impossible owing to the distances, disorientation and the hostile Sudan People's Liberation Army).

In addition to violence and disorientation, misinformation was used to promote fear and loyalty. Abductees were told that, if they escaped, rebels would return and kill them or their family. Youth forced to kill were also told that they would be exiled from their home communities. Another example comes from the LRA's reaction to the Ugandan government's offer of amnesty to all but the most senior LRA officers (first extended in 2000). In response, interviews suggest that Kony immediately banned the possession of radios by his troops and kept the amnesty a closely held secret, even from officers. Abductees who had heard of the amnesty were told that it was a ruse and that any who escaped would be killed by the army.

Finally, spiritual practices were central to motivating recruits – a clear attempt to create new social bonds and loyalty based on a shared cosmology (as well as fear). Kony created a cult of mystery and spiritual power which few abductees or civilians question even now. The Acholi informants with whom we spoke disagreed not on whether Kony possesses spiritual power, but whether these spirits can be overcome. Within the LRA, these purported powers were used to the rebel group's advantage. A spiritual initiation ceremony, typically featuring prayers and anointment with oil, was reported by the vast majority (70 per cent) of males taken for two weeks or longer. The group is highly structured, with detailed spiritual restrictions on personal conduct (e.g. eating, drinking and bathing) and on military practices. Kony is also feared and respected as a prophet. Three long-term bodyguards to Kony described a catalogue of prophecies coming to pass. They also described displays of power, such as the ability to vanish. Through the power of the spirits Kony was also perceived to be omnipresent and able to track down escapees by the smell of the holy oil with which they were anointed.

It is important not to overstate the importance of religious propaganda, however. Some of the spiritual messages commonly reported in the media find little support in the data. For instance, while abductees readily admitted to one-time loyalty to the LRA or acceptance of other spiritual practices, virtually none reported that there was a time when they believed that they had magical protection from bullets. Moreover, while spiritual messages and initiation were commonly received, former abductees were at least as likely to report political propaganda and the promise of material rewards as spiritual dogma. The feasibility and importance of overthrowing the government appear to be the most common throughout the data, followed by the crimes committed by Museveni and promises of government positions and loot.

The effectiveness of indoctrination and control How effective was this focus on fear, punishment, dogma, misinformation and disorientation? Some degree of indoctrination is apparent. According to one informant, abducted for two years,

> I became like a real soldier. I was spying for them [...] There you do things just for survival. I started staying like any of them but I knew in the back of my mind I was just doing it for survival. But for a point I forgot the survival and became a part of them. I was abducting and stealing just like them.

Such 'forgetting' and shift in identity were reported in in-depth interviews. In some cases this was associated with Kony's spiritual powers. According to one informant, 'In the bush, there is something that confused people. There is certain type of [holy] oil which they put on you. It confused you and you could never think of home.'

As a consequence, many abductees stayed for long periods. Two-thirds remained more than two weeks, nearly a quarter remained for a year or more, and an eighth remained for at least two years (Table 7.1). The average abduction lasted nine months. Half of all male youths who stayed at least two weeks with the group received a gun, usually after only two months. Four-fifths of those that ever received a gun were eventually allowed to sleep with the gun, a clear signal of trust (Table 7.1).

Levels of self-reported loyalty and comfort with the LRA appear quite high. Of those abducted for more than two weeks, 44 per cent claim to have ever felt allegiance to Kony, 41 per cent felt like an important member of the LRA at some time, 28 per cent perceived themselves as dependable fighters, 19 per cent admitted there was a time they felt like staying with the LRA, and 10 per cent admitted that they aspired to become a commander one day. These quantities increase steadily among those that stayed longer than a year, as seen in Table 7.1.

Ultimately, the majority of forcible recruits appear to either escape or perish. Four-fifths of abducted youths return. More than nine in ten of the fifth that did not return can probably (and tragically) be assumed perished, as few remain with the LRA (relative, that is, to the estimated 66,000 abducted). Of those that do return, just 5 per cent were rescued and 15 per cent were released. The remaining 81 per cent escaped, almost always during an unsupervised moment (such as in the heat of battle).

For those who remain with the LRA for long periods of time, the decision to escape is usually explained as being preceded by a moment of 'awakening':

> When I grew up I started seeing that whatever Kony says was not true. If it were really true then the government could have been overthrown. And here the people he abducted before I was had all escaped. This made me think of escaping which I finally did.

Some of these stories reflect a realization that the promised benefits would not be received. According to one abductee, 'We would ambush and carry things but then I wouldn't benefit. It was the leaders who benefited. Then I thought I should escape because I had not gone on my own but had been abducted.' From another,

> When I was just abducted I was optimistic that we would win this war because the commanders kept on telling us that we would overthrow the government soon. But after seeing what atrocities these rebels were doing, like killing many civilians, looting and continuous fighting without any success, I realized the rebels are wasting time and we'll not overthrow the government. This made me think of escaping, which I eventually did, and came back home.

Why these methods of indoctrination and disorientation were effective, as well as upon whom they were most successful, are admittedly still poorly understood. Below we suggest that age of abduction is a significant correlate, and offer partial explanations as to why this might be the case.

The strategic value of adolescent abduction

In guerrilla fighting, the effectiveness of children is questionable at best; young adult volunteers are plausibly the most effective recruits, and – all other things being equal – should be the primary targets of abduction. If so, how does one explain the behaviour of the LRA, who preferred young adolescents over young adults for almost all military tasks?

Simply put, all other things are seldom equal. The evidence suggests that young children and adolescents are more easily indoctrinated and controlled than young adults, and so tend to remain much longer once abducted. Children and adolescents are also in much greater supply than adults owing to the demographics of the region. The evidence suggests that young children were militarily less useful than adolescents, however. If true, then adolescents may make the 'optimal' forced recruits when too few volunteers are available.

Alternative theories of child soldiering Dozens of explanations for under-age recruitment have been offered by the vast child soldier literature.[10] Beber and Blattman (2009) develop a formal model that rationalizes and systematizes the barrage of theories in a single logical framework. Here we summarize four broad classes that capture the vast majority of these explanations.

First, some scholars emphasize the relative supply of children. In many poor countries there has been a demographic shift (exacerbated by AIDS) that has created the largest population of young people in history (Singer 2005; Rosen 2005). Similarly, other studies note that the recruitment of children is said to have increased as adults were killed or displaced (e.g. Becker 2004; Machel 1996; Cohn and Goodwin-Gill 1994).

A second class emphasizes the functional value of child recruits. Their usefulness for menial tasks is widely noted.[11] There is little consensus, however, on the military value of children. Some argue that children lack the necessary fortitude (e.g. Guttiérez 2006; Wessells 2006) while others argue the opposite, quoting rebel commanders across Africa who attest to children's stamina, survival and stealth (e.g. ILO 2003; Boyden 2003; Cohn and Goodwin-Gill 1994).

Such testimony is consistent with psychological evidence from US-based studies that find that adolescents have an underdeveloped concept of death, feelings of strength and power, the impression of invulnerability, an inability to assess risks and shortsightedness.[12]

Also in the military value vein, several authors link the increase in the use of child soldiers to rises in the affordability and supply of light weaponry (Coalition to Stop the Use of Child Soldiers 2006; Singer 2005; Machel 1996). By this argument, lighter and cheaper automatic firearms disproportionately increase the relative combat effectiveness of child combatants and thereby raise their usefulness.

A third set of explanations emphasize the costs of recruitment, hypothesizing that children require little material remuneration in absolute and relative terms. Several scholars argue that hunger, poverty, youth unemployment and the absence of educational opportunities may make soldiering a relatively attractive (or even the only) opportunity for youth, thereby reducing the material incentives required (e.g. Honwana 2006; ILO 2003; Brett and Specht 2004; Machel 1996). Another variant of this cost argument suggests that children may be inexpensive recruits because they are more willing to fight for non-pecuniary rewards such as honour and duty, revenge, a sense of purpose, or protection from violence.[13] The vast majority of the evidence to support these claims, however, is largely anecdotal.[14]

Finally, children may be easier to retain. Several studies emphasize the exploitability of children, suggesting that the young are more malleable, adaptable, more easily indoctrinated, more easily deceived, or less likely to question authority (e.g. Guttiérez 2006; Honwana 2006; Singer 2005; Peters et al. 2003; Cohn and Goodwin-Gill 1994). The bulk of this evidence is taken from interviews with rebel officers.[15] Others have framed this argument in terms of developmental psychology. Guttiérez (2006) and Peters (2004), for instance, argue that children are in different stages of moral development and do not make decisions in the sense adults do.

What each of these explanations has in common is an implicit emphasis on the strategic value of child recruitment. Very simply, rebel leaders are interested in recruiting civilians for the military value they yield. Limited resources or a limited ability to monitor and manage a force imply that most rebel groups are constrained in their ability to recruit, however. Thus such groups have an incentive to target those civilians who are expected to offer the highest expected benefits – an amount determined largely by their military value, their cost of recruitment and maintenance, and their likelihood of desertion. By this logic, children will be recruited when they are expected to be as or more valuable than adults, or when they yield less value but adults are in short supply.

Why adolescents? The war in northern Uganda provides a tragic opportunity to weigh these competing explanations. By examining the differences in the self-reported actions, attitudes and experiences of former abductees by the age of their abduction, we can obtain indications of the relative effectiveness, cost and retention of children under coercion.

For instance, comparisons of remuneration by age should reflect differences in relative cost, comparisons of gun receipt and self-reported dependability should indicate military effectiveness, while comparisons of abduction length and allegiance should indicate differences in ease of indoctrination and retention. Beber and Blattman (2009) examine alternative theories of child soldiering using both cross-country data as well as individual survey data from Uganda. We summarize these results below.

Note, however, measures of cost, effectiveness and ease of retention are of course only proxies for the real underlying variables, and so must be interpreted with some caution. The cross-age comparisons, however, are plausibly unbiased and well identified. Thus while attitudes and behaviours as a rebel are undoubtedly reported with some error or bias, so long as this measurement error or bias does not change with age of abduction, any bias will cancel itself out in cross-age comparisons.[16]

The results suggest that, at least when participation is coerced, young adolescents aged roughly twelve to sixteen appear to be the most plentiful, effective and reliable recruits – a fact that is largely due to their supply, their pliability and their low likelihood of desertion. Children below the age of twelve appear at least as easily manipulated as adolescents (or even more so), but do not appear as militarily effective. Adults appear at least as militarily effective as adolescents, but seem much more difficult to disorient, intimidate and indoctrinate. The LRA's expectation of benefits from forced recruits thus peaks around the age of fourteen or fifteen – a configuration that corresponds closely to the LRA abduction pattern seen in Figure 7.1.

Relative supply Simple demographics can explain part of the LRA's focus on adolescents. Looking back to 1995, 21 per cent of our sample population was between the ages of five and nine, while males aged ten to nineteen composed 14 per cent. Thus by 2003 (the year that abductions peaked) there were roughly 50 per cent more adolescents than young adults in the population. If LRA abduction were simply a random draw of the population under thirty, then this difference in supply could account for some of the emphasis on adolescent males seen in Figure 7.1 (the vertical bars).

To account for the potential influence of supply, a population-adjusted likelihood of abduction can be calculated, and is illustrated by the connected line in Figure 7.1. The connected line displays the average probability that a youth of a particular age was abducted in a given year between 1989 and 2004. Note that this population-adjusted figure demonstrates a preference for adolescents – the probability of abduction is increasing up to age thirteen, where it peaks at over 5 per cent, and is decreasing in age thereafter. Even so, the emphasis on adolescents is significantly less pronounced in the population-adjusted line than in the unadjusted vertical bars. In northern Uganda, demographics would appear to account for roughly a third of the excess abduction of adolescents over adults.

Relative remuneration and cost The cost of recruiting does not seem to have played a role in targeting adolescents. The survey data and interviews suggest that child and adult abductees were equally cheap in the eyes of rebel commanders. Food and water were typically pillaged, and so seem unlikely to materially influence the relative cost of children, adolescents and adults. That said, we do not have detailed data on food and water consumption by age, and it is possible that adults were more expensive to maintain. Interviews with former commanders, however, suggest that food and water consumption were not a primary concern.

The most significant cost of labour is, in most instances, direct remuneration – whether in the form of wages, loot or extra rations. Material rewards were relatively uncommon in the LRA, however, and rewards varied little with age of abduction. A simple regression of the receipt of rewards or remuneration on age yields a relationship that is close to zero and statistically insignificant, a finding that holds even after accounting for possible confounding factors such as abduction year, location, length and pre-war characteristics. Thus we see little evidence of the cost argument so often emphasized in the literature.

Relative ease of retention Ultimately, most of the emphasis on young adolescents over adults seems to be explained by differences in ease of retention – very simply, adolescents were the preferred forcible recruits because they stayed longer once captured. The inverse relationship between age and abduction length is illustrated Figure 7.2.[17] Average length of stay declined from an average of a year for a child of eleven, to just five months for a youth in his late twenties. After adjusting for abduction year and location, an abductee's average length of abduction appears to fall by an average of 0.4 months for every additional year of age.[18] Given that the average abduction length is just 8.5 months, this implies that lowering the age of abduction by ten years increases the average length of stay by more than a third.

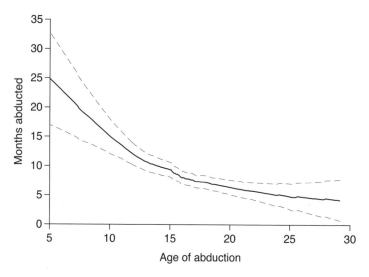

Figure 7.2 Length of abduction, by age of abduction[19]

The interview and survey data support three explanations for the positive relationship between age and the propensity for escape. First, the ease of disorientation appears to be falling with age. Rebel leaders and long-term abductees commonly explained that younger abductees were most fearful of escape, either because their surroundings were more unfamiliar or because they were insufficiently cunning. For instance, according to a seven-year servant of Kony's, 'Old people like escaping, but for the children it is difficult because they do not know how.'

Such claims can be tested indirectly. If fear or disorientation lead children to be less likely to escape on their own initiative, then on average they should be more likely to be rescued or to escape in battle (where less initiative is required). They should also be less likely to know their location at the time of escape. These predictions are borne out by the data. Young children (those abducted before age eleven) were seven times more likely to be rescued than adults (those taken in their late twenties), as seen in Figure 7.3. Moreover, familiarity with the location of escape is rising with age, with adults 40 per cent more likely to know their location at the time of escape compared to young children (see Figure 7.4). There is also weak evidence that adults were a third less likely to have escaped during battle – that is, they are more likely to have snuck away at night or while left alone.[20] These results are robust to controlling for potentially confounding factors, such as abduction length, year and location.

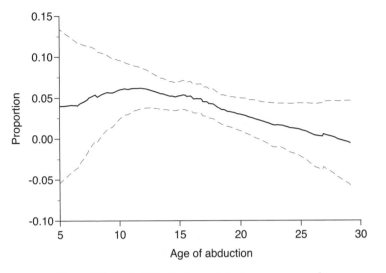

Figure 7.3 Probability that an abductee was rescued (versus escaping)[21]

Second, children and adolescents appear more easily indoctrinated and controlled. Interviews suggest that children and adolescents were more easily indoctrinated and deceived, more trustworthy, and less likely to question authority. According to one youth, who was abducted for six months:

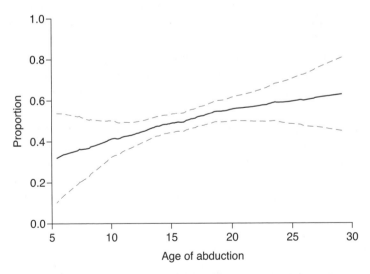

Figure 7.4 Probability that an abductee who escaped knew his location at the time of escape

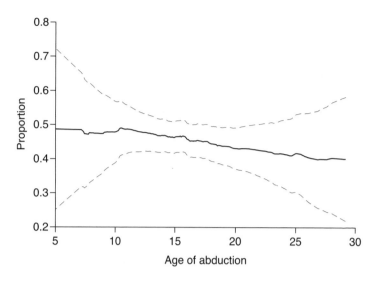

Figure 7.5 Probability that the youth 'ever felt allegiance to Kony'

> You know, it is easy to convince a child of twelve years of anything.
> He will believe any promises made and does not know the difference
> between good and bad. But if you are mature, you know they will not
> overthrow the government.

Similarly, speaking to another long-term abductee, 'A child can be
deceived into thinking that you know something and did something bad
at his place. A child can not change his mind easily if somebody else
gives a different view.'[22] In general, the survey data support these accounts. The proportion of youth reporting that they 'ever felt allegiance
to Kony' is nearly 50 per cent among young children and declines to
roughly 40 per cent for adults (Figure 7.5). Adolescents were also the
most likely to report ever feeling like staying with the LRA. Twenty per
cent of young adolescents reported having such feelings, compared
to roughly 10 per cent of young children and even fewer young adults
(Figure 7.6). Younger abductees are also somewhat more likely to feel
safer inside the LRA. While only 7 per cent claimed to feel this way
overall, the level is roughly 10 per cent for young children and nearly
zero for adults.[23] Such accounts of adolescent malleability are largely
consistent with a growing body of psychological and neurological research on adolescent behaviour and development.[24]

Relative military value Finally, we turn to assessing relative military
value. Several participants emphasized children's traits that were use-

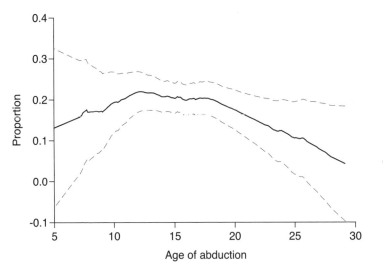

Figure 7.6 Probability that the youth 'ever felt like staying with the LRA'

ful for combat. One long-term abductee interviewed, for instance, emphasized children's agility: 'The children were of ages six to seventeen years, and if taken to fight could not easily be shot at because they could easily run in the bushes to confuse the government soldiers.' A bodyguard to Kony, meanwhile, emphasized their fearlessness: 'When fighting, everyone does it equally. However, children are strong hearted because they are short. Since you fight while standing, it gives them a chance to fire without fear. But those who are old normally have fear compared to children.'

Other accounts, however, stress that small children were less trusted with military tasks and, when abducted, played a servile role. Rebel officers questioned a young child's ability to handle a firearm, or be an effective fighter. Another widely noted limitation on the use of children was their inability to carry heavy loads. The LRA typically travelled in small bands, carrying everything on their backs. Members were expected to carry food, supplies, ammunition and even heavy artillery over long distances, and groups were renowned for their ability to move hundreds of kilometres in a few days. In this regard children appeared less able.

In general, the survey evidence suggests that young children below the age of eleven or twelve were entrusted with military tasks less frequently than older youth, while adolescents seem to have been at least as dependable and effective as young adults (and in some cases more so). First, the self-reported reliability and effectiveness of recruits appears

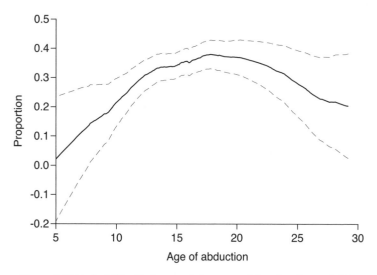

Figure 7.7 Probability that a youth 'was considered a dependable member of the group'

to increase with age of abduction, as seen in Figure 7.7. Second, older abductees were also more likely to receive a rank. Eight per cent of youth abducted after age twenty-one received a rank – more than twice as often as youth under eleven.

Third, adolescents appear to have been most likely to receive a gun and report ever killing a soldier or civilian, as seen in Figures 7.8 and

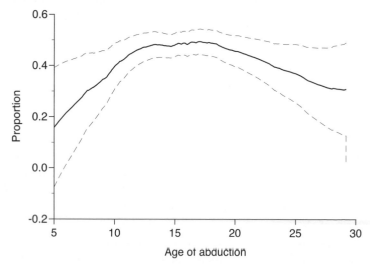

Figure 7.8 Probability that an abductee was allowed to keep a gun

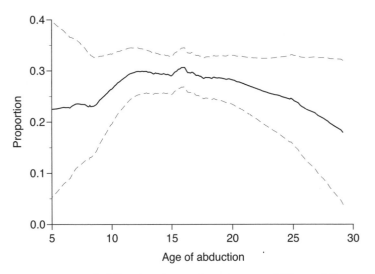

Figure 7.9 Probability that the youth reports ever killing (soldiers and civilians)

7.9.[25] Younger abductees also take much longer to receive a gun – children abducted at age eight to ten received a gun after an average of nine months, while youth abducted at age sixteen to eighteen received one after just 1.7 months on average. Adolescents are also the most likely to have committed killings on behalf of the group (Figure 7.9). Parametric fits of these relationships suggest that each is statistically significant.

Finally, there is suggestive (but not conclusive) evidence for the 'heavy loads' argument. Younger children reported carrying heavy loads 84 per cent of the time, compared to 88 per cent for adults. Linear regression estimates suggest that the probability of carrying heavy loads increased roughly half a percentage point with each additional year of age, yet this figure is not statistically significant.

Discussion and conclusions

This chapter has reviewed systematic survey data and in-depth interviews with formerly abducted youth with two aims in mind: one, to provide a sense of proportion to abduction experiences; and two, to weigh the influence between competing theories of LRA behaviour, in particular the targeting of young adolescents.

These data present a somewhat different picture of the LRA and abduction. Elsewhere we have argued that the long-term impacts of abduction have been misconstrued – in particular, psychological trauma and social dislocation have been overestimated, and the economic and educational consequences underestimated (Annan et al. 2006; Annan 2007; Blattman and Annan, forthcoming). This chapter, meanwhile, has investigated LRA tactics and abduction experiences. While the scale of abduction appears to have been underestimated, other crimes, such as the abduction of very young children or the forced commission of violence – especially the forced killing of relatives or the abuse of dead bodies – are less common than often feared. Rather, the LRA seems to have focused primarily on the abduction of adolescents, and to have used disorientation, the threat of violence and political propaganda at least as commonly as spiritual persuasion, and much more commonly than the forced commission of violence. The emphasis on political propaganda and the promise of future material rewards are reported at least as frequently as spiritual messages and dogma, presenting the LRA as more idea- and cause-driven than is typically reported in the media. Overall, these various forms of propaganda seem to have been fairly effective, at least for a time – a near-majority of abductees report one-time loyalty to Kony and dependability as members of the LRA.

The LRA also comes across as more strategic and coldly rational in its tactics than commonly supposed. The rebel group's emphasis on abduction of adolescents is consistent with evidence that adolescents provided the optimal combination of military effectiveness and longevity – a balance between size and ability, and ease of indoctrination and disorientation.

The LRA's internal emphasis on political ideology is consistent with arguments made by long-time observers such as anthropologist Sverker Finnström (2003). Its use of violence and human rights abuse for strategic purposes has likewise been noted by Doom and Vlassenroot (1999), Van Acker (2004) and Vinci (2005) – part of a broader swing in political science towards recognizing the logic of violence in civil war (Kalyvas 2005).

As noted in the introduction, such accounts lie in stark contrast to the all-too-common presentation of the LRA as criminals, cult leaders and irrational actors. This treatment is exemplary of a larger trend to regard current conflicts as criminal and depoliticized 'new wars' (Kaldor 1999) and rebel groups as predatory or cult-like – sometimes called the 'new barbarism' (Richards 1996).[26] The evidence to support such claims is thin, however, and the case against them is ever growing. Why, then, do they persist?

The LRA has been a fluid organization, a factor that may account for some of its seeming incoherence and inconsistency. The leadership has also expended little effort in presenting a coherent and rational face to the world, or even to their Acholi brethren. Indeed, they may even have benefited from the aura of spiritual mystery and power that surrounds their movement. Nevertheless, it is also worth noting that the view of the LRA as barbaric and irrational has suited most parties to the conflict. For the journalists there are unspeakable (but not unwriteable) horrors to report. For the international donor and the human rights advocate, the image of the victimized child and the vicious rebel force suit both fund-raising and programming biases. For the government, the image of their enemy as barbaric and irrational yields obvious benefits in rallying international support and, perhaps, military aid.

As audiences, we ourselves may be excessively open to the rebel-as-barbarian narrative. Stathis Kalyvas (2003) has argued that the end of the Cold War robbed analysts and audiences of a clear and simple framework for characterizing conflict, and the 'new wars' and 'new barbarism' thesis presents an orderly, if ultimately flawed, means of understanding violent civil wars. Our mistake is simply a failure of imagination, and the desire for simple and orderly accounts of inherently complex conflicts and histories.

Psychological evidence also suggests that humans may be inherently biased towards remembering and highlighting traumatic events more vividly than other memories (see, for example, McGaugh 1992). Further, feeling that the acts themselves are 'barbaric', people may have difficulty in associating cruelty and violence – particularly towards children – with rational and conscious political intent.

Finally, the academics who collect evidence and develop more complex theories of behaviour, including these authors, are often guilty of writing for a narrow audience, and expending little effort at pushing their alternative message to the media and general public. This chapter and this volume hopefully represent a step in the opposite direction.

8 · Between two worlds: former LRA soldiers in northern Uganda

BEN MERGELSBERG

Introduction

In 2008, a religious organization reports on the LRA:

The perpetrators commit atrocities with such malevolence that even the most irreligious people familiar with their acts describe them as 'unrestrained evil'. The targets of the butchery are children. They rape, mutilate, and kill them with a rapaciousness that staggers the imagination. Worse, they compel children to kill one another and their own families, fighting as 'soldiers' in an armed force deliberately composed of children.[1]

Views of the LRA as an anarchic group with criminal energy are frequently supported by accounts of how it makes use of child soldiers. The narrative of the LRA abducting young, innocent children, brainwashing them and forcing them to fight is common in the media. It evokes a generalized image of the child soldier as a vulnerable innocent without any agency, brutally abducted, drugged and turned into a monster. In the words of former CNN Africa correspondent Jeff Koinange:

The education system breaks down when there is civil war and the children get bored and they are doing nothing, easily recruitable by these so called rebel leaders who are going to villages [...] they kill the parents, they take the kids, they brainwash them, sometimes they inject them with drugs. Once that is done, the kids literally can do anything for these rebel leaders. From Uganda to Sudan, from Somalia to Sierra Leone, you name it, I saw them, we had counted them. I tell you, you can almost write the same script and go from country to country and you will all inevitably see the same kind of child soldier.[2]

In this chapter, it will be my aim to challenge such statements. I will present material from the six months of fieldwork I did in northern Uganda. By giving my informants the voices to tell their own stories, I will contrast their experiences with narratives that reiterate the stereotype of the innocent child soldier. I want to argue that the view of helpless children without agency in what has happened to them often does not correspond to their actual experiences. Passive victims on first sight, they turned out during my fieldwork to be active survivors with a good sense of why they were fighting, how they survived and what they needed most after their return from the LRA.

Fieldwork

After several weeks of preparation in Gulu, northern Uganda, I decided to carry out qualitative fieldwork by living with a small number of returned LRA fighters in Pabbo internal displaced people (IDP) camp, located north of Gulu town. There were numerous obstacles I had to overcome to be able to live in the IDP camp. Yet the opportunities my approach offered were valuable. By living as a guest in their family huts, I could share to a large extent the ordinary lives of my informants. I also learned the local language, Acholi, and was able to collect information in an informal way.

In the main part of my study, I focused on four principal informants in Pabbo IDP camp. I lived with each of their families for some time and I had many interviews with my main informants and people from their surroundings. Additionally we had several group discussions facilitated by a translator. These discussions developed a very good dynamic, which enabled us to have very relaxed and open conversations. The degree of trust and mutual appreciation we developed was a remarkable experience in the environment of a war zone that is often marked by barriers between the suffering local population and the white expatriates working for aid agencies.

I will introduce my key informants here, to give a short overview of their past experiences.[3] *Owot Francis* was abducted at the age of ten and later worked as the chief escort of Vincent Otti, the LRA's second-in-command until his death. At the time of the fieldwork, Francis was nineteen years old, having returned recently from ten years spent with the LRA. *Abonga George* was abducted when he was twelve. During the seven years he spent with the LRA he worked as the chief escort for another high commander. He was twenty years old and had a wife and one son. *Okello Simon* was abducted when he was eleven years old and surrendered during battle after about three years. Having spent only three days in the community he was again taken into the LRA and spent one more year with them. Simon has two wives and he was twenty-two during the fieldwork. One wife bore him a daughter and the second one was pregnant during the time of my fieldwork. *Ocan William* lived with the rebels from the age of fourteen. He worked in the training wing of the LRA for three years. He has one wife and a son. During my stay in Pabbo, his wife gave birth to a stillborn child. He was twenty-four.

This chapter largely reflects material I have collected with these main informants, and most of the quotes below come from fieldwork with them. I was able to study their cases in great detail, but the small size of my sample might compromise the general validity of some of my observations. I also did some work to widen my focus. I interviewed and lived with young people who have not been with the LRA; I had several group discussions with other formerly abducted persons (FAPs in what follows)[4] and I carried out an in-depth questionnaire survey on seventy FAPs in several different IDP camps with the help of research assistants. This enabled me to compare my main informants' statements with the narratives of others to some extent. I remain wary of generalizing about the experiences of FAPs, however. The conditions of life with the LRA need to be seen in a dynamic perspective. What life was like for LRA soldiers depended on many aspects, such as the location of the fighters, the abundance of food and other resources, the work they had to do, the intensity of enemy attacks, the leadership of their military unit, etc. Three of my main informants left the LRA before or during Operation Iron Fist, a government offensive that dramatically changed the living conditions for the LRA. Because they all stayed for several years with the LRA, the level of their integration into the group seems to have been rather high compared to the experiences of others. Their perspectives are extreme, one could argue. While this is true in some cases, their opinions are nevertheless no exceptions: they are mirrored in a less dramatic fashion by the opinions of others I have talked to.

Experience of forced recruitment

Life was hard, it would rain on us and the nights were very cold. We new abductees were forced to kill. I was given load to carry and I was forced to walk distances I was not used to. If I got weak I would be beaten. I was just realizing things are not good [...][5]

The transition from civilian to LRA fighter is a painful experience. Most informants I talked to were taken from their community, tied up with other abductees and forced to carry looted food to a hideout in the bush. In the following weeks they had to get used to a completely new life. They quickly had to learn how to live in their new environment: how to sleep without shelter, where to fetch water, how to cope with the long walking distances, etc. They were very vulnerable when the group was attacked by the government army, the Ugandan People's Defence

Force (UPDF): they had no experience of battle, and being tied together they could not easily escape an approaching gunship or mobile UPDF soldiers. They were killed if they tried to escape, were not able to walk any longer or refused an order. They were left alone, far away from all who could provide them with a sense of security. One informant told me he had the feeling he was suddenly living in a different world altogether.

> They say they are removing the civilian type of life from you; they want to change you into a military person. So instead of giving me a gun, I was given a lock wire. Then we got some six people and I was told to use the lock wire to beat these people. And I had to do it, because if you don't do it you are the next person.[6]

Such terrifying experiences are common during the abductee's initial time with the LRA. But my informants also narrated how this horrible situation could improve, if the abductee was ready to take on his new role as a soldier.

> Very many people die on the way. I think what made me come back alive is luck; maybe it is just luck from God that I survived. Then again I had done good work as a well-trained soldier. When I was told to go to a certain position, I would always keep the position, if I was told that the enemy would come from this side, I would wait on this side – I would actually follow the orders. When I did that, it contributed to my survival.[7]
>
> The time you are threatened all the time is when you are still new. But when you are a real soldier, good fighter already been trained, you are now respected.[8]

Spiritual beliefs and practices

> There is always a reason for whatever happens. And always Joseph Kony explains.[9]

Before the abductee could eat with the other LRA soldiers he had to be anointed with the local oil, Moo ya. With this and other following rituals, the new soldier is incorporated into the group of the LRA. The LRA's spiritual observances consisted of rituals, regular prayers and a great number of rules ranging from military regulations to spiritual prohibitions. I asked Abonga George what he did in order to endure the danger and hardship he experienced living in the bush:[10]

> When we were in the bush, the only method we used to survive was prayer. So every Sunday we used to pray.[11]

Aspects of the LRA's spiritual beliefs and practices are rooted in religious elements that emerged in the Acholi society over a long time. Rebel leader Kony is a spirit medium and is visited by several spirits who fight with the LRA. There are also elements of Catholic, Pentecostal and Muslim faith to be found in the LRA's spiritual practices. Here I can pick only a few examples from the wealth of stories my informants gave me. For a more complete account of the LRA's spiritual practices, see Titeca's chapter in this volume.

There was a range of 'holy rules', as my informants called them. They had to be followed closely by the LRA fighters. Even if no one was around, it was believed that the spirits could see everything and would punish disobedient soldiers, often by death from an enemy gun.

> One time, we were crossing a road; a mamba entered our group and started firing. We were firing back with our small guns. One of our commanders took cover and when he did so, the person in the mamba shot his head; the rest of us were not hurt. If you do something you should not do, you may be hurt or shot. That is an example showing that you have to follow.[12]

Punishments by the commanders were frequent, too. They could have a cleansing function and prevent the person from being punished more harshly by the spirits. In the following story the rule about not having sex except when it is sanctioned by the commanders was violated:

> One of my friends had sex with a certain woman who was not his wife. So when we went for battle, among everybody who went there, the two of them were the only ones being shot, the boy and the girl. The boy was shot through the waist and it came through his private part and the girl was shot dead. So we believe, if these rules are not followed, something happens.[13]

I came back to this story later in the discussion. 'You told me of the friend who slept with the woman. The two were killed in the battle, but how did you find out they have actually had sex?'

> I know that those people had sex with one another. Because somebody from Control Alter[14] who said the Holy Spirit came on him and told him that the two have had sex, so they had to confess. When they were asked, they refused. They were beaten and tortured to tell them the truth. When they still refused, they were told: 'you will see what is going to happen. If you have refused, you are the one who is going to suffer the consequences. Because we would have beaten and therefore cleansed you.' After some days, we were just in a certain home, preparing our

food, the UPDF attacked us and the first bullets just got the boy and the girl. I did not witness that they had sex, but when the Holy Spirit talked through the Controller, he would tell them that after two days, this would happen. And it happened.[15]

Belief in the powers Kony derives from the spirits is widespread among the local population. I came across very few FAPs who denied them. One day during my fieldwork in Pabbo I visited an 'ajwaka'[16] in the outskirts of the camp. She was a friendly young woman with a walking disability. When I asked her about Kony's powers, she told me:

At this moment as we are talking I believe Kony has no powers, but he is trying to keep his people in the bush, saying 'if you catch somebody escaping, kill him'. He has made them watchmen over each other. Each one of them now fears that if he is caught, he will be killed. But actually, Kony has no power. The soldiers in the bush fear one another but most of them are now coming back. They realize that they were staying in the bush for no good reason.[17]

Abonga George, whom I lived with during that time, came with me to meet the 'ajwaka' and had listened to the conversation that took place in Lwo with translation into English. He remained silent during the conversation, but when I later asked him about his opinion of what the 'ajwaka' had said, he told me:

That lady is not speaking the truth because she was not there, she does not know what is happening there, but we who were there: we know that there is a spirit with Kony.[18]

Owot Francis told me about other rituals performed in the bush during the time of Operation Iron Fist:

One time in the Imatong Mountains, Kony told us to get grass, everybody should put it around their arms and leave it until the next morning. When it came to morning, we found a dog. We got the dog and started praying, we prayed over the dog. We were throwing small stones to the dog, not actually hurting it, in order to win the war. After we did that, when the battle came, immediately we were able to overrun our enemies.[19]

When I asked him about the origin of that dog, he could not tell me where it came from. Awil Joseph, my co-worker, suggested it could be a dog the UPDF was using to track the LRA. Owot Francis answered:

When that happened, we had not heard that the UPDF was also

following us with dogs. Only later, we heard it was happening. Maybe we did that because Kony already knew that these people are using dogs.[20]

Part of the LRA

Cut off from their former lives, my informants had to build up a new life within the LRA, a life that was dominated by military order and conventions embedded in the spiritual beliefs and practices. The following quotes reflect how my informants were able to accommodate themselves within this new life and how aspects of the LRA helped them to do so. Some of the statements might sound rather surprising. I will comment on them in the second part of my chapter when I discuss the material presented.

> The rules strengthened me a lot. Because I saw that if I follow the things, there was nothing. I would stay alive, be safe. I did not have fear, was always strong hearted. It kept me living with no fear.[21]

> Everything there was done in order. You would be told you are not allowed to break any order. They would tell you today there is no cooking, so you don't cook. They tell you let us go and fight, so you go and fight; today you go and kill so-and-so, you go and kill. There was just order. We kept on doing these orders.[22]

> I was striving so much to get a rank. That is why when they send me, to go and lay an ambush, I would go. I was given difficult tasks. I would perform them. When I was given the rank I started feeling that maybe this was a step ahead and at least respect was given now to me by the other soldiers, the young ones. It gave me a certain way of behaviour in a leadership way.[23]

> Fighting was very nice for us, especially when we were on the winning side. If you go and find you have killed many of your opponents you are very happy. It was not bad, we felt it was nice.[24]

> Fighting was very good for me, because it was part of my work. And if I had stayed for maybe two weeks without firing, I would feel something was missing, something is not very normal.[25]

> If you kill in battle, it is just like a snake comes into your house and you kill the snake to save your life.[26]

> I thought of the war and I was proud, because I thought for a long time that I was fighting for the people to overthrow the government.[27]

> This war, to me, it was justifiable. For example Alice Lakwena – when all

were following her rules, they overran the NRA[28] very well and had gone very far. But when her commander started breaking some of the rules, they started falling back.[29]

This abduction was not something bad, because that is a way of recruiting, they don't have an open way of recruiting. But the problem comes when you get tired of the war, you are weak and they can just kill you. And then maybe sometimes when you come to your family members, you are asked to kill your family members, so that you don't go back. That is the bad part of it. But otherwise it was not bad.[30]

If everything had gone on well, I would not have seen a reason to escape. They promised we would be the ones leading the government and we would have free education by now, everything was fine.[31]

I grew up knowing the use of gun. That was the only source of life; it was an instrument to be used. That war was everything in my life. I did not think about any type of life. I grew up knowing only war, no experience besides having the gun all the time.[32]

Escape

What made me think of coming back: lack of food, no medicine [...][33]

What is often referred to as escape from the LRA might in fact include very many different situations. Sometimes abductees are sent back home (especially those people who were abducted only to carry looted food). LRA fighters might also be captured by the UPDF or brought into a situation in which surrender is the only sensible thing to do. Nevertheless, there are great numbers of those who actively escape, some out of opportunity (for example, when the group passes one's home area), some planning it beforehand. I was told many reasons for such a decision. The common motif in most accounts was that the FAP felt tired of the war that seemed all too meaningless.

I was tired of the war. First they promised: next year they'll overthrow the government. Next year comes and there is nothing that happens. Then they say another year, another month [...] they keep on saying. I knew these things were not true.[34]

LRA leaders used highly effective threats to deter fighters from surrendering to the UPDF. Many fighters were killed if caught escaping, and my informants witnessed several executions of escapees. The threat was a spiritual as much as a military one, however.

If you thought about escaping, the Holy Spirit could identify you, pick you out and kill you even before you escape. That was our fear.[35]

Owot Francis was shot during battle as he was planning to escape. To him, this was clearly the punishment of the holy spirits:

I have been fighting in the bush for nine years, I only got a small wound on the chest; all those nine years there was nothing. But this time when I was shot, there was a reason behind it and the reason was my plan to escape.[36]

There was great fear among my informants of what the military enemy would do with them once they surrendered.

I had much fear. In the bush, when I came across UPDF and I was alone, they shot a bomb at me. That gave me fear: a whole bomb for me alone, so what will they do with all of us? And what if I arrive there? Will they just kill me?[37]

The LRA leadership propagated wild fantasies of the conditions in the IDP camps among my informants.

I thought people were in a sort of prison, being tortured, being punished [...][38]

In the bush I heard that people in the camp were already trained as soldiers, the rest has been taken as slaves.[39]

We were told these people in the camps are given plates which have chemicals in them. So when you keep on eating, you are poisoning yourself slowly.[40]

Ironically, given the appalling conditions in the camps, such fantasies are not completely out of place. Yet my informants' imaginations certainly did not correspond to reality. Escape, for my informants, was a large risk, and there are many who died in such an attempt.

Escape was putting your life into total danger. When we escaped, I made an address to my friends and said: 'now we are escaping. The civilians are our enemies, UPDF soldiers are also our enemies and now that we have escaped from our own army, even they are our enemies. If you meet any of those people you just fire at them until when we reach a place where we want to come out.'[41]

Back 'home'

Life in the beginning was very difficult. The whole reason I had come back was to come home. But I found that now they were taking so much time: going to the barracks, taking me to Gusco;[42] they were just delaying and it was a hard time.[43]

Having escaped, most informants reported to the UPDF or another administrative unit in the IDP camps. From military barracks they were brought to the governmental child protection unit (CPU) run by the army and then to one of the reception centres run by an NGO. Often, only after several months, they were unified with their families.[44]

During this transition my informants seemed to leave behind most of what they connected with their life as a soldier. I asked my informants why they were no longer afraid of being punished by the holy spirits for having escaped. I was told:

Only when you are still in the bush, the Holy Spirit has power over you. When you come back, you are now like a civilian, there's nothing which happens to you.[45]

And when I asked in a group discussion whether they still obeyed the rules they had to follow in the bush, Abonga George said, to the laughter of the others:

Those are rules which are just very stupid rules to follow. I have my own wife now. For instance, when my wife is under menstruation, do I separate with her and stop eating her food? They are just stupid rules, I cannot follow them.[46, 47]

Much of what was before accepted and encouraged was considered mad, stupid or evil in this new life. In the reception centres, my informants were told that to have been part of the LRA was not their fault, since they were innocent victims, abducted and made to do things they had never wanted to do. Owot Francis's words reflect this perspective:

We were living in the bush like people who had closed their eyes. It was as if we were being used, we couldn't reason, we couldn't look any further; just like somebody whose eyes have been closed. You are moving and you cannot see where you are going. All those things are painful, but now after reopening your eyes you can see something. It is painful when I am reminded.[48]

Being reunited with the family meant in most cases starting an existence in one of the IDP camps. Having lived for some time in this environment, I could grasp a little bit of the tremendous suffering this life imposes on the local population. Being squashed together in the camp and controlled in their mobility, people do not have enough space to live, nor to cultivate; they are exposed to alarming sanitary hazards, threatened by major epidemics and rebel attacks. My informants felt much discomfort about life in their new 'homes'.

Formerly we knew the boundaries of where to play. The different families knew their neighbours and that they were not having witchcraft. But now we are in the camp, we don't know the immediate person who is next to us, they may be from another parish, another village. They may come with witchcraft. And when something happens, you cannot even imagine who is responsible. So we just fear.[49]

There is the problem of not being allowed to move at night in the camp, but formerly we used to do it.[50]

We have to wait for food supplied by the WFP. Sometimes the food delays, if you don't have any garden, you have to starve or stay hungry.[51]

While I was in the bush, I was a soldier. I was well protected and I had my ammunition. But when I came back home, I am now a civilian. Now they [the UPDF] have to protect me, I am not protecting myself, like I did it.[52]

The community in the bush is very strong. Everybody had the same laws and the same order. Here some people think to be more equal [...][53]

In the camp, there is no appreciation. You are digging your own garden, nobody is appreciating that. In the bush there, you go to battle, maybe you are successful, and they appreciate you for that. Life here, there's nobody who appreciates.[54]

The feeling of being a stranger here is still there, especially when I am alone at home. Because somebody may come and ask something I don't know. There's nothing I can say. Maybe a relative comes and I don't know him. When I am with friends and we are busy talking, that feeling goes away.[55]

Discussion

In the course of my fieldwork, I was often surprised by what my informants told me. Several quotes I have given above mirror perspectives that are fundamentally different from common ideas about child soldiers within the LRA. At times they could also appear quite inconsistent. For example, Okello Simon, having given me a detailed description of his brutal abduction some time before, said 'abduction was not something bad, because this is a way of recruiting' (see quote above). To make sense of the material presented above, the notion of child soldiers needs to be re-examined in the northern Ugandan context.

Allen and Schomerus (2006) have pointed out that the number of children involved in the recruitments for the LRA has been exaggerated. While my informants may well have fitted into the category of a helpless child at the moment of their abduction, most of them returned as young adults with certain capacities, a sense of independence and self-esteem, and more or less clear reasons as to why they were fighting with the LRA. To understand my informants' accounts, I believe, one must adopt a dynamic perspective of their life trajectories. Such a view emphasizes a time perspective, but it goes beyond that: not only did my informants' experiences change over time; their perspectives on their life are dynamic and can adapt to their social environment. As a general framework, I find it helpful to see FAPs' past as a process of going through two different worlds. Both worlds can have their pleasant sides and both worlds can be terrifying to the FAP. What the experience is like depends on the specific situational context.

The quotes given above underline the profound differences between my informants' lives with the LRA and in their home communities. They frequently used the terms *Kit kwo ma ilum* and *kit kwo ma gang* – 'the type of life in the bush' and 'the type of life at home' – to make this distinction. What defines these two forms of life is not merely two distinct roles within a group (i.e. 'soldier' and 'civilian'). The process of entering into the LRA marks a break with the former life which enables the new soldier to become part of a world with a very distinct social reality. Clearly, such a process of transition is painful and unsettling. This suggests an alternative account of the times of immense suffering and threat in the FAP's life. Instead of conceiving of the soldiers' experience with the LRA as a 'traumatizing' time in the bush that is over once the former fighter has returned home, I want to suggest that the most painful times are periods of transition from one world to the other.

Transition into the LRA

The first period of transition is the time after abduction in which the FAP is forced to leave his former life behind. Richards, in the case of recruitment into the RUF in Sierra Leone, stresses the importance of the fact that the new fighters were stripped of their former life, so that they '"died" to their former existence and the movement was henceforth their life' (Richards 2006). This notion applies to some of my informants in a quite literal sense. Family members of several FAPs told me they did not expect them to come back any more. The parents of Owot Francis did not even come to the reception centre where they were told their son would be. 'We thought Francis wasn't there, we had forgotten all about him, because he was taken when he was very young,'[56] his mother explained to me. In his new life, the abductee is confronted with a whole range of new threats: the brutal LRA abductors, the military enemy (the UPDF) and the hardships of life in the environment of the bush. He can defend himself against these threats only by turning towards the LRA – living with them as one of them. He needs to learn from his group how to live in the bush, he must become a good soldier in order to meet the threat of the UPDF, and must appeal to his leaders in order to get accepted and evade the threat of being killed. These are the forces underlying the process of becoming part of the LRA.

Vinci has emphasized the use of fear by the LRA leadership against the new abducted in a process of what he calls 'initiation through traumatization' (Vinci 2005). While I do not want to deny the important role of fear in controlling LRA fighters, I think that the process of becoming part of the LRA cannot be described merely in these terms. In a situation of danger from within as well as from without the group, the new abducted person's turn towards the LRA is no act of madness or result of his traumatization for that matter. Much of what my informants told me about this time suggested that their behaviour reflected conscious actions of individuals who find themselves in a situation characterized by threats from several sides and by a very limited number of available guarantees for protection and meaning. This process of becoming part of the LRA evolves around the spiritual space the LRA constitutes.

Clearly, the belief system itself is a well-functioning system of fear and control. The fighters in the bush, as the 'ajwaka' put it, are made watchmen over each other. Yet the spiritual dimension goes beyond rules and sanctions. It underpins every aspect of life as an LRA soldier and acts as a powerful force establishing the fact that the abductee now lives in a new world with distinct beliefs and practices. They facilitate the process of becoming part of the LRA and enhance the young abductee's sense of establishing a new identity. The initiation rituals reflect rites of passage from one life to another. They emphasize the continuity of belief patterns the abductee is already familiar with, yet establish the distinctiveness of the new group from the civilian population. When I asked Owot Francis what he thought about the rituals in the very beginning, he answered that he took them 'maybe as a miracle'.[57] To be part of this 'miracle', it seems, made it easier for him to accept all the other exceptional aspects of his new life – the killing, the great threats he was exposed to, and so on. Richards, leaning on Durkheim,

invokes the notion of *group improvisatory performance*: 'the group be-
lieves because it acts together' (Richards 2006). The system of belief in
the LRA established a strong sense of group identity, separated those
inside the LRA from those outside it, and thus created a new moral
space that justified the LRA's actions.

'Mindless' violence

From this perspective, my informants' views of fighting, abduction
and regulations in the bush might seem less surprising. Military and
religious regulation could give a sense of security: if one was a good
soldier and followed the rules there was little to fear. Many deaths
in battle were referred to as the spirits' punishment of the fighter's
disobedience. Good performance was rewarded with military ranks,
which promised a more pleasant life. Many of my informants told me
they were striving to become an officer. Even abductions and killings
of civilians could be perceived as legitimate practices. Owot Francis
told me in an interview:

> Whatever killing, there is a reason why such thing happened. They may
> do this to provoke and hurt the government. The more you do that by
> brutalizing, the more famous you become.[58]

He offered possible explanations for every atrocity by the LRA I
could recall having been reported in the national newspapers during
the months before.[59] Even if not every soldier could know about all
reasons, the spiritual and military organization provided a universe
within which the LRA's fight made sense.

That acts of extreme violence, as unsettling as they appear, might
follow clear rationales has been suggested by several authors before.
Richards argued on Sierra Leonean examples that acts against civilians
often follow a clear reasoning by the acting military group: '[The rebels']
actions are not the actions of madmen or mindless savages. Once a decision to resort to violence had been taken, hand cutting, throat slitting
and other actions of terror become rational ways of achieving intended
strategic outcomes' (ibid.).

Somewhat similar points have been made about the northern Ugandan case (Doom and Vlassenroot 1999; Van Acker 2003; Vinci 2005). For
a group with minimal training and military equipment, 'blind' terror is
a way of gaining control over the population and of undermining the
government's position.

My informants' descriptions of the rituals within the LRA might also
be seen as an interesting contribution to the current discussions about

traditional healing and reconciliation in Acholiland. Rituals can indeed be effective in shaping values and attitudes, but not only for what might be regarded as desirable objectives.[60]

Transition back 'home'

The time of returning home is another painful and challenging time for the FAP. As I have tried to demonstrate, life with the LRA in my informants' accounts was a time of order and discipline, strict rules and harsh sanctions. It was maintained by prayers, rituals and prohibitions and by threats from inside and from outside. To a certain degree it provided the soldiers with a sense of security, of meaning and of independence. This stands in clear contrast to life in the crowded and congested IDP camps, with the constant threat of attack, the restrictions of mobility, extreme poverty and terrible sanitary conditions. In the eyes of some of my informants, *anarchic* would be a description of the IDP camps and not the LRA.

During his escape, the LRA fighter experiences almost the same threats as during the first period of transition: he has to fear the LRA, the UPDF and civilians, and he may not survive alone in the bush. Establishing themselves as civilians, the returned soldiers are stripped of their former identity for a second time. They experience the destruction of the moral space that provided the framework for their actions as a soldier. Some FAPs may have been excellent fighters or commanders, yet their skills are no longer appreciated in the IDP camp (some of them join the UPDF or other military groups, however). Being left with little beyond some material support from reception centres and their family network (if still intact), my informants had to struggle to start a new existence. Having been soldiers, they have also abandoned their ordinary civilian lives. They have not gone to school, and they have lost their friends and many of the social contacts essential for survival in their environment. Having turned their back on their former army, FAPs are often the first ones to be killed in the case of an attack (given that they are recognized as deserters). They cannot defend themselves as they did before. Their struggle to get used to this life and their estrangement from their own community mirrors the harsh conditions the general population in the IDP camps has to endure. The problems of FAPs must be seen in the context of the destruction of social and economic life in northern Uganda. The greatest challenges for their 'reintegration' (if this is how one wants to describe the herding of FAPs into crowded IDP camps) are challenges for the majority of the population in northern Uganda.

Helpless children?

My observations suggest caution regarding what one might call the discourse of the innocent and victimized child soldier without agency. This discourse is reflected in many child soldier testimonies quoted in NGO campaigns or the media. The period of transition when abductees are mistreated, forced to kill, etc., receives most attention, while the fighter's identification with his new life is either ignored or considered not the individual's active decision (for example, a World Vision official spoke of a 'robot state'[61]). After the return from the LRA, FAPs become part of the discourse of the innocent child soldier, especially during the time they spend in the reception centre. They are encouraged to understand their experiences in these terms, and many of the narratives recorded by NGOs and the media are formed in such an atmosphere. A statement to the effect that it was also nice to fight and to receive a rank are inappropriate in this context.

The following testimony, taken from an article on Amnesty International's website, is typical of the accounts quoted in the media and many NGO reports:

> The first time I killed was when I was sent to Lira District. I was told to put a baby in a large pounding mortar and kill it. My commander handed me a large wooden pestle used for pounding grain. I felt so bad when he gave me the order. I was terrified because I knew, if I did not follow the order, I would be killed. So I did as I was told. Killing at the start was difficult, but it became easy when I got used to it. I still have nightmares about the bad things I did in the bush.[62]

Two British journalists in Pabbo IDP camp recorded the testimony during my fieldwork there. They spent one night in the Catholic mission and learned that one of the women working there had been with the LRA. They arranged for a translator and sat in the compound to talk to her. During the interview another woman from the mission came to me and asked what the *muzungus* were doing with her: 'are they counselling her?' This was the first and the last time the journalists came to see her. Many people, especially in the more accessible IDP camps, are used to white visitors conducting some interviews and then leaving. 'You come to ask questions and you say you'll return, but we never see you again,' a woman told me when I visited a camp north of Pabbo for the first time.

A number of abductees seem to have only horrible memories from the bush (especially those who stayed for only a short time with the rebels). For others this is not the case, however. It is common to hear negative accounts of their sojourn with the LRA when talking to a person for the first time. In my experience, some degree of trust between interviewer and FAP is essential to touch on more sensitive questions, such as if the FAP also enjoyed being an LRA combatant. This was very evident in the case of my key informants. Only after some weeks, when my informants and I were somewhat familiar with each other and our discussions had a more relaxed atmosphere, were my informants willing to talk about the degree to which they had identified themselves with the LRA. I remember talking to my co-worker Joseph Awil, a teacher from Pabbo, after a group discussion with my main informants in which we spoke about whether or not the actions of LRA were justifiable. Clearly impressed by the statements we had heard before, he told me: 'at any time I expected these guys to realize where they were going and to back out. But they didn't do it.'

The ambiguity is that, on one hand, my informants considered themselves good soldiers who would have stayed with the LRA had everything gone well. On the other hand, they felt they were abducted as innocent children and that in the bush they were turned into someone they did not want to be – the discourse largely encouraged by their surroundings. These positions mirror the experience of living in two worlds. Owot Francis, who told me he had lived in the bush with 'closed eyes', unable to see what he was doing (see quote above), also seems to fit well with what Peters and Richards (1998) called fighters 'with open eyes' when at another moment he gives convincing reasons for fighting a war:

> I wanted my people to be free, have a good life which they are not having now. Secondly, if I see the soldiers who joined the bush some time back, they have nice houses, a lot of things, nice vehicles, whatever. So I also thought that if we had succeeded, we would be big commanders as well and we would now have the same big homes [...] And then on top of that I would also be earning salary which I am not having now.[63]

Traumatized children?

In harmony with the discourse of the victimized child is the focus on the 'traumatization' of child soldiers. Where the FAP is considered an innocent child without agency abducted by the brutal LRA, its past is frequently seen in the light of the trauma it has suffered. Discourse of trauma in general and or more specifically disorders such as depression or post-traumatic stress disorder (PTSD) are commonly used to describe the suffering of war-affected people. There are research efforts enquiring into the levels of PTSD among FAPs and psychosocial programmes run by NGOs with the aim of healing those with mental disorders resulting from war.

There is a large body of literature that suggests caution regarding an approach towards trauma from the perspective of Western psychiatry (Kleinmann 1977). Writers such as Bracken and Summerfield have questioned assumptions in psychiatry that PTSD is a universal phenomenon and that it can be applied in a meaningful way in any cultural context (Bracken 1998; Kleinmann 1977; Summerfield 1998, 1999, 2000). This chapter supports several of the reservations these authors have mentioned.

Young (1995) wrote an ethnographic account of what he calls the invention of PTSD. He writes: 'The disorder is not timeless, nor does it possess an intrinsic unity. Rather it is glued together by the practices, technologies, and narratives with which it is diagnosed, studied, treated, and presented and by the various interests, institutions, and moral arguments that mobilized these efforts and resources' (ibid.).

Young's thesis illuminates the problems of narratives of PTSD among FAPs in northern Uganda. PTSD is invoked in the context of a discourse that is dominated by ideas of an innocent and victimized 'child soldier'. My discussion suggests that this discourse might not necessarily mirror the FAP's own view of his past. The concept of PTSD is based on assumptions, some of which should be challenged in the context of northern Uganda. Parker, reflecting on mental health in the context of north-east Africa, writes: 'One of the most important issues which requires attention includes the following: PTSD is imbued with culturally specific conceptions of normality and deviance and it is thus difficult to make appropriate diagnosis' (Parker 1996).

An essential feature of PTSD is an aetiological event in the past – a distressing experience that lies outside the range of usual human experience. The problem, of course, is that what my informants would consider a usual experience is probably quite distinct from the usual human experience of someone living in the Western world. In fact, the narratives presented here suggest that even within their own life the idea of normality is a shifting category. In the latest version of the American Psychiatric Association's *Diagnostic and Statistical Manual of Mental Disorders*, the *DSM-IV* (2000), attempts are made to overcome the ambiguity of the notion of usual human experience. The description of the aetiological event now avoids such a general formulation and is given in the following two criteria. One, the traumatized person experiences, witnesses or is confronted with an event involving death or serious injury. Two, the person's response to this event involves intense fear, helplessness or horror. As Young (1995) points out, however, this new definition is by no means more clear cut than the previous one. In a place like Pabbo IDP camp, almost every inhabitant has frequently been confronted with death or serious injury. The way they react to such events might largely be determined by how far this is perceived as a normal experience. An old man in the camp told me: '[...] war? I can't see war. After twenty years I don't see the war any more.'[64]

Further, many of the conditions experienced might be conceptualized in a way not easily applicable to Western psychiatric categories. Above, I quoted Abonga George talking about witchcraft. The threat of evil witches was in fact among the most pressing concerns for my informants and many people in Pabbo IDP camp.

Another issue is that the disorder works within a temporal framework: the diagnosis of PTSD follows the logic of a traumatic event in the past that is connected to the present in forms of defined symptoms. As Young puts it: '[PTSD's] distinctive pathology is that it permits the past (memory) to relieve itself in the present [...] The space occupied in the DSM-III classificatory system depends on this temporal-causal relation: aetiological event → symptoms' (ibid.: 7).

In Uganda, narratives of PTSD go hand in hand with ideas that locate the FAP's traumatic experiences in the past with the LRA. An alternative view suggested in this chapter emphasizes the periods of transition. While one period of transition takes place with the LRA after abduction, another distressing time might be experienced after return from the bush when the LRA fighter witnesses further threats and the breakdown of the moral space in which he acted as an LRA combatant. Thus, what could be described as a traumatizing time lies not only in the FAP's past with the LRA, but also in the present. To diagnose PTSD against a background of continued insecurity, terror and fear is difficult, Parker writes: '– especially as some of the primary symptoms may be adaptive responses to particularly awful circumstances' (Parker 1996: 226).

To conceptualize my informants' suffering along the lines of psychological trauma is problematic. Returning LRA fighters continue living in a place shaken by the effects of the war. Some might feel more helpless and threatened in the camp than as a soldier in the bush. Hardly any of the FAPs living in IDP camps I talked to have received assistance that would give them perspectives for their future. They were more concerned with skill training, security from LRA attacks and the opportunity to move freely and cultivate than with how to deal with their memories. Many of them were responsible heads of a family concerned with nourishing their families, and it was their success in meeting these challenges which gave them a good or a hard time.

Summerfield pointed out the frequently indiscriminate and expansive ways in which we apply the category of trauma, in order to come to terms with experiences of war that are difficult for us to grasp. He calls this the medicalization of a social problem:

> This is the objectification of suffering as an entity apart, relabelling it as a technical problem – 'trauma' – to which technical solutions (like counselling or other psychosocial approaches) are supposedly applicable. However, misery or distress per se is surely not psychological disturbance in any meaningful sense and for the vast majority of survivors, 'traumatization' is a pseudocondition. (Summerfield 1999: 1452)

As I have argued above, issues of returning LRA fighters cannot be separated from the general problem of a population living in the extreme conditions of the IDP camps. Summerfield writes: 'War is a collective experience and perhaps its primary impact on victims is through their witnessing the destruction of a social world embodying their history, identity and living values and roles' (ibid.: 1455).

For many of my informants this is true in a double sense: on one hand they do witness the destruction of their home communities, and on the other hand they did lose part of their identity and living values and roles as they left the LRA.

Conclusion

In this chapter I have presented the accounts of so-called 'child soldiers'. I have shown that the way their lives are narrated in media and NGO accounts is frequently distorted. What has emerged from their quotes is a picture of individuals who have been part of two very distinct worlds. I have suggested that we need to adopt a dynamic perspective of their life trajectory. During one of our group discussions, I asked my informants whether they could kill someone now. They replied by asking back: 'If we were still in the bush or as civilians?' It is easier to kill with a uniform, I was told. I have also quoted my informants above, saying that the spirits from the bush do not have power to punish them any more, because they are civilians now.

These examples suggest two very different life conditions, but also two distinct systems of accountability. What is a right and normal thing to do in one might be punished in the other. Thus, not only my informants' life conditions changed, but also the background through which they made sense of them. Periods of transition between the two are then potential times of conflict. My informants' quotes demonstrate this. They suggest that the hardship of FAPs cannot simply be located in the past with the LRA and call for caution with regard to psychological approaches medicalizing what is ultimately a social problem. To describe FAPs as innocent and helpless children might be a well-meant move to emphasize the fact that they did not choose the life they have lived. But it does not correspond to the lived experiences of many and ignores their potentials in shaping their lives.

9 · Encountering Kony: a Madi perspective

RONALD IYA

Owing partly to the lobbying around issues of traditional justice in Gulu and other parts of Acholiland, leading to the (re-)establishing of a council of Acholi rwodi ('traditional chiefs'), similar processes have occurred among some neighbouring populations. Among the Madi people there is now a college of opi (the Madi equivalent of rwodi), and a council of elders, with a status recognized by the government. In August 2006, Ronald Iya, the opi of Dzaipi in Adjumani District, was elected as leader of these cultural institutions. The choice was appropriate, because it was his home area which was adversely affected by LRA attacks. Most of the population remain in displacement camps. Since his appointment as the senior opi, Iya has become a member of the group of traditional leaders that have been asked to participate in the Juba negotiations. This has placed him in the slightly anomalous position of being a representative of traditional authority who is not from a Lwo-speaking area (i.e. he is neither an Acholi nor a Langi). In the summer of 2008, this book's editors travelled with him through the war-affected areas of northern Uganda, meeting chiefs and elders, including several of those who had travelled with him to Garamba in 2007 to meet the LRA commanders. He was also interviewed again in 2009 following his last visit to Garamaba the previous November. What follows is his own account of his role as a cultural leader and of his encounters with Kony and Otti.

The origins of what is called today the Madi Cultural Institution go back long before British rule. The many clans of the Madi each had an *opi*. None was superior to the others in the past, and all clans were equal too. Some *opi* were rainmakers, as well as administrators, but not all of them. That is how things were until Milton Obote banned the system in the 1960s. When it was revived by the NRM government, it was changed a little by the clan elders for ease of administration and communication. The *opi* in those days did not have a written constitution for ruling or guiding their subjects, nor was it defined who should assist the *opi* in his tasks. But now things are in place, such as a College of Opi, a

177

Council of Elders and a cabinet. These arrangements may be seen as leaving the women out of the proceedings, but it has always been the case that no woman can be a cultural leader. Also, in the Council of Elders the women are represented, and in the cabinet the minister for women is a woman. It was on 18 August 2006 that I officially assumed the leadership of the Madi Cultural Institution.

For my people, this senseless war of the LRA started in August 1986, when Dzaipi sub-county was attacked by the rebels. It has continued up to the last attack on Dzaipi on 10 March 2005, in which thirteen people were murdered and eighty-six huts burnt. Although the UPDF were 300 metres away, they remained in their barracks and left the rebels to do what they wanted. From that day, the community lost trust in the UPDF, and most people left Dzaipi for other places.

When peace talks started between the rebels and the government, the people of Madi were not involved. They followed the talks only on Radio Mega, which broadcast programmes about the Juba negotiations from Gulu. On 10 August 2007, however, I was invited to a peace conference in Lira. From that day I have been attending meetings connected with the Juba talks, and it has been possible to inform my people about how things are proceeding.

In September 2007, seven of us went to Garamba for consultations with the LRA. I alone was from Madi. The other traditional leaders were from Acholi. We stayed in Garamba for eight days. On our arrival in what the rebels called 'Garamba One', we were welcomed by Vincent Otti, Odhiambo and two other rebels with senior positions. They received us very well and we stayed with them, sleeping in the same compound, but in different tents. They fed us on wild meat, *angara* (a bony but tasty kind of fish), beans, greens, posho and rice. I asked Otti how they got the *angara* fish, as I thought it was caught only in Pakwach (a town in northern Uganda located at the point where the River Nile joins Lake Albert). He said, 'What you have in Uganda, we also have in Garamba.'

On the fourth day of our stay, Joseph Kony arrived from his base at 'Garamba Two'. He told us that it took him five and a half hours to walk between the two camps. He came with many LRA soldiers, and they took over the security of the area. We consulted with him from 2 p.m. until 6.30 p.m. He said he was serious about the peace talks, and that he wanted to resolve the issues by talking, not by the gun. But he stressed that he was not militarily weak. He had decided to stop the fighting and to talk because he had seen people of northern Uganda suffering enough. He stressed that if the talks fail, however, he will resume the war. In less than ten years, he claimed, he will win it.

I asked Kony, 'If you fought for twenty years and could not end the war, how is it possible that it take less than ten years for you to win?' He replied that he will change tactics. He will abduct, but not kill. This statement contradicted his claim that he had not killed in the past.

He also told us to tell our people to go back home whether the peace talks fail or not. If talks fail and war resumes and he finds people in the displacement camps, he will send them back to their villages. The people will not forget what he does – even if other people tell lies about him. It was hard to take some of the things he said seriously. What I saw from my time with the LRA commanders was that the late Vincent Otti was the force behind the peace talks. Now that he is believed to be dead, time will be wasted – witness how Kony has delayed the signing of the agreement.

I spoke at length with Otti – who revealed to me that he had commanded two attacks on my people in Dzaipi. The first one was in 1989, in which all the shops were looted, and more than thirty huts burnt. The LRA were not chased by government soldiers, but left the place in their own time, taking all their loot with them. The second was in 2004. This was the hardest day for them as the UPDF fought them, using two helicopters. Otti told me that many died that day. I asked him what their aim was, did they intend to attack Dzaipi? He replied that they had not planned an attack on that day, they were just caught moving through the area from Sudan.

In the seven days we spent at Garamba, I asked all sorts of questions. Some of the reactions were revealing. Odhiambo told us that the people of Lango and Teso 'will not forget him'. I asked him why that was so. He said that he had 'really killed them'. In general, what I found from my discussion in the bush is that the rebels are not sorry for what they have done.

I demanded to see and talk to the rebels who were abducted from my area. I was able to find and talk to three boys, who were abducted at the ages of five, six and seven. One, called Swaib Aimani from Obongi, had at the time of my visit the rank of major. Acholikanzo was a lieutenant and Oryem was a private. Although they were in good health when I was talking to them, they were not free. There was fear in them. I was very sorry and sad when they asked whether their parents, brothers, sisters and relatives were still alive. They were lacking many things that they wanted me to bring them if I ever came back. A bad part of my experience is that these boys from Madi are now probably all dead. That will have happened when Vincent Otti was killed. They were the ones who escorted Otti from Garamba One to Garamba Two, where

Otti was executed. I am sure Swaib has been killed. He apparently shot two rebels dead when he saw Otti being killed, so they also killed him.

My second visit to Garamba was on 10 April 2008, when the Comprehensive Peace Agreement was to be signed. We waited in Rikwamba from 8 a.m. to 4 p.m. But Joseph Kony failed to show up. At 4 p.m., Colonel Odek and another captain came from Garamba to Rikwamba, saying Kony wanted to talk to cultural and religious leaders in Garamba. Eight of us then walked to Garamba One, the very place where we had stayed in September 2007. Was this the home of Vincent Otti? It did not look like a home. Otti's two huts had been turned into stores for food given by the UN. We thought Kony was going to talk to us face to face. Instead he talked to us on the phone, which was stupid, because we could have done that in Rikwamba instead of walking for forty-five minutes. He told us that he could not sign the agreement, because he was ten days' walk away. Another stupid thing was that Dr Matsanga, who was the chairman of the LRA delegation in the peace talks, knew that Kony was not in Garamba, yet kept saying that the agreement was about to be signed.

On the morning of the 11th, the mediator (Reik Machar) asked us to return to Rikwamba. Soon after we left, Dr Matsanga called a press conference at Nabanga, where he and the journalists were based. He declared that he was resigning from the LRA delegation because Kony had told him to tell lies to the world. Yet this very man has now been reinstated as chairman of the LRA delegation! I now think the LRA are just buying time, and the world should know it. Later I heard that Kony had intended that we should have been killed on arrival at Garamba, but that he was dissuaded at the last moment from giving the order. I do not know whether it is true.

After the failed meeting on the 10th, events indicated that the LRA were wasting our time. On 18 April, Kony phoned to again demand a meeting with the cultural and religious leaders to take place on 10 May in Garamba. He also told us that his delegation had not kept him fully informed about the negotiations in Juba, and that they feared to meet him at his base. So we all went back to Nabanga on the 9th in preparation for the meeting on the following day. We waited until the 17th. On each day Kony was rung more than five times, but did not answer.

On the 17th a meeting was held with the LRA delegation, and it was explained that maybe Kony was annoyed, because all the things that he wanted had not been taken to him. We asked what those things were. They said, 'ceremonial army uniforms – which cannot be purchased in Nairobi, because they are too expensive, as well as ropes, and sheer butternut oil'. We knew that the butternut oil was for ceremonies. But everyone was concerned to know what the ropes were for. No answer was forthcoming. I believe they were meant for crossing rivers or for tying up abducted people. After returning from these failed consultations with the LRA, I had lost faith in them, and decided to refuse to go again to Garamba. I thought perhaps I would be willing to go to Juba (i.e. the capital of southern Sudan) for negotiations, but why should I put my life in the hands of Kony in the bush. I realized that he was unpredictable, and could do anything. Nevertheless, six months later I found myself again making the long walk from Rikwamba to Kony's camp at Garamba, this time in the dark.

It is hard to explain why I decided to join that last attempt to persuade Kony to sign the peace deal. My family and friends thought I was extremely foolish. At the end of September 2008, I had discussed the situation with the Acholi paramount chief, Rwot David Onen Acana II, in Gulu. By that point, Kony had not indicated why he had failed to turn up to sign the Juba agreement. Indeed, it seemed that no one had heard from him for months. It turned out, however, that Acana had spoken to Kony by satellite phone a couple of days before. He had sent a message saying that if Kony wanted the cultural leaders to remain committed to the peace talks, he would have to communicate directly and explain his actions. Acana had demanded to hear Kony's own voice.

When he rang Acana, Kony claimed that he had feared to come to the meetings, because he thought he would be attacked. Acana told Kony that everyone thought he was a liar. Kony replied that he was telling the truth and said, 'I started the fighting from your home, how can I deceive you?' Acana told him that he needed to be 'straight'. Kony then said that he was tired of fighting, and did not want to face MONUC forces. 'I want peace talks back on the table.' He also explained that he had not understood about the ICC and the warrants. Acana told him that the ICC could not just be brushed off, and there could not be a proper discussion of the warrants while the LRA was refusing to sign the peace agreement. Kony went on to complain about a lack of airtime for phone calls (i.e. that no one was paying for them), and that he did not have enough food, because the SPLA had taken what the LRA had been given.

Acana commented to me that he was not very excited about the phone call. He was not convinced that Kony was serious about making peace, but he did not want to lose hope completely. In the weeks that followed, there were some further communications. In early November, a meeting was convened by the mediator, Reik Machar, for those involved in the peace talks. The former president of Mozambique, Joaquim Chissano, was also there as the UN secretary-general's representative. No one had heard from the LRA about what they wanted to do, and the mediator did not want to react to this silence on his own. We all agreed that Kony would be told that he had to sign the agreement by the end of November. Masanga, the head of the LRA delegation, agreed to communicate this to Kony. As a result, on the last day of November 2008, another meeting was organized between cultural and religious leaders from northern Uganda and Joseph Kony at Garamba. It was made clear to Kony that this was his last chance to sign. I felt I had to join the group as the cultural leader of the Madi people. Also I still wanted to know what had happened to those Madi boys whom I had met at Vincent Otti's camp in September 2007. As I walked for hours in the dark to see Kony again, however, I have to admit that I felt I may have been as foolish as my friends and relatives suggested. All of us who went were not sure whether we would come back.

A condition that Kony gave for the meeting was that food would have to be delivered to Rikwamba first. He said that no one should try to reach him before that. When we arrived in Juba, we had to wait until food had reached Nabanga, where our helicopter landed. It was then transported to Rikwamba ahead of us. Our intention was to meet Kony briefly and sign the next day. Chissano remained in Nabanga and we entered the bush after 7 p.m. There was checking by the LRA, and they removed telephones and other valuables. Kony was 50–60 metres away from where we stayed at the LRA camp. There was no sign of any abducted Madi, or indeed of Vincent Otti. Okot Odhiambo and Bok Abudema were additionally absent.

The following day, Kony greeted us cordially and raised a number of issues. He looked much the same as he did in 2007. He was at first relaxed, but as he spoke, continuously repeating himself, he became more and more angry. Much of what he said was not coherent; at times he seemed not to remember things he had just said. He went on and on for literally hours – from 9.30 until 2.45. I know the exact times because I was the only one who had managed to keep a watch. The watches of all the others had been confiscated. For some reason they had missed mine. In summary, Kony made five points. First, he complained about the mediator, saying he was biased towards Uganda, and gave preferential treatment to Uganda. Second, he talked about fighting with the SPLA and the Congolese. He said he was attacked and returned fire. He said that no one condemned attacks on them, but he was blamed if attacks were made on others. Third, he raised the issue of the ICC. At first he said that he did not fear it, because the ICC would do nothing

182

to him. Then he said he would not sign until the indictment was lifted. He reminded us that he was the one who called for peace talks in the first place. Fourth, he had not seen all the things agreed on his behalf. Fifth, he said that Museveni was not so bad, but it was those around him who were bad. When I had a chance, I asked about all the missing people, but was told that they were deployed elsewhere. No one would even admit that Otti had been killed. Those asked just refused to give any information. Kony himself dodged such specific enquiries by saying that he had lost many soldiers in attacks by the SPLA and the Congolese army.

Afterwards, at around 4 p.m., Kony called back his negotiator, Matsanga, together with Rwot Acana and Rwot Jimmy Luwala (the chief of Kony's clan) for further private discussions. I was not at this meeting, but Acana reported that Kony asked for direct discussions with President Museveni. He also confirmed Matsanga as his negotiator, and said that in future his delegation should be small, just three or four. To Acana he said that he should not turn his back on the peace process. He could still be of help, and he should not mind about any false allegations. Kony also claimed that, even if he did not sign, he would release abducted children. Then he said he had to hurry away. He needed to be with his fighters. Apparently, those wanting to attack the LRA were fearful if he was present, because he had spiritual as well as military means of defence.

Next day, Caesar Acellam, who was the second-in-command at that time (having succeeded the previous second-in-command, Odhiambo, who had himself replaced the assassinated Otti), came back and emphasized the points Kony had made to us the previous day. He told us Kony could not come for the second meeting. He said Kony had other duties to perform. But he also said that Kony would not sign the agreement after all. The reason given was that the top commanders would not allow him to do so, because there was nothing in it for him or them. The agreement had been made by the delegation, but they were thieves. Acellam also complained on Kony's behalf that no mobile airtime had been sent to him in order for him to participate in the talks himself. It all seemed a bit peculiar. I suspected Kony had really left the previous night, and had wanted to keep us at the camp so that there was no attack. I said this to Rwot Jimmy Luwala, who had been present at the closed meeting with Kony in the late afternoon of the previous day. We realized that we were going to be kept at Garamba for hours, so that Kony would have plenty of time to relocate. In the end we were released at 3.30 p.m., and made our way back to Rikwamba.

All confiscated property was then returned, including the watches and phones of the other cultural and religious leaders. I even got back my spectacles and cigarettes!

What do all these experiences make me feel about the peace talks and the traditional mechanisms for reconciliation that have been given so much emphasis? As far as the talks are concerned, I am not sure whether Kony was ever really committed to them. They were always one of a number of options that he was exploring. Also, he was being given lots of things to encourage him to participate in them. Perhaps if he was really sure that he would not be punished for his crimes, awarded large amounts of money and given an influential job he might have signed a peace agreement. But really there was not much in the one on offer for him personally, and it left the whole issue of the ICC warrant to one side.

When it comes to traditional mechanisms of reconciliation, according to Madi customs, when a clan fights with another clan, then *tolu koka* can be performed. This is similar to the Acholi ritual called *mato oput*. Such rituals can be shown to have stood the test of time, and they may help in promoting reconciliation in some instances. But the crimes that they can deal with are not the kind of crimes committed by the LRA rebels. Perhaps they can assist the return of those who have been abducted and forced to do terrible things. What I have gathered from my people, however, is that the acts committed by the LRA commanders are too grave to be treated in this way. It may be that people will agree to say that they forgive so that there might be peace. But they will not forget. What they really want is for the ICC to have the capacity to arrest Kony and the others most responsible for what has happened.

PART THREE

Peace and justice

7 On 13 October 2005, a pre-trial chamber of the International Criminal Court unsealed warrants of arrest for Joseph Kony and four other senior commanders of the Lord's Resistance Army: Okot Odiambo, Dominic Ongwen, Vincent Otti and Raska Lukwiya. Vincent Otti was reportedly killed at Kony's command in October 2007. Raska Lukwiya had been killed while fighting the Ugandan army the previous year. The news of his death was taken to his family in Uganda on 16 August 2006. They fought to maintain their composure until government officials and UPDF officers had left, at which point the women broke into inconsolable wails (Adam Pletts).

10 · Northern Uganda: a 'forgotten conflict', again? The impact of the internationalization of the resolution process[1]

SANDRINE PERROT

'There is shortage of soft drinks in the north as most of them are ferried to Juba, Southern Sudan. This comes six days to the Christmas day. [...] Most of the outlets in Gulu and other towns were empty yesterday.'[2]

The shortage of soft drinks was topic A on the veranda of the Gulu radio station, where I was seated a few days before Christmas 2006. For months, every day, dozens of trucks, their tyres squashed by overloads of mattresses, consumer goods, boxes of bottled water and crates of sodas, had crossed the Sudanese border directly from Kampala and driven by the shops of Gulu, Kitgum and Pader. This new non-stop route to southern Sudan was a telling sign. A new international effervescence had been instigated farther north, in the brand-new southern Sudanese capital of Juba, by two major events: the signature of the 2005 Comprehensive Peace Agreement between Khartoum and the Sudan People's Liberation Army (SPLA) and the peace talks held there between the Lord's Resistance Army and the Ugandan government since 14 July 2006. Juba had become a hot spot for diplomats, UN representatives, local and international journalists, traders and local investors speculating on one of the most promising peace initiatives ever. Hence, the need for all the sodas.

The international community had turned a blind eye to the northern Ugandan conflict for over fifteen years.[3] UN Under-Secretary-General for Humanitarian Affairs and Emergency Relief Coordinator Jan Egeland's visit to IDP camps in northern Uganda in November 2003 marked a turning point. His endlessly quoted statement on 'the biggest forgotten, neglected humanitarian emergency in the world today' both raised international awareness and prompted the intervention of hundreds of state and non-state external actors.[4] This chapter questions the impact of this long-awaited and massive internationalization on the conflict resolution process in northern Uganda. It argues that, on the one hand, the pressure created by the work of diplomat activists and the hardline political course of action assumed by emerging donors (Nordic countries and Canada, particularly) partly broke the blind-eye diplomacy usually adopted by the Ugandan regime's main backers towards its shared responsibility in the perpetuation of the conflict (Furley 1989). It surely was highly influential in the government's decision to take part in the peace negotiations in Juba. But on the other hand, the humanitarian and regional approach to the conflict by external actors diluted its accountability. The lack of cohesion of donors and the return, within a few months, to a more realist and collaborative diplomacy towards Museveni's government have delayed the Ugandan government's ownership of the conflict resolution process. This gave the regime leverage to resist a UN militarized intervention and to overshadow the local and national political issues that need addressing in order to foster a long-term peace process in Acholiland.

A late internationalization of the conflict

Until 2003, both diplomatic and international financial and media investment in the conflict had been very low. The extra-moral violence used by the LRA (forced child conscription, exactions on civilians, maiming ...), the absence of a clearly articulated political agenda, its constant reference to supernatural forces – often hermetical to a Western rationality of warfare – had partly obscured the complexity of the political and social processes the LRA has developed. The conflict used to be considered as localized and residual violence, left in the shadow of the pacification and state rebuilding model Uganda had developed in the rest of the territory since the beginning of the 1990s. But the humanitarian crisis provoked by Operation Iron Fist (OIF) shed new light on the conflict. This Uganda People's Defence Forces (UPDF) 2002 offensive on the LRA rear bases in southern Sudan caused a radicalized reaction of the LRA and an alarming increase in attacks and abductions in northern Uganda in the following weeks. In a few months, it prompted the displacement of more than 90 per cent of the population of northern Uganda. The number of IDPs skyrocketed from 400,000 in 2002 to 1.6 million in 2005, gathered in 218 official and dozens of ungazetted camps (Parliament of Uganda 2004).[5] Jan Egeland's ensuing floodlighting of the Ugandan humanitarian crisis hastened an unprecedented, uncoordinated and fragmented rush of hundreds of UN agencies, local and international NGOs, journalists, consultants and researchers.[6]

From 'invisible children' to highly visible teenagers

For local actors and peace activists, the internationalization of the conflict was expected to raise international awareness of a humanitarian and security situation heretofore barely reported in brief articles in the regional section of the national newspapers. There was hope also that donors and multilateral institutions' intervention would soften the government policy on the northern conflict and bring alternative solutions to the unlevel dialogue between the military option prioritized by the government since 1986 and the negotiated solution put forward by northern NGOs and civil society organizations. From the beginning of 2004 onwards, the northern conflict became a magnet for international attention and funding. Total humanitarian assistance increased from US$19.5 million in 2000 to US$56 million in 2002 and US$119.5 million in 2007 (UNOCHA [United Nations Office for the Coordination of Humanitarian Affairs] 2000, 2002, 2007). At the same time, total official development assistance and official aid increased from US$817 million in 2000 to US$1.2 billion in 2005 (World Bank 2007). Ten years before, Comboni fathers and a few NGO representatives were the only *Bazungu* (white people) in towns. Today, bars and chic hotels are mushrooming in Gulu, four-by-fours ride up and down its main streets, NGO signs thrive on every corner. 'Gulu has become NGO city! One day NGOs will displace us from Gulu to get more space for their offices and compounds,' ironically joked one of my Acholi friends.

The national and international media coverage brought the conflict to the front burner with dozens of articles on the IDPs' squalid living conditions, children abducted by the LRA or night commuters who used to transit after sunset from their village to sleep on verandas or in the few shelters provided in the more secure trading centres. Rushing into the humanitarian breach opened by Egeland, an impressive increase in more or less good-quality international informing, sensitizing, lobbying and fund-raising initiatives have flourished on the Web. There is a long list: Uganda Conflict Action Network-Uganda-CAN, the joint International Crisis Group-Center for American Progress's ENOUGH project 'to abolish genocide and mass atrocities', the Gulu Walk initiated by two Canadians,[7] or the International Rescue Committee's campaign: 'Stop the violence in Uganda!', to mention only a few. In a confused mishmash, college students, Hollywood actors and peace activists produced documentaries on the northern Ugandan 'plight', such as the Canadian seven-award-winner *Uganda Rising*,[8] Daniel Simpson and Matthew Green's *Rebels without a Cause* or *Journey into Sunset*, produced by former special adviser to the president at the International Crisis Group, John Pendergast.[9] The controversial 2004 documentary film *Invisible Children (Rough Cut)*, dedicated to night commuters, has been shown on almost every campus in California, 'from suburban living rooms to Capitol Hill, with coverage on Oprah, CNN, the National Geographic Channel', comments their website.[10] Directed by three college students from San Diego originally 'in search of adventure', according to their own words, *Invisible Children* generated a series of events and by-products including commuting-like marches, school twinning and even charity water sold to contribute to the building of wells in Uganda. Amazed by the mobilization capacity of their documentary and highly professional website, the movie-makers, converted into humanitarian workers, were completely overwhelmed by the youth movement they have initiated. Unexpectedly, the eponymous NGO (Invisible Children) they created in Gulu had to cope with continuous flows of young, and in this case highly visible, well-intentioned Western teenagers knocking on their door, willing to help and wanting a humanitarian life experience in Uganda.[11]

Far from being marginal and limited to non-state actors, this emergence of public awareness and international civil mobilization converged at top levels with growing political support from the highest international forums, UN members and diplomatic circles for a quick resolution of the conflict (Security Council 2006).[12] This shift indicates a major change in the diplomatic strategy towards Museveni's government, reflecting the arrival and growing influence of new actors in the diplomatic landscape in Uganda and in the UN institutions.

A major shift in Uganda's diplomatic landscape

At the beginning of the 2000s, the main donors in Uganda followed two different strategies: first, the government's military option, backed by the US Department of Defense and reinforced in the aftermath of 9/11 when the LRA was added, on the Ugandan government's initiative, to the State Department's terrorist organizations list. The second option, mainly supported by the US and UK development agencies in Kampala, was to promote a peaceful resolution of the conflict to put an end to the human suffering. Since 1999, the Deparment for International Development's (DfID) Conflict Reduction and Peace Building Program (CRPB) had been working on protection, reintegration of ex-combatants, information and human rights, especially UPDF abuses in the north, etc. On the US side, state and non-state actors had been involved in the mediation process between the LRA and the government. Experienced in the Sudanese conflict resolution, former US president Jimmy Carter and his Conflict Resolution Program were asked in 1999 to restore diplomatic relations between Khartoum and Kampala to try to build confidence with the LRA to bring them to the negotiating table (Neu 2002).[13] The main obstacle for donors and mediators was in creating contacts with the LRA leadership. USAID kept on working on this issue. Worried by the humanitarian issues in northern Uganda and their spillovers into southern Sudan, Roger Winter, then USAID Assistant Administrator for Democracy, Conflict and Humanitarian Assistance in Southern Sudan,[14] tried to organize tripartite peace talks with the LRA and the Ugandan government and wrote a letter to the LRA leadership in mid-2003.

The cumulative impact of this unrequited letter, however, and of the February 2004 Barlonyo massacre that clearly questioned the military capacity of the government to protect civilians, prompted a shift in the USAID strategy. 'We thought at that time that we should not be as proactive in promoting negotiations. We were not opposed to negotiations but we didn't want to promote them any more,' comments a USAID representative.[15] The US government was then focused on finding a 'quick and permanent' solution to the conflict, considering the physical removal of the LRA leadership as a worthwhile option (Jansen et al. 2007).[16] The back-seat stance adopted by USAID created some confusion. Ironically, it stepped aside from the negotiations while the USAID-supported Northern Uganda Peace Initiative (NUPI) – created to build confidence among stakeholders and advise the Ugandan government on conflict resolution – opened its office in Gulu in August 2004, concomitantly with former Ugandan minister and independent mediator Betty Bigombe's arrival in northern Uganda as a NUPI consultant. It also created a vacuum quickly filled by the rise of smaller, very active, although discreet, emerging external actors, with Nordic countries leading the pack. Between late 2004 and 2005, efforts to open dialogue between the government and the LRA resumed with political, technical and financial support from the newly created Core Group, initiated by one of the oldest Ugandan allies, the UK, with Norway (also very involved in the Sudanese conflict resolution process) and the Netherlands. They were later joined by Ireland, Germany, Sweden and Canada.[17]

'Naive' versus realist donors

The major evolution of donors' identity and the harsher diplomacy of newcomers partly broke the status quo policy towards government responsibility in the conflict that had been implemented by traditional donors. Heretofore, Uganda's success story of the 1990s had given strong credibility to Museveni's governance and military strategy in northern Uganda. But the convergence of frustrations regarding the military interventionism in the Congo, the constantly increasing defence expenditures, corruption scandals involving Ugandan officials, and the slow democratic consolidation process mobilized growing criticism of the regime's humanitarian laissez-faire and obstinacy in pursuing a military option which, until then, had brought only modest results. Imposing an 'ethical' and Pearsonian conception of international relations, Nordic country representatives had been among the most vocal in denouncing the regime's democratic approximations and military policy in northern Uganda.[18] In the summer of 2005, with the humanitarian crisis worsening and the conflict growing visibly, the option of mediation and negotiation with the LRA gradually became a compelling one.[19] Embarrassing reports of the appalling humanitarian situation started piling up. Most prominently, the July 2005 Ministry of Health report on mortality rates in the IDP camps, known as the 'WHO report' (Ugandan Ministry of Health 2005),[20] and the Human Rights Watch report on the UPDF exactions on civilians (Human Rights Watch 2005b) were issued in succession. With rival emotional declarations concerning the Ugandan plight, ambassadors and foreign representatives called for action to put an end to the conflict.[21] The flow of international personalities and diplomats visiting IDP camps was such that a Ugandan journalist cynically suggested the IDP camps 'be handed over to the Ministry of Tourism'.[22]

The last months of 2005 marked a clear fissure in the government and donors' relationship. On the political scene, despite the reintroduction of multiparty democracy, Museveni's desire to run for a third term was an open secret and the violent repressive policy against his political opposition during the pre-electoral campaign stirred up tensions with donors. The arrest of his main political opponent, the opposition leader Kiiza Besigye, in November 2005, on accusations of treason and in particular for collusion with the LRA, mobilized opposition and by extension enhanced focus on the government's policy in northern Uganda. For the first time, the conflict became a major irritant in Uganda's relationships with donors. The $350,000 public relations initiative launched on Museveni's demand by his son-in-law, Odrek Rwabwogo's, local public relations firm, Terp Group, in November 2005 to polish Uganda's image still could not prevent the political and aid crisis that was about to take place.[23] At the end of 2005, DfID, Norway and Ireland, followed by the Netherlands and Sweden, reduced their financial budget support over concerns about Uganda's political transition, press freedom and public administration expenditure. They partly reallocated the funds to humanitarian relief in northern Uganda.[24] Apart from this strong symbolic but also short-term action, there was a growing consensus that the government's firm resistance to donors' pressure (partly explained by these countries' constant military and financial support) should be softened by a more robust diplomacy. Pressures from international NGOs, diplomats and UN activists converged in favour of a referral to the UN Security Council.[25]

The emergent donors: a 'UNly incorrect style'

Previous attempts to internationalize the conflict had been resisted by Uganda's closest allies in the UN (the USA and the UK), supported by Russia and China as unconditional advocates of non-interference in national sovereignty. For years, the Ugandan government had with some success endlessly repeated that it could resolve this localized internal conflict by its own military means in a matter of weeks.[26] Efforts to place the issue on the UN agenda were spearheaded by two strong and atypical peace activists: the Norwegian Jan Egeland , who, since the first press statement on northern Uganda issued by the Security Council president on 14 April 2004, had regularly pushed for his briefings to be presented before the Security Council; and Allan Rock, the ambassador and representative to the Canadian permanent mission to the UN, a long-standing and pugnacious activist against child soldiering, champion of the UN reform and of the UN 'responsibility to protect' in cases of genocide, human rights violations or great humanitarian crisis. Since 2004, he had led a behind-the-scenes lobbying by creating a 'Group of Friends of Northern Uganda' around Canada, Ireland, the Netherlands, Sweden and Norway, but also the USA and the UK, reluctant but too influential to be left out. 'The government of Uganda was not very comfortable with the idea of this lobbying group. It's too damned bad, but people are dying there,' proclaimed Allan Rock with an assumed rough and 'UNly incorrect' style.[27]

In the very last months of 2005, the major modification of the regional security environment livened up the debates within the Security Council to facilitate the resolution of the conflict. Concerns that neither the Ugandan government nor any other state actor in the region would be able to implement the arrest warrants issued by the International Criminal Court (ICC) against the LRA leaders in July 2005 added an incentive in favour of a UN military intervention. Two factors contributed significantly to the attempts to put rhetoric into action: the signing of a Comprehensive Peace Agreement (CPA) between Khartoum and the Sudanese armed rebellion in January 2005, and the physical move of the LRA from its Sudanese rear bases to south-western Sudan and eastern Congo in mid-September 2005. There were fears that the havoc created by the LRA could jeopardize the fragile ongoing construction processes in the neighbouring countries. The LRA activities in southern Sudan had created more displacement. The armed group committed abductions and attacks on civilians. For the first time since the beginning of the war, the LRA also allegedly targeted five humanitarian workers, including a foreign national, between October and November 2005, probably in retaliation for the ICC indictments of the LRA leaders. The neutralization of the LRA's nuisance capacity in southern Sudan and in the Congo, where MONUC – the UN's largest and most expensive mission – had been struggling for five years to impose a settlement of the conflict, was perceived as essential for the stability and economic development of the subregion.

The intervention of the ICC in the peace-building efforts spurred another heated debate that divided international actors (including researchers).[28] There was mainly a communication gap between UN agencies, international NGOs and think tanks firmly sticking to the human rights and international justice principles on the one hand, and on the other local NGOs and field representatives arguing for a more careful approach, given the potential impact of the ICC on short-term peace-building dynamics. DfID, together with the British High Commission, sided with the Netherlands, Norway, Ireland and other 'like minded donors' in pushing on the ground for a negotiated solution. But in the UN, as such, 'there was [then] not a lot of support for peace talks in northern Uganda. [...] Northern Uganda was seen as a diversion: people who were supporting peace talks in Sudan didn't want any diversion. But CPA depended on peace and stability in northern Uganda.'[29]

The mounting pressure for a UN intervention reached a climax in January 2006 when Allan Rock urged the Security Council to place northern Uganda on its agenda for immediate consideration.[30] Interestingly, the conflict was addressed as 'a massive and compelling humanitarian emergency' but also as 'a violent conflict that threatens regional peace and security in an area that is one of the most fragile and troubled in the world' (Security Council 2006). Using the deteriorating humanitarian situation as an entry point, Allan Rock clearly pointed to the inappropriate response of the Ugandan government in terms of civilians' protection. In a letter addressed to the president of the Security Council in November 2005, he asked for more robust diplomacy. For the first time, the possibility of the Security Council using 'the full range of instruments at its disposal should the parties not cooperate with the diplomatic efforts of the United Nations' was mentioned.

The debates in the UN, though short lived, dealt with the government's capacity (and/or willingness) to handle the humanitarian situation and to bring a quick end to the conflict. The whole issue was revolving around one central question: is President Museveni a good or a bad boy? The cumulated effect of the media coverage and the presence of humanitarian workers on the ground gave a voice to the victims of the conflict. The 2005 UN report on IDPs compared northern Uganda to eastern Congo and Darfur and depicted the Ugandan laissez-faire in terms of the humanitarian crisis (UN Secretary-General 2005). It pointed to the forcible displacement of civilians by the Ugandan military in poorly protected camps with no adequate sanitation, highly dependent on international food delivery and whose movements were severely restricted by free-fire zones. The shortcomings of the military in terms of internal protection were brought into crude light, just as Uganda was hit with a condemnation by the International Court of Justice in December 2005 for its military violation of Congolese sovereignty between 1998 and 2003.[31]

This international focus on the conflict was highly challenging for the Ugandan government. Of course, it gave high visibility to the UPDF exactions and military business in the north. Mainly, the confidence crisis called into question the process of modernization and equipment of the military, which remains a pillar of the regime. It also jeopardized its grip on the conflict resolution process and therefore on the post-conflict resettlement of power relations in the area, a stronghold of opposition. The most interesting aspect, however, is that even though the northern conflict was talked about in the Security Council, it only remained at that level: talk. The deployment of a UN peace operation itself has never been seriously considered. The epistolary exchange that followed Allan Rock's request to the Council illustrates the sophisticated resistance mechanisms used by Ugandan representatives to dismiss the calls for UN intervention. 'Uganda has a very good communication policy,' a top UN representative told me when asked about the non-deployment of a UN mission in Uganda.[32] Complaining that she was painted 'as the perpetrator of injustice rather than the victim',[33] Uganda indeed immediately displayed a wealth of diplomatic public relations exercises.

The UN intervention: a matter of communication policy?

With pictures and a few figures and statistics carefully picked to back up its case, Uganda succeeded in painting itself as the victim, a feat that could be realized only by portraying the LRA as criminal – an easy task before an already largely convinced audience. The Ugandan argument was threefold: first, as it had done for the last twenty years, it strove to convince UN members that a military victory was imminent:

'it is now clear that the LRA [is] in the throes of extermination [...] A real possibility of the end of their senseless war is finally in sight [...] The rank of this leadership and a few troops have run to the DRC while others are roaming the bushes of Southern Sudan and Northern Uganda in small bands,' it insisted.[34] The government had to show that it and its army were in control of the situation and that 'any international intervention at the tail end of the conflict will not be useful but only "create unnecessary complications"'.

Second, in a classic strategy of laying the blame on donors, the Ugandan government diverted attention from its own suspected laissez-faire and individual responsibility by drawing the Security Council members' focus to UNMIS (the UN Mission in Sudan), MONUC and Kinshasa's inability to contain the presence of the LRA in the Sudan and the DRC. Not only did it defuse tensions in the internal political scene but it also tugged at the UN heartstrings. President Museveni repeatedly threatened to intervene again in the DRC to solve this security problem, raising concerns that this new military interference could thwart MONUC's objective of securing the volatile political and security transitions in the DRC. The killing of eight MONUC peacekeepers by the LRA on 23 January 2006 in the Garamba National Park occurred almost in a timely manner to back up Museveni's claims against the UN missions. It gave credit to the perception of the LRA as a serious military threat to the region.

Third, the Ugandan government worked on restoring confidence by using consensual instruments to show that it was complying with UN requests and obligations. It insisted on its concerted action with donors to provide humanitarian aid (even though almost all humanitarian and development aid is provided by external actors: WFP food distribution, the Work Bank-supported Northern Uganda Social Action Fund – NUSAF – the IDP policy adopted under UNOCHA's pressure, the UNDP-backed Rehabilitation and Development Plan, etc.). But it also committed to giving regular briefings on the situation in northern Uganda and initiated a Joint Monitoring Committee (JMC) with donors to concoct an emergency humanitarian plan for northern Uganda.[35] Even though the JMC mechanism proposed by the Ugandan government still had to prove its pertinence and effectiveness, within the Core Group, the Security Council and the UN Secretariat there was a degree of appreciation for Kampala's efforts to offer a new initiative. As the design and materialization of the JMC progressed, the pressure to place northern Uganda on the Council's agenda lessened (Security Council 2006).[36]

Within six months, the UN Security Council had gone back to a collaborative approach with Museveni's regime. As a consequence, in June 2006 the UN secretary-general recommended pursuing collaboration between donors and the government in order to achieve national peace, and implement a recovery and development plan for northern Uganda. This quest for an effective solution to the LRA issue materialized in the Juba Peace Initiative under the leadership of the South Sudanese vice-president Riek Machar. The opening of the talks on 14 July 2006 was, certainly, the major outcome of repeated and convergent pressure by external actors. Their main success consists in having convinced the foot-dragging Ugandan government to come to the negotiating table. So far, for the government and the UPDF, only a resounding military victory against the LRA could bring a definitive and acceptable end to the conflict.

Which path for conflict resolution?

So why did these mechanisms of resistance to a UN military intervention work so well? Why did they have such an effective impact? Fundamentally, because Uganda played on donors' uncoordinated positions on the best path for conflict resolution. Repeatedly, the UN Ugandan representatives referred to Canada's position as 'misplaced political activism'. It criticized the alarmist tone of the debates about northern Uganda and the 'self serving' attitude of Jan Egeland.[37] These criticisms struck a chord within UN circles, because they concurred with pre-existent sharp stylistic, structural and political divisions between donors and UN agencies. Stylistic, first, between traditional diplomacy and the tougher policy of new external actors: some prominent members of the Security Council, as well as some ambassadors, were irritated by the aggressive and jostling post-Westphalian style of these 'non P5 members'.[38] The issue of the motivation of Nordic countries and Canada in solving the northern Ugandan conflict was often summed up as a 'Nobel seeking' strategy. This would explain, the theory goes, their jealously kept leadership of the peace initiatives. Generally speaking, traditional powers used to consider these small emerging international actors as 'generous naïve donors', with good humanitarian intentions but no political sense.[39]

More generally speaking, there is no cohesion and there is even competition among donors (the Nordic and more generally northern European countries group is no exception), either in delivering humanitarian assistance or in working on peace initiatives. The external actors who proliferated in the aftermath of the shrill cry made by Egeland had a poor knowledge of the political and humanitarian situation on the ground. Dozens of redundant consultancy and research reports were commissioned, postponing the efficient implementation of humanitarian programmes and fuelling the frustrations of the Acholi population. 'I have hundreds of consultancy reports on my desk. We don't need any report any more. We all know what is happening. What we need now is a policy,' commented one of the government's independent consultants.[40] Although gathered in the Dutch-led Core Group, donors have taken endless joint and/or unilateral initiatives in a disordered hustle and bustle. DfID elaborated closer coordination mechanisms to foster concerted approaches. UNOCHA tried to rationalize the mapping of humanitarian aid. The European Commission compiled a matrix of donors' programmes to improve knowledge distribution. But despite these harmonization efforts in the field, the lack of consultation and information-sharing hindered the adoption of a consensual and common overall strategy. Structurally, headquarters and in-country offices work on a different scale, which added another communication gap. 'While these platforms provided an opportunity for more cohesion and harmonization between the donors, directives from capitals – which often are not informed by up-to-date issues – and the often volatile attention span of some countries' policies – e.g. the US – meant that these platforms were reduced to only a façade.'[41]

The proliferation of individual initiatives led to cross-cutting and duplicative programmes. Given the high level of competition among donors, (international) NGOs and agencies seek to develop niches, sometimes creating programmes where they are not necessarily needed (Ginifer 2006). The late arrival of some donors and UN agencies, in a context where others such as DfID or USAID had been involved in the conflict resolution process since the end of the 1990s, created tensions between old actors and newcomers, but also among newcomers.[42] For instance, Canada was a late entry, in November 2006, in the donor group. The level of funding offered by Canada was a way to demonstrate its commitment to the cause. 'The Canadian representative was based in Nairobi till mid-2006, when we opened an office in Kampala. We had to prove that northern Uganda was not only the flavour of the month for Canada and that we were serious about our involvement,' comments the Canadian representative.[43]

Donors, international NGOs and UN agencies also disagreed on the political position to adopt on central issues, such as the Juba peace talks.[44] The Juba Initiative Fund, launched by Jan Egeland in October 2006, created huge controversy. UNOCHA then sought funding to facilitate the ongoing Juba talks with limited logistical and technical back-up and to cover the running costs of the GoSS Peace Secretariat and the Cessation of Hostilities Monitoring Team. So far, the Juba peace talks, kept afloat by donors, have been the most encouraging (though fragile) sign in the conflict resolution process. But there were concerns over the use of the funds by local actors, not to mention strong criticisms of the idea of giving humanitarian assistance to non-officially demobilized combatants. Finally, the fund was directly managed by UNOCHA international staff in Juba, even though there was some reluctance to see UNOCHA coming out of its humanitarian role to play the cashier role for the funds raised for the talks (a role that the UN Department of Political Affairs refused to play).[45]

UN agencies (including UNOCHA) specifically pointed out the contradiction between the Juba peace talks and the issuance of arrest warrants by the ICC. There was clear tension between those who believed in a negotiated solution and those who didn't want to sit with 'criminals'.[46] Donors and UN agencies were caught in a dilemma between supporting the promising Juba peace process or supporting the ICC implementation of the arrest warrants. After Norway gave the first half, 'schizophrenic donors' – as a UN official called them – (Canada, the Netherlands, France and the UK) provided the rest of the $4.8 million asked for by Egeland. They decided not to directly intervene in the talks but didn't want to be left out. Ironically, there was even stiff competition over who would give the biggest amount to the second Juba fund launched in mid-2007 to succeed the first. Even in terms of strategy, some actors decided to exert a go-it-alone, behind-the-scene influence in Juba. Others opted for a multiple-track strategy, creating some confusion about who was doing what in the mediation process. Interestingly, the USA has long remained noticeably absent from the Juba Initiative Fund.[47] The anticipated failure of the Juba peace talks at the end of 2006, however, created a growing consensus concerning the implementation of the ICC's arrest warrants. In November 2006, even the USA unofficially recognized the role of the ICC. In a closed-door meeting in The Hague, the US representative in charge of eastern Africa in the State Department recommended the execution of the arrest warrants. She noticeably invited the ICC prosecutor not to deal with UPDF activities, however.[48]

For its part, the Security Council was more concerned by the regional threat posed by the LRA, its impact on the peace processes in both Sudan and the DRC, and the danger that it could pose to the UN missions' achievements. 'The LRA is not a major security threat any more. The black belt of two million IDPs around Khartoum and in Darfur is a much bigger problem for the UN,' commented a UN official in 2007.[49] Apart from a military intervention in northern Uganda, the UN had the option to mandate MONUC and the UN Mission in Sudan (UNMIS) to deal with the LRA.[50] But at that time, it would certainly have overstretched both missions' costs and mandate (Security Council 2006). In a way, donors adopted a 'better than nothing' option, allowing them at least to take care of the humanitarian situation and to keep President Museveni from destabilizing the whole region with an unilateral attack on the LRA's hideout in the Garamba National Park, across the border in the DRC. In late November 2006 the secretary-general, as a lower-cost solution, appointed former Mozambican president Joaquim Chissano as his special envoy instead. Unsurprisingly, Ugandan pressures made sure his mandate didn't refer to northern Uganda specifically but to 'LRA-affected areas', which also covered the Congo and southern Sudan.[51]

The end of a blind-eye diplomacy?

Basically, the government of Uganda has capitalized on the incapacity of donors to reach consensus and advocacy positions on core issues to maintain its sovereignty and strict independence in its policy choices. So, is Museveni a good or a bad boy? Among external actors, the answer is not clear. Most of them would probably reply 'not that bad'. There had been a large consensus indeed that the government benefits from an indisputable comparative advantage over the LRA. Clearly understanding the UN mechanisms and machinery, the Ugandan government speaks the language of international institutions. It developed a great ability to do the splits in publicizing the humanitarian crisis and soundly arguing that it would resolve it with its own means.[52] In so doing, it ensured that vital foreign aid was not cut off and encouraged UN agencies and NGOs to address the problems (Chabal 2005; Dolan and Howel 2006). So far Uganda has even used the war against the LRA and the high levels of defence spending it entails as an argument to relinquish any responsibility for IDP protection.[53] It is only recently that the Ugandan budget has allocated funds to northern Uganda. As an act of goodwill, President Museveni launched the Peace and Recovery Development Project (PRDP) in October 2008, as a three-year Shs1.1 trillion ($606.5 million) programme for a reconstruction programme in insecurity-affected areas including, but not restricted to, northern Uganda. The government was supposed to provide 30 per cent of the funding, the rest being financed by donors. Some was released immediately, but effective implementation was delayed by difficult funding procedures. The government had also dragged its feet in paying the one-million-dollar contribution it pledged to the Juba peace fund.[54] Given its presence in the Juba peace talks, however, nobody could accuse the government of having been disengaged. No matter that Museveni's representatives, since then, had tried to rally members of the Council to shift back to a military option if the peace talks failed.

And indeed, in spite of the March 2008 agreements on all substantive issues in Juba, the execution of LRA second-in-command Vincent Otti in October 2007, ordered by Kony, and the move of the LRA to north-eastern Congo and south Central African Republic at the beginning of 2008, cast more doubt on the peace talks outcome. New setbacks in negotiation in November 2008, with Kony's repeated failure to keep appointments with peace representatives in Juba and the increasing activities of the LRA in the DRC, led to the collapse of the attempt of the main actors to pursue a peaceful solution. On 14 December, the joint Operation Lightning Thunder was launched by Ugandan, Congolese and South Sudanese troops on the LRA bases in the Garamba National Park with the respectively military and logistical support of MONUC and the Pentagon New African Command.[55] Unsurprisingly, this operation led to a new surge of LRA reprisal attacks against civilians in Haut and Bas Uélé in eastern DRC. As a consequence of the failure by Kony to honour his commitments, and of renewed attacks by the LRA in the DRC, South Sudan and CAR, Chissano's assignment as a special envoy was suspended on 30 June 2009, six months before its originally planned ending (Security Council 2009).

At than time, even though donors and UN agencies had realized the limits of the regime's good governance, and the cost to them of providing core functions and vital humanitarian assistance, they gave preference to a collaborative and concerted approach with the Ugandan government.[56] They had already expressed their discontent with the undemocratic developments of the regime by partly and temporarily cutting aid, but they weren't geared up to cut additional funds in relation to the government's policy in northern Uganda, as Sarah Bayne notes (Bayne 2007).[57] After the government announced in January 2009 deferral of the PRDP to the 2009/10 financial year because it was unable to secure its 30 per cent contribution, the UK temporarily threatened to make its support conditional on implementation of the project and regional equity in Uganda.[58] Indeed, its postponement was likely then to delay the return of IDPs back home. But generally speaking, relations with donor countries have remained stable. The current decrease in donors' aid is more dependent on deteriorating economic global conditions. Donors' twofold diplomatic strategy has been relying on support for and collaboration with the government on the one hand and constructive pressure on the other. This collaborative approach was linked to the firm belief that it is possible to affect the government's conception of the appropriate ways to bring the conflict to an end (ibid.). But fundamentally, the UN and donors shifted back to a pragmatic and realist diplomacy because there was really no option other than conciliating Museveni. Most of the external aid in Uganda is provided through budget support, and is therefore linked to the government's willingness to allot and manage it properly. On the humanitarian side, the appointment of the new humanitarian coordinator, the UK's John Holmes, was very indicative of the shift back to a realist approach. Allan Rock was on the list of potential successors, but Holmes was chosen. 'Holmes is more a humanitarian diplomat than a diplomat humanitarian. He doesn't see things the same way,' commented a UNOCHA official. Moreover, the absence of credible political alternatives as state leader makes any confrontational policy with the incumbent regime vain and pointless. Museveni won the February 2006 presidential elections with more than 60 per cent of the votes, although more than 90 per cent of the Acholi voted for his opponent, Kiiza Besigye.[59]

For the past twenty years, the regime's leader walked a tightrope, oscillating between authoritarianism and democracy, restricting political liberties but enhancing freedom of speech, and using a very sophisticated grammar of half-restraint violence.[60] But fundamentally, the persistence of the image of Uganda's success story of the 1990s still impacts on the perceptions of the donors, including the newcomers. 'The US and UK like Museveni very much, and indeed a part of me likes him too,' a Canadian representative confessed. 'Uganda has a relatively good performance in the fight against HIV/AIDS, even if the credit is not wholly deserved; Uganda is stable and prosperous compared with Kenya, where criminality is more rampant.'[61] Through its joint operation in the DRC and CAR,[62] Uganda succeeded in presenting itself as a pillar of stability, a pivotal peace provider in the region. For the US State Department, and to a lesser extent for the UK, Uganda was still a strong ally in the war against terrorism. In 2006, Washington worried much more about guaranteeing the participation of Ugandan soldiers in the peace mission of the African Union in Somalia than about calling into question the management of the northern Uganda conflict by the government since 1986. Additionally, the deployment of 1,600 Ugandan soldiers in March 2007 gave more international credibility to the Ugandan government and military. In this pattern, the LRA acts as a foil to the government. The armed group leaders failed their internationalization and media exposure test and the reductionist view in the international community of the LRA 'as a dying, ragtag gang' is still the norm (Perrat 2008).[63] And yet, basically, we still don't know much about the LRA or, rather, the different groups of the LRA forming alliances in 2009 with Congolese armed groups to gain control of mines in eastern Congo, establishing new bases in south-eastern CAR and being active not only in Equatoria but also in Bahr el Gazhal state in southern Sudan. And yet these new avatars of the original armed group are further proofs of its amazing regenerative capacity.

Conclusion

Just like the trucks full of soda passing by Acholiland to go to Juba, the international focus quickly shifted from northern Uganda to southern Sudan and north-eastern Congo. And yet, rumours of the LRA rearming in the Congo with the renewed support of Khartoum were already growing in October 2007 and were soon seen to be true. Acholi civilians, who had expected that external actors would have served their cause, now claimed to have been used as a foil by humanitarian NGOs and international agencies: 'We see four-by-fours going from the NGO compound to their office then back home. Why don't they go to the camps? [...] People come here, make reports, go away and we never hear about the report any more. We still die here and nothing happens. People just make money out of the conflict,' said a local actor.[64] The LRA has now left northern Uganda and the number of IDPs has officially dropped to 437,000 as of December 2009.[65] Ironically, although there is a need for public service rebuilding in the region, and multi-year projects for the returnees going back to their vilage of origin, NGOs have started to divert their funds to other 'new' emergencies, such as the Karamoja food security issue in eastern Uganda.[66]

The unclear labelling of the conflict as a local, humanitarian, regional crisis biased the formulation of a clear policy by external actors towards northern Uganda. The ongoing humanitarian bias used by external actors to analyse the conflict adds to the depoliticizing of the conflict and of its resolution. On the Ugandan side, despite the fourfold media, humanitarian, diplomatic and judicial internationalization of the conflict, the Ugandan government's responsibility in the conflict remains mainly unquestioned. The northern insurgency has been diluted in regional dynamics that enabled the government to distract international attention from internal military and political developments and to prevent donors from intervening diretly in the political sphere. Needless to say, the LRA is responsible for the most horrendous atrocities and human suffering in northern Uganda. But the sustainable resolution of the conflict is not only about resolving a humanitarian crisis, and probably not only about disbanding and disarming the LRA. It also depends on the way the regime will address the huge political opposition in northern Uganda.[67] The confrontational policies towards the regime's opponents, the north–south divide, the increasing militarization of the regime, the government's divisive politics, which fuels local tensions in Acholi, and the fact that the army remains the chief actor in the north will all have to be addressed. The humanitarian and regional bias used by external actors to analyse the conflict adds to the depoliticizing of the conflict and of its resolution. The northern insurgency has been diluted in regional dynamics that have enabled the government to distract international attention from internal military and political developments and to prevent donors from intervening directly in the Ugandan political sphere. International forums have included the northern conflict in the 'Great Lakes' and even the 'Greater Great Lakes' conflict system, extending from the Lakes region to Angola, Congo-Brazzaville and Sudan. The sympathy shown for Ugandan security concerns, the support given to the simplistic criminalizing analysis of the LRA, and the lenient attitude of donors regarding the regime's misconduct have dampened donors' leverage to sway the political developments of the regime. In sum, the conflict resolution process is linked to a scale issue. Before 2003, the Ugandan government was presenting the LRA as a local problem that could easily be resolved with its own military means in a matter of weeks. Then the support of the Sudanese government for the LRA was put forward to underline the regional dimensions of the conflict. Finally, only one scale has always been ignored: the national one.

11 · 'The realists in Juba'? An analysis of the Juba peace talks

RONALD R. ATKINSON

On 14 July 2006, peace talks began between the Government of Uganda (GoU) and the rebel Lord's Resistance Army (LRA) to end the twenty-year war in northern Uganda. The talks were mediated by the recently instituted, semi-autonomous Government of Southern Sudan (GoSS) and held in the GoSS capital, Juba. For the first time since the war began, direct talks between the GoU and LRA were being held outside Uganda and under the leadership of an outside mediator, with its own vested interest in helping negotiate an end to the conflict. This led many, both in and outside Uganda, to see the Juba talks as the best hope to end the war in over a decade, and perhaps since it began. This chapter describes the talks, outlines what they achieved, and comments on their ultimate failure.

Historical background

In late 1993, the then GoU minister of state resident in Gulu, Betty Bigombe, initiated talks between the GoU and LRA. In January 1994, Bigombe, with a team of elders and religious leaders, met with the LRA leader, Joseph Kony. A group meeting was followed by a private, tape-recorded session between Kony and Bigombe. In this session, Kony insisted on a comprehensive peace agreement to end the rebellion, requiring the involvement of both the Acholi community as a whole and members of the political wing of the rebel movement living outside Uganda. He argued that this would take six months to organize and asked for this amount of time. Reportedly, after reading a transcript of the private session, President Museveni rejected the idea and gave the rebels a seven-day deadline to assemble and surrender, a condition that effectively ended the peace process.[1]

The widely circulated GoU explanation for Museveni's abrupt announcement of the one-week deadline was military intelligence of LRA contact with the Sudanese government in Khartoum, leading to arms and other support from that source. There is no doubt that such contact had been established, although it was not until after the collapse of the talks that Sudan began providing the rebel group with significant financial assistance, military training, weapons, other supplies and sanctuary. On the oft-invoked principle of 'my enemy's enemy is my friend', Khartoum supported the LRA in part because Uganda backed the Sudan People's Liberation Army/Movement (SPLA/M), Khartoum's main enemy in the long north–south Sudan civil war. The LRA also served as yet one more southern Sudan-based group allied with Khartoum in fighting the SPLA.

The LRA in southern Sudan were typically based near Khartoum military installations and/or in areas of the divided southern Sudan that did not (or did not consistently) support the SPLA, especially in Eastern Equatoria. And the LRA presence as a pro-Khartoum military force in southern Sudan was more than symbolic. LRA fighters seem to have been engaged in more – and more conventional – battles against the SPLA in Sudan than against the Ugandan army (the Ugandan People's Defence Force, or UPDF) in Uganda. In return, support from Khartoum helped enable the LRA to become what a number of analysts claim was a better-trained, better-equipped and more effective fighting force than the UPDF.[2]

Meanwhile, the Sudan government repeatedly denied that they supported the LRA, although virtually no one accepted the denials as justified. As early as 1995, the Ugandan government cut off diplomatic relations with Khartoum over the issue, but international pressure on Sudan to cease their support of the LRA was minimal. Following the 11 September 2001 attacks in the USA, however, the State Department added the LRA to its terrorist watch list. Attempting to improve relations with Washington, the Sudan government 'quietly claimed that it had cut off supplies to the LRA' (see International Crisis Group 2004: 7, 2005a). Shortly after, in January 2002, the Sudanese president, Omar el-Bashir, agreed in a meeting with Ugandan president Museveni to plan joint military operations 'to wipe them [the LRA] off their borders before the end of this dry season'.[3]

The next month, Sudan's chargé d'affaires in Kampala, Mohammed Sirajuddin, publicly admitted that there 'was a relationship in the past. We would provide assistance like foodstuff, maybe some weapons, anything.' 'But', he added, 'that relationship ceased completely. There is no food, medicine, ammunition or other assistance from Khartoum to LRA.'[4] Each of these Sudanese responses – agreeing to work with the Ugandan government against the LRA and claiming that they had ceased supporting the LRA – would be repeated again and again over the next several years. Evidence to the contrary often surfaced, however, leading to frequent challenges by the GoU and others about Khartoum's genuine behaviour and intentions.[5]

In mid-March 2002, however, the two governments announced an agreement whereby Khartoum allowed the Ugandan army to enter Sudan to conduct 'a limited military operation' against the LRA.[6] Later that month, the UPDF began an offensive code-named 'Operation Iron Fist', intended to deliver a final blow to the rebels by stepping up military actions against them in both northern Uganda and southern Sudan, the first major UPDF offensive against the LRA since 1994.[7] Operation Iron Fist undoubtedly produced heavy LRA casualties, although army claims of crippling the rebel organization were wildly exaggerated. And rather than delivering a 'final blow' to the LRA, rebel activity – and violence against civilians – spiked to levels not seen for many years. LRA attacks also extended farther outside the Acholi subregion than ever before, reaching deep into Lango and Teso.[8]

The UPDF entry into southern Sudan established a Ugandan military presence there that has continued into the present, with UPDF numbers in late 2006 reportedly in the 10,000–15,000 range.[9] Despite this presence, for which the Sudanese government regularly extended permission and promised cooperation, the LRA remained a potent and destabilizing force in southern Sudan as long as the Sudan civil war lasted. And despite frequent claims to the contrary, Khartoum's direct or indirect support of the rebels also continued. The LRA remained useful allies.

Then, in January 2005, the Khartoum government and the SPLA/M signed a Comprehensive Peace Agreement (CPA) that formally ended the north–south Sudan civil war. This ended the direct contribution that LRA fighters had made to Khartoum's military struggle inside southern Sudan. The Sudan government's ever more vehement insistence from that point on that they no longer supported the northern Ugandan rebels, however, seems unlikely to have been justified, at least until late 2005 or early 2006.[10]

In any case, even after the signing of the CPA, the LRA's presence in the still-fragmented and fragile southern Sudan not only continued, but spread. From their initial moves into southern Sudan, the LRA had been based mainly in Eastern Equatoria, across the border from north-central Uganda. In August 2005, substantial numbers of LRA fighters began moving across the Nile into Central and Western Equatoria. There they were accused of numerous attacks against civilians over the next several months, but they also established relations with a number of militias and other local leaders. This move was accompanied by the founding, under deputy-commander Vincent Otti, of an LRA base across the Sudan border in Garamba National Park in north-eastern Democratic Republic of Congo (DRC). Neither the SPLA (in the early stages of a difficult, problem-plagued transition to a smaller, professional army) nor the large UPDF contingent inside southern Sudan presented an effective counter to these LRA activities (International Crisis Group 2006: 4–5).

Developments leading to the Juba peace talks

When the CPA ending the Sudan civil war was signed on 9 January 2005, its many provisions included the creation of a semi-autonomous Government of South Sudan (GoSS), formally instituted six months later in July. Its first president – who under the CPA was also the first vice-president of the Republic of Sudan – was Dr John Garang di Mabior, who had led the SPLA/M in its fight against Khartoum since its founding twenty-one years before.

The new CPA-mandated, semi-autonomous GoSS faced massive challenges, both immediate and long term, including the need to: (1) work with Khartoum to monitor and implement the CPA; (2) begin reconstructing the devastated infrastructure of southern Sudan (education, roads, healthcare – indeed, almost everything); (3) build human capacity, in government, business and elsewhere; (4) deal effectively with the international community (the UN, NGOs and donors); (5) cope with the internal politics and divisions within the GoSS and SPLA/M, heightened by moves to transform the SPLA into a smaller, more professional army, which in turn required the disarmament, demobilization and reintegration (DDR) of many SPLA soldiers; (6) begin building peace and trust among a fragmented, heavily armed population, deeply divided by years of civil war – both across ethnic and linguistic lines, and within – which would eventually entail the DDR of the many militia groups throughout the southern Sudan; and, finally, (7) deal with the thorny problems caused by the northern Uganda war and the threats to peace and stability caused by the presence in southern Sudan of large numbers of fighters from both the LRA and the UPDF.[11]

An indication of how seriously the new GoSS took the last of these issues, particularly the LRA, was highlighted by John Garang in three statements made in July 2005: just prior to his inauguration as GoSS president; in the inauguration speech itself; and in his last public comments before his death. In each, Garang emphasized that a continuing LRA presence represented an unacceptable threat to the people and government of South Sudan, and they would have to leave.[12]

The crash on 30 July 2005 that took Garang's life occurred just three weeks after his inauguration as GoSS president. He was returning to the southern Sudan after a meeting with his long-time friend and ally

Ugandan president Yoweri Museveni, when bad weather and pilot error seem to have combined to bring down the Ugandan military helicopter he was riding in just north of the Sudan/Uganda border (though variant rumours of assassination persist).

The person who succeeded Garang as both head of the SPLM and president of the GoSS was Salva Kiir Mayardit, Garang's long-time deputy and already head of the military wing of the movement, the SPLA. Kiir's vice-president was Dr Riek Machar Teny Dhurgon, who had been some-times a key ally of Garang and sometimes a bitter rival and enemy. Each was in his own way controversial (especially Machar), but they provided a leadership style widely recognized as less authoritarian, more open to dialogue and more inclusive than Garang's had been. By January 2006 this new approach helped bring Paulino Matiep Nhial into the new GoSS as Kiir's deputy commander (and effective military head) of the SPLA. Matiep had been the most powerful leader of the many southern Sudanese militia groups aligned with Khartoum and against the SPLA during the civil war, in direct command of the South Sudan Defence Force (SSDF) and with significant influence over a number of others.[13]

In addition to a contrasting style of leadership, the new GoSS leaders had a very different relationship with President Museveni and the GoU than had the late John Garang. Garang and Museveni had been friends since their undergraduate days in Tanzania during the late 1960s, and Museveni had been one of Garang's – and the SPLA/M's – closest allies ever since he came to power in Uganda in 1986.

None of the new GoSS leaders had the personal connection with Museveni that Garang did. And Machar and Matiep, while fighting against the Garang-led SPLA during the Sudan civil war, had both had substantial dealings with the LRA. This distance from Museveni on the part of the post-Garang GoSS leadership, and previous contact between two of them and the LRA, opened up new space for the GoSS and LRA to work with one another. It was, moreover, in the self-interest of each to do so. The LRA had been exploring avenues for peace talks since the failure of the last Betty Bigombe-led attempts in 2004, and the GoSS began seeking contact in late 2005.[14]

For the GoSS, three overarching and related considerations were most important. First was the security threat posed by the rebels to the new GoSS, its army and its citizens. Second was the LRA threat to the GoSS's challenging task of building trust and peace with the numerous groups in southern Sudan that were not clearly or reliably in their camp. Such communities had not been allies of the SPLA during all or part of the Sudan civil war; many were home to militias that had fought against the SPLA; and many had been the targets of SPLA attacks, with children abducted, cattle stolen, and homes and fields destroyed. Almost all remained widely and heavily armed. And it was precisely in communities such as these that most of the four thousand or more LRA fighters in southern Sudan were located. Some of these local groups (or their militias) had reportedly reached accords with the LRA in their midst to establish what were essentially mutual defence pacts, agreeing to oppose jointly attacks on either.[15]

A third major consideration was the untenable situation of having large numbers of 'foreign' fighters operating inside the territory of what was at least a semi-autonomous GoSS (with a referendum on whether to become fully independent scheduled for 2011). For different reasons, both the LRA and the UPDF had been invited into southern Sudan by Khartoum, *not* the GoSS. And even though attention has focused on problems caused by the LRA, having the UPDF remain in GoSS-controlled territory has also contributed to security and other concerns (significantly, when Khartoum's protocol allowing UPDF operations inside southern Sudan expired in February 2006, the GoSS did not renew it). A 2006 International Crisis Group report notes that many in the SPLA/M had come to worry 'that the conflict was slowly shifting from northern Uganda to southern Sudan'. 'The [Ugandan army] brought the battle from Uganda to southern Sudan, but they didn't succeed in defeating the LRA,' said a senior SPLM official. The UPDF presence also raises issues of GoSS sovereignty and legitimacy, for as Kenyan-based journalist Charles Onyango-Obbo argues, the GoSS 'can't credibly portray the Arab regime as northern occupiers, while at the same time allowing the Ugandan army to maintain bases'.[16]

The GoSS leadership reasoned that talks with the LRA offered the chance to begin addressing all three of these problems. By February 2006, GoSS–LRA discussions had produced a formal accord. In addition to subsidiary clauses, the agreement had three main provisions: (1) the GoSS would serve as mediators in peace negotiations between the LRA and the GoU; (2) the LRA would cease initiating hostile activities inside southern Sudan; and (3) if the LRA could not accept these two provisions, then the GoSS would force them to leave.[17]

Aware of the risks that forcibly moving against the LRA would pose to their efforts to build peace and trust in areas not yet firmly committed to the government, the GoSS made clear to the LRA that they wanted to avoid using such force, and would do so only very reluctantly. The GoSS was also clear about the following: (1) they acknowledged that the LRA had a legitimate cause, (2) they accepted that the GoU had not been sufficiently committed to resolving the conflict, (3) they made assurances that they would support the withdrawal of the warrants issued in October 2005 against the top LRA leaders by the International Criminal Court (ICC), and (4) they pledged their absolute commitment to doing everything they could to make the peace talks successful.[18]

Having explored avenues for peace talks since 2004, the LRA leadership by late 2005/early 2006 seem to have viewed such talks as the best option then available to them, and that working with the GoSS was the best, most viable way to pursue that option. Such an assessment seems based, most essentially, on LRA calculations that the GoSS were serious about both the carrots that they were offering (the four points listed just above) and the stick (that the GoSS would, however reluctantly, use force if the LRA would not enter into talks). The relative peace that followed the signing of the CPA had greatly diminished the operating space offered to the LRA as just one of a complex and shifting array of active militias and other armed groups in southern Sudan. This made the threat of the GoSS stick a serious one. If it were used, the LRA ran the serious risk of being isolated and destroyed, or being forced out of their long-term and relatively secure southern Sudan sanctuaries. Only if southern Sudan again descended into widespread conflict did it seem likely that the LRA could re-establish itself as an effective fighting force there (allying with various dissident groups against the GoSS and SPLA), which in turn could provide a way to maintain, or re-establish, an effective insurgency in north-central Uganda.[19]

This related set of assessments provides a more compelling explanation for LRA engagement with the GoSS and then entering into the Juba peace talks than three arguments more commonly put forth. The first, derived from GoU propaganda (purportedly based on GoU military intelligence), is simply wrong. This asserts that the LRA entered into peace talks because UPDF military pressure had reduced the LRA to a ragtag dying force of only several hundred, or at most a thousand or so.[20]

The second and third alternative explanations for LRA participation in peace talks have greater credibility, although the significance of each has often been exaggerated. One is that the top LRA leaders feared the ICC warrants handed down against them in October 2005 and saw peace talks as a possible means to avoid, or at least postpone, arrest. This has been put forth by the court itself, and seems to have become part of accepted wisdom, repeated over and over again in the media, various reports and public comments from a wide range of people both in and outside Uganda. Although the ICC warrants have clearly been a concern for the LRA during the talks (and at the end were an insurmountable stumbling block), there is little evidence that they played a significant role in the rebels' decision to pursue those talks. The third, often coupled with one or both of the first two, has been that the LRA engaged in negotiations merely to buy time 'to reorganize and rearm'.[21]

Even though the GoSS–LRA agreement leading to the Juba peace talks had been reached by late February 2006, the former was not then ready to make the agreement – or their lead role in it – widely public. Indeed, GoSS president Kiir gave no hint of such negotiations in a 22 February press conference, when he 'affirmed' that SPLA and Khartoum forces had joint responsibility for 'expelling' the LRA from southern Sudan.[22]

By early March, however, GoSS leaders had begun quietly making their agreement with the LRA known, using private channels to pass information to local political and community leaders in northern Uganda, and beyond.[23]

An earlier public GoSS offer to mediate between the LRA and GoU was made by Riek Machar in mid-November 2005, prompting a positive rebel response in a press release the next day. Then nothing was heard until five months later, in a *Sudan Tribune* telephone interview with Machar on 20 April 2006, following an 11 April meeting with LRA deputy-commander Vincent Otti. Without acknowledging that the GoSS and LRA had already reached agreement, Machar said that the GoSS had offered themselves as mediators to the rebels and GoU, and 'both sides seemed open to the overture'. When the *Sudan Tribune* approached GoU presidential spokesman Onapito Ekomoloit, however, his response was: 'I don't think any previous overtures to the LRA have yielded positive results [...] I don't think they are interested in dialogue.' He then added a typical GoU refrain: 'They are militarily defeated [...]'[24]

Shortly after, on 1 May, GoU defence minister Amama Mbabazi flew to Khartoum to meet the Sudanese president and UN officials to discuss regional means to 'handle' the LRA, and on the 3rd, Ugandan president Museveni categorically ruled out talks with the rebels.[25]

That same week, unbeknownst to the GoU, GoSS vice-president Machar met with Joseph Kony and Vincent Otti near the DRC/Sudan border. There, in a videotaped session, Machar spoke directly to the top LRA leaders about the GoSS offer to negotiate peace between them and the GoU. Both Kony and Otti agreed to the negotiations and affirmed that they too wanted peace. As shown at the end of the video, Machar opened a black bag, took out two bundles of money, placed them in an envelope, walked over to Kony, and handed the envelope over. It was $20,000 in $100 bills. Machar said that his president had asked him to deliver it, emphasizing that it was for food, not arms or ammunition.

But none of this would become public for another three weeks (and when it did, controversy swirled most strongly around the $20,000).[26]

Just ten days after Machar met the rebel leaders (and another ten before it became public), another – and in many ways parallel – meeting occurred in Kampala. While attending Ugandan president Museveni's 12 May inauguration ceremonies, GoSS president Salva Kiir informed Museveni officially of both the existence of the GoSS–LRA agreement and its three major provisions, and presented a request from Joseph Kony asking the GoU to enter into GoSS-mediated peace talks in Juba.[27]

President Museveni's initial public response, on 16 May, began by refering to the ICC warrants against the top rebel leaders, but then stated that if Kony was 'serious about a peaceful settlement', the GoU 'would guarantee his safety'. He then declared a 1 August deadline on Kony to end the insurgency, adding that if the offer was not taken up, the UPDF and SPLA 'would jointly handle him militarily'. Thus, in almost literally one breath, Museveni (1) completely reversed his categorical rejection of talks made less than two weeks earlier; (2) essentially re-buffed (and offended) the ICC; (3) offered what seemed an olive branch and an opening for dialogue to the LRA leadership; and (4) effectively negated those openings by imposing a deadline that was both unrealistic and unilateral.[28]

The day after Museveni's statement appeared in the press, the ICC responded by insisting that Uganda honour its commitment to the ICC process and that the indicted LRA leaders must be arrested. This position was backed over the next week by both the US government and the European Union. All of this dampened prospects for the success of the GoSS initiatives to get peace talks under way, and resurrected doubts that the GoU and its president really supported such talks.[29]

It was at this stage that news of the Machar meeting with Kony and Otti hit the newspapers. As noted above, immediate controversy focused on the money that the GoSS had given the LRA. But this faded as the historic nature of the meeting began to sink in: the first public appearance of Joseph Kony in many years; the GoSS directly offering itself as mediators to the LRA top leader; and the latter's stated willingness to accept that offer and enter peace talks. The nature of public discourse on the northern Uganda war, as well as the dynamics among the three sides most directly engaged, shifted dramatically.

Momentum, at least for the moment, swung towards the GoSS and LRA, and the peace talks that they in tandem supported. As would be the case from then on, however, such momentum did not last. In-stead, developments both on the ground and in negotiations, as well as assessments of those developments, sometimes pointed to progress towards peace and sometimes the opposite. Accounts in the *New Vision* from the last two days of May alone illustrate the frequently wildly swinging pendulum. On 30 May Ugandan president Museveni was reported to have asked the USA 'to facilitate Uganda, the DR Congo, Sudan and the UN to agree on a joint hunt for LRA chief Joseph Kony'. The next day, GoSS president Salva Kiir, and Vice-President Riek Machar, emphasized both their belief that peace talks would soon begin and their commitment to the talks' success.[30]

Over the month of June, negotiations, developments on the ground and public discourse all continued to swing back and forth. The thirty articles and opinion pieces devoted to the war and proposed peace talks in the independent *Monitor* and the twenty-five in the government-sponsored *New Vision* were divided almost equally between those more or less favourable to and optimistic about peace talks and those that were pessimistic. Several times, the GoU raised doubts or obstacles, with Museveni stating flatly in mid-month that the GoU would not send a delegation to Juba and then repeating his desire to go after the LRA in the Congo.[31]

By late June, however, momentum again lay on the side of the talks, as most clearly and importantly indicated by the GoU decision – reversing its earlier stance – to send a delegation to peace talks in Juba.[32]

The first six months of the Juba talks – achievements and difficulties

When the talks formally opened on 14 July 2006, hopes were high. As noted above, for the first time during the war, an outside mediator, with vested interests in helping navigate an end to the conflict, was leading the talks. A statement by the LRA delegation claimed: 'Never before has there been such an opportunity as this,' and many people both inside and outside Uganda expressed similar sentiments.[33]

The talks were rocky and often raucous. The delegations exchanged accusations and demands from the opening session, and took turns walking out. The first major sticking point was the rebel demand for a ceasefire and the GoU's rejection of the idea. As the two sides danced around the issue, the UPDF continued military activities and on 12 August killed the LRA's third-ranking commander, Raska Lukwiya (included among those targeted by the ICC). This led to yet another break in the talks, more harsh language on both sides, and widespread concern about the talks' future. Then, quite suddenly, the two delegations produced a Cessation of Hostilities Agreement (CoH; on 26 August), quickly hailed as 'a historical development [...] the first time ever a bilateral accord of any sort has been signed' by the LRA and the GoU.[34]

Other stumbling blocks arose during the first six weeks. These included the ICC warrants (with the GoU offering amnesty to Kony and the other top rebel leaders and the ICC insisting on implementing the warrants), accusations from southern Sudan community leaders of human rights violations by both the LRA and the UPDF, and questions about the legitimacy of the LRA delegation, often dismissed as long-time exiles cut off from both Ugandan realities and the LRA military leadership. Early public rifts between the LRA and the GoSS chief mediator, Riek Machar, also surfaced, accompanied by the first rebel demands for a different mediator and GoU rejection of a change.[35]

The same issues continued to resurface, if in sometimes modified form, over the next three and a half months. But the most serious and frequent cause for the talks' many halts and stumbles over that period were violations (or accusations of violations) of the CoH. Although both sides clearly breached the agreement, many accusations against the LRA of doing so seemed dubious; conversely, violations by the UPDF were seemingly both more frequent and more serious.[36] Still, the CoH basically held, a crucial achievement of the talks. The agreement was subsequently amended on 1 November, in an attempt to address difficulties that had arisen, and was extended on 16 December to the end of February 2007.[37]

Then, while the talks were on Christmas recess, Sudanese president Omar el-Bashir suddenly intruded into the process, after virtual silence up to that point. He was in Juba on 9 January 2007 with Salva Kiir to commemorate the second anniversary of the CPA. After Kiir commented that he was losing patience with the LRA over delays in the talks, el-Bashir added: 'We are prepared to constitute a joint force to eliminate the LRA. We do not want them. If we cannot find a peaceful solution to the LRA conflict, then we must pursue a military solution.'[38]

The leader of the LRA delegation, Martin Ojul, quickly reacted, announcing to reporters in Nairobi on 12 January, the day that talks were to resume: 'In view of the statements by the two leaders and security considerations, the LRA delegation for the peace talks are not going back to Juba.' Two days later, the *Sunday Vision* editorial lamented that the LRA 'high command had ordered its delegates not to return to Juba for the peace talks'. A flurry of activity by a host of Ugandan and international actors ensued to get the talks back on track. Despite this, the LRA in late February rejected renewal of the CoH, just days before it was set to expire. For those committed to the Juba process this was very disheartening.[39]

What had gone wrong? Many blamed the LRA, questioning whether they were ever serious about the talks, challenging their credibility to be negotiating peace on behalf of people they had terrorized, and denigrating or dismissing the delegation as long-term exiles cut off from both Uganda and the 'real' (read military) rebel leadership. From the LRA perspective, however, many of the problems resulted from an increasingly biased and otherwise problematic GoSS mediation of the talks. Before turning to rebel criticisms, however, four broad structural obstacles adversely affecting the GoSS performance should be noted.

The first was the multiplicity of other, often intractable, problems confronting the GoSS, the seriousness and immediacy of which frequently overshadowed the talks and took the lead mediator, Vice-President Machar, away from the negotiations. Next was the limited capacity of the new government to deal with those problems. Third, even though some donor funds were made available to help finance the talks, the international community largely failed to provide sufficient technical, logistical and – especially – political support to the talks in general and the GoSS in particular. And fourth was the inconsistent, contradictory and frequently belligerent stance taken towards the talks by the GoU, its army and its president, which strained the patience and skills of both the mediators and the rebels.

In addition to these difficulties, which were daunting enough on their own, numerous problems developed between the LRA delegation and the GoSS (Riek Machar in particular), some surfacing even before the talks opened. Among the most significant of these, as identified in their 5 February statement,[40] were:

- First, the GoSS imposed Machar as chief mediator over the expressed wishes of the delegation for two other mediators, whom the GoSS had originally approved.
- Then, just as the talks got under way, chief mediator Machar insisted that the rebels' second-in-command, Vincent Otti, attend the talks, raising the issue of the credibility of the largely exile LRA delegation. Citing security concerns (especially the ICC warrants), Otti refused, causing the first of many halts to the talks. During the stand-off, which ended with Machar dropping his demand, the LRA delegation was detained and verbally abused at an SPLA military outpost on the Sudan/DRC border for several days.
- Another early issue, despite apparent initial agreement, was the agenda. Agenda item 2 concerned comprehensive issues contributing to the war that should be addressed in the final peace agreement (item

1 was a CoH agreement). But the GoU argued from the outset that this was not necessary, and wanted to 'merge' items 1 and 2, which really meant leaving out item 2. Many international (and domestic) observers and commentators essentially agreed with the GoU on this matter. Sometimes this was based on the sense that the LRA lacked credibility to address such matters; others argued that the Juba talks should focus on a peace deal only and leave consideration of broader issues for later. The GoSS and Machar took the GoU side, and pressured the LRA delegation to abandon their position, sometimes in ways that seemed to the delegation disrespectful and dismissive.[41]

- Security, for both the delegation and the fighters, was another issue of concern, one never fully resolved by the CoH. As part of that agreement, LRA fighters were to congregate at two assembly points, one in Western Equatoria at Ri-Kwangba and the other in Eastern Equatoria at Owiny-Kibul. As noted above, UPDF violations of the CoH were common, and Eastern Equatoria and particularly Owiny-Kibul were especially insecure from the rebel perspective.[42]
- Factional differences within the GoSS and SPLA bled over into the mediation team, both complicating and undermining the talks.
- Finally, over time the LRA delegation grew increasingly disenchanted with what they perceived as the ineffectiveness, volatile personal style and lack of even-handedness of the lead mediator.

The end result of all this – by late 2006 – was the loss of LRA trust and confidence in the GoSS, both to ensure security and to provide fair and impartial mediation. This strained, almost to the breaking point, what had been a positive and mutually beneficial – if never an equal or unequivocal – year-long alliance. The Juba talks were suspended, and both Vincent Otti of the military high command and the peace delegation asserted again and again that the LRA would continue the talks only if their concerns were addressed. They also insisted that they would not accept Machar and the GoSS as mediators or Juba as the venue for continued talks.

Resumption of the Juba talks (March–May 2007)

By late March things had changed.

A sustained flurry of activity by a range of concerned groups – Acholi cultural, religious and parliamentary leaders, local government, local and international NGOs, donors and other concerned governments, the UN – worked both publicly and privately to get the talks back on track. Among these was the UN Special Envoy for LRA-Affected Areas, former president Joaquim Chissano of Mozambique. Along with many others he helped to keep lines of communication open among the GoSS, GoU and LRA. Meanwhile, many people in Acholi and the rest of northern Uganda, after nearly a year of de facto peace, worried that their hopes might be dashed once again, as had happened so many times before during the long years of war. Politicians and pundits expressed opinions that ranged across the spectrum, from (mostly hedged and cautious) optimism to more frequent expressions of resignation, despair, or assertions that they had never believed in the talks in the first place.

On 23 March, Chissano briefed the UN Security Council on his discussions with all the major actors to get the peace talks back on track, which included addressing the reasons for the LRA decision to pull out. That same day, GoU chief negotiator Ruhakana Rugunda announced in a press briefing that a tentative date of 13 April had been agreed upon for resuming the talks.[43]

Before that 13 April date, however, a series of meetings, unannounced to the public, were held in Mombasa from 31 March to 6 April. Hosted by Pax Christi Netherlands (with whom the LRA had periodically explored peace talks since 1995), a GoU team led by President Museveni's brother, Salim Saleh, met with a subset of the LRA Juba delegation. Exactly what took place in these meetings is disputed; reactions to the meetings and what happened there among the broader LRA delegation and the fighters in Garamba were divided; and the 11 April press release by Pax Christi on the meetings was not supposed to have been distributed. But numerous issues that had stalled the peace process for months were clearly discussed – including the expired CoH, bringing others into the mediation process, and addressing broader issues surrounding the war and its conclusion.[44]

Within a week of the Mombasa meetings, Chissano had met for two days with the LRA in Ri-Kwangba, reporting on 15 April that talks in Juba would resume on the 26th of that month. Four countries – Kenya, Tanzania, Mozambique and South Africa – sent representatives to the Ri-Kwangba meetings, and it was announced that they would both act as observers when the Juba talks resumed and provide military delegations to join the CoH monitoring team. It was also announced that the LRA and GoU had extended the CoH; Chissano would co-mediate with Machar; and Ri-Kwangba would serve as the sole LRA assembly point, the insecure Owiny-Kibul site in the east being abandoned – all of which had been called for by the rebels as necessary for their returning to the talks.[45]

Then, shortly after the talks officially resumed on 2 May, a 'landmark'

Agenda Item 2 was signed by the GoU and the LRA on 'comprehensive solutions' to ending the war. Reported initially by the *Monitor* the next day, a nearly complete copy of the text was reproduced in the *Sunday Vision* of 6 May. The issues addressed ranged from broad principles of inclusive and democratic governance to such specific LRA concerns as integrating their fighters into the army and other security agencies; restocking; assessing and remedying regional disparities in government institutions, including the armed forces; assisting people's voluntary and secure return from camps; and implementing (even 'fast-tracking') recovery programmes for northern Uganda.[46]

This was a major step forward. When this paper was originally submitted, however (mid-May 2007), a final peace agreement had yet to be negotiated and signed. Major sticking points remained, especially with respect to issues of accountability and reconciliation, including the ICC warrants, and other obstacles loomed over a consistently difficult and fractious process. But despite all the difficulties (and along with many others), the three main parties in the negotiations – the LRA, GoSS and GoU – persisted, even if sometimes haltingly. Perhaps they would prove to be the 'realists in Juba' after all.[47]

The unravelling of the Juba peace process

The hope expressed in the last sentence was bolstered when on 29 June 2007 GoU and LRA negotiators signed Juba Agenda Item 3 on accountability and reconciliation. This identified in principle a combination of local and national justice mechanisms – already in place or to be instituted – to promote reconciliation and address issues of accountability for wrongs committed by both rebel and state actors (with hints that this combination of mechanisms might satisfy the ICC).

After that, unfortunately, progress became even more halting than before, with formal talks rarely in session and internal divisions within the LRA increasingly evident. Rumours abound that these divisions were created, or at least exacerbated, by GoU manipulations, including secret cash payments to certain LRA members that both divided the rebels and undermined the peace process. The LRA's long-time second-in-command, Vincent Otti, was caught up in the intrigue and executed by Kony in October 2007, which Kony finally confirmed in January 2008, just as he reshuffled the LRA Juba delegation, asserting that a number of them had taken GoU money.

Under the delegation's new head, David Matsanga, the Juba talks resumed in January 2008 after a six-months hiatus. Within weeks, in early February, addenda to the major agenda items 2 and 3 were negotiated, as was a permanent ceasefire and – the talks' final agenda item – an agreement on disarmament, demobilization and reintegration (DDR) of the rebel fighters. Suddenly, a final peace agreement looked imminent.

On 10 April, after a number of delays, Kony was to have added his signature, and President Museveni was to sign four days later. In confused circumstances that reflected continuing divisions both between and within the rebel delegation and fighters – including the firing of Matsanga (although he would resurface later) – Kony did not sign. Although disappointing, this was in some ways not entirely surprising, given the internal dissension within rebel ranks and Kony's request for further clarification about DDR and the mix of 'traditional' and formal legal proceedings that he and his fighters faced, including the role of the ICC.

Kony did quickly appoint deputy leader James Obita as new head of the rebel delegation and invited leaders and elders from northern Uganda for a meeting in South Sudan in early May to discuss the contested issues of restorative and retributive justice. On 13 May, however, after four days of waiting, the assembled leaders who had come to meet the rebel leader issued a communiqué that lamented his failure to show up; commended the patience and efforts of chief mediator Riek Machar (who had waited with the group); urged Kony to sign the peace agreement; and also urged continued commitment to peace on the part of all concerned.

Then, on 25 May, news was released that Kony had finally rejected signing any peace agreement with the GoU, saying that he would rather die in the bush than turn himself over to the GoU or ICC and 'be hanged'. The Juba peace process, after nearly two years of talks that had produced truly landmark agreements, was sent reeling.

Still, efforts to keep the process alive continued. Chissano publicly continued to hold out hope. The GoSS worked to set up a meeting between Machar and Kony in late July (although it failed to come off owing to 'logistical problems').

In October, however, after two months more had passed with no apparent progress, GoSS president Salva Kiir signalled an end to South Sudan's open-ended commitment to the Juba talks. In a message to the GoSS National Assembly, he stated that Kony should no longer have indefinite time to sign the peace deal and insisted on setting a final deadline for signing.

In northern Uganda, meanwhile, even with the uncertainty caused by the often halting nature of the Juba talks, a transition on the ground from war to peace was under way. In Acholi, people were no longer being forcibly kept in camps and were leaving in ever-growing numbers – although many, disappointed so many times before over the long course of the war, remained in the camps through 2008, or at best moved to smaller satellite or 'decongestion' camps. But even many of those who had not yet gone home had begun to go out to farm once again. The roads were busy as people travelled freely, without fear. The relative peace that had come to northern Uganda since late 2005, when the GoSS and the LRA began negotiations that led to the Juba peace talks, remained fragile, but it was real and palpable. Peace was returning to northern Uganda.

At the same time, the situation for the rebels in Garamba was also changing. For more than two years, as the LRA established and built up their base in the expansive Garamba forest, rebel attacks and abductions were relatively rare, although certainly not absent. This was accompanied by a de facto arrangement between the DRC government and the LRA to leave each other alone. But in July/August 2008, the DRC army (the FARDC) began deploying along two sides of the forest. The rebels, according to various reports, took this as provocation. In retaliation the LRA in September began attacking both Congolese and nearby South Sudanese civilians, while sometimes engaging FARDC and SPLA troops as well.

As these developments were unfolding in the DRC, a two-day meeting of 'stakeholders' in the 'Juba dialogue' was held in Kampala in early November. This ended with a joint communiqué from Machar and Chissano giving Kony a 30 November deadline to sign the Final Peace Agreement. After Kony signalled a willingness to do so, a meeting was set up for 29/30 November.

In the intervening weeks, the DRC announced that it would cease military operations against the LRA to enable Kony to sign. Museveni and other GoU spokesmen reiterated several times that once Kony appended his signature, they would request that the ICC defer or 'lift' their warrants. Meanwhile, the spokesman for the UPDF denied that there were 'active plans' to attack the LRA inside the DRC, even as newspaper reports cited credible information that plans for such an attack had already been drawn up. The DRC and South Sudan governments had supposedly agreed, and the US government and army were actively on board.

Over 29/30 November, a large contingent of Ugandan and international delegates gathered and waited at the designated LRA assembly point in Ri-Kwangba. Kony once more failed to show up. For almost all concerned the Juba peace process had reached a dead end. There were a few feints suggesting otherwise over the next ten days (including Museveni saying that he would agree to talk directly by phone with Kony). But immediately after the 30 November deadline passed, Uganda began implementing plans to send the UPDF into Congo on a military mission to attack the LRA, while continuing to deny numerous media reports that such plans were under way. Reports from the rebel camp indicate that they too were preparing for war.

On Sunday, 14 December, the UPDF began bombing LRA camps in Garamba. Proclaimed as a joint operation with the armies of the DRC and GoSS, but an overwhelmingly UPDF affair in fact, 'Operation Lightning Thunder' was designed to kill or capture Kony and his top commanders and cripple or destroy the LRA. As with other flawed and failed Ugandan attempts to deal with the LRA militarily over the past two decades, these objectives were not achieved. Instead, as has typically occurred, the LRA managed to elude and thwart UPDF efforts against them while also launching retaliatory attacks against civilian soft targets. Over the nine months since Operation Lightning Thunder began, various estimates indicate that the LRA have killed more than a thousand people, abducted many hundreds, and displaced up to half a million across a huge swathe of territory in north-eastern DRC, parts of Western Equatoria in South Sudan, and adjacent areas of the Central African Republic.

Operation Lightning Thunder also sounded the death knell of the Juba peace process. The realists involved in the tough negotiations that made up this process – representatives from the GoSS, the GoU and the LRA – helped create a space for at least a fragile peace to take root in northern Uganda, and also crafted a blueprint that could serve as the foundation for a lasting, sustainable peace.[48]

The fate of those achievements is now – sadly – unclear.

12 · NGO involvement in the Juba peace talks: the role and dilemmas of IKV Pax Christi[1]

SIMON SIMONSE, WILLEMIJN VERKOREN
AND GERD JUNNE

Introduction

This chapter offers a background on the early history of the Juba peace process. It describes how an initially low-profile civil society initiative evolved into a hugely publicized negotiation process chaired and overseen by six African and three Western governments as well as by representatives of the United Nations and the European Union. It analyses some of the dilemmas the initiators of the process were faced with and concludes with an assessment of the role of non-governmental actors in peace negotiations. In addition, the chapter contributes to thinking about the role of non-governmental organizations (NGOs) in peace negotiations. Most people agree that NGOs have many roles to play in peace processes, aside from direct mediation, such as bringing issues to the attention of the international public and getting them on to political agendas; building local constituencies for peace by organizing dialogues with civil society leaders and at the grass roots; and working with media and schools.[2] But what can – and should – be their role in peace negotiations more directly?

The role of NGOs in peace negotiations

NGOs can make a contribution in situations in which traditional diplomacy is unable to take an initiative or to proceed further. Especially faith-based organizations at a certain distance from governments but with good access to politicians and with good links to indigenous religious institutions can adopt a credible position to act as mediators in all phases of conflict (Natsios 2003: 346). They can establish contacts with the conflicting parties, initiate and facilitate talks, and help the parties to implement an agreement.

Several authors cite the chaotic nature of contemporary conflict as a reason why NGOs should be directly involved in peacemaking (ibid.; Aall 2007). Since the elites that ruled conflict-ridden countries are often in exile, dead or traumatized, diplomats have lost their traditional counterparts. The leaders of guerrilla movements do not reside in the capital. They may be dispersed in inaccessible areas. NGOs familiar with the countryside and with a good network of local contacts which can act as an intermediary may be better able to get into contact with the different factions. And in 'the case of societies whose government has entirely collapsed, NGOs and religious institutions may be the only sources of authority that have any influence' (Natsios 2003: 338–40). Peace processes necessarily reflect the confused reality of these conflicts. There has to be 'a mixture of de-centralized, flexible, adaptable, and multi-pronged efforts loosely organized in the pursuit of a common goal'. This requires cooperation between official and non-official actors (Aall 2007: 491–2).

NGOs also add an important element to official peace processes, namely the connection to local communities on the ground. The philosophies of most NGOs emphasize that grassroots people know best, that solutions need the backing of local communities, and that indigenous culture and authority have to be respected. This approach creates loyalty and trust between NGOs and communities (Natsios 2003: 343–4). More particularly, faith-based NGOs with deep roots in indigenous religious institutions can use those connections. Another potential strength of NGOs is that they have no formal connection to government, and, generally, an aversion to military force. This frees them from direct political interest in the outcome of the conflict (ibid.: 345–7).

That said, as with other mediators, a degree of self-interest is at play with NGOs as well. 'At the very least non-state mediators have a role and a reputation to establish or defend and thus an interest in appearing as good and successful mediators' (Zartman and Touval 2007: 442). NGOs may have an organizational interest in establishing a presence in a region. As far as the content of the peace process is concerned, NGOs tend to be 'interested in a particular outcome, [...] because they believe in its inherent desirability' (ibid.: 442). In line with NGOs' value orientation, such a particular outcome could, for example, be a peace agreement that is inclusive and that tackles the root causes of a conflict.

Compared to states, NGOs have fewer sources of power at their disposal. They are less able to reward parties for complying, or to coerce them into cooperating by threatening sanctions, the use of force, or even an escalation of the conflict. NGOs have other sources of power, however, such as informational power (being a communication link between the parties) and expert power (based on the knowledge and experience of the mediator) (Aall 2007: 481–6). As we shall see, IKV Pax Christi used both in northern Uganda. Still, there are usually points in a peace process at which state involvement is needed, because:

- *Credible security guarantees* are imperative. Adversaries must have access to a safe location.
- *Additional force is sometimes required* when dealing with parties not stirred by moral or political considerations.
- *Monitoring of ceasefire agreements* demands independent intelligence and military capacity.
- *Negotiation results must be implemented.* This often makes the commitment of members of the international community necessary to support and finance activities intended to consolidate the fragile peace. (As we shall see below, however, the involvement of NGOs is also vital in the implementation stage.)
- *The financial costs of negotiations* surpass the capacity of civil society organizations. As it is not predictable how long negotiations will take, the decision of civil society organizations to engage in these complex processes is not only a political challenge, but also a financial adventure.

Even if NGOs are usually not the primary mediators, and states are needed at some point along the way, efforts by NGOs often help to 'strengthen the context and prepare the terrain for official mediation' (Zartman and Touval 2007: 451). This, however, requires cooperation among different NGOs involved, which is a serious point of weakness: NGOs' proliferation and highly guarded autonomy often leads to competition and contradictory approaches (Natsios 2003: 344). This issue, too, was apparent in the northern Ugandan peace process, especially prior to the Juba negotiations, when different organizations employed parallel initiatives to get the parties to the table.

Often, NGOs are needed to implement agreements, for example with regard to demobilization and reintegration, because they may be the only ones with operational capabilities in the area. Diplomats are good at negotiation, but they are generally less apt at the logistics of implementation amid difficult conditions (ibid.: 342). This suggests that, if and when a northern Ugandan peace agreement is concluded, the role for NGOs will not end.

Start of Pax Christi's involvement

The NGO that brought the parties to the northern Ugandan conflict to the table is Pax Christi Netherlands. Its involvement in the peace process started in 1997, when, after contacts with the Ugandan Catholic Episcopal Conference, Pax Christi commissioned Dr Simon Simonse as an independent consultant to carry out a study (Pax Christi Netherlands

1998) about the possibilities of it contributing to efforts to bring the conflict in northern Uganda to an end. At that time, an initiative to explore possibilities for mediation was under way, led by Dr Leonzio Onek, a biochemistry lecturer in a Kenyan university and a Sudanese Acholi. Seed money for this initiative from the British NGO Comic Relief had dried up and Pax Christi stepping in was welcomed. By then Dr Onek was working with Hizkias Assefa, Professor of Conflict Studies at Eastern Mennonite University (Virginia, USA), an internationally known mediator with a record of successfully dealing with notoriously intransigent rebels such as Foday Sankoh and Alfonso Dhlakama.

Preliminary talks between the Ugandan Minister of the North and Dr James Obita, the external representative of the Lord's Resistance Army (LRA), took place in Lancaster with Professor Assefa as mediator. Dutch Interchurch Aid made arrangements for a second secret round of talks in the Netherlands in March 1998. The Dutch government arranged for travel documents for the rebels, including Joseph Kony. An intra-LRA conflict brought this initiative to a sudden halt, however. Without the knowledge of Dr Onek and Professor Assefa, Dr Obita, the LRA contact person, was involved in a parallel process facilitated by the Community of Sant'Egidio in Rome. Although it was agreed that he would carry a letter from President Museveni to LRA leader Joseph Kony, he went instead to Rome, and had talks with the Ugandan Minister of State for Foreign Affairs. When Professor Assefa and Dr Onek enquired with the Khartoum LRA office about his delay and whereabouts, it was discovered that he was running two peace processes.[3] When he finally arrived at Kony's headquarters in the bush, he was accused of turning peace into a business and nearly executed. Both sides withdrew from the peace initiative and the process stalled.

Together with Dr Onek, Pax Christi continued to explore new openings. With the help of the United Nations High Commissioner for Refugees (UNHCR), Dr Onek and Dr Simonse (who later became a staff member of Pax Christi) paid a visit to Alice Lakwena, the prophetess-leader of the insurgency that preceded the LRA, in her shrine in a refugee camp in north-eastern Kenya. Her return would have been a powerful gesture given her continued support among the Acholi, but she was unwilling and made unrealistic demands.

Upon the completion of a three-year inter-communal peace-building programme by Pax Christi in Eastern Equatoria, Sudan, a meeting was organized in December 2003 with all local partners in order to discuss results and develop strategies for the future. Among those present were Dr Onek (as chairman of the partner organization Equatoria Civic

Fund), Professor Assefa (as keynote speaker) and Dr Simonse (as organizer). During this meeting, the partners called on Pax Christi to find a negotiated end to the conflict in northern Uganda. The reason was that Juba, Magwi and parts of Torit county had become a battleground between the LRA and the South Sudanese rebel group Sudan People's Liberation Army (SPLA) since late 1994, and between the LRA and the Ugandan army (Uganda People's Defence Force or UPDF) since 2002. These clashes often caused greater suffering to the local population than the Sudanese war. Northern Ugandan church leaders also encouraged Pax Christi to re-engage, with public opinion in northern Uganda overwhelmingly against the war and in favour of a negotiated solution. These calls from the grass roots made Pax Christi decide to become involved once again. Pax Christi formulated an opening document which contained the crucial principle that justice should be done for victims of war crimes and human rights violations irrespective of who had been the perpetrator. As old contact lines were reactivated, it became apparent that there was willingness on both sides of the conflict to re-engage.

Around the same time a mediation attempt was undertaken by Betty Bigombe, a former Ugandan Minister for the North.[4] Her initiative received active support from five donor countries organized in a Core Group, formally a subcommittee of the technical donor group. The British and Norwegian governments sent diplomats to help facilitate the mediations. Pax Christi had direct access to the Dutch Minister of Development Cooperation in that period and regularly exchanged strategic information. The Dutch government, the lead country in the Core Group, requested that Pax Christi take a step back in its initiative to give Mrs Bigombe a chance of succeeding. Pax Christi complied, in spite of its analysis that the Bigombe process was going to fail because in the eyes of the LRA Bigombe was too close to the Ugandan government. Her efforts were focused on getting the LRA to accept government amnesty in return for peace. It seems indeed to have been Bigombe's close association with the government which made the process lose steam after a while. Finally, the indictment of five LRA leaders by the International Criminal Court (ICC) in 2005 made it impossible for her to proceed (considering that the Ugandan government was the party that had asked the ICC to investigate the LRA).

The ICC arrest warrants

In October 2005 the ICC issued arrest warrants for the five indicted LRA leaders. This completely changed the space for peace initiatives in northern Uganda. People involved disagree as to whether the indictments hampered the peace process – by causing the LRA to withdraw – or whether they may actually have contributed to a willingness on the part of the LRA to achieve a negotiated agreement in the hope that this would provide a way to get out of the ICC charges.

IKV Pax Christi has been an ardent advocate of the creation of the ICC. But in the case of Uganda, there was an obvious tension between the objectives of both organizations. Pax Christi wanted the LRA leadership to talk to the government, the ICC wanted the leaders to be arrested. According to the ICC, the arrest of the leaders would decapitate the LRA, which might lead the other members to abandon the struggle. According to Pax Christi, the arrest of the leaders would make negotiations more difficult, because it would make the rest of the LRA even more suspicious and more difficult to deal with.[5] In any case, it was clear that the ICC was unable to arrest the five at short notice. Meanwhile, the humanitarian crisis in northern Uganda continued unabated and civil society in Uganda was crying out for a negotiated solution. Against this background and in view of the encouragement of its efforts by the government of Uganda (GoU) and the willingness of the LRA to enter peace talks, Pax Christi saw a continuation of its efforts to reach a negotiated peace as the only option.

In response to the indictments, Pax Christi clarified its position on the issue of justice and reconciliation in a strategy document (Pax Christi Netherlands 2006). The paper recognizes the importance of justice but argues in favour of *restorative* rather than *retributive* justice. Restorative justice also establishes the responsibility of the accused, but instead of focusing on punishing the convicted perpetrators, it emphasizes the public recognition of the victim as a victim of injustice, the compensation of victims and, particularly, reconciliation with the objective that both parties can resume living together. The paper explores the value of traditional methods of justice and reconciliation from this perspective and identifies the conditions that would give restorative justice the highest possible legitimacy, drawing from the experience of the South African Truth and Reconcilation Process as well as the ideas of international legal experts.

The run-up to Juba

With the arrest warrants out, Pax Christi had to abandon the idea of organizing secret negotiations in a quiet location far away from the scene of war. To make it possible for the government and the rebels to talk, a space had to be found that was not accessible to arrest teams which states that are signatories of the Rome Statute were expected to put in place. In addition, in order to reach the venue one should not have to make stops in third countries that had signed the Rome Statute. It turned out that Pax Christi did not have to look far to find such a country. Since the government of Sudan, and by implication the Government of Southern Sudan (GoSS), had not ratified the Rome Statute, they could be expected not to collaborate with arrests under the Rome Statute. This made Sudan a place where it was safe to talk. In addition, Pax Christi soon learnt that the GoSS was keen on stopping the war between the Ugandan army and the LRA, which was being fought on its territory and continuing to cause great loss of life and suffering to its citizens. At the time the LRA also kept the two main roads connecting South Sudan with Uganda and Kenya blocked. In January 2005 North and South Sudan signed the Comprehensive Peace Agreement which also stipulated the withdrawal of the Sudan Armed Forces (SAF), the LRA's main support, from the south. In a mass rally in August 2005, the new president of the GoSS, Lieutenant General Salva Kiir, gave the LRA and the UPDF (the Ugandan army) three options: negotiate peace, leave our territory, or be chased from Sudanese territory by the SPLA.

Over the years Pax Christi had developed contacts with a number of persons who directly or indirectly had access to the LRA leadership. The contacts were cultivated in anticipation of a request for mediation. Most of the contact persons were motivated by the distressing situation of the people of northern Uganda. They tried to use their family relations, former business contacts and other connections to help find an opening for peace. The group that contacted Pax Christi around Christmas 2005, however, with a request to arrange peace talks with the Ugandan government, was new to Pax Christi. It claimed to be sent by the LRA high command. Since people with similar claims had approached Pax Christi before, the mission was met with scepticism. Only when one of Pax Christi's earlier contacts confirmed that the leadership had sent a group on a peace mission did Pax Christi engage. Dr Riek Machar, vice-president of the GoSS, was then requested to co-operate in establishing the necessary contacts with the LRA leadership. Since the LRA leaders were believed to be in an area still protected by the SAF, contacts would have to be arranged as a collaborative effort of SPLA, SAF and the Joint Integrated Units that had been created out of both armies as a result of the peace agreement between them. Dr Riek Machar agreed, and on 14 February 2006 Pax Christi flew the LRA delegation to Juba to meet with the vice-president and the Minister of Internal Security, Daniel Awet. The meeting was most successful. Within a month, follow-up meetings with the intelligence chiefs of the three armies were held, followed by a reconnaissance field trip to fix the venue for a first meeting.

Pax Christi's understanding of the collaboration with GoSS was that Pax Christi – in the persons of Dr Onek, Professor Assefa and Dr Simonse – was to be responsible for the mediation of the peace talks while GoSS would be the host. This division of roles was in line with the wishes of the LRA leadership.

It took two more months before the first meetings with the LRA leaders Lieutenant General Vincent Otti (11 April 2006) and Joseph Kony (5 May) took place. Later it became clear that during this period the leadership was moved from the East Bank to their later location near Nabanga in Western Equatoria. The GoU, in the person of the Minister of Internal Affairs, Dr Ruhakana Rugunda, had encouraged the initiative from the start. The GoU, however, did not fully get on board until they had been shown the video of the meeting with Kony on 5 May, which had been attended by the LRA leadership, the LRA contact group in Juba, Dr Machar, and the Pax Christi team. LRA leader Joseph Kony had been invisible to the outside world for twelve years until he appeared in this meeting.

The video inaugurated a new phase in the peace process. The GoSS delegation that attended the celebrations of Ugandan president Museveni's third term installation left the video, unedited, with the GoU. It ended up in the Government Media Centre, which put it on the Internet. From that day the peace initiative has been surrounded by journalists and people working with other NGOs. Pax Christi had to abandon the idea of having a quiet process screened off from the media. At that point the Community of Sant'Egidio, which had been involved in parallel peace initiatives, and representatives of the Swiss government joined the process.[6]

In 2006 war-torn South Sudan hardly had any facilities to host the talks. As it gradually became clear that the vice-president was to play a central role, the only option was to hold the talks in sweltering Juba. At the time there was only one hotel that had a meeting room with a steady power supply and air conditioning. It was in the centre of Juba and the hotel rooms were canvas tents, often shared. Ugandan reporters were permanently stationed in the hotel, making sure the talks made headlines in Kampala.

During the meetings on 11 April and 5 May, the mediation team had spent a lot of time explaining to the LRA leaders the importance of a small, effective, trusted delegation. Professor Assefa recommended a group not larger than seven persons, balanced between military and civilians, with a solid mandate. In June two visits were made to Nabanga to obtain a definitive list from the leaders. Meanwhile, however, since its first successful visit to South Sudan, the contact group had steadily grown. After the 5 May meeting had been in the news and the video of the event was made available on the Internet, more LRA sympathizers flew in from Europe and North America and the LRA contact group snowballed to almost twenty people, all of them from the diaspora overseas and in East Africa. While the purpose of the Nabanga trips was to discuss the nature, size and composition of the delegation, the presence of traditional, church and civil society leaders, politicians and a swarm of journalists created an atmosphere that was festive and confused, not businesslike. As a result, all the members of the contact group were confirmed as members of the LRA delegation. The vice-president and Pax Christi insisted that members of the leadership, preferably Lieutenant General Otti, should be part of the delegation, but this request was not met. Instead the promise was made that two military commanders would join the negotiations later. These gentlemen indeed came, but they offered little input and returned to the bush after a while.

In an effort to match the numbers of the LRA delegation the GoU sent a sixteen-man delegation, without consulting the mediation team. The result was that the mediation room was packed from the start, each delegation occupying two rows. As mentioned, the majority of the LRA delegates were overseas diaspora members without experience of war or the deprivations of bush life. By contrast, the majority of the government delegates (thirteen out of sixteen) were officers in the different security forces. As partners in a dialogue this was a most unlikely match.

The Juba negotiations

On 14 July 2006, the negotiations in Juba were officially opened in the Assembly Hall of the South Sudanese parliament to enormous public attention. After some days of experimenting with the cast of the mediation team, Dr Riek Machar invited Professor Assefa to be his co-chair and head of the Resource Group. The Pax Christi team members Dr Onek, Dr Simonse and Nico Plooijer became members of the Resource Group, together with two representatives of the Swiss government and two members of the Sant'Egidio community. The Resource Group, chaired by Professor Assefa, met after every negotiating session and was occasionally consulted during sessions to help unblock progress. It helped the mediators to sound out ideas, drafted texts, and provided expert advice. In the course of the talks other experts and representatives of United Nations (UN) organizations were added to the group.

An agreement on the cessation of hostilities was reached and came into force on 26 August 2006. This agreement convinced a number of governments of the seriousness of the negotiations, in spite of the ICC indictments.

The talks meant hard work, in a hostile climate, at irregular hours, and for the first three months without a break. A key figure in GoSS, the vice-president could often make himself available only at odd hours.

Professor Assefa co-chaired the negotiations up to the first break in October. Dr Riek Machar started to be referred to as the 'Chief Mediator' – a role the Sudan People's Liberation Movement, the political wing of the SPLA, had assigned to him. In response to a growing adversarial atmosphere, Dr Machar tried to get a firmer grip on the process, and increasingly dominated the mediation. This rendered the effective participation of the co-mediators, including his fellow ministers in the team, difficult. From that point onwards, the Pax Christi team repeatedly wondered whether it still added enough value. Frustration increased, while the Pax Christi head office in the Netherlands continued to receive the bills for the presence and activities of its employees in Juba. Dr Machar continued to add members to the Resource Group, sometimes people whom the LRA considered partisan. Complaints and accusations that the Chief Mediator was adopting a pro-GoU position became more frequent. A breaking point was the discussions regarding the UPDF presence close to the East Bank assembly point of LRA forces. On 31 October, the LRA delegation declared that they had lost confidence in Machar as the mediator. In November, however, the talks resumed with a mediation team that was strengthened with other GoSS ministers. For a while noticeable progress was made on agenda item 2, 'Comprehensive solutions',[7] but when everyone expected the LRA to sign the agreement on this item just before Christmas, the delegation protested that the text had been changed without their knowledge and they refused to sign. Then the negotiations stalled more permanently.

On 12 November 2006, the UN Coordinator of Humanitarian Affairs, Jan Egeland, visited South Sudan. The Pax Christi peace team accompanied him when he visited the LRA leadership in Ri-Kwangba. Upon their return to Juba, Professor Assefa and Dr Simonse discussed with Egeland the causes of the lack of progress in the negotiations and shared with him the idea of a back-channel process to unblock the talks. Egeland encouraged the option and proposed to stay in touch in case his cooperation could help. Professor Assefa had regular telephone conversations with Mr Egeland until shortly before the end of his term of office on 12 December.

On 4 December 2006, the UN appointed former Mozambican president Joaquim Chissano as a special envoy to northern Uganda to overlook the peace process. Pax Christi informed Chissano of its plans to help unblock the talks using a back-channel process and expressed the wish to meet with him. Mr Chissano did not respond to Pax Christi's letter. He also appeared uninterested later. Mr Chissano's strategy to unblock the Juba talks was the diametrical opposite of Pax Christi's low-profile approach. To ensure the impartiality of the mediation he included representatives of the governments of Kenya, Tanzania, the Democratic Republic of Congo and Mozambique in the mediation team and opened the door of the mediation room to observers from the United States, the European Union, South Africa, Canada and Norway. In this way he was able to boost international political and financial support for the process.

The back-channel talks in Mombasa and Nairobi

The loss of confidence and repeated walkouts by the LRA, and the growing misunderstanding more generally, were challenging for Pax Christi. The problems presented the organization with an opportunity to take up its original role, however: working behind the scenes to bring the parties together. Pax Christi still had the confidence of both sides, and as the Juba negotiations stalled, it became clear that both parties supported the idea of a back-channel process to work through the thorny issues that hindered progress in the negotiations. Dr Simonse and Professor Assefa began to prepare such a back-channel process. They visited President Museveni, who made it clear that the GoU welcomed an additional effort. The president's brother, retired general and Minister of Micro-Finance Caleb Akandwanaho, better known as Salim Saleh, was mandated by the president to lead the government delegation. The president informed Dr Machar of the back-channel process.

The government and the LRA sent small core delegations and a quiet mediation took place in Mombasa and Nairobi, Kenya, in April 2007. The talks were organized by IKV Pax Christi and mediated by Professor Assefa. They were not intended to replace the Juba process, but to help it along by inserting the outcomes of the back-channel process. The Mombasa–Nairobi talks provided a safe space away from political pressures and public scrutiny. This mattered because the atmosphere in the Juba process had become highly charged and adversarial owing to intense media attention and the large number of parties involved, each with its own interests.

Before setting off for Mombasa, Salim Saleh had convinced the UPDF top command to drop Owiny-Kubul as one of the two assembly points of the LRA stipulated in the Cessation of Hostilities Agreement (CoH) and to give safe passage to the LRA who were still on the East Bank to join the combatants assembled near Ri-Kwangba. As an opening move of the Mombasa round of talks, the adjustment of the CoH did a lot to improve the atmosphere between the parties. If we wanted to identify a point in time where the deadlock was broken, this important concession, engineered by Salim Saleh, would probably best qualify. The amended CoH was signed by the parties on 14 April 2007 in Ri-Kwangba during the meeting at which Mr Chissano was introduced to the LRA leadership. The Mombasa meeting then tackled the sticking points that had prevented the LRA from signing the Agreement on Comprehensive Solutions (agenda item 2) in Juba. There were four issues: the system of government, inclusiveness in participation in government, participation in state institutions, and the institutional framework for economic and social development in north and north-eastern Uganda. Each of the points was thoroughly discussed and on all but the first the parties reached agreement.

The atmosphere in Mombasa was friendlier and more conducive to mutual understanding than the prickly climate of Juba. This was due to the smaller number of delegates. On the LRA side there were five people. Except for the lawyer Ayena-Odongo all had been part of the LRA contact group that had established the first contacts with Pax Christi around Christmas 2005. On the government side there were four people, General Salim Saleh, his assistant Captain Ruhinda Maguru, Dr Sam Kagoda, Permanent Secretary in the Ministry of Internal Affairs, and Joseph Ocwet, former Ugandan ambassador to the United Kingdom. Ambassador Ocwet, who had been one of the initiators of the Betty Bigombe initiative, played an important role in mobilizing his government to support the back-channel initiative. With the exception of Dr Rugunda, the leader of the government delegation in Juba, the key people from both Juba delegations were present. Those who were considered 'hardliners', army officers and chiefs of security services on the government side and the LRA delegates from the overseas diaspora, were not there. The approachability of General Saleh and the comfort of a luxury beach hotel further contributed to the relaxed work atmosphere.

Apart from an addendum to the CoH stipulating a single assembly point, the Mombasa talks resulted in an agreement that covered much of the ground of the negotiation agenda. Agreement in principle was reached on outstanding issues in agenda items 2 (Comprehensive solutions) and 3 (Reconciliation, accountability, amnesty). The agree-

ment on items 2 and 3 was ready to be signed when the LRA delegation suddenly announced that they had to show the document to their
superiors first. Three weeks later, in Nairobi, the delegations consulted
on disarmament, demobilization and reintegration (DDR) issues (item
4). The Nairobi talks could not be finalized, as the LRA delegation did
not have sufficient expertise on DDR.

When comparing the successive texts of the agreement on agenda
item 2 – the text rejected by the LRA on 22 December 2006, the Mombasa
text of 6 April 2006, and the text signed in Juba on 2 May 2007 – it is
striking that the last text is the most top-down and state-centred. In
the last text there is no mention of a role for civil society while the
rehabilitation payments, supposedly from international donors, are
channelled through the state apparatus and do not go directly to victims and their communities. Provisions in the texts of 22 December
and 6 April stipulated the 'autonomy' of the institution allocating the
resources for recovery (10.1.b), 'the use of existing structures in IDP
camps' (10.2.i) as implementing agencies, and a 'heavy involvement of
the local population' in the policy and management structures (10.3).
These had all been deleted in the final agreement. The Implementation
Protocol of agenda item 2, signed on 22 February 2008, substantiated
and elaborated on the top-down character of the mechanisms to be
put in place.

On agenda item 3, 'Accountability and reconciliation', in Mombasa
the parties were able to agree on a comprehensive first text. When we
compare the text agreed in Mombasa with the Juba 2 document, the
five pages of Mombasa appear very roughly hewn in contrast to the
legal finesse of its Juba counterpart signed on 29 June 2007. The Juba
Agreement takes a lot of trouble to reaffirm existing legal institutions,
including penal law and the amnesty legislation, while opening a door
for alternative justice mechanisms, including traditional reconciliation.
In Mombasa the government commits itself in a few brief points to enact
a law that makes it possible to apply alternative justice mechanisms. In
comparison with the Juba Agreement, the Mombasa text is refreshingly
straightforward, with the LRA committing itself to the unconditional
submission of its members to processes of accountability and reconciliation and to owning up to the wrongs it has committed. Its plain
language may have been more adequate, at least for the non-state party
to the agreement. It is further noteworthy that in Mombasa the parties
agreed to a forum for national reconciliation, an element missing from
the Juba text.[8]

Given the progress that had been made in Mombasa, there was

fertile ground for continuing the Juba negotiations. No one in Juba explicitly mentioned the Mombasa process, however. Those who had been involved acted as if it had not happened. At the resumption of the Juba talks on 26 April 2007, Professor Assefa informed the special UN Envoy for LRA-Affected Areas, Mr Chissano, the Chief Mediator, Dr Machar, the members of the mediation team, the Resource Group, the parties and observers present of the results of the back-channel process. No questions were asked, nor were comments raised, except by Archbishop Odama, who wanted to know whether the Chief Mediator had been informed of the side process. Dr Machar did not comment on Professor Assefa's affirmative answer. Discarding the outcome of Mombasa served the perception of Juba, and of the many parties who had a stake in the talks there, as being right on track. Knowing that many questions regarding the content of a final agreement had basically been settled, reports on the negotiations in May and June 2007 sounded sometimes strange. Perhaps at this stage the main challenge was no longer to come to a definitive agreement, but to reaffirm ownership and commitment of the UN and state actors involved in the Juba process and 'sell' the agreement to the public and to the respective constituencies and stakeholders. IKV Pax Christi decided to withdraw from the negotiating table.

The process in Juba was slow and cumbersome. The delegations were very large, there was a big mediation team, and there were many others present. There seemed to be a belief that the more high-profile the actors involved, the better it was. There may have been advantages from the perspective of creating a peace constituency and ensuring compliance with an agreement, once concluded, but it also made the negotiations more complex and expensive.

Dilemmas

Over the course of the negotiation process, Pax Christi Netherlands saw itself confronted with a number of dilemmas.

Peace versus justice The more general peace-building dilemma of whether to prioritize justice (trying war criminals) or peace (ending the violence) was, and still is, the most hotly debated issue with regard to the northern Ugandan process. The ICC was unwilling to compromise on the justice issue, emphasizing that without justice there would be no true peace. Local civil society groups in northern Uganda were divided, but many took a surprisingly forgiving stance towards the LRA and stated that ending the violence was most important, at whatever cost. Pax Christi tended towards the latter position: the everyday costs of the war were simply too high. In its contributions to the debate it emphasized the importance of the possibility for the victims of injustice of 'owning', identifying with, the justice meted out to those responsible for the war crimes. Furthermore, bringing the five LRA leaders to court would by definition be a limited and one-sided way to ensure justice for the victims of crimes committed by both sides.

Trust-building versus legitimizing criminals That 'addressing the root causes of the conflict' was put on the agenda was largely due to Pax Christi, which had stressed these issues already in its reaction to the Bigombe process. In retrospect, Pax Christi's insistence on dealing with the root causes of the conflict, which is crucial for the sustainability of peace, might have given the LRA a legitimacy which it claimed, but no longer deserved.

Confidentiality versus transparency When Pax Christi engaged in the peace process, it had the intention to keep the negotiations confidential, if possible until the day an agreement was reached. By severely limiting the choice of venues, the ICC indictments frustrated this plan. Under normal circumstances Juba would never have been an option. The visibility of the talks hindered informal contacts and confidence-building between the members of the delegations. Fear of being suspected of a lack of loyalty restricted the interaction between the individual members of the two delegations. The presence of the press sometimes gave delegates the opportunity to turn the negotiations into an unhelpful public drama. The back-channel negotiations at Mombasa and Nairobi were insulated from the media in order to encourage the parties to participate freely. Though IKV Pax Christi prefers such a quiet approach, it can conflict with its need to account for its actions to its constituency and donors. Transparency does not necessarily imply immediate openness of transactions, however. It is necessary for accountability and future credibility, but it can also come when the work is done.

The war and peace economy War can become a way of life – but so can protracted peace negotiations. Rebels with no other income than what they get from looting and extortion cannot pay hotel bills. Somebody has to shoulder these costs during peace negotiations. It is also necessary that delegations have good contact with their leaders; otherwise negotiation results might not be accepted. So communication equipment and airtime have to be provided. However, peace negotiations can become another method for obtaining resources. Endless discussions with the LRA about money and their sky-high financial demands were a heavy burden for the process. Some delegates would have risked the failure of the peace process, because they were not satisfied with the daily allowances. There is a very thin line between not paying enough and thereby jeopardizing the peace process, and paying too much, making delegates addicted to the process and interested in prolonging the negotiations endlessly to reap additional benefits. Cautious financing can incite parties to shop for other partners. The LRA at one moment did so. The flirt was rather short when it turned out that the other party did not have the money. There is a kind of 'market for peace', in which interested parties may pay 'higher rates' to play a crucial role in the process. IKV Pax Christi has always been very conscious of the danger of misappropriation of funds and did not get involved in such bargains.

Avoiding reputation damage There are risks associated with NGOs engaging with rebel forces to try to draw them into a peace process. IKV Pax Christi repeatedly asked itself how it could avoid being taken advantage of by the LRA or other parties. The payment of hotel bills, sitting allowances and the facilitation of telephone communication made Pax Christi vulnerable to criticism, especially in the early stages of the peace process. Reputation damage was a concern for Pax Christi when the arrest warrants came out, and it was not clear whether the negotiations would receive any support from countries that had signed the Rome Statute. Pax Christi staff were aware that they might be blamed for carrying out activities that would be seen to run counter to the ICC. Later, when the international support for the Juba talks grew and hundreds of thousands of IDPs started to go home, this fear dissipated.

Negotiations on the basis of values or on the basis of power As a peace actor IKV Pax Christi is motivated by considerations deriving from its commitment to values. In negotiating an end to conflicts between governments and rebel movements, power inevitably plays a role. In mediating for a government party there is always a risk for the non-governmental actor of being compromised by favours and threats from that government, which may use its power to obstruct the involvement of the NGO. Instead of acting as an impartial mediator, the NGO risks becoming a power broker. Rebels can also exercise power over their mediator. They can use the good intentions as well as the NGO's desire for success to blackmail it. In co-mediating a conflict with a state actor, as with GoSS in Juba, contradictions may arise between the values of the NGO and the interests of the co-mediating state actor. In Juba, the obvious interest of GoSS in maintaining relations of good neighbourliness with GoU made it vulnerable to LRA accusations of partiality, especially in the confusion surrounding the eastern assembly point. As a co-mediator, IKV Pax Christi had to stay clear of endorsing any such bias.

Concluding reflections: NGOs in peace processes

The previous section ended with reflections on the role of power in peace processes. At the outset of this chapter, a number of sources of power by mediators were mentioned: coercive and reward powers, which state actors usually possess more than NGOs, and informational and expert powers, which NGOs can have as well, sometimes even more than states. Pax Christi employed both sources of power. It actively played the role of communicator, and this was valued by the parties. Because states were afraid of what being in contact with the LRA could do to their reputation, only an NGO could initiate such contacts. Pax Christi's expert power was exercised by making suggestions in the Resource Group, by offering to provide training of delegates, and, particularly, during the Mombasa–Nairobi side process, when Professor Assefa could make optimal use of his extensive experience and skill as a mediator.

Competition and lack of coordination among different groups involved, considered by Natsios as a weakness of NGOs, were indeed issues in this case. Prior to the Juba negotiations, different organizations employed parallel initiatives to get the parties to the table. This is related to NGOs' funding structure and the need they have to profile themselves in order to secure future support. Competition among peacemakers played a role more broadly as well. Many groups involved were preoccupied with their reputations and with positioning themselves in such a way that they could claim responsibility for successful outcomes. Thus, the Chief Mediator claimed an increasingly central role for himself. Nearly all persons involved in the Juba mediation chose to ignore the results of Mombasa, partly because there was no credit to claim for them, and partly, because there were no signatures, they could afford to ignore the achievement and maybe claim the credit for it for themselves. This highlights the importance of 'face' in peace negotiations (and sometimes even its pre-eminence over content and outcomes) – something that does not prominently appear in the literature.

Another issue that emerges from the case is rather specific but, as the ICC expands its activities, may come to play a role in many future conflicts. It concerns the various tensions between official and unofficial actors, particularly when the ICC enters the scene. The engagement of the ICC in northern Uganda has given the peace versus justice debate particular salience in this case, and has forced all involved to take a stance in this debate. While IKV Pax Christi took a nuanced view, most states were tied by being signatories of the Rome Statute. The growing number of governments represented at Juba, however, illustrates that also among (and within) states that had ratified the Rome Statute there were different positions, and some were more prepared to accept a compromise than others. Also within governments, diplomats and jurists often had different opinions.

The literature suggests that, although NGOs, too, have self-interest, they tend not to have any direct connection to the stakes in the conflict and to be relatively free from political pressures. This was the case for IKV Pax Christi as well. The organization was independent in relation to the interests of the parties and had no other agenda than to advance the peace process. The conflicts of interest that existed between the LRA and Pax Christi related to what the Pax Christi team perceived as unnecessary delays, the courting by the delegation of other peace organizations, and the financial claims made by the delegation – not to political issues. The NGO's value orientation and its good relations with religious leaders also helped create legitimacy and trust. Moral authority is important in a context where everyone else is tainted by the conflict. In addition, IKV Pax Christi, being at home in the region, was well connected to its communities and had profound background knowledge of the history of the conflict. This resonates with theoretical reflections about the added value of NGOs, which are aware of the diversity of local situations and can link local communities to global and regional networks.

Although independence mattered, political connections did as well. IKV Pax Christi was accepted as a mediating agency by the LRA in part because of its ability to reach government authorities. Parties in the region recognized that it was well connected in Europe and could talk to the ICC and to donor governments.

What, then, can and should the role of an NGO be in peace processes, and how does this role relate to that of state actors? In northern Uganda, IKV Pax Christi was particularly able to contribute *before* the official negotiations (getting the parties to agree to the negotiation process, securing a venue) and at times *when the negotiations stalled* (organizing side meetings). This suggests the role of an NGO like IKV Pax Christi to be complementary to that of states. As the literature cited at the start of this chapter suggests, complex conflicts need both official and non-official actors to be part of their solution. They are both good at different and complementary parts of a peace process. In addition, in a negotiation between a state and a rebel movement, the rebel movement has an interest in a civil society actor as a mediator.[9] States have common interests and a common modus operandi. A government may therefore beforehand be biased in favour of the other state.

Government and NGOs still have to find appropriate cooperation arrangements, however, combining NGO independence and government capacity. Recognition of the expertise and independence of NGOs and of governments should be the foundation of complementary cooperation. A common understanding with regard to the overall goals is a precondition. Government support is indispensable to create an enabling environment for civic mediation. Government support may include reliable security guarantees, political support, intelligence and monitoring capacity, commitment to the implementation of results and the availability of a financial safety net.

The UN Department for Political Affairs has created a stand-by mediation team with experts in ceasefire, transitional justice and power-sharing constitutional arrangements, which can quickly be on the ground. This will not do away, however, with the need to involve NGOs in peace processes. They are needed to take initiatives when there is no call from governments or international organizations. Diplomats would not be able to carry out such inherently secretive and politically sensitive activities as talking to the LRA to get them to agree to the idea of talks. NGOs also play an important role by creating grassroots support for the peace process. A more explicit arrangement between governments and NGOs is needed, which recognizes the complementarity of their roles.

13 · Bitter roots: the 'invention' of Acholi traditional justice

TIM ALLEN

When the situation in the north of Uganda was referred to the International Criminal Court (ICC) in late 2003, the Lord's Resistance Army (LRA) had been fighting the government for over fifteen years. The ICC chief prosecutor, Luis Moreno Ocampo, anticipated that a focus on the LRA as the ICC's first big case would be widely welcomed. After all, there was no doubt that grievous crimes had occurred, many of them involving children.[1] On 29 January 2004, Ocampo publicly announced the referral at a joint press conference in London with the Ugandan president, Yoweri Museveni, reflecting the confidence of both of them that it would be possible to secure quick convictions.[2] Things did not work out as expected, however. The court confronted a barrage of criticisms, and Uganda became something of a quagmire.[3] Warrants were issued for Joseph Kony and four of his senior commanders in 2005, but none has been arrested, and an underlying issue at the peace negotiations held in Juba, southern Sudan, between 2006 and 2008, was how the ICC legal process might be stopped or sidestepped. Much of the antipathy to the ICC's role focused on an alleged bias in the proceedings and on the court's capacities to enforce its decisions. Also, many activists and analysts took the view that ending the atrocities in the region required room for compromise over the LRA senior commanders' accountability. Ocampo himself became a controversial figure, and matters were not helped by the fact that the ICC as a whole was poor at explaining what it was doing or defending its actions. There was, in addition, a more fundamental kind of objection. The ICC's role in Uganda was attacked as an effort to impose a partial and compromised 'Western' form of 'justice', one which sets aside or ignores local mechanisms for conflict resolution and social reconciliation.

A similar point has, of course, been made in other places where international criminal justice mechanisms have been introduced. Both the Special Court for Sierra Leone and the International Criminal Tribunal for Rwanda have been castigated as unhelpful to social reintegration and a dreadful waste of much-needed finance. They are dismissed by many analysts as a sop to the conscience of people living in rich countries, whose governments have done so little to prevent genocide and comparable atrocities occurring in a continent that basically does not matter very much. Their perceived inadequacies are contrasted with the apparent success of amnesty procedures in other places, notably South Africa and Mozambique (Cobban 2007).[4] It is suggested that these examples show that in Africa justice is essentially restorative rather than retributive.[5]

Thus, to a large extent the case for recognition of local, African and traditional judicial approaches in northern Uganda was nothing new. The ICC, however, has been found to be more vulnerable to the argument than the other international courts and tribunals. This is because the ICC statute requires it to complement national judicial processes whenever possible, and also to act both 'in the interests of victims' and 'in the interests of justice' without explaining precisely how those phrases should be interpreted.[6] A result has been collaboration between some very odd bedfellows. Traditional justice has been espoused by peace mediators and aid workers, by clergy of the established churches and by representatives of the LRA. Even members of the Ugandan government and armed forces declared a willingness to consider it – especially once the full implications of public trials at The Hague became clearer, notably that the defence counsel of the accused could raise embarrassing issues.[7] Particularly in the years immediately after the ICC referral 'received wisdom' about local justice became so entrenched that it was provocative to raise questions about it. As late as the summer of 2008, the Acholi paramount chief accused the author of 'dehumanizing society' for having suggested that there was a great deal of what Hobsbawm and Ranger aptly called 'the invention of tradition' going on (Hobsbawm and Ranger 1993).[8]

One consequence of the lobbying has been the June 2007 'Agreement on Accountability and Reconciliation' between the LRA and the Ugandan government. This formed a component of the overall peace agreement being negotiated in Juba. It proposed that justice measures drawn from the customs of the Acholi people and their neighbours should be officially recognized, and incorporated into Ugandan law. The agreement raised expectations of a formal challenge being made to the jurisdiction of the ICC on grounds of 'complementarity' (i.e. that there is no longer a need for the ICC to be involved, because Ugandan judicial processes are adequate).[9] This is one of two ways in which the ICC's warrants might not be executed – assuming that the LRA commanders remain alive and that Uganda upholds its commitments under the ICC statute. Either an annual stay of execution can be placed on the warrants by the UN Security Council, or there will have to be a successful complementarity challenge made in an ICC pre-trial chamber. If the latter occurs, it is anticipated that the case would be based on the legal competence of the mechanisms proposed in Juba, specifically a special division of the Ugandan High Court which in some way incorporates forms of traditional justice. Towards the end of 2008, a model for a hybrid arrangement along these lines was outlined by James Ogoola, the Ugandan Principal High Court Judge given responsibility for setting up the procedures.[10] How things reached this point and the implications of the process are the subject of this chapter.

Drinking the bitter root

In 2004, I was asked to assess the implications of the ICC referral in northern Uganda by Save the Children. The agency had made public its concern about the risks that might be incurred by abducted children. When I arrived in Gulu, the largest town in the war-affected region, I was immediately struck by a consensus among aid workers that the ICC intervention was likely to be unhelpful. Their views were reiterated by almost all the urban-based 'opinion leaders' I interviewed, including human rights activists and Christian clergy. Many were vigorous in their opposition.[11] Essentially their argument was the following: convictions in criminal trials are not a universally recognized approach to justice, and among the Acholi there are other ways of doing things; reconciliation is preferred to retribution, and amnesty and truth-telling are much more acceptable than punishment of the guilty, particularly if those who have suffered can receive some form of compensation. 'Justice', one local human rights activist told me, does not just come from the 'briefcase of the white man', and cannot be established by international decree. It has to be locally grounded to have meaning.[12] People are willing to welcome back those who have been with the LRA, because they view the rebels as their children. They forgive even those who have done the most terrible things. The ICC intervention is therefore a neocolonial experiment that ignores the realities and understandings of the victims. Instead, traditional justice measures should be embraced as a more appropriate and viable alternative, contributing to social reconciliation and peace.

At the time, the case for local – or more accurately Acholi – justice tended to focus on just one ritual, *mato oput* (drinking the bitter root). It was maintained that this was the ancient rite that allows for reconciliation with compensation, rather than revenge. Aid funds had been made available to support *mato oput* rituals, and a council of 'traditional chiefs' or *rwodi* was being created to perform them. It was suggested that David Acana, the person who had been chosen by the council to take on the new role of Acholi paramount chief, would perform collective *mato oput* ceremonies, at which even the LRA senior commanders could be accepted back into society.

Mato oput was talked about as if it was something unique, but it was actually similar to scores of other African rituals associated with conflict resolution and payment of compensation following a killing. It involved the killer and the family of the bereaved drinking a concoction made from the blood of sacrificed sheep and a bitter root in such a way as to indicate that their dispute had been set aside, following agreement about compensation. In the past, compensation in such a situation would probably have involved the giving of a girl to the family of the bereaved, both to bind the families together, and so that a child could be born to the bereaved lineage to replace the one that had died. It was quite a rare kind of ritual, as compensation arrangements were not common for a killing that had occurred in a local war or clan feud. They were negotiated where the killing was a murder within the immediate moral community.

A reason why this particular ritual had been singled out to represent traditional justice was connected with an influential report, written by Dennis Pain, an anthropologist who had carried out fieldwork in Gulu town at the end of the 1960s and who had been the head of Oxfam in Uganda in the mid-1980s (Pain 1997). He was also a devout Christian with a close relationship with the Acholi Anglican community. The report was commissioned from International Alert following the 1997 *Kacoke Madit* (Big Meeting) in London. *Kacoke Madit* was a gathering of over three hundred Acholi from Uganda and the diaspora, including government ministers, church leaders and LRA representatives. Funded by voluntary contributions, its aim was to raise international awareness of the conflict in northern Uganda, and generate a consensus for peace and reconciliation among the Acholi, or at least among 'opinion leaders'. Much of the discussion at the meeting was about the erosion of Acholi values as a result of the war, and a decision was made to promote Acholi unity and strengthen the Acholi cultural heritage. Research was commissioned to elicit the views of Acholi 'opinion leaders' in Uganda on what would constitute a substantive talks agenda and a process for reconciliation, and Dennis Pain was contracted to write it up.

Pain's Christian beliefs are evident right at the start of his report. Under the title he wrote: *'Lacwec tye!'* ('The Creator exists'), and he then

245

dedicated it to 'the one who has inspired it and is alone responsible for creating the consensus which it represents'. Although he did not make the link explicit in the text, he viewed Acholi values as resembling Christian ideals. He argued that the way forward in northern Uganda was to combine a formal amnesty with support for the performance of *mato oput* for LRA combatants, and to eventually combine these reconciliation rites for individuals with the performance of another, even rarer, ritual called *gomo tong*, 'bending the spears'. This was a ceremony that occurred at the end of a war, symbolizing the termination of the fighting. To do this, it would be necessary for donors to fund the provision of compensation to victims, and for support to be provided for the reinvigoration of the traditional chiefs (*Rwodi-mo*), whose influence had been eroded but whose moral authority remained intact. According to Pain:

> Acholi traditional resolution of conflict and violence stands among the highest practices anywhere in the world. After factual investigation, it requires acknowledgement of responsibility by the offender, followed by repentance and then payment of compensation, leading to reconciliation through *mato oput*, the shared drinking of a bitter juice from a common gourd. This practice of reconciliation lies at the heart of a traditional approach to 'cooling' the situation and healing the land and restoring relationships, far beyond the limited approaches of conservative western legal systems and a formal amnesty for offences against the state. [...] All Acholi know that because of atrocities [...] all involved must go through *mato oput* reconciliation. Lacking the means for those returning from the bush to pay compensation, the international community is asked to supply the means along with resettling former fighters, avoiding the impossible task of differentiating the coerced from the instigators of violence. By going through this process it is intended that the offenders will no longer be open to fresh charges in the national courts. This prospect will create the climate in which children will be released to return home and be reconciled. (Ibid.: 3)

Pain's specific recommendations included the following:

> International NGOs [...] should be asked to liaise with any peace and reconciliation infrastructure as part of their legitimate brief in addition to their aid and development functions. [...] The Uganda Joint Christian Council could evaluate its potential to become the main independent coordinating and umbrella body for the purposes of monitoring the peace in coordination with others. [...] The *Rwodi-mo* [...] should now

take advice in drafting proposals for how to deal with violent personal offences by traditional means involving confessions and compensation. [...] The Attorney General may wish to obtain the support of the legal community for a radical law enabling traditional resolution of violent personal offences to be effected in special circumstances of social breakdown and then advise on the way forward under the Constitution. [...] The *Rwodi-mo* should be encouraged to seek and offer appropriate reconciliation outside Acholi, providing a lead for others to follow across Uganda. [...] Churches in Uganda should take a lead in authentic preaching and teaching in Acholi from a perspective of hope within suffering. [...] An international donor or NGO should be approached as a matter of urgency to support the traditional authorities in establishing the reconciliation procedures to be used in resolving the conflict. (Ibid.: 65, 87, 90, 110–15)

The next step was to investigate if this 'consensus' among 'opinion leaders' really reflected the attitudes of the Acholi people as a whole, and in January 1999 the Belgian government offered resources to undertake research on the chieftaincy system and its capacity to implement the agenda that Pain had proposed. An international NGO, the Agency for Cooperation and Research in Development (Acord), took charge of this programme. Pain's arguments were also investigated by an independent researcher, Mark Bradbury, as part of a comparative study of peace practice funded by several donors, including the governments of Sweden, Norway, the Netherlands, Germany, Australia and the United Kingdom (Bradbury 1999).

Both the Acord findings and Bradbury's were highly critical. Acord concluded that traditional structures were weak and fragmented; that many of the 'elders' were themselves not sure how to carry out traditional rituals; that there was widespread disagreement about who were the *real* traditional leaders; and that few people considered the traditional structures a key priority (Dolan 2000a; Acord 2000). Bradbury concurred, also noting that there were tensions between elders over the possible financial benefits; and that there were concerns that the external support for traditional chiefs was just another way of trying to bring the region under closer government control without contributing to improved education and economic development. In addition, he suggested that support for Acholi traditional chieftainship was as much a response by certain interested parties to the contemporary restoration of the Buganda kingdom in southern Uganda as anything to do with more local political dynamics (Bradbury 1999: 17–20). It was also obvious to anyone who had read historical studies and early sources on the region that claims about the Acholi people forgiving offenders and accepting compensation were overblown. Punitive measures were common. It depended on the crime, who had committed it, and who was arbitrating.

Nevertheless, the notion of Acholi traditional leaders promoting traditional reconciliation proved popular with international agencies looking for local representatives with which to work.[13] It was also seized upon by influential Christian leaders, such as the former Anglican bishop of Gulu, Baker Ochola, and the Catholic archbishop, John Baptist Odama, who, like Pain, found Christian virtues in the local customs.[14] In addition, it was taken up by important Uganda-based human rights campaigners, including the widely respected legal authority, Barney Afako, the charismatic head of Human Rights Focus, James Otto, and Zachary Lomo, the director of the Refugee Law Project of Makerere University in Kampala.[15]

For a few years things moved slowly, owing partly to the worsening security situation. Nevertheless, some Christian leaders and Acholi traditional elders continued to promote Pain's proposals. In 2000, an organization called Ker Kwaro Acholi ('authority of Acholi grandfathers/elders') was set up, under the terms of Article 246 of the 1995 Ugandan constitution, which allows for the institution of traditional or cultural leaders. Although evidence was lacking, it was claimed by some supporters that this was actually a reconstitution of an organization dating back to the early fifteenth century. During this period, efforts were made to keep communication open with the LRA, and certain individuals gained widespread respect for their courageous attempts to recover abducted children, publicly forgive those who caused them harm, and even meet with rebel commanders in the bush without any protection.

At the time that the ICC referral became public in early 2004, these people seemed to offer the only available route by which to start negotiations. The prospects of them doing so, however, appeared to many peace activists to have been undermined by the threat of arrests and prosecutions. One aspect of the controversy that ensued was an injection of funding and increased external support for the implementation of the traditional justice agenda, premised on the assumption that local rituals performed under the auspices of chiefs and elders would, in some undefined way, lead to social reconciliation. The Liu Institute for Global Issues (a research centre based in Canada), Caritas (a Catholic aid agency) and USAID's Northern Ugandan Peace Initiative (NUPI) were among internationally funded institutions that engaged in participatory investigation and facilitation of the traditional justice approach, especially in the vicinity of Gulu town.[16]

By mid-2005, dozens of *mato oput* ceremonies were being performed, occasionally attended by a host of aid workers and journalists. The Acholi paramount chief (David Onen Acana II) had also started to perform larger-scale public rituals. Remarkable claims were made about the effectiveness of these activities, which were taken at face value by international visitors, including many journalists and researchers – most of whom went only to places close to Gulu, where the paramount chief and the main local enthusiasts of traditional justice were based. An example of the kind of perception being promoted is reflected in a *New York Times* article of April 2005:

> The International Criminal Court at The Hague represents one way of holding those who commit atrocities responsible for their crimes. The raw eggs, twigs and livestock that the Acholi people of northern Uganda use in their traditional reconciliation ceremonies represent another. The two very different systems – one based on Western notions of justice, the other on a deep African tradition of forgiveness – are clashing in their response to one of this continent's most bizarre and brutal guerrilla wars [...][17]

The reification of rituals

My own local-level research in the camps for displaced people, however, indicated something very different. By mid-2005, there was more interest in traditional rituals than at the time of the Acord research in the late 1990s, probably because of all the external support. But I found no evidence of an emerging, or re-emerging, tradition system of Acholi justice. On the contrary, some of those spoken to were adamant that public rituals were useless, or could make things worse by concentrating polluting spirits (*cen*). Not surprisingly, Madi and Langi informants were even more dismissive. They had also suffered at the hands of the LRA, so why should it be the Acholi who do the forgiving? Overall, most of those talked to in the camps mixed concern about the security implications of issuing warrants for the arrest of Kony and his senior commanders with a willingness to see them prosecuted and punished. Certainly there was no general rejection of international justice. Often there was concern about how such legal measures were going to be applied, and why it had taken so long for their plight to be noticed.

With respect to *mato oput* ceremonies, I was told several times in 2005 that one had been performed to reconcile a woman with her relatives after her escape from the LRA. She had been made to kill her uncle, and the ritual was deemed a necessary part of her return home.[18] I was unable to interview the people involved, however, and none of the *mato oput* ceremonies actually observed or investigated in the course of my field research was directly connected with the LRA. They all related to homicides that had occurred within the population, sometimes many years ago. It was difficult to avoid the conclusion that most were being performed now because of the availability of donations from aid agencies to pay for the sacrificed sheep and to have a party.

The collective rituals being performed by the paramount chief and the council of elders did involve former LRA combatants, but they were not *mato oput* ceremonies of the kind reportedly performed in the past. Those observed involved no compensation, no killing of sheep and no drinking of any bitter root. The ceremony may have been called *mato oput*, but it was in fact based on an altogether different ritual, one that involves stepping on eggs – something that is actually indicated in the *New York Times* article quoted above. This is a common welcoming rite, and is not normally connected with the reintegration of killers. It was revealing that on one occasion, organized by USAID-funded NUPI (Northern Uganda Peace Initiative) for 'elders' to explain Acholi forgiveness rituals to representatives of 'the youth', the paramount chief admitted that he did not know how to perform the traditional *mato oput* ceremony. My impression was that the public welcoming ceremonies were not really very significant for many of those attending. When I interviewed the LRA brigadier Sam Kolo in May 2005, soon after he had surrendered,[19] I asked whether he would perform *mato oput*. He replied that he would, but when asked whether he would look into the eyes of those he had harmed, request reconciliation and pay compensation for what he had done, he just laughed, saying that he would not do that, but would do the *mato oput* that the paramount chief performed. I asked whether he thought that the public ceremony was really something serious. He laughed again, saying nothing.

Another reason for scepticism about the alleged traditional Acholi desire to forgive relates to the word 'forgive' itself. A few months after my interview with Kolo, he was present at an event organized to publicize the official amnesty process. He gave a short speech explaining what 'forgiveness' *really* meant, and telling the audience how to go about it. At one level this seemed an extraordinarily inappropriate topic for him to choose, and some listeners found it hard not to laugh. What he meant to communicate, however, was probably something different to how it sounded. The incident was one of many that highlighted ambiguities with the connotations of the concept. In the Acholi language, the term *timokeca* is used for the English word 'forgiveness', but it is also used for 'amnesty' and 'reconciliation'. This means that discussions about Acholi 'forgiveness' might refer to a range of things, from formal amnesty arrangements to just having a formerly abducted person living in the community.

In order to try to make a more objective assessment of the prevalence of forgiveness rituals and traditional restorative justice, in June 2005 my research team created a sample of formerly abducted people who had returned from the LRA. This was derived from the records of reception centres that had been set up to receive them and assist their reintegration. Over a three-month period, it proved possible to locate 238 of them. They were all living in displacement camps or in the main towns in the war zone. None had performed *mato oput*, and only sixty-nine had been involved in any kind of reconciliation ceremony. The results confirmed that there was little general enthusiasm for *mato oput* or other ceremonies performed by the paramount chief.

In response to these findings, and also those of some other researchers,[20] during the past few years those seeking to promote local justice have made efforts to refine their position. One way in which this has been done is to broaden the range of rituals that might be incorporated into a recognized Acholi system of traditional justice (Baines 2005; Harlacher et al. 2007).[21] Rituals mentioned in various recent reports and articles include *lwako pik wang* (washing away the tears), *mayo tipu* (cleansing the spirit/ghost), *tamu kir* (cleansing for an abominable act), *mayo piny* (cleansing a specific area), *ryemo gemo* (chasing spirits from a wide area), *moyo kom* (a general cleansing ritual), *kwero merok* (cleansing someone who has been killed in war) and *ryemo jok* (chasing out a 'free' spirit). In addition to these, the June 2007 'Agreement on Accountability and Reconciliation' between the LRA and the Ugandan government mentions *culo kwor*, and defines it as 'compensation to atone for homicide, as practiced in Acholi and Lango cultures, and to any other forms of reparation, after full accountability' (Government of Uganda and Lord's Resistance Army/Movement 2007). The agreement also mentions a selection of non-Acholi rituals: *kayo cuk*, *tonu ci koka* and *ailuc*. These are defined as 'traditional rituals' performed by the Langi, Madi and Iteso peoples 'to reconcile parties formerly in conflict, after full accountability'.

The elaboration of the traditional justice argument to include these other Acholi rituals as well as a few rituals of neighbouring groups is a positive step. It is at least recognition that things are much more complicated than had initially been suggested. The proliferation of recognized, named rituals, however, does not resolve the basic difficulty of turning selected local practices into something new. Listing them in this way takes them out of the contexts in which they have been used and adapted flexibly to specific circumstances, and reifies them. If they are categorized and institutionalized into a semi-formal judicial system, they will inevitably be very different to what they were to start with.

The 'invention' of traditional justice

My doubts about codifying ceremonies partly stem from personal experience. I spent four years living in Acholi and Madi villages in the 1980s.[22] At that time it was rare for rituals to be given special names. It was more common for there to be a view that a home or a person should be ritually cleansed, or a sacrifice performed at a shrine to mark a collective response to a particular problem. Sometimes a sheep, or a chicken, or a goat, or a bull, would be sacrificed. At other times there would be a sprinkling of water, or an anointing with oil, or a smearing with herbs and roots. Certain male elders were known to be effective at calling on ancestors to bless the living, and they would be asked to do it on all sorts of occasions. There were women, too, both young and old, who were understood to have special powers to heal and cleanse, and there were Christian and Muslim ceremonies that also played a part in daily life. Therapies for ailments, disputes and misfortunes ranged from spirit invocation to rubbing magical substances into the skin to injections of drugs bought in the market. Several strategies might be tried to deal with the same problem, and ritual acts, many of them small and habitual, were performed frequently. When someone was asked what a particular ritual was called they were likely to find the question a bit strange. The answer was usually a straightforward description of what has happened: 'we have cleansed a spirit from the compound', 'we have blessed the returned hunter', 'we have sucked witchcraft from the body', 'we have paid compensation', 'we have washed away the tears', 'we have stepped on an egg', etc. But different people might give different descriptions, and asking if there is going to be another 'cleansing the spirit from the compound' ritual might not make much sense. When there was a compound that was thought to be affected by a malevolent spirit, a ritual might be performed to cleanse it. Precisely what that ritual involved could vary.

This does not mean, of course, that selected rituals cannot be codified. If there is external support for doing so, and figures of authority are created to perform them, then they may become formalized into a pseudo-traditional system. Not surprisingly, among the activists in northern Uganda who are openly promoting such an agenda are those who might gain local political influence, notably the newly created council of 'traditional' chiefs. The practices that are coded and turned into such a system, however, will be altered in the process. They will lose their flexibility, and will no longer have all the many resonances and associations of lived ritual actions. They will have status that is at least partly based on their externally supported authority. They will become privileged rites, and most likely the preserve of certain figures of male authority recognized by the government. It is worth bearing in mind that efforts were made to do the same thing rather more systematically in the past, when 'tribal' customs were incorporated into the indirect administration of the British protectorate through government-appointed chiefs and other local agents.

To the extent that it is possible to reconstruct what ways of life were like in the region of northern Uganda in the nineteenth century, it seems that there was a wide range of customs and rituals that varied from place to place and from one social network to another. Some practices may have been associated with long-established hierarchies, notably those connected with lineage patriarchies or rainmaking, but there were no large kingdoms of the kind that existed to the south. Although the new cohort of traditional chiefs claims to have royal ancestries that reach far back in time, they are mostly the descendants of people who were recognized or selected as government chiefs in the first decades of the twentieth century. In some instances, members of their families had previously acted as local allies of slave and ivory traders, or of the armed forces sent to the area to impose Egyptian rule. Others were rainmakers or clan elders who Postelthwaite, the first district commissioner, chose to use in the years after the First World War. That is why Okot p'Bitek, the well-known Acholi poet and essayist, claimed that the British invented the Acholi 'tribe' in the 1920s (p'Bitek 1980a).[23] The term Acholi itself was a late-nineteenth-century introduction, probably derived from the local word for 'black' (*chol*). Thus, if there has ever been a system of 'traditional justice', in the sense of a standard range of rules and regulations for dealing with offences that were applied beyond the immediate moral community of neighbouring lineages, it was to a large extent the product of British indirect administration. By the late protectorate period, customary laws had become quite well established at the local courts of chiefs, and there were mechanisms for externally regulating their application.[24]

The protectorate system of customary justice was not accepted without dissent. Some clan elders opposed the selection of others to represent them, and 'common' lineages resented attempts by 'royal' ones to rule them or interpret the spirit world on their behalf. As the years passed, there were pressures to appoint chiefs with a relatively high level of formal education, something which was provided at mission schools. This meant that many chiefs became closely connected with the established Christian churches, as well as with the government's regulations and tax collection. It made them ever more like government officials, and increasingly compromised as local ritual specialists. This was one reason why there was a proliferation of alternative kinds of both rituals and specialists in the years before and after independence, including the emergence of powerful *ajwaki* (witch doctors/diviners/ healers) who did not represent the privileged patrilineages, and could perhaps better comprehend and interpret the various social upheavals of the later decades of the twentieth century. These new *ajwaki* similarly tended to link themselves with formal religion, partly as a way of asserting their moral probity, but they emphasized alternative approaches to spirituality, associated with critical and reforming movements. In particular they drew on or replicated aspects of 'born again' and Pentecostal Christianity. Both Joseph Kony and Alice Lakwena (the leader of the Holy Spirit Movement of the mid-1980s) arose from among such specialists (Allen 1991b; Behrend 1999a).

Dilemmas of hybrid accountability

Thus, at one level, the current debates about traditional justice are part of a longer-standing local contest about who should interpret the Acholi spirit world and traditional customs of social life. Discussion of ritual practices in recent publications about northern Uganda, however, largely overlooks these tensions, and suggests far greater consensus than is actually the case. The selection of rituals is also revealing. Those chosen for definition and description are mostly connected with negotiating misfortune and promoting well-being. They help connect individuals with a wider community. They are actually the same sorts of activities that have been noted in Uganda and elsewhere by researchers and professionals working on public health. Ritual specialists are commonly involved in both individual and collective therapies, and can be viewed as dispensers of 'traditional healing' as well as 'traditional justice'. It is worth noting that, where medical personnel have made efforts to professionalize 'traditional healers' and collaborate with them, new kinds of hybrid therapists have tended to emerge, such as so-called 'TBAs' (traditional birth attendants) or 'herbalists' or '*daktari*' (Swahili for doctor). Their credibility might draw on local practice, but it is also related to external linkages with aid agencies and the formal healthcare services.[25] Supporting the performance of selected rituals as 'traditional justice' will, at best, have the same effects.

Not far away from Uganda, in Rwanda, the *gacaca* courts have become a national project (Karekezi and Nshimiyimana 2004; Cobban 2007).[26] Serious problems have been noted with their operation, but arguably they have been more successful than the International Criminal Tribunal for Rwanda in dealing with the perpetrators of the 1994 genocide. When it finishes its remaining trials, the latter will have dealt with only a few of the worst offenders, and will have cost a huge amount of money. Might it not have been better to use those funds to support the Rwandan judiciary and the *gacaca* courts, which is where thousands of others are being held to account and mostly reintegrated into Rwandan society? Enthusiasts of traditional justice working in northern Uganda view what has been achieved in Rwanda as a model ready for importing. But it would be wrong to imagine that the newly established *gacaca* courts would have emerged in their current form without the active support of the Rwandan government, and more locally grounded and unofficial *gacaca* continue to operate at the same time. The state-sponsored *gacaca* are inspired by local customs, but are a different kind of institution.[27] Also, a major difficulty in replicating something like the semi-formal *gacaca* courts in northern Uganda is that the area is far more ethnically diverse than Rwanda, and was not a single political unit in pre-colonial times. The kind of administrative structures that existed in the Rwandan kingdom required certain broadly accepted rules, and it is possible to make a case that the sharing of mechanisms for mediating conflicts comprised a sort of judicial system. But there was never an integrated Acholi, or Madi, or Langi, or Iteso political entity of that kind, let alone one that covered the whole region.

Creating viable new hybrid judicial mechanisms in northern Uganda is nevertheless feasible, if there is sufficient external support. Any potentially useful system would have to be constrained and carefully monitored (presumably by the government), just as was the case in the protectorate era, and as is meant to have occurred more recently in Rwanda. Without regulation, rituals and customs may not be used in the ways that enthusiasts expect. Just as the activities of 'traditional healers' can have very counterproductive effects from a biomedical point of view, those dispensing 'traditional justice' might not adhere to modes of interpreting acts that outsiders deem appropriate. Social cleansing in particular can be very violent, and traditional courts are as likely to be adapted to interpret and punish witchcraft and sorcery as they are to deal with instrumental killings and mutilations. A traditional punishment for a certain kind of witchcraft among the Acholi was to kill the culprit immediately by inserting an arrow into the person's anus. One locally perceived limitation of chief's courts under British rule was that such acts had to be treated as murder, and it was not even allowed to make accusations of witchcraft in legal proceedings. The latter was a reason why there were so many cases of 'poisoning'. After independence the restrictions on witchcraft accusation were lifted, and there was quite a bit of violent witch-cleansing under the auspices of chiefs in the 1960s (described among the Langi by Abrahams 1985). It has continued to occur from time to time, adapting over the years to changes in Uganda's local administration.

Recent examples include those described in Madi areas, immediately to the west of the Acholi homelands. Here, the setting up of locally elected councils by President Museveni's government in the late 1980s, as well as the early HIV/AIDS awareness campaigns, inadvertently lent credibility to the practice. In the absence of a functioning judiciary, the village-level councils tended to represent local patrilineages, and became involved in hearing disputes, including those related to conflicts within homes. In the fraught period of opening up farmland and reasserting gendered hierarchies after the return of the population from refugee settlements in Sudan, there were inevitably accusations of witchcraft. Accusations were especially common when there were women living in the home for whom no bride-price had been paid. At the same time, the councils were taking on a role in trying to constrain sexual activity, a strategy that was primarily focused on women. A local term for witchcraft became connected with AIDS, and appeared to lend government support for witch-cleansing. In some domestic disputes, especially those in which there were accusations about the death of a child, the councils found individuals guilty of witchcraft, and on several occasions the accused was ritually tortured and killed (Allen 1991a, 1992, 1997). In 2009, further research by the author and one of his students at the same locations revealed that the connection with the local councils has continued, incorporating ideas about democracy. All adults in a village write the name of someone they believe to be a witch on a piece of paper, which they then place in a pot. The names are added up like votes. Those with a high number of votes are publicly named and their photographs taken and displayed. Several of those accused are severely beaten or chased away from their homes, and in one case investigated a named person committed suicide. Those involved in running the proceedings have no doubt that they are acting in a socially beneficial way, and explained with pride how they had harnessed traditional knowledge to modern practices. The point is that there are serious risks in local customs and rituals being interpreted as inherently benign.

The collective performance of rituals tends to be connected with the implicit and explicit expression of moral values. The rituals are also used to shape those values, because when ritual practices are frequently repeated, and when they are connected with locally powerful ideas, people and institutions, they can affect the way participants think about things. Many groups use ceremonies to do this, from the Boy Scouts and Christian churches, to armies and schools. If certain rituals are effectively adapted and institutionalized in ways that have local resonances, and are associated with accepted hierarchies, then they may shape the understandings of those who participate in them. This suggests that who regulates the rituals and to what purpose are very important. The power that rituals of social cleansing and incorporation can have as a tool for social engineering is evident from the success of both the Holy Spirit Mobile Forces and the LRA in securing the cooperation and indeed the loyalty of their recruits. They have adapted Acholi ceremonies and have combined them with Christian (and to a lesser extent Muslim) rites of worship. It has been a heady mix, and one that has had a deep impact on many of the impressionable young people who have chosen or been forced to join their ranks. In this context, it is not surprising that the promotion of *mato oput* and certain other rituals by traditional authority figures and Christian activists seems to mirror the rebel movement's own use of comparable techniques of cleansing and incorporation.[28]

Prospects for Acholi traditional justice

Let us assume that concerns raised above can be dealt with – that adequate monitoring can be put in place and that there is enough funding and external support to create a viable hybrid system of 'traditional justice' in northern Uganda that is not just co-opted by local elites. Would this lead to peace, or perhaps a better kind of peace? Advocates seem to believe it would with a passion. Some imagine that the ICC has a capacity to withdraw its warrants, and should be made to cease its activities in favour of vaguely formulated conceptions about African ways of doing things.[29] Others more familiar with the ICC statute continue to assert that Acholi (and now also Madi, Langi and Iteso) mechanisms of traditional justice and accountability have been reinvigorated, so a case can be made that the ICC process is unnecessary. They point out that the ICC statute requires it to act in a way that is complementary with national judicial systems, and additionally draw attention to those articles of the ICC statute that refer to 'the interests of justice' and 'the interests of victims'.[30] Efforts have been made to make the court accept an alternative, local conception of justice, and for the Ugandan government to formally challenge the ICC's jurisdiction. Initially it was human rights activists, conciliation groups and humanitarian aid workers who promoted these agendas, but the LRA delegation at the peace talks in Juba also adopted them.[31] The June 2007 'Agreement on Accountability and Reconciliation' between the LRA and the government of Uganda was a fruit of all this lobbying, although it is important to note that it was not quite the breakthrough that has been suggested. Joseph Kony was not wrong when he complained in 2008 that the peace deal he was being asked to sign seemed to have left aside issues relating to him and his senior commanders.

The 'Agreement on Accountability' mentions a selection of rituals that will be appropriate to deal with those returning from the LRA. It does not explain how this will happen, however, and it excludes those for whom warrants have been issued, as well as the Ugandan army. Essentially what the LRA delegation had achieved was an alternative to the amnesty arrangements, to which they objected on the grounds that it implicitly criminalized their campaign. Thus, it provided a degree of official recognition for those wanting to perform reconciliation rituals, but it actually added little to the existing situation. Even the proposed alternative to the amnesty is rather limp, given the fact that most people who have returned from the LRA have never actually applied for it, let alone received it. Doubtless those keen on traditional justice arrangements hope that if the agreement becomes part of Ugandan law, there will be a stronger case for the warrants to be set aside on complementarity grounds. At present, however, it seems very unlikely that the ICC judges could accept that argument. Certainly no case could be presented without a clear and convincing explanation of what 'after full accountability' means in the agreement's definitions of local rituals.

There is in addition a further problem with all this, one which for me renders the project of establishing an official system of traditional justice in northern Uganda deeply flawed: it is not a national project. Even if LRA commanders are willing to submit to local rituals in a serious way, genuinely seeking 'forgiveness' or 'reconciliation' and offering acceptable compensation for what they have done, the effect is to throw the horrors of the region on to the people who live there. It suggests that the government and the rest of the country have nothing to do with what has happened, and implies that people in northern Uganda have their own 'primitive' justice measures, whereas those in the south have modern ones. No one expects President Museveni and Joseph Kony to perform *mato oput* with each other. If the institutionalizing of traditional justice is to be a national project, what are the rituals from the Baganda or Banyoro or Banyankole that are to be used? Judge Ogoola, who is in charge of setting up the legal mechanisms outlined in the Juba Agreement, comes from Busia in the south-east of the country, but made no mention of the healing rituals of his own people when outlining his plans at the end of 2008, and when asked about it, linked *mato oput* with a generalized notion of restorative justice shared by all Africans.[32]

There is a real prospect that the linking of traditional justice with the proposed special division of the Ugandan High Court will end up reinforcing the view that the people of northern Uganda are responsible for the violence of their home areas, and that they have their own ways of dealing with it. The LRA may reject the blanket amnesty, because it criminalizes their movement, but there is a danger that the institutionalization of local justice will socially infantilize the whole of the war-affected north if it implies that the people of the region are at an earlier stage of development, and are not ready for modern forms of governance. To use the classifications of the Ugandan scholar, Mahmood Mamdani, the emphasis on *mato oput* and other northern rituals suggests that the people of the region should remain 'subjects' rather than claim the full rights of 'citizens' (Mamdani 1996). Surely that cannot be the way forward. Most northern Ugandans I know would like the same kind of legal protection enjoyed by people in other parts of the world, and they are certainly no more 'traditional' than people in southern Uganda.

Debates about the relevance of international criminal trials have occurred in each situation in which they have been introduced. It is obvious that there is inconsistency in the way rules established in conventions and treaties are applied, and that there is a great deal of hypocrisy in the human rights discourse of powerful states – something that is well illustrated by the US attitude to the ICC.[33] It is also not certain, even in Europe, that the ritual humiliation of a small group of individuals, who are held to be most responsible for terrible acts, contributes to social healing. Perhaps the proceedings of courts and tribunals just remind people why they hate each other so much. It is misleading, however, to dismiss the ICC approach as simply being a form of discredited neocolonialism. It is actually more appropriate to direct that reproach at those attempting to institutionalize local rituals in a similar manner to the protectorate administration's use of indirect governance measures.

It is feasible that the current interest in establishing such a system will result in the emergence of new modes of conflict resolution, and that these may be appealing to at least some of those affected by the war. Public welcoming ceremonies for LRA combatants under the auspices of the paramount chief and his council may prove useful. Evidence from fieldwork in the region does not suggest that they are particularly significant at the moment, but things may change if traditional justice procedures are incorporated into Ugandan law. Incorporating local justice will come with risks, however. It might have the effect of entrenching gendered hierarchies associated with particular lineages. Their externally supported powers may be resented, and may not necessarily promote the forms of reconciliation enthusiasts anticipate.

Whatever happens with respect to the setting up of the special division of the Ugandan High Court, there are many who have come back from the LRA and have been accepted by their loved ones without any rites being performed at all. There is also no doubt that others have been – or will at some point be – purified. It is likely that those who are known to have committed terrible acts will have to submit to such processes if they want to live in their former homes. The cleansing rituals will be performed by a variety of specialists, from *rwodi* (traditional chiefs), to clan elders, to female *ajwaki*, to charismatic Christian preachers and Catholic priests. It may be that individuals will have to go though several kinds of rituals until there is consensus that their *cen* (polluting spiritual emanations) are contained. A few may have to find ways of paying compensation for what they have done, and it is likely that there will also be those who find themselves in difficult circumstances when they are no longer protected by aid agencies, soldiers or government officials. Most of those interviewed who have held senior rank in the LRA are fearful of what might happen if they are exposed to the fury of people they have bereaved, and have no confidence in assertions about Acholi 'forgiveness'. They will live in places where their acts are not known, in the towns, and or in other parts of the country. Several have chosen to live at army barracks.

Conclusion

When David Acana, the Acholi paramount chief, was interviewed by this book's editors about *mato oput* and traditional justice measures in September 2008, his position had become significantly more restrained than it had appeared to be three years previously. He had seen an earlier version of this chapter, and he began by expressing irritation about what I had written. As the discussion continued, however, he became amused when we repeated to him some of the far-reaching, and contradictory, claims still being made about *mato oput* by other cultural leaders and activists.[34] He said that the traditional customs were something that people could draw upon if it helped them, but they were not an adequate alternative to formal processes where the most serious crimes had been committed. To our surprise, he had now come to regard the ICC process as broadly beneficial, and took the view that Kony and the other senior LRA commanders should be prosecuted for what they had done.

Exaggerated claims about *mato oput* and other local modes of allocating accountability have suggested that the Acholi and other groups in northern Uganda are in some special way different. Of course, they have their own unique ways of life, but like decent people everywhere else, they require a functioning state to make the best of their lives. The obsession of so many concerned about the suffering in northern Uganda with 'traditional justice' inadvertently reinforces a tendency to demonize the people of the region.[35] For political and cultural reasons, the Acholi in particular are caricatured in Uganda as innately violent, and less concerned about terrible acts than other populations. In Kampala, this is offered as an explanation for their willingness to forgive, and it is common to hear comments about leaving the uncivilized northerners to their own devices. The campaign for regionally and 'tribally' specific traditional justice has done nothing to promote national integration, and the commitment of those who have so assiduously promoted it for selfless reasons has been worthy of a better cause. The Acholi paramount chief himself now recognizes this. Sustainable peace in northern Uganda is going to be possible when there is the necessary political will, relative stability across the border in Sudan, adequate investment in services, improvements in livelihoods and, above all, the deployment of adequate legitimate force to guarantee security. For a long time it was hard to see how government soldiers deployed in the war zone could have had protection of the population as their primary objective. During the past few years the situation has changed. At least in part, that is due to greater international scrutiny of human rights issues directly and indirectly associated with the ICC involvement. Has that really been such a bad thing?

14 · The ICC investigation of the Lord's Resistance Army: an insider's view

MATTHEW BRUBACHER

The involvement of the ICC in northern Uganda has renewed debate over balancing the needs of peace and justice. While often presented as an unprecedented contest between the two goals, the inclusion of justice mechanisms within peace agreements has been growing since the 1990s, as has the involvement of international criminal courts in ongoing armed conflicts (Vinjamuri and Boesenecher 2007: 5). While pursuing justice in these contexts is difficult, the interplay between international courts and conflict is becoming increasingly sophisticated.

Unlike the Nuremberg and Tokyo tribunals, which were established in the wake of a clear military victory, international criminal courts today increasingly operate within ongoing armed conflicts. From the establishment of the International Tribunal for the Former Yugoslavia (ICTY) during the conflicts in the former Yugoslavia to the impact of the Special Court for Sierra Leone (SCSL) on the conflict in Liberia, to the International Criminal Court's (ICC) intervention in Darfur, the Democratic Republic of Congo (DRC) and northern Uganda, international criminal investigations are becoming part of the landscape of armed conflict and altering the manner in which conflicts are managed.

The creation of the ICC as the first permanent international criminal court able to independently select its cases, and the increasing number of state parties, reflect the growing will of the international community to hold individuals accountable for serious crimes. Beyond accountability, however, an almost equally significant narrative justifies the creation of these courts on the basis that justice contributes to establishing peace.[1] The implementation of these twin objectives is, however, complex.

This chapter will focus on the experience of the ICC in northern Uganda. The chapter will look briefly at the experience of other international criminal courts in ongoing armed conflict then take a more in-depth look at the dynamics that existed in the conflict in northern Uganda and assess how the ICC-OTP (Office of the Prosecutor) attempted to develop a comprehensive approach in order to pursue its mandate.

Peace and accountability: the dual purpose of international criminal courts

As international criminal courts operate either within or in the wake of armed conflict, they operate among a multitude of other diplomatic, humanitarian and military-related initiatives each pursuing their respective initiatives. While international criminal courts are established primarily to enforce individual criminal responsibility, those promoting international justice frequently profess that by holding individuals accountable, international criminal courts contribute to creating the basis for peace.

The dual purpose of building peace through accountability was given as a justification for the creation of the ad hoc tribunals both of which were created subsequent to UN Security Council determinations that the situations in the former Yugoslavia and Rwanda were threats to international peace and security.[2] In a report recommending the establishment of the ICTY, the UN secretary-general stated, '[...] that it was convinced that in the particular circumstances of the former Yugoslavia, the establishment of an international tribunal would bring about the achievement of the aim of putting an end to such crimes and of taking effective measures to bring to justice the persons responsible for them, and would contribute to the restoration and maintenance of peace'.[3]

In 1994, this reasoning was echoed by the ICTY itself when it stated that 'Far from being a vehicle for revenge, [the ICTY] is a tool for promoting reconciliation and restoring true peace'.[4]

Similarly, the Security Council, in authorizing the creation of the SCSL, stated that '[...] a credible system of justice and accountability for the very serious crimes committed there would end impunity and would contribute to the process of national reconciliation and to the restoration and maintenance of peace [...]'[5]

Legal authorities, such as Taylor (1992: 634–41), Bassiouni (1998: 1211) and Goldstone (1995) also claim that international courts are vital to peace inasmuch as without fair and impartial justice there can be no reconciliation between peoples, even if there is a political settlement between leaders. The Preamble of the Rome Statute recognizes that grave crimes threaten the peace, security and well-being of the world and that lasting peace requires that there be no impunity for crimes of concern to the international community.[6]

Among the many reasons given for the ability of international criminal courts to contribute to building peace is that the courts contribute to a process of national reconciliation by substituting individual guilt for the collective guilt (Goldstone 1995: 183; S. Johnson 2003: 488), provide justice for victim communities, re-establish the legal order in post-conflict environments, provide a forum for truth-telling that creates an authoritative and shared record of history (International Crisis Group 2002: 12), deter future crimes by strengthening legal enforcement procedures[7] and raise the normative level of acceptable behaviour.[8] The reasoning continues that the punishment of criminal actions contributes to establishing 'real peace' by aiding the national transition process and restoring social equilibrium through the ability to impose the rule of law (Scharf and Rodley 2002).

While international courts may contribute to the above attributes, most of these benefits presume that there is a sufficient degree of stability and security within the country as well as a sufficient degree of consensus as to what constitutes the most appropriate mechanism of justice. In environments where the crimes are still being perpetrated and the societal views and interests fragmented, pursuing these goals is more difficult.

The tensions between accountability and peace

The fundamental quandary that confronts all international criminal courts which intervene in ongoing armed conflicts is that those they identify as suspects are often the same individuals who could be involved in negotiating a political settlement. Those involved in the negotiations will often state that during a process of political negotiation, a public arrest warrant against members of a party to the negotiations may cause that party to retrench its positions and deter its willingness to commit to a peaceful settlement. A public arrest warrant may also complicate efforts of negotiators to include indicted persons in talks. As stated by one British official involved in negotiations during the conflict in the former Yugoslavia, the problem was 'indicting people [when] you may be negotiating with them' (Bass 2000: 222). In such conditions, parties may demand immunity from prosecution as a condition to concluding an agreement and negotiators will be tempted to provide some degree of assurance as a means to increase trust and build incentives to concluding an agreement.

The other danger is that the suspect may also use the issuing of a warrant as a justification to escalate hostilities, both as a protest and as a means to raise his profile and complicate efforts for authorities to execute the warrant. States, on which international courts rely to execute their warrants, may also be reluctant to execute warrants if they perceive it as politically inexpedient, particularly if executing that warrant puts their nationals in danger (Bell 2000: 270–3). Accommodating these interests and allowing suspected criminals to participate in negotiations, however, creates an array of political and legal difficulties.

Politically, allowing a suspect to participate in negotiations will result in conferring upon that individual a greater degree of political, if not moral, legitimacy as well as give credibility to the agenda that they brought to the negotiating table. When that individual is suspected of committing serious crimes and furthering policies suspected of fomenting systemic and widespread atrocities, such a decision sets an uncomfortable precedent.

Legally, prosecutors have no ability to engage in political negotiations and must act according to their statutory duties. As stated by the ICC prosecutor, Luis Moreno-Ocampo, 'My duty is to apply the law without political considerations. I will present evidence to the Judges and they will decide on the merits of such evidence.'[9] As judicial organs, prosecutors must remain independent and impartial in the execution of their responsibilities – obligations that would be challenged were prosecutors to be perceived as being involved in negotiations.

There is also a growing body of normative international law promoting the obligation to prosecute those suspected of committing serious crimes[10] as well as a growing resolve by the international community not to recognize unqualified amnesties in international peace agreements.[11] Negotiated agreements therefore have increasingly included either provisions identifying accountability mechanisms or wording that would not prevent such a mechanism from operating in the future.

In addition, while pursuing justice in the midst of ongoing armed conflicts may complicate efforts to achieve a solution, the effect is not necessarily negative. One immediate effect international arrest warrants have is to marginalize the target politically and increase the costs associated with supporting or harbouring that individual. This marginalization was illustrated when the ICTY issued its indictments against the Bosnian Serb leaders Radovan Karadzic and Ratko Mladic in 1995. Although both Karadzic and Mladic enjoyed a high level of support within their constituencies and both were scheduled to participate in the Dayton peace negotiations, the indictments served to exclude them from the political discourse and undermined their power base. Despite concerns that the indictments would jeopardize the peace process (Boyd 1998; Schrag 2004), the Dayton negotiations were successfully concluded.[12] The negotiators were even able to include within the Dayton Accords a provision obliging 'all parties to cooperate in the investigation and prosecution of war crimes and other violations of international humanitarian law'.[13] For these reasons, the Dayton Accords are often cited as an example where peace and justice were pursued in a complementary manner (S. Johnson 2003: 188).

Similarly, during the 1998 Kosovo conflict, the ICTY, in a real-time law enforcement role, unsealed indictments against Zeljko Raznatovic, the leader of a notorious Serb paramilitary organization known as 'Arkan's Tigers', in an attempt to stigmatize him and his associates.[14] Again, on 27 May 1999 the ICTY issued indictments against Slobodan Milosevic and four other high-level leaders (Arbour 2004: 402). These indictments were issued at a time when Serb forces had committed new atrocities[15] and Milosevic had refused to commit himself to a negotiated solution, developments which were increasingly positing Milosevic as a spoiler.[16] Issuing indictments at this time served to further strengthen the already growing resolve of the international community to take more forceful steps to sideline spoilers to the peace process and stop the criminal activity.

The legal regime of the Rome Statute

For the prosecutor of the ICC, the legal regime differs in several areas from those of previous international criminal courts. The prosecutor can receive notice of crimes from three different sources but then needs to follow the same analytical process in making the decision on whether to investigate.[17] The crime must have occurred after 1 July 2002, the date the statute entered into force.[18] In addition, the crime must have been committed by a person either in the territory of states parties or a national of a state party.[19] This territorial jurisdiction, however, can be expanded when the UN Security Council, acting under Chapter VII, refers the matter to the ICC.[20] With 110 states parties, this jurisdictional regime gives the prosecutor much broader jurisdiction than the ICTY, which was limited to crimes that occurred in the territory of the former Yugoslavia.

In addition to these jurisdictional criteria, the prosecutor has several admissibility criteria that need to be taken into consideration. The first criterion, gravity, is given particular emphasis in the Rome Statute.[21] The gravity criterion is applied both to the alleged crime and to the person believed to be the most responsible for committing that crime. In regard to assessing the gravity of the crimes themselves, the prosecutor has identified four indicia to guide this analysis, including the scale of crimes, the nature of crimes, the manner of their commission and their impact.

The second criterion of admissibility, complementarity, refers to the relationship of the ICC to national jurisdictions. This system is also markedly different to the ICTY, which had primacy over national courts. Unlike this vertical relationship with states, the ICC cannot simply order national systems to hand over a particular case but must instead defer to genuine national proceedings.[22] The principle of complementarity works on the premise that states have the primary obligation to enforce the law and the ICC is only a court of last resort if the state that has jurisdiction over the crime is either unable or unwilling to prosecute the crimes itself.

This more horizontal relationship with state jurisdictions encourages states to comply with their obligation to enforce the law rather than be a substitute for national proceedings (Zolo 2004: 402). Although it is currently unclear what type of proceeding is sufficient to satisfy the court's emerging definition of a 'genuine proceeding', this system allows the court to work in a manner that appreciates national justice initiatives.

The third element to be considered is the 'interests of justice' criterion. The 'interests of justice' is a countervailing consideration that requires the prosecutor to consider certain factors that may produce a reason *not* to proceed with an investigation or prosecution. This consideration is made only once a positive decision to proceed has already been made. 'In deciding whether to initiate an investigation, the Prosecutor shall consider whether: [...] Taking into account the gravity of the crime and the interests of victims, there are nonetheless substantial reasons to believe that an investigation would not serve the interests of justice.'[23]

The definition and scope of the 'interests of justice' have been a matter of considerable debate. Initially, some authors argued that this provision could apply if the pursuit of justice impaired peace and security (Cassese et al. 2001; Brubacher 2004).[24] Others, however, particularly from the human rights community, argue for a more restrictive interpretation (Human Rights Watch 2005a). This second, more restrictive interpretation is the direction in which the OTP is going. In its policy paper on the 'interests of justice', the OTP cites the need to provide redress to victims and the object and purpose of the statute in pursuing accountability as the basis for interpreting this provision, and states that the exercise of this provision would be exceptional in nature.[25]

In its policy paper the OTP states that 'it would be misleading to equate the interests of justice with the interests of peace'.[26] For cases where a situation should arise whereby ICC involvement directly threatened peace and stability, the authors of the statute included Article 16, which obliges the court to defer an investigation or prosecution for one year in the event the UN Security Council finds that these proceedings are a threat to international peace and security by issuing a Chapter VII resolution. The insertion of this provision is significant as the mandate and capacities of the UN Security Council are more capable of dealing with resolving conflicts between peace, justice and security than a judicial body such as the ICC. It should also be noted that any decision by the prosecutor not to proceed based solely on the 'interests of justice' is reviewable by the judges.[27]

While broader issues of peace and security may not directly factor into decisions, however, the paper goes on to state that in assessing the 'interests of victims', an element of the interests of justice, the OTP will take into consideration the victims' personal security as well as the obligation of the court to protect victims and witnesses.[28] As such, while the prosecutor is not able to change its decisions in light of the effect of its investigations on peace processes or the general security situation, the prosecutor may take certain precautionary measures regarding security, including witness protection measures and modifying its public messages and profile.

Investigating the situation regarding northern Uganda

Opening the investigation Soon after the ICC became functional in 2003, the OTP began receiving information about crimes being committed in northern Uganda, and the situation quickly became an area of focus.[29] At that time, the LRA had just returned to northern Uganda en masse after the Ugandan national army, the Uganda People's Defence Force (UPDF), routed LRA bases in southern Sudan in what was termed Operation Iron Fist. Although this military operation eventually contributed to undermining the ability of the LRA to operate in northern Uganda and Sudan, in the short term LRA attacks in northern Uganda increased dramatically.

On 16 December 2003, the Office received a referral from the government of Uganda regarding 'the situation of the Lord's Resistance Army'.[30] Under the Rome Statute, 'a State can refer to the Prosecutor a situation in which one or more crimes within the jurisdiction of the Court appear to have been committed [...]'[31] This referral does not automatically trigger an investigation nor an obligation on the prosecutor to launch an investigation but, like any other source, merely provides the prosecutor with notice that crimes may have been committed. It is also important to understand that a 'situation' under the Rome Statute is a broad term that encompasses all crimes within ICC jurisdiction within certain temporal, territorial or personal parameters rather than those of a particular individual or group.[32] In interpreting the Ugandan referral, the prosecutor also had to be mindful of his duty to independently and objectively analyse the information provided to him. As such the prosecutor interpreted the referral to include all crimes committed in the conflict of northern Uganda regardless of the party that committed them. The prosecutor informed the government of Uganda of this fact prior to opening the investigation.[33]

As the Office began to collect information it quickly became apparent that a reasonable basis existed to believe crimes were committed within ICC jurisdiction and that the crimes committed by the LRA were significantly more grave than those committed by other parties. Among all the thousands of crimes the prosecutor can investigate only those most responsible for the worst crimes. Between July 2002 and June 2004, the LRA was allegedly responsible for at least 2,200 killings and 3,200 abductions in over 850 attacks, as well as a high number of sexual crimes, including rape and sexual enslavement.[34] There was also information to indicate that many of these crimes, such as sexual enslavement and child abduction, were being committed as part of an organizational policy and were systemic in nature.

The focus of the OTP on LRA crimes caused concern among the affected population, who often view themselves as being victims of both the LRA and the UPDF.[35] This is an understandable view given the proximity of the civilians to the UPDF, their being corralled into IDP camps and the strict restrictions, such as curfews, imposed on them for such an extended period of time. The OTP received information regarding alleged crimes committed by security forces of the Ugandan government and these were analysed and information was actively collected in the field. At the time of writing no final decision regarding alleged crimes by Ugandan authorities had been taken by the OTP.

As a judicial body the OTP must use objective criteria in the selection of situations and cases. In this regard, the maintenance of impartiality cannot be equated with equality of blame. The use of objective standards to guide case selection may result in public perceptions of bias, particularly when the crimes of one party are significantly worse than the of other, as in the case of northern Uganda. Although justice needs to be seen to be done, however, the prosecutor's office cannot open itself to being influenced by popular sentiment, as to do so would subject the ICC to subjectivity, incoherence and external pressure. Moreover, it would detract from the ability of the ICC to enforce a defined level of normative behaviour across the different situations in which investigations are being conducted.

The situation in northern Uganda at the launch of the ICC investigation When the OTP launched its investigation into the situation of northern Uganda on 28 July 2004, the conflict was entering its nineteenth year. At this time, LRA crimes in northern Uganda, while still occurring on a daily basis, were decreasing. Although there was no peace process per se in mid-2004, the local community expressed concerns regarding the possible negative effect an ICC investigation might have on the prospects for future negotiations, as well as its effect on the security situation. Having regard to these concerns, the OTP maintained a low profile in its investigation, and the announcement on 28 July 2004 at the launch of the investigation was deliberately anodyne.[36]

At the time the investigation was launched the UPDF had renewed its 'Iron Fist' offensive, crossing the so-called Red Line for the first time.[37] The Red Line had been the northernmost point of deployment for the UPDF under the terms of the agreement entered into with the Sudanese government in 2002. The LRA had moved its bases and its leadership above the line to protect itself from UPDF attack, but in March 2004 the Sudanese government gave the UPDF permission to move farther north, although the actual operation was delayed for several months. It was only on 29 July 2004 that the UPDF were able to launch an operation to rout the last three remaining permanent LRA bases, nearly killing its leader, Joseph Kony, who by several accounts appears only to have narrowly escaped.[38] At the same time, the main block of the Equatorial Defence Force (EDF), a government-backed militia that had worked closely with the LRA since their move into southern Sudan, had joined the SPLA in March 2004 and was now openly fighting its former ally.[39] The tide was shifting against the LRA and their overall capacity was eroding.

After the investigation was opened, the Uganda investigation team was formed with approximately fifteen professionals from a diverse array of backgrounds and nationalities.[40] The investigation team quickly established an infrastructure in Uganda to support its activities, including the establishment of a witness protection system. Although many local groups expressed concerns regarding the OTP's impact on security, future peace processes and the perceived clash of the ICC with traditional justice mechanisms, the cooperation from the ground was and for the most part remained consistent. During the first few months, the prosecutor selected six crime incidents from the 850 possible LRA attacks.[41] This focused the investigation and allowed the team to proceed more rapidly. It would take the team only nine months to collect a sufficient amount of information to apply to the judges for five arrest warrants against the LRA commanders who bore the greatest responsibility for some of the worst attacks.[42]

The five arrest warrants targeted the top commanders of the LRA, which operated on a military structure similar to the Ugandan People's Democratic Army (UPDA), which was itself fashioned on a simple British infantry command structure. At the time of the warrants, the LRA operated with Joseph Kony as chairman of the LRA and the overall commander; Vincent Otti as deputy chairman; Okot Odhiambo as army commander; and Raska Lukwiya as deputy army commander. Beneath these positions there were four brigades with Dominic Ongwen, the fifth target of the warrants, being the commanding officer of the notorious Sinia Brigade.

Developing a comprehensive approach The interplay of conflict resolution initiatives and justice is manifest in all of the situations under ICC investigation as all four of its current investigations, northern Uganda, DRC, Darfur and the Central African Republic, take place within ongoing armed conflicts. This not only creates logistical and security issues for the office staff, its partners and witnesses, but it also means that the Office will be operating alongside a wide array of other actors working to manage the conflict and restore civilian livelihoods.

Broadly, these initiatives include efforts to provide security, humanitarian relief, peace-building and justice. The OTP views itself as part of this justice component alongside national proceedings and other community initiatives. It recognizes that, while each actor needs to pursue its respective initiatives, each initiative affects the others and there is a need to attempt a harmonization of efforts. In order to preserve its impartiality, however, the OTP cannot be a component of the other initiatives. The OTP policy is to maintain its independence and pursue its mandate to investigate and prosecute, but to do so in a manner that respects the mandates of others in order to maximize the positive impact of all.[43] Although many observers state that there needs to be peace before justice, the problem with this approach is that many of the conflicts are endemic and may last for an indefinite period of time. So this raises the question of how long victims need to wait until justice is pursued. Also, stating openly that the parties will be prosecuted only after they sign up to a peace deal does little to encourage either process and does not address the issue. A more constructive question would be to ask how justice and security can be pursued in a manner that addresses the totality of concerns of victims.

Since the beginning of 2004, the OTP has had frequent discussions with states and international organizations involved in the Ugandan situation. In addition, the OTP sent numerous missions to the country to consult with the government and local community. Although security concerns and the need to maintain a low profile[44] limited the ability of the team to consult widely with the affected community, the team identified various representatives of the affected communities and listened to their concerns. In northern Uganda a number of ethnic groups were affected by the conflict, including the Madi, Acholi, Langi, Teso and Kumam. It is important to note that during the period covered by the main OTP investigation, July 2002–July 2004, the Acholi, Langi and Teso people were nearly equally victimized in terms of the number of killings and abductions.

The prosecutor took a broad-based approach in consulting with representatives of the victim population and established relationships with various levels of local governance, including the religious and traditional structures, as well as local government, members of parliament and civil society. In consulting these stakeholders, the prosecutor invited local leaders to The Hague. The first delegation, which was composed of Acholi leaders, arrived in March 2005.[45] After this meeting the invitation was expanded to include the Langi and Teso leaderships, each sector being given the discretion to choose their representatives.[46] Although there were a variety of different views and concerns both within and between the delegations, there was unity on the need to end the commission of crimes and to restore a semblance of justice to the affected communities. The various actors also left with an appreciation that each actor had a role to play and that further consultation would be needed in order to complement each other's respective initiatives.

LRA activity during the ICC investigation

During the period of focus for the OTP investigation between July 2002 and July 2004, LRA attacks in Uganda were at their peak. Although LRA attacks were decreasing by the time the investigation opened, however, the OTP continued to carefully assess the security situation.

As can be seen in Figure 14.1 (derived from security reports made available to the OTP), after the investigation was launched LRA crimes continued to decline and the LRA were also decreasing in number. By the end of 2004, the LRA, while still dangerous, were experiencing difficulties and entered into peace talks with Betty Bigombe in November. This peace process resulted in a ceasefire which lasted until the end of the year and was very briefly revived the following year. This process, however, ended in February 2005 when two high-level LRA commanders, including the head of the LRA negotiating delegation, defected.[47]

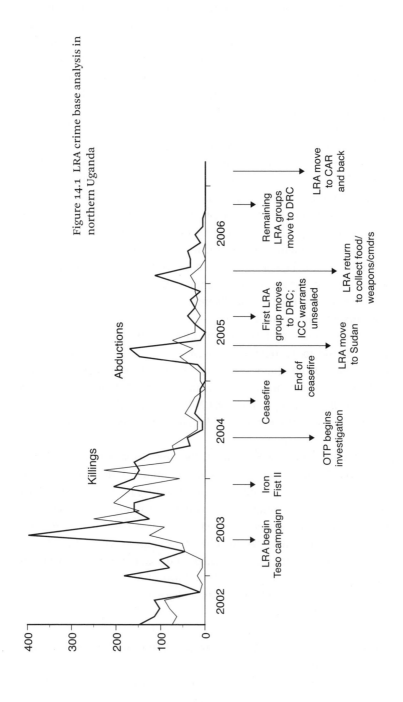

Figure 14.1 LRA crime base analysis in northern Uganda

Defections were always of great concern for the LRA leadership during previous peace talks, and the LRA resumed attacks in retaliation for the betrayal. By this time, however, the LRA was very exposed, and within a few weeks three major LRA commanders had been killed, with more being captured. With the constant pressure and the depleting officer corps, the LRA was no longer able to abduct for the purposes of recruitment. The continued existence of the LRA in northern Uganda was ending and the LRA knew it.

By 6 May 2005, the prosecutor was ready to make his application for arrest warrants against five senior members of the LRA, including the top two members, Joseph Kony and his number two, Vincent Otti. In his application for the warrants, the prosecutor requested that they be sealed owing to security concerns.[48] Although there would never be a perfect time to unseal the warrants, the OTP wanted to wait until the LRA capacity to inflict violence was low relative to the ability of the Ugandan government to provide security. The application also requested that the warrants be sealed to allow time for the OTP and the Registry's Victims and Witnesses Unit to ensure that all prosecutorial witnesses were protected.[49] The Pre-Trial Chamber subsequently issued five sealed warrants on 8 July 2005.[50]

Between March and August, the LRA prepared for its move to the DRC. In June 2005, commanders were called for meetings in Sudan to plan the move and orders were given to gather food and other supplies, including plastic containers (jerrycans) which would be used to make rafts for the crossing of the River Nile. Around this time there was a temporary rise in abductions as LRA kidnapped people to use them to carry food and weapons.

At the beginning of September, the first crossing took place. This group was led by the LRA's second-in-command, Vincent Otti, and included most of Control Alter, the administrative body of the LRA which controls everything from finance and political affairs to arms supply, as well as several brigade commanders. The movement of that group to DRC revealed the LRA plan to shift its geographic centre. Otti crossed into the DRC around mid-September and made several contacts with DRC officials in the area around the town of Aba, in north-east DRC. Otti requested that the LRA be granted leave to remain in DRC with its weapons, but this request was denied. The LRA then moved to establish a base on the remote western edge of Garamba National Park, a heavily forested area in the Haut Uele Province of DRC, where there was little government presence.

This movement was significant in the prosecutor's decision to unseal the warrants as the movement of these key commanders to the DRC decreased the military capacity of the LRA in northern Uganda, thereby improving security there. The ability of Ugandan security forces to protect had also improved in the latter part of 2004 after the UPDF implemented a new protection strategy for the IDP camps. As the capacity to protect was relatively high and the LRA capacity relatively low, the general security situation was assessed as having improved. Also, by this time the necessary measures to ensure the security of witnesses had been taken.[51]

With the improved security conditions in northern Uganda and the movement of one of the suspects to a state that was a party to the ICC, the OTP requested the Pre-Trial Chamber to unseal the warrants and to transmit them to the DRC, Sudan and Uganda. The judges authorized the Registry to transmit the arrest warrants on 27 September 2005.[52] The warrants and the requests for arrest and surrender were transmitted to the three territorial states in which the LRA were present, namely Uganda, DRC and the Sudan. The first two states were parties to the ICC Statute and thereby had an obligation to arrest. As Sudan was not a state party, the OTP approached the government for support and in October 2005 concluded an agreement whereby the government agreed to arrest members of the LRA named in ICC arrest warrants. After the warrants were transmitted, the prosecutor requested that the judges unseal the warrants fully, which they did on 13 October 2005.[53]

After the LRA had established a base in Garamba National Park, several other LRA groups, and Kony himself, crossed the Nile and made their way down to the new headquarters. The River Nile had been the principal geographical boundary in southern Sudan that had limited the LRA's movement. Owing to the size of the river and the constant military pressure, the move was dangerous for the LRA and several groups had difficulty leaving northern Uganda to rejoin the main force. The LRA needed space to finish its regrouping effort. After numerous failed attempts at contacting possible mediators to restart peace talks, the LRA found a willing party in the Government of Southern Sudan. The current peace talks in Juba thus began in July 2006 and eventually resulted in a ceasefire.

Under the initial ceasefire agreement, the LRA were supposed to assemble in two assembly points, one on the east side of the Nile at Owiny-Kibul and the other to the west at Ri-Kwangba. Security monitoring showed, however, that LRA groups continually made attempts to cross from the east bank of the Nile in order to join the main LRA group in Garamba. In January 2007, using the cover of the ceasefire, the remaining senior LRA commanders finally managed to make the journey. As a result, the LRA succeeded in their efforts to regroup their forces, which was a primary goal of entering the talks in the first place.

Soon after the LRA regrouped in Garamba at the end of 2007, a group was sent off westward along the border between DRC and Sudan to the Central African Republic. There were several reasons for the LRA to move to a largely unmonitored and under-administered region of this country, including a wish to link with other rebel groups, but the LRA moved back by the beginning of March and talks with the government of Uganda resumed. The LRA would, however, keep the Central African Republic as a back-up option should the situation in the DRC become insecure.

The negotiation process continued in Juba with various personalities, primarily from the Acholi diaspora in London and Nairobi, brought in to develop a political agenda for the LRA. Although these individuals largely operated in their own capacities and almost none had spent much time with the real LRA, or even met its leader, Joseph Kony, many had been financiers of the LRA for years. The connection between these individuals and the real LRA, however, is intermittent and dubious at best, and the real LRA fired and changed members of the delegation on many occasions.

While the talks were ongoing, the OTP continued to rally states to enforce the warrants. Several positive steps were taken in this regard, including the 8 September 2007 Ngurdoto Agreement between the DRC and Uganda wherein the two countries agreed to conduct joint military operations against the LRA in collaboration with the UN peacekeeping force in the DRC, MONUC (Mission de l'Organisation des Nations Unies en RD Congo).[54] MONUC forces had been involved in a failed attempt to arrest senior commanders of the LRA in January 2006, in which eight Guatemalan UN peacekeepers were killed. In July 2007, however, MONUC set up a forward base just south of the main LRA base in a town called Dungu in the south-west corner of Garamba.[55] It is important to note that MONUC has a robust mandate to use force and has an agreement with the OTP to assist in arrest efforts.

As the talks dragged on, divisions began to appear within the LRA and on 2 October 2007 Vincent Otti and several other commanders were executed, reportedly pursuant to orders of Joseph Kony.[56] Numerous LRA members defected soon after but Kony was able to reassert control.[57] In February 2008, as the dry season set in and after the LRA delegation had concluded all major parts of the negotiation process, the LRA moved back into the Central African Republic. Unlike in the previous movement to the Central African Republic, however, the LRA began a mass abduction campaign, taking civilians from the Central African Republic, Sudan and the DRC.[58] At the end of March, the LRA brought hundreds of these new abductees back to their base in Garamba and began to give them military training. This latest move by the LRA is as significant as their move to Sudan in 1994 or their move to DRC in 2005, as it indicates that they are attempting not only to rebuild their forces but to transform themselves into a regional military force rather than one focused on northern Uganda.

Making justice a component of peace

The experience of previous international criminal courts demonstrates that the pursuit of justice is linked with the efforts of other actors in any given context, including peace processes (Horowitz 1985; Mark 1995; Sisk 1996; Lake and Rothchild 1996; Williams and Scharf 2002: 32). Maintaining a complementary relationship between the two is not easy but it is possible (Sapira 2003: 1011). International criminal courts can contribute to efforts to achieve a sustainable peace that includes the re-establishment of legal order and the rule of law.

As experienced by the ICTY, those most responsible for committing systematic and widespread crimes are often those who are reluctant to genuinely commit to peaceful negotiations. By issuing warrants, international courts can isolate leaders who act as spoilers to a peace process, focus public attention, galvanize international cooperation and apply pressure to deter those funding the organization.[59] As stated by the ICC prosecutor, making justice a part of peace is a challenge, but one that is necessary.

> Dealing with the new legal reality is not easy. It needs political commitment; it needs hard and costly operational decisions: arresting criminals in the context of ongoing conflicts is a difficult endeavour. Individuals sought by the Court often enjoy the protection of armies or militias, some of them are members of governments eager to shield them from justice. Those difficulties are real. They can however not lead us to change the content of the law and our commitment to implement it.[60]

In regard to the situation in northern Uganda, although a durable peace remains elusive, the facts on the ground demonstrate that since the ICC investigation began the security situation has improved dramatically, and processes to achieve a negotiated settlement have increased.[61] While the end result has yet to be determined, the strategy of the prosecutor demonstrates that there can be synergy between the dual purpose of international criminal courts.

8 A returned LRA rebel takes part in a cleansing ceremony. This is not *mato oput*, the ritual that has been given such emphasis by those promoting so called traditional justice, but a version of a cermony called *lakare kat*. It involves the ritual slaughter of goats and chickens as determined by local elders as a way of returned rebels confronting their fears and memories in front of the community. Afterwards the animals are roasted and the meat is shared among the returnees' relatives and neighbours. Amuru Camp, 28 August 2006 (Adam Pletts).

Postscript: a kind of peace and an exported war

TIM ALLEN, FREDERICK LAKER, HOLLY PORTER
AND MAREIKE SCHOMERUS

Since 2006, an unfamiliar degree of stability and order has been sustained in northern Uganda. The problem of the LRA has been exported. Gulu town, the largest urban centre in the former war zone, is the fastest-growing city in the country. Large numbers of IDPs have been leaving the camps, and the process has accelerated since the government announced 'voluntary' return and a camp phase-out operation in 2007. The discovery of oil in Amuru district in January 2009; new investments in roads, health centres and school buildings; the continued presence of international aid agencies; the opening of new hotels and banks; the demand for agricultural produce across the border in Sudan; and the presence of foreign military personnel have created a palpable and widespread sense of change. The United States has increased its presence in the region with a variety of high-profile operations. The newly formed US Africa Command (AFRICOM), which cooperated in Operation Lightning Thunder with mixed results, has also been involved in 'humanitarian' activities. These have included immunization of children and veterinary services in March and April 2009, and the joint military exercises code-named Natural Fire, which brought together soldiers from Uganda, Burundi, Kenya, Tanzania and Rwanda in October 2009, to practise and test disaster relief capabilities.[1] Quite suddenly, northern Uganda has morphed from its long-prevailing image as the country's chaotic and violent backwater into a place of untapped economic potential and of strategic and political interest to the world's most powerful state. Of course, appearances can be deceptive, and President Museveni's government has confidently proclaimed the war in the north to be over more than once before. Events proved otherwise. But things do seem different this time.[2]

Christmas

'We would hear them say "it's over" on radio, but then within two or three days we would hear gunshots and the rebels would pass our house or sit in our compound. So, we were slow to trust this time. But now …' The young woman shrugged as if the sound of children laughing, goats running through the compound and the absence of explosions sufficiently completed her statement. 'It's been three years,' she finally concluded. 'But we were worried. We always had that thought, "maybe they [the LRA] will come back" in our minds.'

This was Christmas Day, 2009, being celebrated in a village a few kilometres from Gulu town. Since 2006 the guns have mostly been silent in Uganda. In 2006 and 2007 people were hopeful but still uncertain of the direction of the Juba talks. In November 2008, when it was clear that they had failed, concern increased as people followed the daily news of Operation Lightning Thunder and LRA attacks on civilians, especially the 'Christmas Massacres' in DRC. In the last months of 2009, the radio reported that the LRA had written several letters threatening a repeat of the previous year's holiday bloodshed. LRA veterans who had recently escaped or been captured, such as 'Lieutenant Colonel' Charles Arop, admitted they had joked about celebrating Christmas as they had the previous year, with killing and abductions.

The father of the house, respectfully referred to as Mzee (a term for a male elder), noted that their Congolese brothers and sisters across the border were not experiencing the same security his family and friends were enjoying. Whenever the news punctuated the music playing on the radio they were keen to listen for any reports of violence. 'Fortunately,' Mzee said, towards the end of the day, 'it seems the LRA decided to celebrate some other way. But,' he shook his head, 'it's not good. They [the Congolese] are suffering while we are here enjoying our chicken.'

There is a comforting distance now between the memory of gunshots and this celebration. The border between DRC and Sudan is a long way away, and it seems the LRA are not coming back. While the women laughed from the kitchen, where they were sweating over charcoal stoves, Mzee recounted past Christmas stories and contrasted them with this year. His favourite Christmas was the first year that they spent with the whole family in this village. They moved here from Atiak in 1995. The war had begun but they had not yet felt its devastation as a family. They moved closer to Gulu town for access to better schools for his six girls and son. 'All my children were home on school holidays that year.' That was the year before he lost his leg when he rode his bicycle over a landmine while collecting wood for charcoal. He regularly jokes that the compensation the government keeps promising landmine victims will help his children pay for his funeral. It was also the year before a massacre in their home village, Atiak, where they lost many relatives.

His eldest daughter had been visiting an aunt in Atiak when the LRA attacked. While she was trying to run away she fell into an old pit latrine where she hid until the sound of killing stopped. She continues to suffer from nightmares, hallucinations and from pain that has been diagnosed as a psychosomatic symptom of trauma.

'This war spoiled everything,' Mzee explained. 'This is the first year since 1995 when we've felt safe and free to celebrate. It has been years we've waited for this celebration.' One of his daughters added, 'Ever since then, there was nothing like dancing, or new dresses and sodas. Sometimes Christmas caught us when we didn't even have batteries for the radio and we had either dried fish or just beans for dinner.' This year they had an incredible spread of food and their neighbour, who works for the local radio station, brought home a massive sound system that competed with Mzee's hand-held radio to play alternating Western Christmas songs and Acholi traditional music. Everyone danced.

Many people in northern Uganda had gone home for Christmas for the first time in decades – not to a camp or a satellite camp, but to their original villages. In the weeks and days leading up to Christmas, the streets of Gulu town were packed with people preparing for festivities. Relatives from Kampala were travelling home. Seats on buses were full, prices inflated, and everyone in a rush to order meat for Christmas dinner, or buy a new outfit, or even a small artificial tree. For this family, Christmases past were defined by violence, death in the family, outbreaks of infectious diseases (including Ebola) and 'night commuting' to the nearby Catechist Centre. 'This Christmas, we are already thinking of the New Year – that means we expect to reach it. We have hope.' They have been discussing plans to move back to Atiak, but like many people they are waiting on land issues to be resolved and services to be provided, especially water. 'When they drill a borehole,' Mzee says, 'we'll go home. It's a very nice place when there's no war in Sudan or in Uganda.'

When asked about their thoughts on the future, someone responded with a statement that is often repeated regarding the war and this ambiguous and fragile kind of peace: 'People are tired.' They all nodded. 'Although,' one woman added after a thoughtful pause, 'there are a lot of politics in fighting.' She recalled the arrests the previous year of two of their neighbours who are still being held in Luzira Prison with a number of other prominent opposition figures. They are accused of involvement with a conspiracy to begin a new rebel movement. On these controversial arrests, the family were quite adamant: 'These arrests weren't arbitrary. They did investigations and there must be some truth in it.'

281

They clicked their tongues and shook their heads at their neighbours' desire to use violence to accomplish political ends after all they have suffered. 'There are some people who simply will never accept to be peaceful while Musevini is in power.' Knowing that most of them are not great supporters of the current government either and are sympathetic to similar political goals, I asked what method of resistance they would support. 'For us – we'll fight with our vote and with our prayers. That's the only way now.' Another woman chimed in, *'Can pwonyi,'* an Acholi saying that literally means that disaster and poverty teach you. 'We have learned.'

Ending internal displacement

All of us who have lived and researched in northern Uganda during the past year or so have had similar conversations. But expressions of guarded optimism do not mean that there is a sense of difficulties evaporating. One huge issue is the ending of internal displacement. If hundreds of thousands of people had crossed an international border in a matter of months, either as refugees or returning refugees, it would be grounds for concern. The resettlement of IDPs is not so different.

In 2007, the Office of the Prime Minister issued the Camp Phase-Out Guidelines. These include bold statements, such as that 'the right to freedom of movement must be respected', and that the 'voluntary character of the return in safety and dignity must be ensured'. Not surprisingly the guidelines do not acknowledge the past horrors of the IDP camps, nor the fact that many had been forced to move there and stay there by the Ugandan army. But, leaving those points aside, a central problem with the guidelines is the treatment of return, resettlement and reintegration of IDPs as a purely technical problem. The guidelines simply call for the population to go back home after fourteen years of encampment. It is acknowledged that there will be vulnerable groups, such as widows and orphans who are not old enough to stand up for their rights, but it is suggested that area land committees, local council courts, clan systems and formal courts should be able to handle such cases. If only things were that straightforward!

It is true that some IDPs have eagerly returned to their homes, but others have been effectively pushed out of camps, with local officials making threats about imminent demolition of huts and the halting of food aid. Some of those who have returned to former family residences have then confronted a decline in access to healthcare at clinics and primary education.[3] Facilities may have been of a low quality in camps, but at least something was available. Many have also faced wrangles over access to land. An example of how bitter these disputes can be was the incident in March 2009, when some 120 people were rendered homeless in Corner Agula village in Gulu's Odek sub-county. Their homes were burnt down during clashes between Lukwo and Palaro clan members, who have been fighting over control of the land that separates the two groups.[4] Another challenge is the rise in prices, especially of food. The demand across the border in Sudan since the signing of the CPA has meant that those with food to sell can make a substantial profit, but those without a ready harvest find it hard to buy what they need. Red beans, for example, went up by 50 per cent in 2009, and sugar by almost the same. A bunch of bananas, which used to cost 100 shillings, now sells for 2,000 shillings.[5]

According to the government of Uganda, 80 per cent of IDPs have now returned home, and several more camps are scheduled for closure in 2010.[6] Even UNHCR estimates that there are still approximately 370,000 IDPs remaining in camps and transition sites,[7] however, and in general the current overall statistics on IDP numbers have to be treated with caution, not least because there are several different kinds of IDPs. Many of those who were forced into camps back in the mid-1990s, for example, may never have lived in rural locations as farmers, and it can be anticipated that considerable numbers will gravitate towards the bigger towns, or to bigger IDP camps which will become permanent urban centres. There is in addition a high degree of mobility between villages. According to an Oxfam report, this has

> blurred the distinction between IDP and returnees, which in turn has complicated interventions by the government and humanitarian agencies. How, for example, should an individual who has returned to his or her home village but can only access services in the camps be characterised? Similarly, how should a camp resident who has chosen to buy or rent land in the camp so as to be permanently based there be classified?[8]

There is also the fact that as many as half a million Acholi people were displaced out of their home region and are living in specific, camp-like urban locations in Jinja, Masindi, Kireka and Entebbe. There has been little recognition of this group, and virtually no assistance.

Thus, there is hope and expectation that sustained peace will co-incide with rapidly improving livelihoods, but experiences among the masses of forcibly displaced have been very mixed. This was predictable, given the limitations of the Peace, Reconstruction and Development Plan (PRDP) and the manner of its implementation. The PRDP was initiated in 2007 to stabilize the north so as to regain peace, recovery and development through four strategic objectives: consolidation of state authority; peace-building and reconciliation; rebuilding and empowering communities; and rebuilding the economy of northern Uganda. Originally intended as a three-year programme, it is behind schedule and is now planned to finish in 2011.

There are signs of its implementation dotted across the region, but the PRDP has several problems. These have included a lack of local ownership of projects, concerns that funds have been abused by politicians and a basic lack of consensus about its management – notably resulting in tensions between the Office of the Prime Minister and the Ministry of Finance, Planning and Economic Development. A further concern is the PRDP's geographic scope, which encompasses thirty-eight districts, and creates the impression that half the country has been engulfed in civil war, as Uganda is comprised of a total of eighty districts. The war-affected parts of northern Uganda are made up of only twelve districts, which raises the question of why and how twenty-six districts have come to be subsumed under northern Ugandan reconstruction. Finally, despite all the fanfare about it, the PRDP's budget is relatively small at $609 million – of which 70 per cent is donor funded and 30 per cent provided by the government of Uganda. To put this into context, Georgia, after the seven days of conflict with Russia in August 2008 over Georgia's separatist regions of Abkhazia and South Ossetia, has been pledged $4 billion in aid[9] and the Palestinian Authority has been pledged $5 billion in aid, after the three-week Israeli offensive in Gaza during 2008.[10]

An exported war

If things remain difficult for many of those affected by the LRA war in Uganda, they are much better off than populations now experiencing the LRA's brand of violence along the borderlands of Sudan, the DRC and the CAR. Those who were with the LRA at the time of Operation Lighting Thunder but subsequently escaped or were captured have described what happened. One of those interviewed by researchers from the United Nations High Commissioner for Human Rights (OHCHR) explained that:

> [...] after the 14th December attack, the LRA dispersed, forming four groups to escape Garamba Park: the first one went to DRC, two other ones went to Southern Sudan and the last one with the high ranking commanders went to Central African Republic. [Joseph] Kony sent a

message to all the LRA commanders to attack the villages in Southern Sudan and kill the villagers. This message was passed on to the fighters [...] I could see they had satellite phones, cell phones, and hand held radios [...][11]

On 1 January 2009 fifteen to twenty men appeared from the bush and attacked locations near Maridi, several miles from the border, in the Western Equatoria state of southern Sudan. This account by a boy living in one of targeted villages was fairly typical of others collected by OHCHR between late 2008 and September 2009.

At 8 pm, a man with an AK-47 entered our tukul [house] and ordered us to remain seated. I saw that other men had surrounded the tukul. We were scared and decided to run away. The man inside the tukul shot my brother in the back as he tried to escape. I ran into the bush. I could hear my relatives screaming as they were attacked. The next morning I came out of my hide-out and found the bodies of my relatives. My uncle had been hacked to death and my sister-in-law had been cut into pieces. My aunty was still alive but had been stabbed with a bayonet [...][12]

During the same attack, another victim was assaulted with an axe and then pushed into a fire while still alive. Since the end of 2008, there have been confirmed LRA attacks on various Sudanese populations, including Azande, Baka, Mundu, Avokaya, Moru and Kakwa groups. The violence has been persistently brutal, with a large number of mutilations and abductions as well as killings. Some of those interviewed by OHCHR researchers after managing to escape described abuses similar to those that used to be reported in northern Uganda. Abducted people, including children, would be given heavy loads to carry, and those unable to do so would be beaten or murdered, usually with a machete. 'Whenever I made a small mistake,' one boy explained, 'I would receive thirty strikes with the flat part of a panga [machete].' There have also been reports of systematic rape. Whereas in northern Uganda there were tight restrictions on LRA combatants' access to women for sexual purposes, these appear to have been largely set aside. According to one woman who had escaped:

[...] at night the fighters used to tie the abducted men one to another, make them lie on the ground and cover them with a plastic sheet. They would then take all the women to the bush and rape us. They barely gave us any food and would beat us on a regular basis with sticks, the butts of the guns or their fists.[13]

In December 2009, OHCR reported that over 38,000 people had been displaced and more than eighty killed in these LRA attacks in Sudan. Meanwhile, across the border in the DRC, things were even worse. According to a report released in the same month by the Office of the High Commissioner for Human Rights (OCHR) and MONUC (the UN Mission in the DRC), the LRA had killed 1,200 and abducted 1,400, including 600 children, in a ten-month rampage. An estimated 230,000 people had been displaced.[14]

UN reports from both Sudan and DRC draw attention to the lack of protection afforded to afflicted populations by the armies that are supposedly there to perform that role.[15] With the official end of Operation Lightning Thunder in May 2009, an offensive code-named Rudia II was initiated from DRC, involving MONUC forces. But its capacity to engage the LRA in terrain they know well has proved to be lacking. In southern Sudan SPLA forces have rarely done any better. The Ugandan army and US advisers for AFRICOM are also still present, and AFRICOM staff claim that levels of attrition against the LRA have again intensified since the end of 2009. But the attacks continue.

Not surprisingly, the role of AFRICOM in Operation Lightning Thunder has been the focus of considerable criticism. Many analysts have complained that it just made the situation worse. It made a return to peace talks impossible and led to attacks on vulnerable civilians. AFRICOM officers have responded by claiming that the attack did not cause the atrocities or casualties; rather it 'diminished the rebel group's ability to abduct children who are forced to serve as fighters'.[16] The blame for the slaughter should be directed at the LRA, who butchered as they fled the Ugandan army. This is hardly an adequate explanation for the botched attack, however. In a statement to the US Congress, Senator Feingold, the chairman of the Subcommittee on African Affairs, made the following observations:

As we have seen too many times, offensive operations that are poorly designed and poorly carried out risk doing more harm than good, inflaming a situation rather than resolving it. Before launching any operation against the rebels, the regional militaries should have ensured that their plan had a high probability of success, anticipated contingencies, and made precautions to minimize dangers to civilians. It is widely known that when facing military offensives in the past, the LRA have quickly dispersed and committed retaliatory attacks against civilians [...]

Mr. President, to put it bluntly, I believe supporting viable and legitimate efforts to disarm and demobilize the LRA is exactly the kind of thing in which AFRICOM should be engaged. Of course, the key words there are viable and legitimate [...] In the case of this current operation against the LRA [...] I do not believe these conditions were met or the necessary due diligence undertaken before its launch.[17]

It also seems reasonable to ask what the US forces were hoping to achieve. When questioned about this, AFRICOM staff state that they were asked to provide assistance by the US ambassador in Uganda and the Ugandan government. But the Ugandan government has signed and ratified the Rome Statute of the International Criminal Court (ICC). The Ugandan army could therefore claim to be attempting to execute the ICC warrants for Joseph Kony and his remaining top commanders. But the USA is not a party to the Rome Treaty, and has generally been opposed to the ICC. So what would have happened if Kony had been captured, something that might still occur? Will the USA support a procedure whereby he is handed over for prosecution in The Hague? No answer has been provided. Perhaps the US position on the ICC is in flux under the new US administration of Barack Obama, and matters may become clearer in 2010. The LRA prosecutions were supposed to be the first cases for the ICC. Quick convictions were going to help establish the credibility of the institution. Those did not happen. But the ICC's link with Uganda and President Museveni has remained very important. In May and June 2010, Kampala will host the first Review Conference to consider amendments to the Rome Statute. On the agenda is the defining of the fourth crime over which the ICC will have jurisdiction, the waging of aggressive war. Unlike in the meeting in Rome, the USA will not have voting rights, because it is not a 'state party', but it will doubtless want to have some kind of voice in proceedings. It will be interesting to hear what representatives of President Obama have to say.

A topic that will doubtless be raised by civil society groups attending the meeting is the role that the ICC played in the Juba process. During those negotiations the government of Uganda was generally clear in the formulation of its goals. It aimed at bringing an end to the LRA conflict without too great a commitment to broad comprehensive solutions. It could be argued, however, that international attention, partly linked to the ICC intervention, pushed the government towards an acceptance that conditions in northern Uganda had to be improved. On the other hand, the threat of ICC prosecutions did little to focus the LRA agenda. Their delegation displayed unreliable negotiating behaviour, and at times buried sensible points under unreasonable claims. Kony himself was, to say the least, equivocal and inconsistent in his engagement. As

David Matsanga, the former delegation leader, has put it, 'Instructions from General Joseph Kony were often at times confusing and he kept on shifting the goal-posts [...] A golden opportunity was thus lost and it's doubtful that any nations of the world will in future pay for any other [LRA] peace talks.'[18] Many of those who were so committed to the peace talks would doubtless concur.

It would be superficial and misleading, however, to suppose that the Juba process collapsed simply because Kony did not really want a resolution. There were other aspects to what happened, some of which have far-reaching implications for future peace talks in central Africa and indeed everywhere else. The introduction of international justice procedures against LRA commanders, supported by the very same international community that also facilitated the peace talks, was not simply a contradiction. It had implications for both how the peace talks were run and how issues of justice were dealt with. Scholarly criticism tends to focus on the question of whether the threat of ICC prosecution acts as a disincentive or an incentive for perpetrators of terrible crimes to enter negotiations or change their behaviour. Whatever the case, it affects the manner in which peace talks are facilitated. The Juba process made clear that the representatives of states that are signatories of the Rome Statute, conciliation organizations, NGOs and UN agencies have not resolved the question of how to adequately support negotiations within the ICC framework. The Juba talks were the first attempt to do so. They failed. But the ICC framework is not going to go away. Hopefully some lessons have been learned.

Meanwhile, in early 2010, Kony remains at large, and UN security maps of south-west Sudan and neighbouring areas of DRC are dotted with indications of LRA attacks. Research in southern Sudan at the end of 2009 revealed that one of the most commonly cited threats to the Comprehensive Peace Agreement is continued insecurity associated with Kony's forces. He is even rumoured to have become a player in the Darfur conflict. LRA capacities are doubtless being exaggerated. But that is the point. The mysterious qualities of their leader are again being invoked. Those who met him during the peace talks found him rather awkward and unimpressive. His power does not arise from his skills in negotiation and certainly not from his ability to find compromises. He is now back in his element, and it would seem that he is running rings around multiple armies and their US advisers. He is not just surviving, he is skilfully terrorizing. Whatever one thinks about Joseph Kony, it is a remarkable achievement.

Notes

Introduction

1 Andrew Mwenda, 'Uganda should have right to invade neighbour DR Congo', *Independent*, 20 February 2009.

2 Quoted in Andrew Mwenda, 'Seven UPDF generals criticise Kony attack', *Independent*, 22 January 2009.

3 There is a rich literature on southern Sudan with many sources available online at www.sudan archive.net/. A good overview of the development in the region up to the CPA is D. H. Johnson (2003).

4 A research team led by Mareike Schomerus and Tim Allen carried out fieldwork during October and November 2009. Over 80 per cent of the 229 people interviewed in different parts of southern Sudan stated that they will vote for independence.

5 A helpful overview of Uganda's post-independence history, written from a southern Ugandan perspective, is Mutibwa (1992). There is no good political history of Tito Okello's government, nor an in-depth analysis of the war in Luwero.

6 The main sources on Alice Lakwena are Allen (1991b) and Behrend (1999a). There are also book-length manuscripts by Catherine Bond and Caroline Lamwaka, two of the journalists who covered events at the time. Hopefully they will at some point be made more widely available.

7 Sources on the LRA war include Allen (2006); Finnström (2003); Dolan (2005; now published as *Social Torture: The case of northern Uganda, 1986–2006*, Berghahn Books, 2009); Gersony (1997, at pdf.usaid.gov/pdf_docs/PNACC245.pdf); Bøås and Hatløy (2006, www.fafo.no/); and Allen and Schomerus (2006, pdf.usaid.gov/pdf_docs/PNADI241.pdf).

8 For an overview see Schomerus (2007).

9 Pax Christi, 'How ENLightning is the Thunder? Study on the Lord's Resistance Army in the border region of DR Congo, Sudan and Uganda', Utrecht, February 2009, p. 10.

10 For an analysis of these units, see ibid.

11 The final decision to enter the DRC was taken without involving the Congolese or Ugandan parliaments. Also MONUC and UN Mission in Sudan (UNMIS) were not informed beforehand.

12 For an analysis of the impact of Operation Lightning Thunder see Schomerus and Tumutegyereize (2009).

13 See *Africa Mining Intelligence*, 213, 28 October 2009.

1 The roots of LRA violence

1 I do not enter into the controversy over the pre-colonial socio-political structure that existed in the area that would come to be known as Acholiland. Given the loaded nature of the term 'chief', I will use the category 'lineage-based authorities' or simply 'elders' in order to include both elders – that is,

those men who hold authority due to seniority, and *rwodi* or 'chiefs' – that is, those men who hold authority due to their lineage and often to some sort of election or appointment. By doing so, however, I elide the important distinction, and tension, between the two groups. For recent contributions to this debate, see Allen (1991b); Atkinson (1999); Bchrcnd (1999a); and Finnström (2003: 61–71).

2 The Acholi had the highest rate of employment of all the peoples of Uganda, and were second only behind the Baganda in terms of their representation in the civil service (Gertzel 1974; Kasfir 1976; Leys 1967; Sathyamurthy 1986).

3 For more on the councils, see Mamdani (1976: 192–5) and Mitchell (1939).

4 The idea that the NRA, and Museveni in particular, were primarily motivated by anti-northern, and especially anti-Acholi, sentiment in launching their rebellion is an article of faith among many Acholi political leaders in Uganda and among those in the diaspora. This meshes with the idea of a Bahima/Tutsi conspiracy led by Museveni, the object of which is to re-create an empire across central Africa, and whose principal obstacle was the northern domination of the Ugandan state and army. For this position, see Nabudere (2003). For academic treatments, see Clark (2001: 269–71) and Jackson (2002). This theory has been hotly contested by NRA/M supporters (Museveni 1997; Amaza 1998: 23–38; Museveni 1986; Mutibwa 1992: 154–5; Ngoga 1998: 91–106); Gerard Prunier, 'Uganda, nearly a miracle', *Le Monde Diplomatique*, 1998.

5 For the importance of anti-northern sentiment in the mobiliza-tion of the Baganda peasantry, see Amaza (1998: 62); Finnström (2003: 108); Okuku (2002: 23); and Omara-Otunnu (1987: 176).

6 'NRA, Okello forces fight for Karuma Falls', *Weekly Focus*, 7 February 1986.

7 'Bazirio, [sic] forces evacuate Kitgum, Arua Towns', *Weekly Focus*, 11 March 1986.

8 'NRA completes liberation struggle', *Weekly Focus*, 27 March 1986.

9 'War gets rough in the North', *Weekly Focus*, 18 February 1986.

10 Confidential interviews, Gulu town, November 2005.

11 'Gulu: the legacy of war', *Financial Times*, 23 August 1986; 'NRA soldier goes on shooting spree', *Weekly Focus*, 18 April 1986.

12 'Four NRA killed in Kitgum', *Financial Times*, 8 July 1986.

13 'Insecurity grips Gulu, Kitgum', *Financial Times*, 14 August 1986.

14 'Rebels harass NRA', *Citizen*, August 1986; 'Thugs terrorise Gulu, Kitgum', *Financial Times*, 10 June 1986.

15 'NRA sweeps North', *New Vision*, 16 September 1986; 'Museveni explains situation in Northern Uganda', *Focus*, 27 February 1987.

16 For the idea of the NRA representing an external enemy, see Behrend (1999a: 23–6).

17 Confidential interviews in internment camps in Gulu District, March 2003; 'Govt. troops close Catholic mission in Northern Uganda', *Focus*, 5 December 1986; 'Horror in Gulu: a personal account', *Weekly Topic*, 25 February 1987.

18 'Gulu: the legacy of war', *Financial Times*, 23 August 1986.

19 See the communiqué released by the Uganda Goodwill

Mission after their trip to Sudan to consult with the UPDA in 'Allimadi is imposter', *New Vision*, 7 April 1987; 'Why Gulu-Kitgum rebels are fighting', *Weekly Topic*, 13 May 1987.

20 'Atrocities shake N. Uganda', *Citizen*, 5 September 1986; 'Amnesty complains of NRA atrocities', *Weekly Topic*, 4 November 1987; 'Violation of human rights: Govt.'s credibility is at stake', *Citizen*, 26 September 1986.

21 'Govt. troops intensify operations', *Focus*, 19 December 1986.

22 'People kill, burn rebels in the North', *Star*, 25 March 1987; 'N. Uganda: Okeny petitions Museveni', *Citizen*, 7 December 1988.

23 'Gulu witnessess brutality and atrocity', *Weekly Topic*, 2 December 1987.

24 In February, according to one account, there were ten major rebel groups; 'Horror in Gulu: a personal account', *Weekly Topic*, 25 February 1987.

25 'Northern rebels now turn against each other', *Focus*, 30 January 1987.

26 'Rebels launch attack on Gulu', *Focus*, 17 July 1987.

27 'Rebel Alice Lakwena sends warning to Mbale', *Focus*, 4 September 1987.

28 Tim Allen calls attention to the more general violence of the HSM (Allen 1991b: 373).

29 'Fighting continues in Lira and Apac', *New Vision*, 21 March 1987.

30 'Rebel Lakwena forces regroup for counterattack', *Focus*, 6 October 1987; 'Rebels from Lakwena-Otai meeting cause panic in Tororo town', *Focus*, 16 October 1987; 'Tororo people take up arms against Lakwena', *Weekly Topic*, 14 October 1987.

31 'Lakwena not a military threat', *New Vision*, 26 October 1987; 'Lakwena affair proved that people are the best soldiers', *Weekly Topic*, 3 February 1988; 'Foreign press meets Lakwena', *New Vision*, 26 October 1987; 'Interview with a rebel', *New Vision*, 26 October 1987; 'Lakwena attacks Magamaga', *New Vision*, 26 October 1987.

32 'Rebel Alice Lakwena sends warning to Mbale', *Focus*, 4 September 1987.

33 'Fighting continues in Lira and Apac', *New Vision*, 21 March 1987.

34 This is subject to much speculation; for the most comprehensive treatment, see Finnström (2006: 373).

35 'A footnote to Lakwena debacle', *Weekly Topic*, 27 January 1988.

36 'Was NRM taken for a ride in N. Uganda?', *Citizen*, 29 August 1988.

37 On negotiations between Kony's forces and the NRA in Gulu, see 'Holy Spirit talks continue', *New Vision*, 16 April 1988, and 'NRA, UPDA in final talks', *New Vision*, 11 April 1988.

38 'War problem of democracy', *Weekly Topic*, 9 September 1987.

39 'More rebels respond to amnesty', *Focus*, 12 January 1988; 'Anti-Lakwena dismissals hit Gulu', *Citizen*, 14 June 1989; 'Army, RCs relations deteriorate in Gulu', *Guide*, 10 May 1990.

40 'Holy Spirit smashed in Kitgum, Latek flees to Sudan', *New Vision*, 22 November 1988.

41 'Kony still in Kitgum', *New Vision*, 5 May 1991.

42 'Kony rallies OK, says Ssemogerere', *New Vision*, 16 April 1996; 'Kony rebels vow to take part in May elections', *Monitor*, 22 April 1996; 'Gulu in big panic: Kony fights for multipartyism', *New Vision*, 6 March

1996; 'Kony rebels hold political rallies', *Sunday Vision*, 14 April 1996.

43 'Kony rebels burn minister's Pajero', *New Vision*, 23 February 1994.

44 'LRA rebels to honour ceasefire – spokesman', *New Vision*, 28 April 1996.

45 'Gulu in big panic: Kony fights for multipartyism', *New Vision*, 6 March 1996; 'Kony rebels hold political rallies', *Sunday Vision*, 14 April 1996; 'Kony rallies OK, says Ssemogerere', *New Vision*, 16 April 1996; 'Kony rebels vow to take part in May elections', *Monitor*, 22 April 1996.

46 'Bloody "battle" at Koch Goma. Peace disrupted again', *Weekly Topic*, 9 March 1988; 'Otunnu to meet Kony in Sudan', *New Vision*, 28 July 1994.

2 Foreign aid and violent conflict

1 Author's interview with Keith Muhakanizi, deputy secretary to the Treasury, Uganda's ministry of finance, planning and economic development, Kampala.

2 Author's interview with Dr Ezra Suruma, current minister of finance (Kampala, 12 July 2003).

3 Informal chat with President Museveni (31 December 1999): he told me that 40 per cent of all the officers they were sending for training to Cuba would be returned because they were tested and found HIV positive and therefore not fit to go through the rigorous training.

4 In 1989, the first attempt to investigate the problem of ghost soldiers on the army register by the government caused officers at army headquarters to burn the entire Records Department offices at Republic House.

5 Author's interview with the current chief of military intelligence, Lt Col. James Mugira (1 February 2005).

6 Uganda became a CIA regional listening hub; the US government trained a Ugandan battalion in peacekeeping skills under the Rapid Africa Response Force programme; Uganda became a beneficiary of US$20 million per annum as 'non lethal weapons military aid'; the government was sure of US backing in international bodies such as the IMF, the World Bank and the UN; the US government began to provide the Ugandan military and security forces with satellite pictures revealing the position of the rebels and equipment to monitor rebel communications.

7 Report of the Commission of Inquiry into the purchase of junk MI24 helicopter gunships chaired by Lady Justice Julia Sebutinde, 2004.

8 'The bank, the president and the country', ITV documentary on the discussions between Museveni and Lynda Chalker on military spending, 1998.

9 Museveni interview on KFM (18 October 2004).

10 For a detailed case study of the depredations of Uganda's military and its corruption, see Tangri and Mwenda (2004).

11 Testimony of Colonel Noble Mayombo, Chief of Military Intelligence, before the Army High Command Committee investigation into the existence of ghost soldiers.

12 This information is taken from testimony by soldiers before the Army High Command Committee on the existence of ghost soldiers. When the *Monitor* newspaper began to serialize the report, government sought and got a permanent court injunction against the paper.

13 Final report of the High Command Committee.

14 These observations were often made by members of parliament

from the region. In a 2003 report to parliament, MPs from the northern region reported that there were no soldiers to defend the camps or fight the rebels. Those that they saw were physically emaciated. Professor Mahmoud Mamdani travelled to the Acholi region in 2004 to undertake an assessment and made similar observations to me.

15 'Ear to the ground', *Monitor*, 23 August 2006.

3 The spiritual order

1 Personal communication (Kampala, 5 April 2007).

2 'Mystic guerillas who deal in bloodshed', *Daily Telegraph*, 20 March 2004.

3 Also the September 2006 edition of the *Review of African Political Economy – ROAPE*, 110(33).

4 In this, this line of thinking is not totally new. It has been widely demonstrated how ethnicity, as another locally embedded social reality, can serve instrumental political and military goals (Lonsdale 1994; Welsh 1996). In her analysis of the conflicts in Liberia and Somalia, Duyvesteyn (2000), for example, analyses ethnicity as a functional tool with a political rationale. Similar analyses have already been undertaken for religion: it has, for example, been demonstrated how religion can play a legitimizing role, as in the 1994 Rwanda genocide (Longman 2005).

5 Interviews conducted in November/December 2005 and September/October 2006, with the generous help of Olyech Kitara and Tony Labol.

6 Kony has about fourteen spirits, which have names such as Juma Oris 'Oriska Debohr', Silly Silindi or Jim Brickey. It is important to emphasize that for people both within and outside the movement, it is the spirits rather than Joseph Kony who are the true agents of the rebellion – just as with Alice Lakwena's HSMF (see Behrend 1999a). Joseph Kony is nothing but the messenger ('laor'), who has no choice but to obey the spirits. Kony emphasizes the separation between the spirits and himself, for example by describing himself as a 'victim' of the spirits.

7 Author's interview with Father Carlos Rodriguez (14 December 2005) and various interviews with ex-commanders, 2005/06.

8 Author's interview with ex-controller S. (28 September 2006).

9 Ben Mergelsberg, 'Crossing boundaries. Experiences of returning "child soldiers"', draft report, 2005 (www.child-soldiers.org/document_get.php?id=1110).

10 Author's interview with ex-controller S. (28 September 2006).

11 These rules are similar to those of Alice Lakwena's HSMF. See Behrend (1999b) or Allen (1991b: 377–8).

12 Mergelsberg, 'Crossing boundaries'.

13 Author's interview with ex-commander J. (16 December 2005).

14 For example, 'As a controller, when you are in the front line, you kneel down, you make a cross, and you take soil, you hold it up and you say: "The power of the world and heaven belong to God", and then you throw it in front of you.' (Author's interview with ex-controller S., 27 September 2006).

15 'Because Kony said: God is standing in front of you, behind you and above you, so why take cover? God is protecting you! God has put you in the world, so why should you fear? If a bullet comes, God will catch it. If you do take cover, you will

be punished. For example, one boy was caught behind a big tree; but the bullet made a big circle, and hit the boy from the back! When you fear and you hide somewhere, the bullet is going to hit you where you hide. So people fear to hide! Instead you stand!' (Author's interview with an ex-commander, 3 October 2006). This rule was also used by Alice Lakwena's HSMF.

16 The order of the spirit Silly Silindi for LRA men not to marry Sudanese women on reaching Sudan can be seen as another pragmatic decision. 'Silly Silindi said "If you go to Sudan, see the beauty of my place, but do not touch anything! Do not even be eager to touch it!" Some boys tried, but they were killed in the battle as a punishment.' Author's interview with ex-commander A. (7 October 2006).

17 This 'new order' can also be seen as a sectarian enclave held together by a charismatic leader and with high costs of entry and exit – as analysed by Mary Douglas (1993).

18 Moo ya or shea nut oil is oil from the sacred shea butter tree. In Acholi culture, it is used to anoint the 'rwodi moo' or 'oil chiefs' who, for example, perform the 'Mato Oput' reconciliation ritual. The oil can be eaten in Acholi culture, but not in the LRA.

19 Author's interview, People's Voice for Peace (Gulu, 14 December 2005).

20 Ajwakas or 'won ngom' are healers or spirit mediums which offer sacrifices and prayers.

21 Author's interview with ex-commander T. (27 September 2006).

22 'Amuru' means 'boiling' and the spring has hot water.

23 Author's interview with ex-controller G. (8 October 2006).

24 Author's interview with ex-commander A. (18 December 2005).

25 The LRA also accuses the Catholic Church of organizing prayers against the LRA. On several occasions, they threatened to kill the Archbishop of Gulu diocese, and in 2003 the LRA ordered that all Catholic priests be killed. In June 2003, the LRA attacked a Catholic mission, killing nineteen people, and in May 2003 forty-five seminarians were abducted. See Allen (2006: 40–2).

26 Author's interview with former chief catechist Abonga Papa (1 October 2006).

27 A similar rationale can be seen with the RUF in Liberia (Richards 2005a: 131).

28 Author's interview, UPDF soldier (21 December 2005).

29 'Govt. plots spiritual war on LRA', *New Vision*, 18 July 2003.

30 'I did not tell the press that the UPDF was going to fight Kony using witchcraft', *New Vision*, 23 July 2003.

31 For example, the Ugandan ambassador to the USA, Edith Ssempala, in: 'Uganda's war with the devil', *The Chalcedon Report*, 23 May 2005, www.chalcedon.edu/articles/article.php?ArticleID=10.

32 Different sources in northern Uganda (religious, journalistic and governmental) claim that in 1993 a prayer rally was organized by high-level government representatives, in which religious leaders from different religious groups gathered for prayers on Odek mountain (where Kony received his spirits). After three days of praying, the religious leaders claimed not to be able to fight evil spirits.

33 E.g. 'The spirit could order you only to use four bullets. If you go there with five bullets, the fifth will be yours, meaning you will be shot! And we would win the war like

that. Because one bullet is able to shoot four people. [...] Rules changed when changing place. When we went to Sudan, we suddenly had many, many bullets: there we could use three magazines of bullets, but not four; and three mortars.' Author's interview with ex-commander A. (10 December 2005).

34 'When fighting and you come across a tree or an anthill, you make the sign of the cross and pray "Please respect me". People are superior to trees and anthills and therefore don't have to ask for mercy but merely respect' (Anonymous 2005: 5).

35 Author's interview with ex-commander C. (30 September 2006).

36 The only (minor) reference to spiritual affairs was made at one of the rebel assembly points, where the LRA requested forty rosaries from the monitoring team. According to the monitoring team, the rebels gathered every evening in smaller groups to hold prayers. (Author's interview with monitoring team officer, 13 April 2007).

37 This is nevertheless in strong contrast with earlier negotiations. For example, Allen notes that in the 1988 peace talks between the UPDA and Kony, attempts to negotiate with Kony's group 'proved impossible, since so many issues had to be referred back to the spirits' (Allen 1991b: 374). In the 1994 peace talks, symbolic cleansing with holy water of the government representatives took place, before the LRA would sit down to discussions with the government representatives. Also, at individual peace initiatives of, for example, Father Carlos Rodrigues during the second half of the nineties, sprinkling had to take place (interview with Father Carlos Rodrigues, 14 December 2005). During the

December 2004 peace talks with the LRA, there were introductory prayers from chief catechist Abonga Papa, but no longer did all the government (or media-) representatives have to be sprinkled individually.

4 An African hell

1 An earlier version of this chapter was published by *Politique Africaine* (Finnström 2008b), and the argument builds partly on material that appears in *Living with Bad Surroundings: War, history, and everyday moments in northern Uganda*, published by Duke University Press (Finnström 2008a). I thank Tim Allen, Koen Vlassenroot, Vincent Foucher and the anonymous reviewers for their critical input. Research in Uganda was endorsed by the Uganda National Council for Science and Technology, and financed by the Department of Research Cooperation of the Swedish International Development Cooperation Agency.

2 *The Times*, 28 June 2006.

3 Quoted by Reuters, 'Uganda resumes peace talks with LRA rebels in Sudan', 14 December 2006.

4 'Armed conflict in the heart of Africa: Sudan's regional war', *Le Monde Diplomatique*, 1 February 1997, mondediplo. com/1997/02/02sudan.

5 'Only one solution to ADF war', *New Vision*, 23 January 2000.

6 'Moving beyond "protected villages" in northern Uganda', www.idpproject.org, p. 11, accessed 6 September 2002.

7 Quoted, e.g., in 'ADF rebels are like hyenas – Museveni', *Daily Monitor*, 16 February 2000.

8 'The stories we must tell: Ugandan children and the atrocities of the Lord's Resistance Army', *Africa Today*, 1998, p. 82.

9 'Moving beyond "protected villages"', p. 13.

10 Women's Commission for Refugee Women and Children, 2001, www.womenscomission.org, p. 82, accessed 10 September 2002.

11 'Moving beyond "protected villages"', p. 9.

12 Letter to author from sixteen-year-old 'Tekkwo Olum' (7 September 2000).

13 Author's interview with 'Martha', an eighteen-year-old female student (Gulu town, 15 February 2000).

14 Quoted in 'Mao demands post-Juba talks implementation plan', *Daily Monitor*, 10 March 2008.

15 Author's interview with 'David', twenty-five-year-old (Gulu town, 30 April 2000).

16 Author's interview with 'Moses', a university student in his mid-twenties (Gulu town, 13 July 2002).

17 Author's interview with 'Peter', a university student in his mid-twenties (Gulu town, 13 July 2002).

18 Author's interview with 'James', a secondary school student in his early twenties (Gulu town, 13 July 2002).

19 Undated LRA letter, distributed locally in late December 1999, translated from the Acholi original.

20 See also Ehrenreich, 'The stories we must tell: Ugandan children and the atrocities of the Lord's Resistance Army', *Africa Today*, 1998, pp. 99–100.

21 International Crisis Group, 'Seizing the opportunity for peace', *Africa Report*, 124, 2007, www.icg.org, accessed 26 April 2007.

22 See Finnström (2008b), where this document is reproduced in its entirety.

23 Author's interview (Gulu town, 30 May 2000).

5 Chasing the Kony story

1 Sam Farmar, 'I will use the Ten Commandments to liberate Uganda', *The Times*, 28 June 2006.

2 Jeffrey Gettleman, 'The perfect weapon for the meanest wars', *New York Times*, 29 April 2007.

3 Having worked in the area for two decades, my academic supervisor Tim Allen of the London School of Economics (LSE) had been asked to conduct a study on the workings of the reintegration procedures for former LRA soldiers. I came along to help. See the outcome in Allen and Schomerus (2006).

4 Sorious Samura, 'Living with refugees – surviving Sudan', *Dispatches*, Channel 4/Insight News, 9 December 2004.

5 Janet Malcolm makes a valid point about the role of the first-person commentator in her excellent study of the relationship between journalists and their subject: 'The "I" character in journalism is almost pure invention [...] The journalistic "I" is an over-reliable narrator, a functionary to whom crucial tasks of narration and argument and tone have been entrusted, an ad-hoc creation, like the chorus of Greek tragedy. He is an emblematic figure, an embodiment of the idea of the dispassionate observer of life. Nevertheless [...] among journalists, there are those who have trouble sorting themselves out from the Supermen of their texts' (Malcolm 1983: 159–60). In time, this assessment would come to strongly resonate with me.

6 In the *Newsnight* piece, Farmar introduces the moment when Kony first appears as having finally man-

aged to meet the man 'he had been chasing for a year'.

7 Personal communication, 8 June 2006.

8 As a result of this set-up, the account of the meeting between Kony and Machar published in a Dutch paper and consequently the UK's *Sunday Telegraph* was the first newspaper report to come directly from the LRA camp (Koert Lindijer and Michael Hirst, 'First sight of rebel leader in 20 years as he tries to broker deal to end bloodshed in Uganda', *Sunday Telegraph*, 18 June 2006).

9 'Words almost failed me' is actually a bit of a euphemism when describing my reaction. In the course of the discussion about the script, I did engage in a shouting match with Farmar in the *Newsnight* open-plan office in which I called him an arsehole.

10 This echoes another bit of Wainaina's advice to the writer on Africa: 'establish early on that your liberalism is impeccable' (Wainaina 2005: 92).

11 Wainaina must be delighted about such a good student. He even took his advice that 'whichever angle you take, be sure to leave the strong impression that without your intervention and your important book, Africa is doomed' (Wainaina 2005: 92–3). Michela Wrong makes an interesting point about the journalistic pursuits of the 'youngster with the accent and confidence of the public-school-educated British male'. For Wrong, the arrogance of Western reporters interpreting events in Africa 'reaches dizzying levels'. For those who do not acquire any in-depth knowledge before writing about an incredibly complex conflict, writes Wrong, there remains only one approach: 'you deliver a manuscript that is all about you, with Africa as a picturesque backdrop to your macho derring-do' (Michela Wrong, 'A bumptious guide to book writing', *New Statesman*, 12 March 2007. In Farmar's *Times* article, he refers to himself (with various pronouns) thirty-seven times. Kony (either named or by use of pronouns) appears sixty times, including when possessive pronouns are used.

12 Sam Farmar, 'Uganda rebel leader breaks silence', BBC News Online/Newsnight, 28 June 2006.

13 I found out about *The Times* article in Nairobi airport, along with the revelation that Farmar had been on the BBC World Service to explain whether Kony's denial of atrocities was true. His activities broke his contractual obligations, and after formal communications with my production company, on 28 June he agreed not to publish the material further. The December 2006 issue of *Harper's* magazine, however, carried a transcript 'from an interview with Kony, conducted last June in Congo by Sam Farmar' in which all my questions are credited to Farmar (Sam Farmar, 'Interview: spirit in the bush', *Harper's*, December 2006). *Harper's* associate editor apologized to me and wrote that Farmar had in all communications with *Harper's* 'maintained that he had asked the questions presented in the transcript we published, which he approved before publication. We acted in good faith, relying on Farmar's previous credits with the *Times* and the BBC' (personal email, Christian Lorentzen to Mareike Schomerus, 17 December 2007). Farmar states that the oversight must have been *Harper's*.

14 Peter Barron, 'The Newsnight mission', BBC News Online/Newsnight, 23 January 2005.

15 An interesting dilemma when covering the LRA arises from the LRA-perpetuated mythology. As Vinci writes, the use of fear and the establishment of Kony as a spiritually powerful figure are among the LRA's strongest propaganda weapons. Yet scores of supposedly objective reporters, including Farmar, have happily perpetuated this LRA propaganda in order to underline their own courage. What was puzzling to me was the complete demystification of Kony that I experienced upon meeting him. In fact, a few years after the interview, an active LRA member said to me that the press exposure had been a mistake because, with it, the LRA had lost its strongest power, the fear that came from being the unknown. Solidifying the LRA image of the mystical rebel leader, rather than questioning it, makes the press complicit in using fear as a weapon of war, as Vinci points out: 'Making Kony a living, breathing human being in the eyes of the people would help […] It is no accident that few outsiders have met him. Bringing Kony into the light would help to end the perception that he is to be feared. This might be accomplished by […] providing simple documentary evidence of his existence, beyond the decade old pictures recycled in newspapers' (Vinci 2006: 97).

16 British Broadcasting Corporation, 2005.

17 This points to a broader problem in how discourse is established as media organizations use each other to prove their own credibility in a kind of what Irving Janis calls 'groupthink' or Stephen van Evera describes as 'non-self-evaluation'. This 'causes decision-makers to abandon their independence of mind and conform to the dominant view in the group', explains van Evera. 'As a result the dominant view is never carefully examined even if it is woefully flawed' (Stephen van Evera, 'Why states believe foolish ideas: non-self-evaluation by states and societies', *Security Studies Program*, 2002, pp. 1–46). *Harper's* had assumed that the BBC and *The Times* would not manipulate material, hence further publication seemed unproblematic. ARD did not dare to question the accuracy of BBC reporting. As a result, the LRA narrative has remained remarkably unchanged for decades.

18 Personal email, my translation.

19 I published an article about the interview in Germany's Weekly *Die Zeit* (Mareike Schomerus, 'Die Geissel seines Volkes [The scourge of his people]', *Die Zeit*, 13 July 2006).

20 Personal email, Peter Barron to Mareike Schomerus, 8 November 2006.

21 In March 2007, I received yet another call from *Newsnight*. Amnesty International, *Newsnight*'s commissioning editor said, had asked to enter the Kony piece for their journalism awards. She was furious when I declined again, calling me 'strange'. She simply could not understand what my objections might be.

22 One example is David Chappell, deputy managing editor of *The Times*. He reacted to criticism that *The Times* article had not covered the humanitarian catastrophe in the Ugandan displacement camps in the following way: 'The difference in views between you and Mr Farmar on the portrayal of the humanitarian conflict in Uganda is a matter of objectivity and perhaps arises from your different approaches – one more academic than the other.

Again that is opinion, not fact, and therefore not a matter for *The Times*' (personal email, David Chappell to Mereike (sic) Schomerus, 4 August 2006). It is an interesting point that, while stylistically subscribing to the personalized and subjective storytelling approach, it is still claimed that this is 'objective' news reporting. For Jeremy Paxman, the policy of forced displacement and the camps did not seem to be a problem at all, as he reiterated in his intro to the *Newsnight* report that 'Some two million people have fled to camps which are patrolled by the Ugandan army'.

23 Similar ethical issues of doing research in violent environments are discussed by Sudhir Venkatesh in his work on Chicago gangs (Venkatesh 2008).

24 The greater implications of this can be seen time and again in coverage of African issues. In 2010, *Newsnight* ran a controversial piece on witchcraft in Uganda, a highly political and complex subject, which also relied on the imagery of the 'first journalist' to interview the witch, along with other clichéd imagery. A heated discussion on the blog of the *London Review of Books* ensued and can be found at www.lrb.co.uk/blog/2010/01/12/adam-kuper/bizarre-rumours/. Along the same lines, US-based Vice TV produced a sensationalist video guide to Liberia (with very courageous reporter Shane Smith at the heart of darkness), using many of the same stereotypes, which caused great debate, yet also some major news coverage. An overview of the blogosphere debate can be found at shelbygrossman.com/2010/01/the-vice-debate/.

25 The LRA has always followed media coverage closely. The more one-sided it has been, the more defiant – and usually violent – they have been.

26 Santo Alit was reportedly killed by the UPDF in CAR in September 2009.

27 See the text of the interview in this volume. The other contributors to this volume – namely Finnström, Perrot and Branch – cover some of these ambiguities in dealing with the LRA in this book or in their other published work.

6 Interview with Joseph Kony

1 The interview was conducted by the author and recorded on video by cameraman Sam Farmar.

2 Kizza Besigye returned from exile in October 2005 to run against President Museveni in the 2006 elections. He was arrested shortly after his return to Uganda and accused of treason, concealment of treason and a case of rape. The treason charges were directly linked to accusations of his cooperation with the LRA. He was cleared of the rape charge and the Constitutional Court ruled that he could not be tried as a terrorist, although the treason accusations still stand. He won 37 per cent in the February 2006 elections, beaten by Museveni's 57 per cent. He contested the elections, which were found by the Supreme Court of Uganda to have been conducted with voter intimidation, violence and irregularities.

3 Will Ross, now covering West Africa for the BBC, said that Kony 'could be referring to a trip organized by the Ugandan army near the beginning of 2002. A group of journalists were driven into Sudan by the Ugandan military with the promise of seeing the "liberated" LRA camps/bases and witnessing progress in the fight against the LRA. We were told we would be there for a few

days. Our first stop was the Ugandan army base at Palotaka in Sudan but after about an hour or two there, we were suddenly ordered back on to the military vehicles and driven back to Uganda. It was difficult to know what was taking place but it was widely believed that at the time the Ugandan troops were being hit hard in the Imatong Mountains and perhaps the Ugandan authorities didn't want us to witness the real situation on the ground. It was a PR flop. So that could marry with Kony's comment that we were stopped from seeing what was happening in Sudan, but during that trip, there was no attempt to meet the LRA leadership so Kony's line, "He refuse Will Ross to come and meet us. He refuse Will Ross to come and get us", is not relevant. On the other hand I made many requests, via Sam Kolo and Vincent Otti, to make contact with Joseph Kony but they never got anywhere. There was a period when the LRA was keen to talk to the media, especially when Sam Kolo [the LRA's former main negotiator] was still in the bush. During that time the Ugandan authorities were clearly not happy that the BBC and other media outlets were broadcasting the LRA version of events.' (Personal email, Will Ross to Mareike Schomerus, 2 April 2008.)

4 Mukura is in what is now Kumi district. It is estimated that between sixty and one hundred people died in the train.

5 Mbara is located in western Uganda and is the home area of President Museveni.

6 The sound of my name and the nickname that followed from it may have had a deeper significance to Kony. In accounts of early LRA initiation rituals, LRA soldiers were told,

after having undergone symbolic ritual, that the ritual had 'loaded [them] with malaika', reminiscent of the blessing at the end of a Christian church service. See Behrend (1999a).

7 What the abductees say

1 See chrisblattman.com/sway for details of SWAY, including questionnaires, reports and ongoing activities.

2 These sub-counties are Acholibur, Akwang, Atanga, Kitgum Matidi, Orom, Pader, Pajule and Palabek.

3 The impacts of war and child soldiering on well-being are discussed in Annan (2007), Blattman and Annan (forthcoming) and Annan et al. (2006).

4 Households were randomly sampled from a 2002 United Nations census, and 95 per cent of these were successfully tracked down. (A possible concern is the disappearance of households between 1996 and the 2002 UN census. We estimate that fewer than 5 per cent of 1996 households disappeared in this manner as most households left some family members behind to collect food aid). Interviewers then developed a roster of youth present in the household in 1996 with the household head. The year 1996 was chosen as it pre-dated more than 90 per cent of abductions and was easily recalled as the time of the first election since 1980. Youth were sampled from this retrospective roster and, as half of survivors had migrated, were tracked across the country. Eighty-five per cent of surviving youth were successfully found. Among abducted youth, 20 per cent never returned from abduction (and are presumed perished), 3 per cent returned but have since died, and 7 per cent survived but could not be found, for a total attrition of

30 per cent. Demographic data on non-survivors and unfound migrants were collected from surviving family members. The potential bias arising from such attrition is discussed below.

5 In all, roughly 10 per cent of reported abductions appeared suspicious owing to discrepancies between the reports of the household head and the youth. For half of these discrepancies, either the abduction period was short (such as a single day) or the youth had left the household some years before, and so we are inclined to believe that the discrepancy is the result of the household head's error. In the other half of cases (fewer than 5 per cent of all abductees) the youth's report is sufficiently divergent from that of the parent that our suspicions are aroused, and it is possible that abductions are overstated by this amount. It is also possible, however, that parents sought to conceal abductions. Fortunately, the estimates of the impact of abduction presented in this chapter do not change materially when these youths are reclassified as 'non-abducted', and so are likely to create little bias.

6 This concern is an important one to some abductees. From one informant, 'The formerly abducted people I know who are here in Acholibur are about seventy-five [in number], but some people just claim they were abducted. Some of them were just taken from the garden and asked to direct the rebels for a distance of about six miles and then told to go back home. Such a person also claims he was abducted, but he has not reached the core that we have reached. Such a person, when asked, cannot tell you the sufferings we have gone through.'

7 See, for instance, Allen and Schomerus (2006). Allen argues that the number of children in the LRA is often exaggerated and that only a third of abductees were likely to be under eighteen (Allen 2005).

8 Data include absentee youth and youth who have since died or did not return from abduction (collected from the household survey). Multiple abductions are included. The proportion of the population abducted by age is calculated by dividing the number of youths abducted at each age in each year by the total number of youths in the population of that age in that year, and calculating the running-mean over all years via symmetric nearest-neighbour smoothing (bandwidth = 0.5).

9 Such self-reported acts of violence may be under-reported, of course. Based on in-depth follow-up interviews with a sub-sample of youth and their families, however, the general accuracy of these self-reports appears substantial. Moreover, when interviewees were asked what other recruits were forced to do, responses followed similar patterns and proportions. Finally, owing perhaps to the widespread abductions in northern Uganda, many of the atrocities committed are openly spoken about and admitted.

10 A current and comprehensive listing of the alternative explanations for child soldiering is provided by Wessells (2006).

11 For example, Shepler (2005) notes that in Sierra Leone children were useful as servants and aides to military officers.

12 See Andvig and Gates (2006), Wessells (2006) or Brett and Specht (2004) for a discussion.

13 E.g. Honwana (2006); Rosen (2005); Brett and Specht (2004);

Machel (1996); Cohn and Goodwin-Gill (1994); 'Children of war', *American Educator: The Professional Journal of the American Federation of Teachers*, 1984.

14 Lab-based psychological evidence from the USA is also sometimes used to bolster these claims. Andvig and Gates (2006), for example, point to evidence from developmental psychology that children have a greater tendency towards altruism and for bonding to a group.

15 For instance, one central African rebel commander quoted by ILO argued that the young 'are docile and can be manipulated', and 'they obey orders to the letter' (ILO 2003: 26).

16 Another source of potential bias could arise from the provision of selective incentives. Consider that, if adults are indeed systematically different from children, a rebel leader might offer adults different incentives to participate and perform. If so, cross-age comparisons would confuse real underlying differences between children and adults with the response to different incentive packages, thereby biasing the result. As we will see below, the evidence points to equally low levels of material incentives offered to both children and adults. The evidence on age-varying non-material incentives and tactics is mixed, however. Adults appear mildly more likely than children to report having been tied up and receiving political propaganda, while they are slightly less likely to be forced to commit gross acts of violence and to be threatened with harm. These differences are neither systematic nor large, however, and so significant bias seems unlikely.

17 The solid line represents the average length of abduction at a given age of abduction, and is calculated as a running mean with a bandwidth of 0.5 years of age. The dashed lines represent the 90 per cent confidence interval.

18 Significant at the 5 per cent level. This estimate comes from a linear regression (not displayed) of abduction length on abduction year and location indicators, as well as pre-war characteristics. In this instance the unit of observation is an individual abduction. Youth may have experienced more than one abduction.

19 The solid line is a running-mean calculated via symmetric nearest-neighbour smoothing with a bandwidth of 0.5. The dotted lines represent the 90 per cent confidence interval. Data include absentee and non-surviving youth, but exclude youth that did not return from abduction. Multiple abductions enter individually.

20 The decline of one third is observed in the data, but is not statistically significant at conventional levels.

21 The solid line is a running-mean calculated via symmetric nearest-neighbour smoothing with a bandwidth of 0.5. The dotted lines represent the 90 per cent confidence interval. Data do not include absentee or non-surviving youth, but are weighted by inverse sampling and attrition probabilities. Multiple abductions enter individually.

22 Adult abductees were also seen as untrustworthy. According to a former bodyguard to Kony, '[Kony] thinks old people can be used to send to go and kill him, and that it's not good for old people to be next to him because they might have bad [subversive] thoughts.' Another bodyguard who served Kony's family for eight years echoed such sentiments.

Adults, he explained, 'can escape any time, and [...] they will reveal their secrets to the government'. Several former abductees also mentioned that adults were feared as possible spies.

23 All results statistically significant at (at least) the 5 per cent level.

24 For instance, studies have suggested that susceptibility to peer influence peaks at age fourteen (Berndt 1979; Steinberg and Silverberg 1986), that adolescents project over shorter horizons and discount the future more than adults (Greene 1986; Nurmi 1991; Gardner and Hermann 1990; Halpern-Felsher and Cauffman 2001), that adolescents place less weight on risks than adults (Halpern-Felsher and Cauffman 2001; Furby and Beyth-Marom 1990), that impulsivity increases between middle adolescence and early adulthood (Greenberger 1982; Steinberg and Cauffman 1996), and that significant adolescent brain development occurs in regions associated with long-term planning, emotion regulation, impulse control and risk evaluation (Spear 2000; Dahl 2001; Giedd et al. 1999).

25 The peaking of gun possession and forced killing in early adolescence, as seen in Figures 7.8 and 7.9, is supported by the results of a linear regression of each dependent variable on a quadratic form of age (i.e. age and age-squared). The coefficients on age and age-squared suggest a peaking of these self-reported behaviours in mid-adolescence (roughly fourteen). These results are robust to the inclusion of potentially confounding factors as controls, including abduction length, year and location.

26 See also Kaplan, 'The coming anarchy', *Atlantic Monthly*, February 1994.

8 Between two worlds

1 Carter Johnson, 'Deliver us from Kony', *Christianity Today*, www.christianitytoday.com/ct/2006/january/18.30.html, accessed 16 May 2008.

2 Audio comment on CNN. com: www.cnn.com/interactive/world/0701/slideshow.audio.soldiers/frameset.exclude.html, accessed 16 May 2008.

3 All names have been changed.

4 This is the expression suggested by Allen and Schomerus (2006).

5 Author's interview with FAP (Pabbo IDP camp, 13 May 2005).

6 Author's interview with Abonga George (Pabbo IDP camp, 25 April 2005).

7 Author's interview with Owot Francis (Pabbo IDP camp, 13 May 2005).

8 Author's interview with Owot Francis (Pabbo IDP camp, 6 May 2005).

9 Author's interview with Owot Francis (Pabbo IDP camp, 7 July 2005).

10 'Live in the bush' is a common expression synonymous with 'life with the LRA'.

11 Author's interview with Abonga George (Pabbo IDP camp, 25 April 2005).

12 Author's interview with Owot Francis (Pabbo IDP camp, 6 May 2005).

13 Author's interview with Okello Simon (Pabbo IDP camp, 6 May 2005).

14 Control Alter: a unit within the LRA fulfilling many spiritual functions and with close relations with the LRA leadership (see Titeca, this volume).

15 Author's interview with Okello Simon (Pabbo IDP camp, 6 May 2005).

16 Girling (1960) translated the word 'ajwaka' as 'medicine women or herbalists'.

17 Author's interview with 'ajwaka' (Pabbo IDP camp, 12 July 2005).

18 Author's interview with Obonga George (Pabbo IDP camp, 12 July 2005).

19 Author's interview with Owot Francis (Pabbo IDP camp, 7 July 2005).

20 Ibid.

21 Author's interview with Okello Simon (Pabbo IDP camp, 6 May 2005).

22 Author's interview with Owot Francis (Pabbo IDP camp, 13 May 2005).

23 Author's interview with Ocan William (Pabbo IDP camp, 26 May 2005).

24 Author's interview with Ocan William (Pabbo IDP camp, 8 July 2005).

25 Author's interview with Owot Francis (Pabbo IDP camp, 8 July 2005).

26 Author's interview with Abonga George (Pabbo IDP camp, 13 May 2005).

27 Author's interview with Abonga George (Pabbo IDP camp, 14 July 2005).

28 NRA: National Resistance Army, later renamed UPDF.

29 Author's interview with Okello Simon (Pabbo IDP camp, 6 May 2005).

30 Ibid.

31 Author's interview with Abonga George (Pabbo IDP camp, 6 June 2005).

32 Author's interview with Owot Francis (Pabbo IDP camp, 25 April 2005).

33 Author's interview with FAP (Atiak IDP camp, 20 June 2005).

34 Author's interview with Owot Francis (Pabbo IDP camp, 27 April 2005).

35 Author's interview with Okello Simon (Pabbo IDP camp, 7 May 2005).

36 Author's interview with Owot Francis (Pabbo IDP camp, 7 July 2005).

37 Ibid.

38 Author's interview with Okello Simon (Pabbo IDP camp, 26 May 2005).

39 Author's interview with Ocan William (Pabbo IDP camp, 26 May 2005).

40 Author's interview with Owot Francis (Pabbo IDP camp, 26 May 2005).

41 Author's interview with Owot Francis (Pabbo IDP camp, 10 July 2005).

42 Gusco is a reception centre run by a local NGO in Gulu town.

43 Author's interview with Okello Simon (Pabbo IDP camp, 10 July 2005).

44 This is the process most of my informants underwent. It should be noted, however, that there might be many others who immediately return to their homes, for example. These people, by the very fact that the regular institutions have not registered them, are less likely to be encountered by researchers.

45 Author's interview with Ocan William (Pabbo IDP camp, 7 May 2005).

46 The informant is referring to the rule in the bush that if a wife is undergoing menstruation she has to separate from the group and no one is allowed to eat her cooked food.

47 Author's interview with Abonga George (Pabbo IDP camp, 7 May 2005).

48 Author's interview with Owot

Francis (Pabbo IDP camp, 13 May 2005).

49 Author's interview with Abonga George (Pabbo IDP camp, 25 April 2005).

50 Author's interview with Okello Simon (Pabbo IDP camp, 13 May 2005).

51 Ibid.

52 Author's interview with Owot Francis (Pabbo IDP camp, 22 May 2005).

53 Author's interview with Ocan William (Pabbo IDP camp, 22 May 2005).

54 Author's interview with Okello Simon (Pabbo IDP camp, 22 May 2005).

55 Author's interview with Owot Francis (Pabbo IDP camp, 8 May 2005).

56 Author's interview with mother of Owot Francis (Pabbo IDP camp, 7 May 2005).

57 Author's interview with Owot Francis (Pabbo IDP camp, 14 July 2005).

58 Author's interview with Owot Francis (Pabbo IDP camp, 6 June 2005).

59 Possible reasons were the violations of the rules the LRA has established for the civilians (such as not riding bicycles, for example), retaliation in the home area of a fighter who has escaped or just to 'hurt the government' as stated in the quote.

60 Tim Allen, personal communication.

61 Joe Mettimano, Child Protection Policy Adviser for World Vision, used this expression in the context of child soldiers in Sierra Leone in a show broadcast by *World Vision Report* (www.worldvision. org/worldvision/radio.nsf/stable/ wvradiostory_022104_joemettimano childsoldiers, accessed 16 May 2008).

62 Richard Lough and Euan

Denholm, 'Violence against women in northern Uganda' (news.amnesty. org/index/ENGAFR590012005, accessed 16 May 2008).

63 Author's interview with Owot Francis (Pabbo IDP camp, 8 July 2005).

64 Author's interview with old man (Pabbo IDP camp, 28 May 2005).

10 A 'forgotten conflict', again?

1 I am very grateful to Gerald Owachi and Jean-François Lisée for the thoughtful proofreading and for their judicious comments. I would like to thank also Mike Otim, James Otto, and other UN officials, government and donors' representatives who chose to remain anonymous in Kampala and northern Uganda for the time spent sharing their ideas with me. This chapter does not necessarily reflect their views.

2 'No soda in Gulu', *New Vision*, 20 December 2006.

3 For explanations on why the Ugandan conflict was 'forgotten' by the international community, see Perrot (2004).

4 'War in northern Uganda world's worst forgotten crisis: UN', Agence France Presse, 11 November 2003.

5 UNOCHA, *2004 Humanitarian Update, Uganda*, VI(VII), www. reliefweb.int/rw/rwb.nsf/.

6 More than 216 NGOs were registered in Gulu NGO Forum's list, fifty in Pader and more than a hundred in Kitgum in October 2005. Interviews with Gulu, Kitgum and Pader NGO forums' representatives, October 2005.

7 In 2006, Gulu walks were organized in over one hundred cities in fifteen countries and raised $500,000 (www.guluwalk.com/blog/, accessed 22 November 2007).

8 *Uganda Rising*'s narratives are told by the actor Kevin Spacey. It won awards in Canada, France, the USA and Norway (www.ugandarising.com/home.html).

9 John Pendergast is a former adviser to the US State Department and Director of African Affairs at the National Security Council. He is now co-chairing the Washington-based Enough project (www.enoughproject.org/node/12).

10 www.invisiblechildren.com/media/assets/file/online_media_kit.pdf. The controversy was raised because of images from the war in Sierra Leone included in the movie and presented as being of the northern insurgency.

11 I am grateful to Ayesha Nibbe for bringing this to my attention.

12 In 2009, Invisible Children, together with Resolve Uganda and the Enough project, initiated lobbying for a 'LRA Disarmament and Northern Uganda Recovery Act' in the US Congress. In October 2009, nearly 150 members of Congress had backed the initiative. See 'Resolve Uganda, persistence pays off for Arkansas activist as key Congressman cosponsors bill', 27 October 2009, available at www.resolveuganda.org/node/912, accessed 27 October 2009.

13 www.c-r.org/our-work/accord/northern-uganda/index.php, accessed 20 April 2008.

14 Roger Winter is also the former executive director of the US Committee on Refugees and has been appointed as the Special Representative of the Deputy Secretary of State for Sudan. He had been involved in the Sudanese conflict resolution process.

15 Phone interview with a USAID representative (13 March 2007).

16 www.channelresearch.com/dwnld/070705_USAID_Uganda_Final_Report.pdf., accessed 28 April 2008.

17 Many countries joined the Core Group later. The United States stepped in again in the first months of 2005, following Betty Bigombe's appeal for greater US involvement.

18 Sigurd Illing, the former head of the European delegation, had been one of the most vocal in criticizing the government military option in northern Uganda. He was followed by Danish representatives.

19 Significantly, in 2004 the Acholi Religious Leaders Peace Initiative (ARLPI) and their spokesperson, Bishop McCloud Baker Ochola, were awarded the prestigious Paul Carus Award for Outstanding Contributions to the Interreligious Movement and the Niwano Peace Prize. ARLPI is an ecumenical organization that was created in 1988. It has, since then, strongly advocated reconciliation, mediation, amnesty and human rights and facilitated contacts between the LRA and the government of Uganda's representatives.

20 See also Civil Society Organizations for Peace in Northern Uganda (CSOPNU) (2006). The CSOPNU report stated that the average mortality rate in Uganda was three times higher than in Iraq.

21 Interestingly, US Assistant Secretary of State for African affairs Jendayi Frazer, moved by her first visit to northern Uganda, urged a quick resolution of the conflict: 'We believe that the priority has to be peace. And so, as for the pursuit of that peace, we are quite open on how we achieve it. But that is the priority: to stop the war. And if the government of Uganda can come to some agreement with the LRA

that has to be the priority.' But a few days later, the State Department denied that this statement should be understood as a support for negotiations (J. Frazer, 'Engaging the Horn of Africa', 2006, www.state.gov/p/af/rls/rm/2006/68759.htm, accessed 17 January 2008).

22 R. Leitch, 'The Elephant in the sitting room', 2005, www.usmedicine.com/column.cfm?columnID=213&issueID=81, accessed 17 January 2008.

23 'The bag man for CNN', *Monitor*, 30 November 2005.

24 DfID had already cut budget support by £5 million in May 2005 to show its concern about the political developments in the regime. In total, the UK cut its aid by £20 million, followed by Norway and Ireland (£2 million), the Netherlands (£5 million) and Sweden (around £7 million) (DfID press release, 'UK cuts direct budget aid to Uganda by £15 million, withholds further £5 million', 20 December 2005).

25 In December 2005, while the UK had the presidency of the Security Council, a group of international NGOs (International Rescue Committee, Oxfam, Save the Children UK, Tearfund, World Vision UK) issued a briefing paper for MPs and peers on 'why should the UN Security Council act now on northern Uganda?' (see IRC, Oxfam, Save the Children UK, Tearfund, World Vision UK, 'Why should the UN Security Council act now in Northern Uganda?', press release, December 2005, www.fonu.org/images2/pdf%20files/N%20Uganda%20Why%20the%20UNSC%20note%20to%20MPs%20FINAL.pdf, accessed 28 April 2008).

26 Global Policy Forum, Uganda (www.globalpolicyforum.org), quoted by Uganda Conflict Action Network,

'The Bush administration and the Juba peace process: missing in action', 2006, www.ugandacan.org/USG_and_Juba_peace_process_brief.pdf, accessed 10 January 2008.

27 Phone interview with Allan Rock (28 February 2007).

28 See the debates between Tim Allen and Erin Baines on traditional and international justice.

29 Phone interviews with a US representative, spring 2007.

30 Allan Rock had delivered a letter in December 2005 to the British president of the Security Council. He presented it in January 2006 to be circulated as a Security Council document (Security Council 2006).

31 International Court of Justice, 'Armed activities on the territory of the Congo', press release, 19 December 2005, www.icj-cij.org/presscom/index.php?pr=995&pt=1&p1=6&p2=1, accessed 28 April 2008.

32 Author's unofficial interview with a top UN representative, New York, April 2007.

33 Uganda Permanent Mission to the United Nations, 'Situation of internally displaced persons in northern Uganda', annexe to the letter dated 13 December 2005 from the chargé d'affaires a.i. of the Permanent Mission of Uganda to the United Nations addressed to the president of the Security Council.

34 Ibid.

35 Author's interview with a UNOCHA representative, December 2006. See also N. L. Harbitz (Human Rights House) 'From iron fists to iron sheets', www.humanrightshouse.org/dllvis 5_print.asp?id=5098&noimages=0, accessed 24 April 2007.

36 www.securitycouncilreport.org/site/c.glKWLeMTIsG/b.1556445/k.9BBC/Update_Report_

No_5BRUgandaBR18_April_2006. htm, accessed 8 January 2008. The JMC was launched on 4 May 2006. It brings together the government, the Core Group, South Africa, the World Bank, the UN Humanitarian Coordinator and two representatives of civil society to provide advice to the government for the implementation of its original six-month action plan. The JMC didn't have unanimous support. 'Egeland and OCHA pushed to create a JMC. It is a nonsense. It is not effective. It's a window dressing in an effort to say they were doing something. But they never created anything,' confided a Canadian diplomat (phone interview, April 2007).

37 Uganda Permanent Mission to the United Nation, 'Situation of internally displaced persons in northern Uganda'.

38 Author's interviews, Kampala, June 2005, December 2006.

39 These words were used by different Western diplomats and UN representatives during our interviews. See also Douma and van Walraven (2000).

40 Author's interview with Raja Jandhyala, senior conflict and development adviser to the office of the Ugandan prime minister (Kampala, September 2005).

41 Written comment of a donor representative (Kampala, November 2007).

42 See the joint analysis conducted by the British High Commission and DfID, 'Conflict reduction strategy for Acholiland', 1999, updated by the 'Conflict analysis and strategy for Acholiland' in June 2003 (Ginifer 2006).

43 The opening of offices in Kampala was one of President Museveni's conditions for accepting Canada's participation in the JMC. Phone interview with Robert Fowler, former Canadian representative at the UN permanent mission (23 March 2007).

44 The southern Sudanese mediation itself was motivated by a need to strengthen the implementation of the CPA in the perspective of the referendum on the independence of southern Sudan expected for 2011.

45 Author's interview with a UN official (Kampala, December 2006).

46 Author's interview with a UN official (Gulu, December 2006).

47 These words were used by a UNOCHA official. As of October 2006, the UK committed up to £250,000 ($520,000), Norway NOK56.6 million ($1.2 million), Sweden SEK7 million ($1 million). See Government of Norway, press release, 24 October 2006, www.reliefweb. int/rw/rwb.nsf/db900sid/EVOD-6UWE2J?OpenDocument, accessed 17 March 2007; DfID, press release, 17 October 2005, www.dfid.gov.uk/ news/files/pressreleases/uganda-peace-deal.asp, accessed 17 March 2007. On 16 November 2006, in a rare declaration, US ambassador to Uganda Stephen Browning announced that the USA would provide '$90 million to address post-conflict challenges if the talks succeed'; see Uganda Conflict Action Network, 'The Bush administration and the Juba peace process'.

48 Unofficial report of the meeting, November 2006.

49 Phone interview with a UN official, December 2006.

50 Resolution 1663 (24 September 2006), in ambiguous terms, urged UNMIS to 'make full use of its current mandate and capabilities' vis-à-vis the LRA.

51 UN Service News quoted by the *New Vision* (4 December 2006). The Ugandan government had

refused to have a 'special envoy for northern Uganda' as was initially planned.

52 Phone interview with a European diplomat in the United Nations, May 2007.

53 The national IDP policy was signed under pressure from UNOCHA in 2004.

54 *Monitor*, 17 May 2007.

55 Jeffrey Gettleman and Eric Schmitt, 'US aided a failed plan to rout Ugandan rebels', *New York Times*, 6 February 2009, available at www.nytimes.com/2009/02/07/world/africa/07congo.html?pagewanted =1&_r=2&sq=uganda&st=cse&scp=2.

56 In October 2006, the International Development Committee, among others, clearly recognized before the House of Commons: 'We accept that the continuing conflict in northern Uganda is not the fault of the Government of Uganda. Nevertheless the Government of Uganda has responsibilities to its population in the north which hitherto it has failed to fulfil. [...] This is costing donors US$200 million per year – money which could make a huge development impact if the conflict was resolved and the resources were spent on post-war reconstruction and on resettling displaced people in their villages ' (House of Commons 2007).

57 In November 2007, the British international development secretary announced that the UK had even agreed to give £700 million in aid to Uganda in a ten-year development partnership (BBC News, 24 November 2007).

58 Economic Intelligence Unit, *Country Report, Uganda*, April 2009.

59 More surprisingly, the NRM won 80 per cent of all seats in the 2009 local government council elec-tions and by-elections, with a high score in northern Uganda probably explicable by restored security.

60 Even the proliferation of NGOs was used by the government to tighten its control on their activities in northern Uganda. In 2006, it promulgated an NGO Registration Act. Although this law aims at limiting the number of 'briefcase NGOs', it also constrains NGO to periodically renew their permit and to give an account of their activities.

61 Phone interview, March 2007.

62 Ugandan military intelligence units were deployed in CAR in August 2009 with the permission of the CAR government (Jack Kimball, 'Uganda hunts LRA rebels in Central African Republic', Reuters, 7 September 2009).

63 Finnström and Atkinson, 'Uganda peace talks: the realists in Juba, 19 September 2006, friendsforpeaceinafrica.org, accessed 20 April 2008.

64 Author's interview with Sister Mary Oker, head of the Gulu Amnesty Commission Office (17 October 2005).

65 See the International Displacement Monitoring Center's website, available at http://www.internal-displacement.org/idmc/website/countries.nsf%28http Envelopes%29/2439C2AC21E16365 C125719C004177C7?OpenDocument (accessed 18 April 2010).

66 A shortage of donations had forced WFP to cut rations given to the displaced people. Germany temporarily provided the lacking funds ($850,000) (*New Vision*, 4 June 2006). A DFID-UNDP £80 million three-year recovery programme, though, was launched in 2009.

67 The political roots of the conflict have been clearly expressed in

the Report to the Secretary-General pursuant to Resolutions 1653 (2006) and 1663 (2006). The report adds, however, that the opening of a national dialogue is reliant on the competence of the Ugandan state (UN Secretary-General 2005).

11 'The realists in Juba'?

1 Reported in Onyango Odongo, 'Facts about Joseph Kony' (unpublished typescript, 2007, pp. 37–43).

2 On the LRA in southern Sudan, see, for example, D. H. Johnson (2003); Schomerus (2007); Finnström (2008a: 84–91); and, for a broad regional account, Prunier (2004: 359–83).

3 'LRA days numbered', *New Vision*, 15 January 2002. This was in many respects a follow-up to the Nairobi Agreement of December 1999 between the governments of Uganda and Sudan to normalize relations between the two countries, with a subsequent implementation meeting in January 2001, both held under the auspices of the Carter Center.

4 'Soudan not in touch with Kony', *New Vision*, 4 February 2002.

5 To illustrate, between January 2002 and January 2006, the Ugandan government newspaper, *New Vision*, ran over sixty stories on the Sudan government's stance viv-à-vis the rebels, nearly equally divided between those indicating improved GoU–Sudan relations and those questioning or criticizing Khartoum for supporting the rebels. Schomerus (2007) presents evidence that the degree of Khartoum–LRA cooperation did in fact fluctuate markedly over time.

6 See 'Sudan clears UPDF on Kony', and accompanying editorial, 'A real breakthrough', *New Vision*, 14 March 2002. Reports from GoSS sources in March 2006 indicate that Khartoum's response was not always as positive as it appeared. UPDF activities inside Sudan required liaison with the Sudanese army. GoSS sources claim that when UPDF forces pursued the LRA inside Sudan, Khartoum soldiers who accompanied them often knew where the LRA were located, and would intentionally lead Ugandan troops in a different direction. In addition, reports widely circulated in Uganda indicate that the large number of UPDF 'ghost soldiers' virtually precluded the operation's military success. The actual number of troops located in the north available for the operation was evidently less than half of those supposedly available.

7 For historical accounts of the war, see, for example, Dolan (2000b); Working Paper no. 11, Refugee Law Project (2004); Branch (2007a, esp. ch. 2).

8 Statistics compiled from *New Vision* indicate that the UPDF reported killing more than 2,500 LRA fighters in 2003/04, during the height of Operation Iron Fist; during this time period, 252 attacks on civilians were attributed to the LRA, resulting in more than 1,500 civilian deaths – see Rogers, 'Statistical evaluation of the war in northern Uganda, 2003–2004' (University of South Carolina, 2006).

9 Interview, GoSS official (November 2006). The LRA claims 'roughly 20,000' UPDF troops in eastern Equatoria state alone – see Lord's Resistance Army (LRA) Peace Delegation, 'A synopsis on Uganda peace talks' (5 February 2007, p. 9).

10 The Sudanese government admitted in July 2003 that 'some Sudanese military officers' continued to give assistance to the LRA – see 'Sudanese

official explains Kony aid', *New Vision*, 13 July 2003, p. 5. Two years later, the ICG noted that: 'Since command and control in the [Sudanese] military is very tight, it is very unlikely that whatever resupply and sanctuary continues is unsanctioned by senior levels in Khartoum' (International Crisis Group 2005a: 4–5). Reported air drops of supplies to the LRA in September and December 2005 were widely attributed to members of the Sudanese military or government (confidential interview, March 2006), and GoSS president Kiir accused the Sudanese army of supporting the LRA in late February 2006 (which the army promptly denied the next day) – see 'Salva Kiir says Sudanese army supports Ugandan LRA', *Sudan Tribune*, 21 February 2006; 'Sudanese army says it has no connection with LRA rebels', *Sudan Tribune*, 22 February 2006. Schomerus states that 'Khartoum apparently did try to re-establish contact in March 2006, but the general consensus is that the relationship is over – the LRA is adamant that they are no longer supplied and do not want a relationship with Khartoum' (Schomerus 2007: 11).

11 John Garang provided his own list of concerns and challenges when he was sworn in as president of the new GoSS – see 'Address on inauguration of the Sudan Collegiate Presidency' (Khartoum, 9 July 2005), available at the website of the South Sudan Institute of Democracy and Peace (www.ssidp.org). The 7th International Sudan Studies Conference, held from 6 to 8 April 2006 in Bergen, Norway, included a wide range of panels and individual papers on issues and problems surrounding the implementation of the CPA a year after its signing.

12 See 'Garang ...', *New Vision*,

4 July 2005; 'Address on inauguration', cited above, which identified expulsion of the LRA as one of five immediate political and security concerns; and 'Garang warns Kony', *New Vision*, 30 July 2005. In his eulogy at Garang's funeral, his successor, Salva Kiir, publicly reiterated the same view, saying that the 'SPLA can't and won't tolerate the LRA presence in the South' – quoted in International Crisis Group (2005b: 8); this source also states that Kiir had told ICG staff in 2004/05 that it was an SPLA 'priority' to deal with the LRA.

13 A general history that places Kiir, Machar and Matiep in historical context is D. H. Johnson (2003); for a partisan account of the bloody split between Machar and Garang, see Nyaba (1997); and for a popular account that highlights that split, see Scroggins (2002). A brief profile of and interview with Matiep can be found in 'South Sudan unity is crucial to protect peace', *Sudan Tribune*, 15 January 2007.

14 Much of this paragraph is based on confidential interviews in Kampala and Gulu in early 2006. See also Schomerus (2007: 11), and the chapter by Simon Simonse et al. in this volume.

15 The 4,000 figure comes from GoSS sources, with some local governments where large numbers of LRA were based asserting that the number was higher (confidential interviews, February and March 2006); 4,000 was confirmed as a reasonable estimate by both GoSS and LRA sources in July 2006. This did not include the thousand or so LRA fighters in the eastern DRC or the unknown number then still in northern Uganda. Reports of what were basically mutual defence agreements were widespread, with

claims that this included LRA pacts with militias in Azande in western Equatoria, one of the three largest ethnic groups in southern Sudan. Again, see Schomerus (2007).

16 International Crisis Group (2006: 7); Onyango-Obbo, 'Panelist view: why Ugandan peace talks go nowhere', PostGlobal, Washington Post online, 12 February 2007, www.washingtonpost.com. See also a vehemently argued commentary against a UPDF presence in southern Sudan by Obargot Paabwola, 'Ugandan army should leave South Sudan', *Sudan Tribune*, 31 October 2006.

17 I was shown a copy of this agreement in early March 2006. The essence of these three main provisions was made widely public in Uganda in mid-May when GoSS president Kiir officially informed Museveni of the agreement and relayed a message from LRA leader Joseph Kony inviting the GoU to enter into GoSS-brokered peace talks in Juba ('Sudan VP gives Kony message to Museveni', *Monitor*, 15 May 2006). Included in the subsidiary clauses was a GoSS request to the LRA to reduce or cease attacks in northern Uganda and eastern DRC as well as southern Sudan, and the rebels responded positively in all. Very few LRA attacks were reported inside Uganda after February and March, and there were reports that LRA leader Joseph Kony had contacted his deputy in the DRC, Vincent Otti, stating specifically that Congolese civilians should be strictly left alone (confidential interview, April 2006).

18 Confidential interviews, March 2006. GoSS assurances to the LRA leaders about not supporting the ICC made it into the Ugandan press ('Sudan VP meets Kony rebels in Juba', *New Vision*, 8 June 2006),

where it was reported that 'Machar assured Kony they [the GoSS] did not mean to cooperate with the ICC'.

19 Deputy commander Vincent Otti's establishment of a base in Garamba forest in eastern DRC in September 2005, however much it might serve as an LRA refuge, does not seem a good base for continuing insurgency in north-central Uganda, given the distances involved and the borders to be navigated.

20 This was both a GoU argument for why the LRA joined in the talks, and the one most widely accepted by the international community – see International Crisis Group (2006: 7–8), which cites a GoU minister of defence briefing to the UN Security Council on 19 April 2006 claiming that the number of LRA fighters had been reduced from 5,000 (of whom 3,000 were armed) in 2002 to around only 400 (120–150 armed). The year before, in July 2005, army spokesman Lieutenant Colonel Shaban Bantazira claimed that 'the rebels had a command structure of brigades with about 8,000 fighters in 2002 before the inception of operation "iron fist", of whom only about 300 fighters are left' – see 'LRA remnants are mere criminals, says UPDF', *New Vision*, 19 July 2005. The ICG report casts doubt on these GoU numbers, citing 'numerous credible eyewitness reports' indicating much higher estimates, though still well below those indicated in n. 15 above.

21 The quotation comes from the chief prosecutor of the ICC in a press release dated 6 July 2006, just prior to the opening of the peace talks in Juba. He also wrote: 'The negotiations currently taking place are partially a result of pressure from the ICC arrest warrants' (available at www.icc-cpi.int/press/

pressreleases/164.html). Use of the term 'partially' makes this a reasonable position to take, unlike many later claims emphasizing the role of the warrants above all others. For example, in an October 2006 meeting in Washington with representatives of donor governments and NGOs operating in northern Uganda, Betty Bigombe (who had initially argued that early ICC involvement had severely undermined her 2004 attempts at peace talks) asserted that the ICC warrants were '80% of the reason' that the LRA were engaged in the peace talks. See also International Crisis Group (2006: 1), which emphasizes military pressure and the ICC warrants as crucial in bringing the LRA into negotiations. The Ocampo argument that the Juba talks were merely intended to buy time has been a favourite of the GoU and UPDF, not only with respect to Juba but earlier talks as well. In contrast, in the eleven-page, thirty-two-point statement by the LRA peace delegation in February 2007 explaining why they were not (then) returning to the Juba talks, the issue of the ICC warrants comes only on p. 7, as item 22.

22 See 'LRA's expulsion is the task of Sudan's army and SPLA-Salva Kiir', *Sudan Tribune*, 22 February 2006.

23 This was the way in which US officials in Uganda were first told of this development, as well as, it seems, the current US ambassador, just prior to his leaving Washington for Uganda. It would turn out that the US government would play little public role in the peace process until its very final stages, purportedly in part because President Museveni asked that it stay in the background.

24 See International Crisis Group (2006: 7) on the November 2005

Machar–LRA exchange. April 2006 information comes from 'South Sudan offers to mediate between Uganda, LRA rebels', *Sudan Tribune*, 21 April 2006.

25 See 'Mbabazi, Wamala in Sudan on Kony', *New Vision*, 2 May 2006; 'Hunt for rebel Kony to go regional', *Sunday Vision*, 7 May 2006; 'Museveni rules out talks with LRA', *New Vision*, 4 May 2006.

26 See 'Kony given Shs36m "to buy food"', *Monitor*, 23 May 2006, which first broke the story. It was picked up the next day in the *Sudan Tribune* ('South Sudan government gives Ugandan LRA rebels 20,000 dollars, and "I want peace", says Ugandan LRA rebel leader', 24 May 2006), and the day after that in *New Vision* ('Army doubts Kony peace offer', *New Vision*, 25 May 2006). See also transcripts from the video ('Exclusive: Inside Kony's camp – details now revealed', *Monitor*, 25 May 2006, and 'It's time for peace, says Machar – Riek Machar–Joseph Kony meeting', *Monitor*, 26 May 2006). An audio of the interview can be heard on the BBC website – see www.bbc.co.uk and search for 'Machar'. On the controversy surrounding the $20,000 GoSS gift to Kony, see 'SPLA cash gift to Kony angers govt.', *Sunday Monitor*, 28 May 2006; 'South Sudan gift to LRA Kony bothers Uganda', *Sudan Tribune*, 28 May 2006; and 'South Sudan's Salva Kiir defends aid to Ugandan rebels', *Sudan Tribune*, 30 May 2006.

27 See 'Sudan VP gives Kony message to Museveni', *Monitor*, 15 May 2006. While the article is accurate in its depiction of the three main provisions of the agreement, the indication that Kony was apprised of the provisions only earlier that month is not. The astute and well-

sourced journalist Charles Onyango-Obbo wrote in late June that Kiir had brought a tape of the Machar–Kony meeting and showed it to Museveni ('Kony is crazy; so why does Riek love him?', *Monitor*, 28 June 2006).

28 The first quotation comes from 'Uganda gives LRA's Kony ultimatum for talks', *Sudan Tribune*, 17 May 2006; the second from 'Breaking news: President Museveni offers Kony peace deal', *Monitor*, 17 May 2006.

29 The ICC announcement was reported by the BBC and repeated in 'Kony must be arrested – ICC', *New Vision*, 18 May 2006; the US position was reported the same day in 'US wants to capture Kony by end of year', *Monitor*, 18 May 2006; and the EU statement appeared in 'EU demands immediate arrest of Kony', *Monitor*, 22 May 2006. Two examples of the doubts noted above, shared by many, can be found in 'Museveni's offer to LRA's Kony sparks new concerns', *Sudan Tribune*, 21 May 2006, and an opinion piece by Godfrey Ayoo Elum, 'Govt. has surrendered another chance to peace in the north', *Monitor*, 22 May 2006.

30 'M7 woos US', *New Vision*, 30 May 2006; 'Kony talks set for Juba', *New Vision*, 31 May 2006.

31 For a sampling of negative stories see 'Interpol starts hunt for Kony', *Monitor*, 3 June 2006; 'No amnesty for Kony, says Amama', *New Vision*, 9 June 2006; 'Sudan agrees to arrest Kony', *Monitor*, 12 June 2006; 'Otafire opposes LRA peace talks', *Monitor*, 26 June 2006. Museveni's statement that the GoU would not send a delegation to Juba is in 'Govt. will not talk to Kony', *New Vision*, 14 June 2006; his threat to 'track down' the LRA is in 'Museveni wants to hunt LRA in Congo', *New Vision*, 19 June 2006.

32 This was announced in 'Rugunda [head of the Ugandan negotiating team] heads to Juba', *New Vision*, 28 June 2006; 'President now sends team to Juba', *Monitor*, 29 June 2006.

33 Ojul's comment is quoted in the *New Vision*'s announcement of the opening of the talks – see 'LRA talks begin in Juba', *New Vision*, 15 July 2006. Sverker Finnström and I were among those arguing that the Juba talks were the best chance to end the war since at least 1994 and perhaps since its beginning in 1986 – see 'Uganda's moment for peace', *International Herald Tribune*, 10 August 2006.

34 Quoted in 'More challenges after cessation', *New Vision*, 27 August 2006. Multiple articles nearly every day over July and August in both the *Monitor* and *New Vision* convey the advances and retreats in the talks, as do numerous other accounts in international media, articles and reports.

35 Again, see numerous articles from the *Monitor*, *New Vision* and *Sudan Tribune* during July and August.

36 Schomerus (2007: 18) notes at least one attack on the LRA by UPDF helicopter gunships, officially confirmed by the UPDF, SPLA, LRA, UN and CoH monitoring team, but denied in UPDF press statements.

37 The amended CoH text can be found in 'The new LRA–Uganda truce', *New Vision*, 2 November 2005; announcement of the CoH's extension is in 'LRA truce extended for 2 months', *New Vision*, 17 December 2006.

38 'Al-Bashir wants Ugandan rebels out of Sudan', *Sudan Tribune*, 11 January 2007.

39 See 'LRA refuse to renew ceasefire agreement', *Monitor*, 23 February 2007; 'LRA wants talks in Kenya', *Sunday Vision*, 14 January 2007; 'Juba: LRA best option', *Sunday Vision*, 14 January 2007.

40 Members of the rebel delegation had earlier discussed several of these same issues in a series of meetings with me in Juba in November 2006, and had also raised them with GoSS officials (with, the delegates felt, little result).

41 The first indication of Machar's position on this came after just four days of talks, and then a week later while the talks were on recess following a GoU walkout. In *New Vision* ('Juba peace talks to resume next Monday', 25 July 2006), Machar claimed substantial progress in the talks, which were to resume the next Monday (31 July). He then indicated that the delegates had discussed three of the five agreed-upon agenda items, including comprehensive solutions, implying that very early brief and preliminary discussion on such a large, complicated and contentious issue had been sufficient.

42 The insecurity of Owiny ki-Bul for LRA fighters is made starkly clear in a front-page graphic on the 16 November 2006 front page of *Monitor*, which shows UPDF bases surrounding the designated assembly site.

43 'Juba talks to resume April 13', *New Vision*, 23 March 2007.

44 The 11 April Pax Christi press release was reported on the Uganda-CAN website the day it was released; the story was reported in the Uganda press the next day ('Gen. Saleh meets Kony team', *Monitor*, 12 April 2007). Again, see also the chapter by Simonse et al., this volume.

45 See 'Govt., LRA talks under-

way', *Sunday Monitor*, 15 April 2007; 'LRA rebels, govt. sign new truce', *Monitor*, 16 April 2007. It had been earlier reported that South Africa, Kenya and Mozambique would be joining the mediation team, and that their inclusion 'was a major condition the LRA set before they return to the negotiating table' ('South Africa, Kenya join Juba peace talks', *Monitor*, 3 April 2007).

46 'Govt., LRA sign second agreement', *Monitor*, 3 May 2007; 'Govt., LRA rebels sign new pact', *Sunday Vision*, 6 May 2007.

47 The phrase comes from Finnström and Atkinson, 'Uganda peace talks – the realists in Juba', *Sudan Tribune*, 19 September 2006.

48 For an analysis of the 'failure' of the Juba talks from the perspective of two members of the early LRA delegation, see Obonyo Olweny and Otim Okullo, 'The reasons Juba peace talks failed and proposal on the way forward for resolving the LRA conflict in Central Africa' (Nairobi, February 2009).

12 NGO involvement in Juba

1 On 1 January 2007, Pax Christi Netherlands merged with the Interchurch Peace Council (IKV) to become IKV Pax Christi. In this chapter the name Pax Christi Netherlands is used when relating to events occurring before 2007.

2 The World Bank report on 'Civil society and peacebuilding' distinguishes 'Seven civil society functions in peacebuilding': protection, monitoring/early warning, advocacy/public communication, socialization, social cohesion, intermediation/facilitation, and service provision (World Bank 2006b: 12).

3 In his statement on the website of Conciliation Resources Dr Obita

admits that after receiving President Museveni's letter, he also contacted the Carter Center as a third party (www.c-r.org/our-work/accord/northern-uganda/peace-efforts-1996-98.php). The Carter Center started its mediation in August 1999 with a meeting between the Sudanese and Ugandan governments.

4 There had actually been several initiatives, among which the following: in March and April 2003, peace talks took place between the LRA and a Presidential Peace Team. A partial ceasefire was agreed upon, but the agreement was constantly violated. Real negotiations did not get off the ground. Bigombe II consisted of on-and-off talks from November 2004 until October 2005, when the ICC warrants made Bigombe's mediation efforts impossible. The ICC had had the sealed warrants ready from 8 July 2005 onwards, and there is some evidence that the public announcements had been adjourned until 13 October 2005 to give the Bigombe II initiative a chance.

5 Natsios (2003: 340) mentions precisely this diffusion of power centres in many post-Cold War conflicts as an important reason to have NGOs involved in conflict resolution.

6 Sant'Egidio connected with Dr Obita during the Kacoke Madit meeting of April 1997 in London after they had been contacted by the Italian headmistress of the Aboke Girls Secondary School, 137 of whose pupils had been abducted by the LRA (De Temmerman 2001). The Swiss government is a good friend of the GoSS and offered its diplomatic services as an intermediary between the mediation team and the ICC.

7 The Juba talks had five agenda items: 1: Cessation of hostilities; 2 Comprehensive solutions to address the root causes of the conflict; 3: Reconciliation and accountability; 4: Permanent ceasefire; 5: Disarmament, demobilization and reintegration.

8 Despite the details of the agreements, much was left to the implementation protocols. These needed extensive consultations. This process, which included haggling about resources, added several months to the Juba peace process from the end of June 2007 until the end of January 2008.

9 This is not always the case, however. Southern Sudan's SPLA was not interested in NGO mediation at all, because that might have undermined its claim to the same status as the (northern) government of Sudan. In the peace process that had ended the first Sudanese War (1955–72), on the other hand, the Sudan Council of Churches had been the primary mediator.

13 Bitter roots

1 Importantly, several alleged crimes were perpetrated in northern Uganda after July 2002, when the International Criminal Court's statute came into force. The court cannot prosecute crimes committed before that date.

2 For a detailed discussion of the ICC's intervention in Uganda, see Allen (2006). An earlier version of this chapter appeared in *Politique africaine*, 107, October 2007, pp. 147–66.

3 One of the best critical pieces on the ICC intervention in Uganda is Branch (2004).

4 A succinct presentation of a similar argument is Dowden (2007). For a response, see Allen (2007a).

5 The contrast between African restorative justice and 'Western' punitive justice is drawn in many pub-

lications. See, for example, Lamony (2007) (www.iccnow.org/), or, for a balanced view, Baines (2007). The distinction was also highlighted in press briefings and reports on the July 2007 Agreement on Accountability. For instance, the government's team leader in the peace talks, Internal Affairs Minister Ruhakana Rugunda, compared the national code, deemed punitive, with *mato oput*, which he considered as 'restorative [and] hence promot[ing] reconciliation'. See IRIN, 'Uganda : penal code to incorporate traditional justice system', 5 July 2007. A very thoughtful discussion of the alleged dichotomy between restorative and retributive justice in northern Uganda and elsewhere is Hovil and Quinn (2005) (www.refugee lawproject.org).

6 ICC Rome Statute Preamble, Articles 1, 53, 54, 55, 61, 65, 67 and 68.

7 Allegations that the Ugandan army played a major role in forced population displacement mostly relate to events before 2002, when the ICC statute came into force. They are, however, likely to be raised in court proceedings.

8 Rwot David Acana made this comment at a discussion that took place at his home in Gulu during September 2008. It was directed at the author in relation to an earlier version of this chapter, published in *Politique africaine*. It should be added that this was a frank exchange of views, not an acrimonious argument. Also, as noted at the end of the chapter, the chief's own views about traditional justice have now become much more moderate than those of other enthusiasts.

9 According to the Ugandan government-owned *New Vision* newspaper, 'The Government plans to ask

[the ICC] to drop the charges against the rebel commanders for war crimes and crimes against humanity once a peace agreement is signed and an alternative justice system agreed' ('LRA accept responsibility for war crimes', *New Vision*, 22 June 2007). A case proposing that the ICC warrants can be set aside on complementarity grounds if traditional accountability mechanisms are incorporated into Ugandan law is set out in the 'LRA/M Position Paper on Accountability and Reconciliation in Relation to the ICC Indictment', 20 June 2007 (www.acholinet.com/).

10 He did so at a meeting held at the offices of Conciliation Resources in London on 11 December 2008.

11 In November 2004, I interviewed retired bishop Baker Ochola. He suspected that I must have a formal connection with the ICC and could barely contain his anger. He lectured me for over an hour about what he saw as local understandings and accused the ICC of trying to make a name for itself out of the suffering of his people – and, indeed, his own suffering: his wife had been killed by an LRA landmine.

12 The quotes are from an interview in May 2005 with James Otto, the head of Human Rights Focus, an organization based in Gulu town.

13 One of the main donors supporting the setting up of a council of traditional chiefs was the Belgian government, in spite of the fact that it had also funded the highly critical Acord assessment. USAID, the Dutch government, the United National Development Programme and several international non-governmental organizations also provided funding. For a good example of the donors' approach, see 'Remarks by Ambassador Sigurd Illing, head of the

European Commission delegation to Uganda at the anniversary of coronation of David Acana II, Paramount Chief, 4 February 2006' (www.deluga. cec.eu.int/en/speeches/Speech_ Coronation_Acholi.doc).

14 Odama is the chairman of the Acholi Religious Leaders Peace Initiative. See his 'Reconciliation process (mato oput) among the Acholi tribe in northern Uganda. A commemorative address made during the ceremony for the 21st Niwano Peace Prize award in Japan' (www.npf.or.jp/).

15 For some positive views about *mato oput* and Acholi reconciliation rituals, see Afako (2002) (www.c-r. org/); and Lomo and Hovil (2004) (www.refugeelawproject.org/).

16 A good example of the kind of approach they promoted is presented in Hansen (2008) (www.geppa.dk/).

17 'Atrocity victims in Uganda choose to forgive', *New York Times*, 18 April 2005.

18 This incident and two other cases involving people who had returned from the LRA were mentioned at a meeting organized in Gulu in June 2005. See Ker Kwaro Acholi and Nupi, 'Report on Acholi youth and chiefs addressing practices of the Acholi culture of reconciliation', Gulu, 3–5 June 2005.

19 During 2004, intermittent communications with the LRA commanders developed into more promising talks with the Ugandan government and Kolo was the main LRA spokesperson. The talks broke down in early 2005, however, and Kolo, who had been offered amnesty and (improperly) immunity from the ICC legal process, surrendered on 16 February. No arrest warrant has been issued for him, and he has been living in Gulu town under Ugandan

army protection. The interview referred to in the text took place in Gulu in March 2005.

20 My own findings were initially circulated in Allen (2005). They were largely corroborated by International Center for Transitional Justice and Human Rights Center (2005) (www.hrcberkeley.org). In that questionnaire-based study, over 2,500 randomly selected adults in Gulu, Pader and Kitgum Districts were asked: 'What is justice?' The most common responses were 'compensation' (8 per cent), 'assistance to victims' (10 per cent), 'truth and fairness' (11 per cent), 'reconciliation' (18 per cent) and 'trials' (31 per cent). Just 7 percent of respondents explicitly mentioned 'traditional justice'. A follow-up study was carried out in 2007, based on interviews with 2,875 people. When asked which mechanisms would be most appropriate to deal with those LRA and UPDF responsible for violations of human rights, equal numbers mentioned the ICC (29 per cent) and the Ugandan national court system (28 per cent). Twenty per cent said the amnesty commission. Only 3 per cent mentioned traditional ceremonies (International Center for Transitional Justice and Human Rights Center 2007) (www. hrcberkeley.org). Interestingly, even the local field research supported by the Liu Institute in collaboration with Ker Kwaro Acholi was unable to find much evidence that *mato oput* was an effective means of reintegrating LRA combatants: 'The majority of respondents argued that Mato Oput could not be adapted straightforwardly to play a role in realizing justice in the current circumstances' (Baines 2005) (www.ligi.ubc.ca/).

21 Both these reports, written by

researchers close to the council of traditional chiefs and Acholi religious leaders, recognize the limitations of *mato oput*, and present a range of other rituals that might be used.

22 I lived and researched in the region from 1982 to 1984, and from 1987 to 1991. I returned to the area in 2004 at the request of Save the Children, initially to explore the possibility that the ICC intervention would jeopardize children who have been abducted by the LRA.

23 Not all historians would agree with this. Some have used oral accounts to trace a proto-Acholi ethnic identity back in time, notably Atkinson (1999). For a critical review of this work, see Allen (1994).

24 Not all of these were effective. There were frequent efforts, for example, to set limits to bride-price payments in marriage disputes. But these were persistently ignored.

25 For a discussion of these issues, see Last and Chavanduka (1986).

26 See also the reports produced by Penal Reform International (www. penalreform.oeg).

27 For a detailed discussion of this hybrid aspect of the *gacaca* courts, see Clark (2007).

28 As M. Bradbury pointed out, 'The traditional ritual practices of elders seem to be being pitched against the rituals of Kony. Perhaps the battle is not just for the hearts and minds of the Acholi, but also for the soul' (Bradbury 1999: 29).

29 The ICC statute does not empower the prosecutor to withdraw warrants. As explained at the start of the chapter, the warrants can be suspended on an annual basis by the UN Security Council, or the jurisdiction of the court can be challenged in a meeting of the court's pre-trial chamber on complementarity grounds (i.e. it could theoretically be argued that the prosecution by the ICC is not necessary, because the crimes will be adequately dealt with by the national judiciary). A case might additionally be made in the pre-trial chamber that prosecution would not be 'in the interests of victims' or 'in the interests of justice', but it is hard to see how a convincing case could be constructed.

30 ICC Statute, Preamble and Articles 1, 53, 54, 55, 61, 65, 67 and 68.

31 LRA Delegation to the Juba Talks (2006); 'LRA accept responsibility for war crimes', *New Vision*, 22 June 2007.

32 This was in response to questions posed by the author at a meeting in London in December 2008. Interestingly, Judge Ogoola took pains to emphasize that, in his view, the special division of the High Court should be a form of 'supplementary' rather than 'complementary' justice. The implication seemed to be that it should be thought of as a kind of 'add-on' for those who needed it, rather than something that was a full partner or component of the formal legal system. He additionally seemed to suggest that the new arrangements would have to replicate in most respects the key components of the ICC prosecution process to be credible. The LRA senior commanders might go through some form of traditional justice, but they would have to be tried in a more conventional court of law as well. The more he spoke, the harder it was to see why Joseph Kony and others would choose to submit to such procedures, rather than go to the ICC in The Hague (where, among other benefits, there would be no threat of a death penalty).

33 The Clinton administration was initially supportive of the idea of a permanent international criminal court, but became concerned that warrants might be issued for US citizens. The US government did sign the treaty, but did not ratify it. The Bush administration was openly hostile. President Bush stated that he would 'unsign' the treaty, and countries that ratified have been required (under the threat of losing US development aid and military assistance) to sign bilateral arrangements with the USA, stating that they would not support the prosecution of US citizens. The US attitude to the ICC has contrasted with its support for the other, regionally and temporally restricted, international courts and tribunals.

34 In September 2008 the book's editors interviewed numerous cultural and religious leaders about *mato oput* to see how things had changed since 2004/05. Attitudes varied from the retired Anglican bishop Baker Ochola, who continues to promote the idea that a big *mato oput* ritual is essential to cleanse the past, to the chief of Joseph Kony's clan, who wanted *mato oput* to be performed by the paramount chief and compensation paid by aid donors, to other *rwodi* (traditional chiefs) who thought it should be performed by Kony's clan and that they should pay compensation to everyone else. Some thought the rituals had to be performed by each clan elder, others at larger meetings. Another view was that of a well-known proponent of traditional Acholi ways who lives in Kitgum, and who advised Dennis Pain, when he was writing his influential *Bending of the Spears* report. Her view was that the real *mato oput* can be performed

only by one particular lineage that lives a few miles from Kitgum town.

35 M. Bradley warned of this back in 1999: 'Celebrating Acholi culture and identity expresses Acholi separateness or difference from the rest of Uganda, and holds the danger of reformulating the war as an internal, intra-Acholi conflict' (Bradbury 1999: 20).

14 The ICC investigation

1 'Recognizing that such grave crimes threaten the peace, security and well-being of the world' (Rome Statute, Preamble).

2 SC Res. 808, UN SCOR, 48th Sess., 3175th mtg, at 1 UN Doc. S/RES/808 (22 February 1993).

3 See Report of the Secretary General (S/25704), at paras 10 and 26.

4 See UN Doc. S/1994/1007 (29 August 1994).

5 SC Res. 1315, UN SCOR, 4186th mtg, UN Doc. S/RES/1315 (2000).

6 Preamble, para. 3.

7 The issue of whether international criminal justice actually deters crime is contested. There is little empirical evidence to support this belief and some criminal behavioural psychologists state that for criminal justice systems to deter, it is necessary that the system has the ability to impose liability and punishments. For an overview, see Zolo (2004: 73); Von Hirsch et al. (1999); Robinson and Darley (2004). For authors who expound the belief that international criminal law deters crime, see Akhavan (2001); Williams and Scharf (2002: 21–2).

8 'Report by UN High-Level Panel on Threats, Challenges and Change. Follow-up to the outcome of the Millennium Summit', UN General Assembly, A/59/65, 2 December 2004, p. 35; Garapon (2004: 716).

9 'Building a future on peace and justice', speech of Luis Moreno-Ocampo, Nuremberg Conference, 27 June 2007.

10 International Covenant of Civil and Political Rights (Article 2), Convention Against Torture (Articles 4, 5 and 7), American Convention on Human Rights (Article 1), Inter-American Convention on Forced Disappearance of Persons (Article 1), Inter-American Convention to Prevent and Punish Torture (Article 1). See also non-treaty human rights standards such as the Declaration on Protection of All Persons from Enforced Disappearance, GA Res. 47/133, 18 December 1992, and the Principles of the Effective Prevention and Investigation of Extra-Legal, Arbitrary and Summary Executions, ECOSOC Res. 1989/65, 24 May 1989; Principles of international cooperation in the detection, arrest, extradition and punishment of persons guilty of war crimes and crimes against humanity, G.A. Res. 3074 (XXVIII), 3 December 1973. See Pejic (2008: 28).

11 While in the early 1990s the UN was involved in negotiating broad amnesties in El Salvador, Haiti and Guatemala, the international community has become increasingly reluctant to grant amnesties for serious crimes, as demonstrated in the peace agreements in the Democratic Republic of Congo, East Timor and Sierra Leone (Martin 1999). For an overview see Stahn (2002). See also Kritz (2002: 82).

12 For an overview of the negotiations see International Crisis Group (2000); Williams and Scharf (2002).

13 Article IX, General Framework Agreement for Peace in Bosnia and Herzegovina, 1 December 1995.

14 ICTY press release, CC/

PIU/391-E, The Hague, 31 March 1999.

15 'Racak massacre haunts Milosevic trial', BBC, 14 February 2002 (news.bbc.co.uk/1/hi/world/europe/1812847.stm).

16 James Rubin, US Department of State daily press briefing, 24 March 1999.

17 Notice of crimes under the statute can be referred by the UN Security Council, a state party or any other source.

18 Article 12, ICCSt.

19 Ibid.

20 Article 13(b), ICCSt.

21 Article 17(1)(d) states that the crimes must be of 'sufficient gravity to justify further action'.

22 Article 17, ICCSt.

23 Article 53(1)(c), ICCSt.

24 The interests of peace and security have additional relevance in that Article 16 allows the Security Council to defer ICC investigations if the Council deems the investigation to be a threat to international peace and security under Chapter 7 of the UN Charter.

25 Para. 4 of the Preamble of the ICC Statute affirms that the most serious crimes of concern to the international community must not go unpunished; while the last states that the authors are resolved to guarantee lasting respect for the enforcement of international criminal justice. This more limited definition may be further evidenced by the use of the 'interests of justice' in Articles 55(2)(c), 65(4), 67(1)(d), all of which use the use the term 'interests of justice' to refer to matters regarding the rights of the accused or victims as affected in the course of an investigation or trial.

26 Policy Paper on the Interests of Justice, Office of the Prosecutor,

International Criminal Court, September 2007 (www.icc-cpi.int/library/organs/otp/ICC-OTP-InterestsOfJustice.pdf).

27 ICC Statute, Article 53(3), (4).

28 The court's obligation to protect victim and witness security and well-being are expressed in Article 68(1) and Article 54(1)(b).

29 At this time the OTP was also seriously analysing the situation of the Democratic Republic of Congo, Colombia and the Côte d'Ivoire.

30 'President of Uganda refers situation concerning the Lord's Resistance Army (LRA) to the ICC', The Hague, 29 January 2004 (www.icc-cpi.int/php/index.php).

31 ICCSt, Article 14.

32 C. K. Hall, in Triffterer (1999: Article 19, 407–408). Cited by ICC Pre-Trial Chamber I, 'Decision on the applications for participation in the proceedings of VPRS1, VPRS2, VPRS3, VPRS4, VPRS5, VPRS6 (public redacted version)', 17 January 2006.

33 The Office of the Prosecutor, 'Report on the activities performed during the first three years (June 2003–June 2006)', 12 September 2006, (www.icc-cpi.int/library/organs/otp/OTP_3-year-report-20060914_English.pdf).

34 Statement by Luis Moreno-Ocampo, Fourth Session of the Assembly of States Parties, 28 November–3 December 2005, The Hague, 28 November 2005.

35 See 'Making peace our own', OHCHR, July 2007.

36 'Prosecutor of the International Criminal Court opens an investigation into Northern Uganda', The Hague, 29 July 2004 (www.icc-cpi.int/press/pressreleases/33.html).

37 The Red Line largely coincided with the Juba–Torit road.

38 'UPDF captures Kony's wives and children', *New Vision*, 29 July 2004; 'Ugandan army says may have killed LRA rebel chief', Reuters, 29 July 2004; 'Uganda raids rebel HQ', Reuters, 29 July 2004; 'Ugandan army claims killing 120 LRA rebels in southern Sudan', AFP, 29 July 2004.

39 'Sudan rebels battle LRA', *Monitor*, 29 July 2004.

40 The Office of the Prosecutor, 'Report on the activities performed during the first three years (June 2003–June 2006)', 12 September 2006.

41 OTP presentation at the time of the warrant unsealing, 14 October 2005 (www.icc-cpi.int/library/organs/otp/Uganda-_PPpresentation.pdf).

42 Ibid.

43 The Office of the Prosecutor, 'Report on the activities performed during the first three years (June 2003–June 2006)', 12 September 2006.

44 Ibid., para. 33.

45 'Statements by ICC Chief Prosecutor and the visiting delegation of Acholi leaders from northern Uganda', OTP press release, 18 March 2005 (www.icc-cpi.int/press/pressreleases/96.htm).

46 'Joint statement by ICC Chief Prosecutor and the visiting delegation of Lango, Acholi, Iteso and Madi community leaders from northern Uganda', OTP press statement, 16 April 2005 (www.icc-cpi.int/press/pressreleases/102.html).

47 Colonel Onen Kamdule, the LRA Director of Operations, defected on 4 February 2005 and Brigadier Sam Kolo, the LRA Political Commissar, defected on 15 February 2005. 'Museveni extends LRA ceasefire to February 22', *New Vision*, 19 February 2005 (www.newvision.co.ug/D/8/12/418947).

48 Decision on the Prosecutor's

Application for Unsealing of the Arrest Warrants, 13 October 2005 (www.icc-cpi.int/library/cases/ICC-02-04-01-05-52_English.pdf).

49 Ibid.

50 Ibid.

51 Ibid.

52 Ibid.

53 Ibid.

54 For a summary of the agreement, see useu.usmission.gov/Article.asp?ID=69478730-aa31-4872-b1ef-7e8abe8ac38e.

55 'Uganda: United Nations prepares to strike LRA', *Monitor*, 25 April 2008.

56 'Uganda: how LRA deputy Vincent Otti was killed', *New Vision*, 9 December 2007.

57 The most significant defector was Colonel Patrick Opio Makasi, then LRA Director of Operations ('Uganda: Uganda wants top LRA rebel extradited', *Monitor*, 22 October 2007).

58 'LRA prepares for war, not peace', IWPR, 24 April 2008; 'Governments and United Nations must push for release of 350 people kidnapped in Central Africa by Lord's Resistance Army', Amnesty International, 22 April 2008 (www.amnestyusa.org/document.php?id=ENGUSA20080422001); 'Uganda: LRA abducts 150 in Central African Republic', *New Vision*, 29 March 2008.

59 Although individuals are presumed innocent before being found guilty in the court of law, in actuality the investigation of and the issuance of a warrant for suspects often results in immediate international stigmatization and political marginalization (Garapon 2004: 717).

60 'Building a future on peace and justice', speech of Luis Moreno-Ocampo, Nuremberg Conference, 27 June 2007.

61 The contribution of the ICC to reducing crime and pushing the LRA into negotiations has been acknowledged by several sources, including: Report of Jan Egeland, p. 4 (Egeland stated that 'the indictments had been a factor in pushing LRA into negotiations, that they should not disrupt the talks, and that there could be no impunity for mass murder and crimes against humanity'); Intervention of Ambassador Mirjam Blaak of Uganda, 25 September 2006 (Blaak stated: 'I would like to emphasize that if it was not for the warrants of arrest hanging over the heads of the indictees, the LRA may not have agreed to the peace process'); International Crisis Group, 2006, stating that the ICC warrants 'rattled the indicted commanders, reduced their opportunity to emerge from the conflict with impunity and put pressure on Khartoum to cut its umbilical cord to the LRA' (www.crisisgroup.org/library/documents/africa/central_africa/b041_peace_in_northern_uganda.pdf).

Postscript

1 Natural Fire 10, www.africom.mil/getArticle.asp?art=3652&lang=0.

2 Information in this postscript is drawn from research carried out in 2009 and 2010 by Tim Allen, Frederick Laker, Holly Porter and Mareike Schomerus. Holly Porter is currently researching in northern Uganda, and has contributed the section about Christmas Day, 2009.

3 'Return to uncertainty? Addressing vulnerabilities in northern Uganda', Republic of Uganda, p. 47.

4 'Uganda: land rows reverse resettlement', IRIN, 17 March 2009.

5 'Uganda: boom time in Gulu', IRIN, 16 October 2007,

www.irinnews.org/Report. aspx?ReportId=74800.

6 'All IDP camps to close by March 2010', 10 Decembe 2009, www.nurep.org.

7 *Uganda Report 2010*, UNHCR, www.unhcr.org/cgi-bin/texis/vtx/page?page=49e483c06.

8 'From emergency to recovery: rescuing northern Uganda's transition', Oxfam Briefing Paper 118, September 2008.

9 'Donors offer $4.5bn in Georgia aid', 22 October 2008, www.aljazeera.net.

10 'Donors pledge aid to build Gaza, shun Hamas', 2 March 2009, www.reuters.com.

11 'Twelfth periodic report of the United Nations High Commissioner for Human Rights on the situation of human rights in the Sudan – Attacks on civilians in Western and Central Equatoria States, Southern Sudan, between 15 December 2008 and 10 March 2009 by the Lord's Resistance Army (LRA)', OHCHR, December 2009, p. 9.

12 Ibid., p. 10.

13 Ibid., p. 11.

14 Information on the LRA in DRC is derived from the United Nations Organization Mission in the Democratic Republic of the Congo and the Office of the High Commissioner for Human Rights, 'Special Report: Summary of fact finding missions on alleged human rights violations committed by the Lord's Resistance Army (LRA) in the districts of Haut-Uélé and Bas-Uélé in Orientale province of the Democratic Republic of Congo', December 2009. Like the above-quoted report on Sudan, this report also describes extremely violent incidents, including rape.

15 This point reiterated concerns raised in previous reports, including Mareike Schomerus and Kennedy Tumutegyereize, 'After Operation Lightning Thunder: protecting communities and building peace', Conciliation Resources, London, 2009.

16 John Vandiver, 'AFRICOM official defends US role in Ugandan mission', *Stars and Stripes*, European edn, 14 February 2009, www.stripes.com/article.asp?section=104&article=60712.

17 Congressional Record Statement of US Senator Russ Feingold on the Lord's Resistance Army, feingold.senate.gov/record.cfm?id=309530.

18 'SUDAN: Southerners still besieged by suspected LRA fighters', IRIN, www.irinnews.org/Report.aspx?ReportId=87173.

Bibliography

Aall, P. (2007) 'The power of nonofficial actors in conflict management', in C. A. Crocker et al. (eds), *Leashing the Dogs of War: Conflict Management in a Divided World*, Washington, DC: US Institute of Peace Press.

Abrahams, R. (1985) 'A modern witch-hunt among the Lango of Uganda', *Cambridge Anthropology*, 10(1): 32–45.

Acord (2000) 'Background papers presented to the conference on "peace research and the reconciliation agenda"', Gulu, northern Uganda, September 1999 (COPE Working Paper no. 32), London: Acord.

Adam, J., B. De Cordier, K. Titeca and K. Vlassenroot (2007) 'In the name of the Father? Christian militantism in Tripura, Northern Uganda and Ambon', *Studies in Conflict & Terrorism*, 30(11): 963–83.

— (2005) 'A land market for poverty eradication? A case study of the impact of Uganda's Land Acts on policy', Kampala: Land and Equity Movement Uganda (LEMU).

Afako, Barney (2002) 'Reconciliation and justice: "Mato Oput" and the Amnesty Act', in O. Lucima (ed.), *Protracted Conflict, Elusive Peace: Initiatives to end the violence in Northern Uganda: Conciliation Resources*, London: Acord.

Akhavan, P. (2001) 'Beyond impunity: can international criminal justice prevent future atrocities?', *American Journal of International Law*, 95(1): 7–31.

Allen, T. (1991a) 'The quest for therapy in Moyo district', in H. B. Hansen and M. Twaddle (eds), *Changing Uganda: Dilemmas of Structural Adjustment and Revolutionary Change*, London: James Currey.

— (1991b) 'Understanding Alice: Uganda's Holy Spirit Movement in context', *Africa*, 61(3): 370–99.

— (1992) 'Upheaval, affliction and health: a Ugandan case study', in H. Bernstein et al. (eds), *Rural Livelihoods: Crises and Responses*, Oxford: Oxford University Press.

— (1994) 'Review of R. R. Atkinson's *The Roots of Ethnicity: The Origins of the Acholi of Uganda before 1800*', *Africa*, 66(3): 370–99.

— (1997) 'The violence of healing', *Sociologus*, 47(2): 101–28.

— (2005) *War and Justice in Northern Uganda: An Assessment of the International Criminal Court's Intervention*, London: London School of Economics (Crisis States Research Centre, Development Studies Institute).

— (2006) *Trial Justice: The International Criminal Court and the Lord's Resistance Army*, London: International African Institute/ Zed Books.

— (2007a) 'Defending the ICC', *Prospect*, 134.

— (2007b) 'The International Criminal Court and the invention of traditional justice in northern

Uganda', *Politique Africaine*, 107: 147–65.

Allen, T. and M. Schomerus (2006) 'A hard homecoming. Lessons learned from the reception centre process in Northern Uganda – an independent study', Kampala: Management Systems International.

Allen, T. and J. Seaton (1999) 'Introduction', in T. Allen and J. Seaton (eds), *The Media of Conflict: War reporting and representations of ethnic violence*, London and New York: Zed Books.

Amaza, O. O. (1998) *Museveni's Long March from Guerilla to Statesman*, Kampala: Fountain Publishers.

Amnesty International (1989) *Uganda: The human rights record (1986–1989)*, London: Amnesty International.

— (1991) *Uganda – Human rights violations by the National Resistance Army*, London: Amnesty International.

— (1992) 'Uganda: The failure to safeguard human rights', London: Amnesty International.

Andvig, J. C. and S. Gates (2006) 'Recruiting children from armed conflict. Child Soldiers Initiative working group session', Pittsburgh, PA.

Annan, J. (2007) 'Self-appraisal, social support, and connectedness as protective factors for youth associated with fighting forces in northern Uganda', Indianapolis: Indiana University.

Annan, J., C. Blattman and R. Horton (2006) 'The state of youth and youth protection in northern Uganda: findings from the survey of war affected youth', Kampala: UNICEF Uganda.

Annan, J. et al. (2009) 'Women and girls at war: "wives", mothers and

fighters in the Lord's Resistance Army', Unpublished working paper, Yale University.

Anonymous (2005) *LRA Religious Practices*, ed. R. Skow, Unpublished.

Appleton, S. (2001) *Poverty Reduction during Growth: The case of Uganda, 1992–2000*, Nottingham: University of Nottingham.

Arbour, L. (2004) 'The crucial years', *Journal of International Criminal Justice*, 2(2): 336–402.

Arendt, H. (1958) *The Human Condition*, Chicago, IL: University of Chicago Press.

— (1970) *On Violence*. New York: Harcourt, Brace & World, Inc.

Atkinson, R. (1999) *The Roots of Ethnicity: The origins of the Acholi of Uganda*, Kampala: Fountain Publishers.

Bach, S. (2007) *Leni: The Life and Work of Leni Riefenstahl*, New York: Alfred A. Knopf.

Baffes, J. (2006) 'Restructuring Uganda's coffee industry: why going back to the basics matters', World Bank Policy Research Working Paper 4020, Washington, DC: World Bank.

Baines, E. (2005) 'Roco Wat I Acoli: restoring relationships in Acholiland: traditional approaches to justice and reintegration', University of British Columbia, Liu Institute for Global Issues, Gulu district NGO Forum, Ker Kwaro Acholi.

— (2007) 'The haunting of Alice: local approaches to justice and reconciliation in northern Uganda', *International Journal of Transitional Justice*, 1: 91–114.

Bass, G. J. (2000) *Stay the Hand of Vengeance: The Politics of War Crimes Tribunals*, Princeton, NJ: Princeton University Press.

Bassiouni, C. (1998) *The Statute of*

the *International Criminal Court: A Documentary History*, New York: Transnational Publishers.

Bauman, Z. (1998) *Globalization: The human consequences*, Cambridge: Polity Press.

Bayne, S. (2007) 'Aid and conflict in Uganda', London: Safer World.

BBC (British Broadcasting Corporation) (2005) 'Editorial guidelines: the BBC's values and standards', London: BBC.

Beber, B. and C. Blattman (2009) 'The industrial organization of rebellion: the logic of forced labor and child soldiering', Unpublished working paper, Yale University.

Becker, J. (2004) 'Children as weapons of war', New York: Human Rights Watch.

Behrend, H. (1998) 'War in northern Uganda: the Holy Spirit movements of Alice Lakwena, Severino Lukoya and Joseph Kony (1987–1997)', in C. Clapham (ed.), *African Guerillas*, Oxford: James Currey.

— (1999a) *Alice Lakwena and the Holy Spirits. War in northern Uganda 1986–97*, Oxford, Kampala, Nairobi and Athens: James Currey/ Fountain Publishers/EAEP/Ohio University Press.

— (1999b) 'Power to heal, power to kill: spirit possession and war in northern Uganda (1986–1994)', in H. Behrend et al. (eds), *Spirit Possession, Modernity and Power in Africa*, Oxford: James Currey.

Bell, C. (2000) *Peace Agreements and Human Rights*, New York: Oxford University Press.

Berndt, T. (1979) 'Developmental changes in conformity to peers and parents', *Developmental Psychology*, 15(6): 608–16.

Blattman, C. and J. Annan (forthcoming) 'The consequences of child soldiering', *Review of Economics and Statistics*.

Bøås, M. and A. Hatløy (2006) 'The Northern Uganda Internally Displaced Persons Profiling Study', New York: UNDP/USAID/Fafo.

Boyd, C. (1998) 'Making Bosnia work', *Foreign Affairs*, 77(1).

Boyden, J. (2003) 'The moral development of child soldiers: what do adults have to fear?', *Peace and Conflict: Journal of Peace Psychology*, 9(4): 343–62.

Bracken, P. (1998) 'Hidden agendas: deconstructing post traumatic stress disorder', in P. Bracken and C. Petty, *Rethinking the Trauma of War*, New York: Free Association Books Ltd.

Bradbury, M. (1999) 'An overview of initiatives for peace in Acholi, northern Uganda', Cambridge: Collaborative for Development Action.

Branch, A. (2004) 'International justice, local injustice', *Dissent*, 51(3).

— (2005) 'Neither peace nor justice: political violence and the peasantry in northern Uganda 1986–1998', *African Studies Quarterly*, 8(2): 1–31.

— (2007a) 'The political dilemma of global justices: anti-civilian violence and the violence of humanitarianism, the case of northern Uganda', PhD dissertation, Columbia University.

— (2007b) 'Uganda's civil war and the politics of ICC intervention', *Ethics and International Affairs*, 21(2): 179–98.

Brett, R. and I. Specht (2004) *Young Soldiers: Why They Choose to Fight*, Boulder, CO: Lynne Rienner.

Browning, C. R. (1992) *Ordinary Men: Reserve Battalion 101 and the Final*

Solution in Poland, New York: Harper Perennial.

Brubacher, M. (2004) 'Prosecutorial discretion in practice', *Journal of International Criminal Justice*, 2(71): 71–95.

Cassese, A., P. Kirsch and B. Le Fraper Du Hellen (2001) 'Round table: prospects for the functioning of the International Criminal Court', in M. Politi and G. Nesi (eds), *The Rome Statute of the International Criminal Court: A Challenge to Impunity*, Burlington, VT: Ashgate Press.

Chabal, P. (2005) 'Introduction: violence, power and rationality: a political analysis in contemporary Africa', in P. Chabal et al. (eds), *Is Violence Inevitable in Africa? Theories of conflict and approaches to conflict prevention*, Boston, MA: Brill.

Chabal, P. and J. P. Daloz (1999) *Africa Works: Disorder as political instrument*, Oxford/Bloomington: International African Institute/James Currey/Indiana University Press.

Clark, J. F. (2001) 'Explaining Ugandan intervention in Congo: evidence and interpretation', *Journal of Modern African Studies*, 39: 269–71.

Clark, P. (2007) 'Hybridity, holism and "traditional" justice: the case of the Gacaca Courts in post-genocide Rwanda', *George Washington International Law Review*, 39(4): 765–837.

— (2008) 'Doing justice during conflict: the International Criminal Court, transnational justice and reconciliation in the Democratic Republic of Congo and Uganda'.

Coalition to Stop the Use of Child Soldiers (2006) 'Child Soldiers Global Report 2004', London: Coalition to Stop the Use of Child Soldiers.

Cobban, H. (2007). *Amnesty after Atrocity? Healing Nations after Genocide and War Crimes*, Boulder, CO: Paradigm.

Cohn, I. and G. S. Goodwin-Gill (1994) *Child Soldiers: The Role of Children in Armed Conflict*, Oxford: Oxford University Press.

Collier, P. and A. Hoeffler (2001) 'Greed and grievance in civil war', Policy Research Working Paper no. 2355, Washington, DC: World Bank.

CSOPNU (Civil Society Organizations for Peace in Northern Uganda) (2004) 'Land matters in displacement: the importance of land rights in Acholiland and what threatens them', Kampala: CSOPNU.

— (2006) 'Counting the cost: twenty years of war in northern Uganda', Kampala: CSOPNU.

Cyanzayire, A. (2002) 'The Gacaca Tribunals: reconciliatory justice', Kampala: National Unity and Reconciliation Summit.

Dahl, R. E. (2001) 'Affect regulation, brain development, and behavioral/emotional health in adolescence', *CNS Spetr.*, 6(1): 60–72.

Ddungu, E. (1994) 'Popular forms and the question of democracy: the case of Resistance Councils in Uganda', in M. Mamdani et al. (eds), *Uganda: Studies in living conditions, popular movements and constitutionalism*, Austria: JEP and Centre for Basic Research (Kampala).

De Temmerman, E. (2001) *Aboke Girls: Children abducted in northern Uganda*, Kampala: Fountain Publishers.

Deininger, K. and R. Castagnini

(2004) 'Incidence and impact of land conflict in Uganda', World Bank Policy Research Working Paper 3248, Washington, DC: World Bank.

Deininger, K. and J. A. Okodi (2003) 'Growth and poverty reduction in Uganda, 1990–2000: panel data evidence', *Development Policy Review*, 21(3): 481–509.

Deininger, K., T. Yamano and D. Ayalew (2006) 'Legal knowledge and economic development: the case of land rights in Uganda', World Bank Policy Research Working Paper 3868, Washington, DC: World Bank.

Diken, B. and C. B. Lausten (2003) *Zones of Indistinction – security, terror, and bare life*, Lancaster: Department of Sociology, Lancaster University.

Dolan, C. (2000a) 'Inventing traditional leadership? A critical assessment of Dennis Pain's *The Bending of the Spears*', COPE Working Paper no. 31, London: Acord.

— (2000b) 'What do you remember? A rough guide to the war in northern Uganda, 1986–2000', London: Acord.

— (2005) 'Understanding war and its continuation: the case of northern Uganda', PhD dissertation, Development Studies Institute, London School of Economics and Political Science, University of London.

— (2009) *Social Torture: The Case of Northern Uganda*, Oxford: Berghahn Books.

Dolan, C. and L. Howel (2006) 'Humanitarian protection in Uganda: a Trojan horse?', London: Human Policy Group.

Doom, R. and K. Vlassenroot (1999) 'Kony's message: a new Koine? The Lord's Resistance Army in northern Uganda', *African Affairs*, 98(390): 5–36.

Douglas, M. (1993) *In the Wilderness: The doctrine of defilement in the Book of Numbers*, Sheffield: Sheffield Academic Press.

Douma, P. and K. van Walraven (2000) 'Between indifference and naïveté, Dutch policy interventions in African conflicts. A synthesis report', The Hague: Conflict Research Unit.

Dowden, R. (2007) 'ICC in the dock', *Prospect*, 134.

Dugard, M. (2003) *Into Africa: The Dramatic Retelling of the Stanley–Livingstone Story*, London: Bantam Books.

Duyvesteyn, I. (2000) 'Contemporary war: ethnic conflict, resource conflict or something else?', *Civil Wars*, 3(1): 92–116.

Ellis, S. and G. Ter Haar (2004) *Worlds of Power: Religious thought and political practice in Africa*, London: Hurst & Co.

Ferguson, J. (1999) *Expectations of Modernity: Myths and meanings of urban life on the Zambian Copperbelt*, Berkeley: University of California Press.

Finnström, S. (2003) *Living with Bad Surroundings. War and existential uncertainty in Acholiland, northern Uganda*, PhD dissertation, University of Uppsala.

— (2006) 'Wars of the past and wars in the present: the Lord's Resistance Movement/Army in Uganda', *Africa*, 76: 200–19.

— (2008a) *Living with Bad Surroundings: War, history, and everyday moments in northern Uganda*, Durham, NC: Duke University Press.

— (2008b) 'An African hell of colonial imagination? The Lord's

Resistance Army/Movement in Uganda, another story', *Politique Africaine*, 112.

— (2009a) 'Fear of the midnight knock: state sovereignty and internal enemies in Uganda', in K. Bruce and B. E. Bertelsen (eds), *Crisis of the State: War and social upheaval*, Oxford/New York: Berghahn Books.

— (2009b) 'Gendered war and rumors of Saddam Hussein in Uganda', *Anthropology and Humanism*, 34(1).

Fithen, C. and P. Richards (2005) 'Making war, crafting peace: militia solidarities and demobilization in Sierra Leone', in P. Richards (ed.), *No Peace, No War: An anthropology of contemporary armed conflicts*, Athens/Oxford: Ohio University Press/James Currey.

Furby, L. and R. Beyth-Marom (1990) 'Risk taking in adolescence: a decision-making perspective', Washington, DC: Carnegie Council on Adolescent Development.

Furley, O. W. (1989) 'Britain and Uganda from Amin to Museveni: blind eyes diplomacy', in K. Rupesinghe (ed.), *Conflict Resolution in Uganda*, Athens: Ohio University Press.

Garapon, A. (2004) 'Three challenges for international criminal justice', *Journal of International Criminal Justice*, 2: 716–26.

Gardner, W. and J. Hermann (1990) 'Adolescents' AIDS risk taking: a rational choice perspective', *New Directions for Child Development*, 50: 17–34.

Geertz, C. (1983) *Local Knowledge*, London: Fontana Press.

Gersony, R. (1997) *The Anguish of Northern Uganda: Results of a field-based assessment of the civil conflicts in Northern Uganda*, Kampala: USAID Mission.

Gertzel, C. (1974) *Party and Locality in Northern Uganda 1945–1962*, London: Athlone Press.

Giedd, J. N., J. Blumenthal and N. Jeffries (1999) 'Brain development during childhood and adolescence: a longitudinal MRI study', *Nature Neuroscience*, 2: 861–3.

Gilligan, J. (1999) *Violence: Reflections on Our Deadliest Epidemic*, London: Jessica Kingsley Publishers.

Gingyera-Pinycwa, A. G. G. (1989) 'Is there a "Northern question"?', in K. Rupesinghe (ed.), *Conflict Resolution in Uganda*, London: James Curry.

— (1992) *Northern Uganda in National Politics*, Kampala: Fountain Publishers.

Ginifer, J. (2006) 'Internal review of DfID's engagement with the conflict in northern Uganda. Evaluation report EV663', London: DfID.

Girling F. K. (1960) 'The Acholi of Uganda', London: Colonial Research Studies.

Goldstone, R. (1995) 'Justice as a tool for peace-making: truth commissions and international tribunals', *NYU Journal of International Law and Politics*, 28: 485–503.

Government of Uganda (2006) 'National Peace, Recovery and Development Plan for Northern Uganda (PRDP) 2006–2009', Kampala: Government of Uganda.

Government of Uganda and Lord's Resistance Army/Movement (2007) 'Agreement on accountability and reconciliation between the government of the Republic of Uganda and the Lord's Resistance Army/Movement', Juba: Government of Uganda.

Green, M. (2006) 'Confronting categorical assumptions about the power of religion in Africa', *Review of African Political Economy*, 110(33): 635–50.

— (2008) *The Wizard of the Nile*, London: Portobello.

Greenberger, E. (1982) 'Education and the acquisition of psycho-social maturity', in D. McClelland (ed.), *The Development of Social Maturity*, New York: Irvington.

Greene, A. L. (1986) 'Future-time perspective in adolescence: the present of things future revisited', *Journal of Youth and Adolescence*, 15(2): 99–113.

Guttiérez, F. (2006) 'Organizing minors. Ford Institute Workshop on Child Soldiers', Pittsburgh, PA: Ford Institute.

Halpern-Felsher, B. L. and E. Cauffman (2001) 'Costs and benefits of a decision. Decision-making competence in adolescents and adults', *Journal of Applied Developmental Psychology*, 22(3): 257–73.

Hansen, S. M. (2008) 'Northern Uganda and the role of non-state actors', Power, Politics and Change in Weak States, 1–2 March 2006, Copenhagen: Danida/GEPPA.

Harlacher, T. et al. (2007) *Traditional Ways of Coping in Acholi: Cultural provisions for reconciliation and healing from war*, Kampala: Caritas Gulu Archiocese.

Hausmann, R., L. Pritchett and D. Rodik (2004) 'Growth accelerations', NBER Working Papers 10566, London: National Bureau of Economic Research.

Hobsbawm, E. and T. Ranger (1993) *The Invention of Tradition*, Cambridge: Cambridge University Press.

Honwana, A. (2006) *Child Soldiers in Africa*, Philadelphia: University of Pennsylvania Press.

Horowitz, D. (1985) *Ethnic Groups in Conflict*, Berkeley: University of California Press.

House of Commons International Development Committee (2007) 'Conflict and development: peacebuilding and post-conflict reconstruction', London: House of Commons International Development Committee.

Hovil, L. and J. R. Quinn (2005) 'Peace first, justice later: traditional justice in northern Uganda', Kampala: Refugee Law Project.

Human Rights Watch (1997) 'The scars of death: children abducted by the Lord's Resistance Army in Uganda', New York: Human Rights Watch.

— (2003) *Abducted and Abused: Renewed conflict in Northern Uganda*, New York: Human Rights Watch.

— (2005a) 'Human Rights Watch policy paper: the meaning of "the interests of justice" in Article 53 of the Rome Statute', New York: Human Rights Watch.

— (2005b) 'Uprooted and forgotten: impunity and human rights abuses in northern Uganda', *Human Rights Watch*, 17 (12A).

Ignatieff, M. (1998) *The Warrior's Honor: Ethnic War and the Modern Conscience*, New York: Metropolitan Books.

ILO (2003) 'Wounded childhood: the use of child soldiers in armed conflict in central Africa', Washington, DC: International Labour Organization.

IMF (2005) 'Uganda: Poverty Reduction Strategy Paper–Joint Staff Advisory Note', IMF Country Report no. 05/308, Washington, DC: IMF.

— (2006) 'Uganda: sixth review under the three-year arrangement under the poverty reduction and growth facility', IMF Country Report no. 06/43, Washington, DC: IMF.

Internal Displacement Monitoring Centre (2006) 'Only peace can restore the confidence of the displaced: update on the implementation of the recommendations made by the UN secretary-general's representative on internally displaced persons following his visit to Uganda', Geneva: Internal Displacement Monitoring Centre.

International Center for Transitional Justice and Human Rights Center (2005) 'Forgotten voices: a population-based survey on attitudes about peace and justice in northern Uganda', New York: ICTJ/HRC.

— (2007) 'New population-based data on attitudes about peace and justice', New York: ICTJ/HRC.

International Crisis Group (2000) 'War criminals in Bosnia's Republika Srpska', Balkans Report no. 103, Brussels: ICG.

— (2002) 'Finding the balance: the scales of justice in Kosovo', ICG Balkans Report no. 134, Brussels: ICG.

— (2004) 'Northern Uganda: understanding and solving the conflict', Africa Report no. 77, Nairobi/Brussels: ICG.

— (2005a) 'Building a Comprehensive Peace Strategy for northern Uganda', African Briefing no. 27, Kampala: ICG.

— (2005b) 'Garang's death: implications for peace in Sudan', Africa Briefing no. 30, Nairobi/Brussels: ICG.

— (2006) 'Peace in northern Uganda?', Africa Briefing no. 41, Nairobi/ Brussels: ICG.

Jackson, S. (2002) Regional Conflict Formation and the 'Bantu/Nilotic' Mythology in the Great Lakes, New York: Centre on International Cooperation, New York University.

Jansen, S., E. Brusset, R. Oywa, F. Viliani and R. Otto (2007) 'Evaluation of the CRD and NUPI, USAID Uganda', New York: USAID.

Johnson, D. H. (2003) The Root Causes of Sudan's Civil Wars, Oxford/Bloomington: James Currey/Indiana University Press.

Johnson, S. (2003) Peace without Justice: Hegemonic instability or international criminal law?, Aldershot: Ashgate.

Kaldor, M. (1999) New and Old Wars. Organized violence in a global era, Cambridge: Polity Press.

Kalyvas, S. N. (2003) 'The ontology of "political violence": action and identity in civil wars', Perspectives on Politics, 1(3): 475–94.

— (2005) 'Warfare in civil wars', in I. Duyvesteyn and J. Angstrom (eds), Rethinking the Nature of War, Abingdon: Frank Cass.

Karekezi, U. A. and A. Nshimiyimana (2004) 'Localizing justice: gacaca courts in post-genocide Rwanda', in E. Stover and H. M. Weinstein (eds), My Neighbour, My Enemy: Justice and Community in the Aftermath of Mass Atrocity, Cambridge: Cambridge University Press.

Karlström M. (2004) 'Modernity and its aspirants: moral community and developmental utopianism in Buganda', Current Anthropology, 45: 595–619.

Kasfir, N. (1976) The Shrinking Political Arena: Participation and ethnicity in African politics, with *a case study of Uganda*, Berkeley: University of California Press.

Kasozi, A. B. K. (1994) *The Social Origins of Violence in Uganda: 1964–1985*, Montreal: McGill-Queen's University Press.

Kastfelt, N. (2005) 'Religion and African civil wars: themes and interpretations', in N. Kastfelt (ed.), *Religion and African Civil Wars*, London: Hurst and Co.

Kayunga, S. S. (2000) 'The impact of armed opposition on the Movement system in Uganda', in J. Mugayu and J. Oloka-Onyango (eds), *No-Party Democracy in Uganda: Myths and realities*, Kampala: Fountain Publishers.

Keen, D. (2006) *Endless War? Hidden functions of the 'War on Terror'*, London: Pluto Press.

Khadiagala, L. (2001) 'The failure of popular justice in Uganda: local councils and women's property rights', *Development and Change*, 32(60).

Kleinmann, A. (1977) 'Depression, somatization and the "new cross-cultural psychiatry"', *Social Science and Medicine*, 11: 3–10.

Knightly, P. (2000) *The First Casualty: The War Correspondent as Hero and Myth-Maker from the Crimea to Kosovo*, London: Prin Books.

Kritz, N. J. (2002) 'Where we are and how we got here: an overview of developments in the search for justice and reconciliation', in A. H. Henkin (ed.), *The Legacy of Abuse – Confronting the Past, Facing the Future*, New York: Aspen Institute and New York University School of Law.

Kuperman, A. J. (2004) 'Provoking genocide: a revised history of the Rwandan patriotic front', *Journal of Genocide Research*, 6(66).

Lake, D. and D. Rothchild (1996) 'Containing fear: the origins and management of ethnic conflict', *International Security*, 21(2): 41–75.

Lamony, S. A. (2007) 'Approaching national reconciliation in Uganda: perspectives on applicable justice systems', Kampala: Uganda Coalition on the International Criminal Court.

Lamwaka, C. (1998) 'Civil war and the peace process in Uganda, 1986–1997', *East African Journal of Peace and Human Rights*, 4(2): 139–69.

— (2000) *Beyond the Face of the Storm: The peace process in northern Uganda 1986–2000* (unpublished MS).

— (2002) 'The peace process in Northern Uganda, 1986–1990', in L. Okello (ed.), *Protracted Conflict, Elusive Peace: Initiatives to end the war in Northern Uganda*, London: Conciliation Resources in collaboration with Kacoke Madit.

Last, M. and G. L. Chavanduka (1986) *The Professionalization of African Medicine*, Manchester: Manchester University Press.

Levi, P. (1989) *The Drowned and the Saved*, London: Vintage.

Leys, C. (1967) *Politicians and Policies: An essay on politics in Acholi, Uganda, 1962–65*, Nairobi: East African Publishing House.

Lindqvist, S. (1997) *Exterminate All the Brutes*, London: Granta Books.

Lomo, Z. and L. Hovil (2004) 'Behind the violence: causes, consequences and the search for solutions to the war in northern Uganda', Kampala: Refugee Law Project.

Longman, T. (2005) 'Churches and social upheaval in Rwanda and Burundi: explaining failures to oppose ethnic violence', in N. Kastfelt (ed.), *Religion and*

African Civil Wars, London: Hurst and Co., pp. 82–101.

Lonsdale, J. (1994) 'Moral ethnicity and political tribalism', in P. Kaarsholm et al. (eds), *Inventions and Boundaries: Historical and anthropological approaches to the study of ethnicity and nationalism*, Roskilde: Roskilde University, pp. 131–50.

Lord's Resistance Army/Movement (n.d.) *Lord's Resistance Movement/Army (LRM/A) Manifesto* (printed document).

— (1996a) *LRA Policy Definitions and Explanations*.

— (1996b) *Manifesto from Lord's Resistance Movement/Army (LRM/A) to all Ugandans*.

— (1997) *An Alternative Programme for a New Uganda. The Lord's Resistance Movement/Army Manifesto 1997*.

— (2006) *Opening Statement of the LRA Peace Delegation Juba – Southern Sudan, 16th July 2006*.

LRA Delegation to the Juba Talks (2006) 'LRA position paper on accountability and reconciliation in the context of alternative justice system for resolving the Northern Ugandan and Southern Sudan conflicts', Juba.

Machel, G. (1996) 'Impact of armed conflict on children', New York: UNICEF.

Malcolm, J. (1983) *The Journalist and the Murderer*, New York: Alfred A. Knopf.

Mamdani, M. (1976) *Politics and Class Formation in Uganda*, Kampala: Fountain Publishers.

— (1995a) *And Fire Does Not Always Beget Ash: Critical reflections on the NRM*, Kampala: Monitor Publications.

— (1995b) 'NRA/NRM: two years in power', in M. Mamdani, *And Fire Does Not Always Beget Ash: Citical reflections on the NRM*, Kampala: Monitor Publications.

— (1996) *Citizen and Subject: Contemporary Africa and the Legacy of Late Colonialism*, Princeton, NJ: Princeton University Press.

Marciano, F. (1999) *Rules of the Wild*, London: Jonathan Cape.

Mark, T. (1995) 'The case against an international war crimes tribunal for former Yugoslavia', *International Peacekeeping*, 2.

Markowitch, H. J. and W. Siefer (2007) *Tatort Gehirn – Auf der Suche nach dem Ursprung des Verbrechens* [Brain as the Scene of the Crime: Searching for the origin of crime], Frankfurt/Main: Campus.

Martin, I. (1999) 'Haiti: international force or national compromise?', *Journal of Latin American Studies*, 31(3): 711–34.

McGee, R. (2000) 'Analysis of participatory poverty assessment and household survey findings on poverty trends in Uganda', Sussex: Institute of Development Studies.

McGaugh, J. L. (1992) 'Affect, neuromodulatory systems, and memory storage', in Lawrence Erlbaum Associates (ed.), *The Handbook of Emotion and Memory: Research and Theory*, Hillsdale, NJ: Lawrence Erlbaum Associates.

McLaughlin, G. (2002) *The War Correspondent*, London: Pluto Press.

Mitchell, P. E. (1939) *Native Administration: Note by the Governor*, Entebbe: Government Printer.

Mucyo, J. (2008) 'Minutes of the symposium on Gacaca'.

Mudoola, D. (1996) *Religion, Ethnicity and Politics in Uganda*, Kampala: Fountain Publishers.

Museveni, Y. K. (1986) *Selected*

Articles on the Uganda Resistance War, Kampala: NRM Publications.

— (1997) *Sowing the Mustard Seed: The struggle for freedom and democracy in Uganda*, London: Macmillan.

Mutibwa, P. M. (1992) *Uganda since Independence: A story of unfulfilled hopes*, London: Hurst and Co.

Nabudere, D. (2003) *The Hidden War, the Forgotten People*, Kampala: Makerere University Human Rights and Peace Centre.

Natsios, A. (2003) 'An NGO perspective', in W. Zartman and L. J. Rasmussen, *Peacemaking in International Conflict. Methods and Techniques*, Washington, DC: US Institute of Peace Press.

Neu, J. (2002) 'Restoring relations between Uganda and Sudan: the Carter Center process leading to the 1999 Nairobi Agreement', *ACCORD*, 11.

Ngoga, P. (1998) 'Uganda: the National Resistance Army', in C. Clapham (ed.), *African Guerillas*, Oxford: James Currey.

Nkonya, E., J. Pender, J. Pamela, D. Sserunkuuma, C. Kaizzi and H. Ssali (2004) 'Strategies for sustainable land management and poverty reduction in Uganda', Research Report 133, Washington, DC: International Food Policy Research Institute.

Nordstrom, C. (1997) *A Different Kind of War Story*, Philadelphia: University of Pennsylvania Press.

NURC (National Unity and Reconciliation Commission) (2003) 'Opinion survey on participation in Gacaca', Kigali: NURC.

Nurmi, J.-E. (1991) 'How do adolescents see their future? A review of the development of future orientation and planning', *Developmental Review*, 11(1): 1–59.

Nyaba, P. A. (1997) *Politics of Liberation in South Sudan: An insider's view*, Kampala: Fountain Publishers.

Nyeko, B. and O. Lucima (2002) 'Profiles of the parties to the conflict', in O. Lucima (ed.), *Protracted Conflict, Elusive Peace: Initiatives to end the violence in northern Uganda*, London: Conciliation Resources in collaboration with Kacoke Madit.

Ocan Odoki, S. (1997) *Death Rituals among the Lwos of Uganda. Their significance for the theology of death*, Gulu: Gulu Catholic Press.

Ochieng, E. O. (1991) 'Economic adjustment programmes in Uganda 1985–89', in H. Hasen and M. Twaddle (eds), *Changing Uganda*, London: James Currey.

Ojur, F. (2006) 'Opening remarks', Traditional Justice in the Northern Ugandan Conflict, International Bar Association.

Okodi, J. A., S. Sseweyana, L. Bategeka and F. Muhumuza (2004) 'Operationalizing pro-poor growth: Uganda case study evaluation report', Kampala: Economic Policy Research Centre.

Okuku, J. (2002) 'Ethnicity, state power, and the democratization process in Uganda', Uppsala: Nordic Africa Institute.

Okumu, Rev. J. (2005) 'Acholi rites of reconciliation', *The Examiner, Human Rights Focus*, 2(15).

Oloka-Onyango, J. (2000) 'New wine or old bottles? Movement politics and one-partyism in Uganda', in J. Mugayu and J. Oloka-Onyango (eds), *No-Party Democracy in Uganda: Myths and realities*, Kampala: Fountain Publishers.

Omara-Otunnu, A. (1987) *Politics and the Military in Uganda (1890–1985)*, Basingstoke: Macmillan.

— (1992) 'The struggle for democracy in Uganda', *Journal of Modern African Studies*, 30: 443–63.

— (1995) 'The dynamics of conflict in Uganda', in O. W. Furley (ed.), *Conflict in Africa*, London/New York: I. B. Tauris.

Onyango-Odongo, J. M. (1998) *The Rebel War in Northern Uganda*, Gulu: The Forum.

Ottemoeller, D. (1998) 'Popular perceptions of democracy: elections and attitudes in Uganda', *Comparative Political Studies*, 31(1): 98–134.

Pain, D. (1997) *The Bending of the Spears: Producing consensus for peace and development in Northern Uganda*, London: International Alert and Kacoke Madit.

Parker, M. (1996) 'Social devastation and mental health in northeast Africa', in T. Allen (ed.), *In Search of Cool Ground*, London: James Currey.

Parliament of Uganda (1997) 'Report of the committee on defence and internal affairs on the war in northern Uganda', Kampala: Parliament of Uganda.

— (2004) 'Report of the Select Committee on humanitarian and security situation in the Acholi, Teso and Lango subregions', Kampala: Parliament of Uganda.

Pax Christi Netherlands (1998) 'Steps towards peace and reconciliation in northern Uganda: an analysis of initiatives to end the armed conflict between the government of Uganda and the Lord's Resistance Army, 1987–1998', Report of a consultancy commissioned by Pax Christi Netherlands, Utrecht: Pax Christi.

— (2006) 'Achieving sustainable peace in the conflict between the Lord's Resistance Army and the government of Uganda', Utrecht: Pax Christi.

p'Bitek, O. (1980a) *African Religions in Western Scholarship*, Kampala: Uganda Literature Bureau.

— (1980b) *Religion of the Central Luo*, Kampala: Uganda Literature Bureau.

Pejic, J. (2008) 'Accountability for international crimes: from conjecture to reality', *International Review of the Red Cross*, 845: 13–33.

Perrot, S. (2004) 'Vers une fin de conflit au Nord de l'Ouganda? La LRA (1987–2005), causes et enjeux d'une guerre prolongée', *L'Annuaire des pays d'Afrique orientale*, pp. 73–139.

— (2008) 'Les sources de l'incompréhension: production et circulation des savoirs sur la Lord's Resistance Army', *Politique africaine*, 112: 140–59.

Peters, K. (2004) 'Re-examining voluntarism: youth combatants in Sierra Leone', Pretoria: Institute for Security Studies.

Peters, K. and P. Richards (1998) 'Fighting with open eyes: youth combatants talking about war in Sierra Leone', in P. Bracken and C. Petty (eds), *Rethinking the Trauma of War*, New York: Free Association Books.

Peters, K., P. Richards and K. Vlassenroot (2003) *What Happens to Youth During and After Wars?*, A Preliminary Review of Literature on Africa and an Assessment of the Debate, RAWOO Working Paper, The Hague: RAWOO.

Pettitt, C. (2007) *Dr Livingstone, I Presume? Missionaries, Journalists, Explorers and Empire*, London: Profile Books.

Pham, P. et al. (2007) 'Abducted: the Lord's Resistance Army and forced conscription in northern Uganda', Berkeley/Tulane: Human Rights Center, University of California/Payson Center for International Development.

Prunier, G. (2004) 'Rebel movements and proxy warfare: Uganda, Sudan and the Congo (1986–99)', *African Affairs*, 103(412): 359–83.

Refugee Law Report (2004) Working Paper no. 11, 'Behind the violence: causes, consequences and the search for solutions to the war in northern Uganda', Kampala, Uganda, February.

Republic of Uganda (1995) 'Constitution of the Republic of Uganda' (Preamble, section XXIV), Kampala: Government of Uganda.

— (2002) 'Second Participatory Poverty Assessment Report: deepening the understanding of poverty', Kampala: Ministry of Finance, Planning and Economic Development.

— (2004) 'Poverty Eradication Action Plan 2004–2007 (PEAP), volume 1', Kampala: Ministry of Finance, Planning and Economic Development.

— (2005) 'Uganda Poverty Status Report', Kampala: Republic of Uganda, Ministry of Finance, Planning and Economic Development.

— (2006) 'Background to the budget financial year 2006/07', Kampala: Ministry of Finance, Planning and Economic Development.

— (2007) 'National household survey 2006', Kampala: Uganda Bureau of Statistics.

Richards, A. I. (1939) *Land, Labour and Diet in Northern Rhodesia: An economic study of the Bemba tribe*, Oxford: Oxford University Press.

Richards, P. (1996) *Fighting for the Rain Forest. War, youth and resources in Sierra Leone*, Oxford: James Currey/Heinemann.

— (2005a) 'Green book millenarians? The Sierra Leone war within the perspective of an anthropology of religion', in N. Kastfelt (ed.), *Religion and African Civil Wars*, London: Hurst and Co., pp. 119–46.

— (2005b) 'Introduction', in P. Richards (ed.), *No Peace, No War: An anthropology of contemporary armed conflicts*, Oxford; OH: James Currey/Ohio University Press.

— (2006) 'An accidental sect: how war made belief in Sierra Leone', *Review of African Political Economy*, 33(110): 651–63.

Robinson, P. and J. Darley (2004) 'Does criminal law deter? A behavioural science investigation', *Oxford Journal of Legal Studies*, 2: 173–205.

Rodriguez, C., K. Smith-Derksen and S. J. Akera (2002) *Seventy Times Seven: The impact of the Amnesty Law in Acholi, Gulu*, Gulu: Acholi Religious Leaders' Peace Initiative, Women's Desk of Caritas Gulu and the Justice and Peace Commission of Gulu Archdiocese.

Rosen, D. M. (2005) *Armies of the Young: Child Soldiers in War and Terrorism*, New Brunswick, NJ/London: Rutgers University Press.

Rugadya, M., E. Obaiko and H. Kamusiime (2004) 'Gender and the land reform process in Uganda: assessing gains and losses for women in Uganda', Kampala: Associates for Development.

Sapira, M. (2003) 'Review of peace with justice? War crimes accountability in the former Yugoslavia', *AJIL*, 97(4).

Sathyamurthy, T. V. (1986) *The

Political Development of Uganda, 1900–1986, Aldershot: Gower.

Save the Children Fund (1998) 'Dispatches from disaster zones: the reporting of humanitarian emergencies', London: Public Conference at Church House.

Scharf, M. and N. Rodley (2002) 'International law principles on accountability', in C. Bassiouni (ed.), *Post Conflict Justice*, New York: Transnational Publishers.

Schipper, Y. and J. G. Hoogeveen (2005) 'Which inequality matters? Growth evidence based on small area welfare estimates in Uganda', World Bank Policy Research Working Paper 3592, Washington, DC: World Bank.

Schomerus, M. (2007) 'The Lord's Resistance Army in Sudan: a history and overview', Geneva: Graduate Institute of International Studies, Small Arms Survey (Sudan Human Security Baseline Assessment Project – HSBA).

Schomerus, M. and K. Tumutegyereize (2009) *After Operation Lightning Thunder: Protecting communities and building peace*, London: Conciliation Resources, http://www.c-r.org/our-work/uganda/ documents/After_Operation_Lightning_Thunder_29April09_lores.pdf.

Schrag, M. (2004) 'Lessons learned from ICTY experience', *Journal of International Criminal Justice*, 2(2): 427–34.

Scroggins, D. (2002) *Emma's War: An aid worker, a warlord, radical Islam, and the politics of oil. A true story of love and death in Sudan*, New York: Pantheon Books.

Security Council (2006) 'Update report no. 5, Uganda, 18 April 2006', New York: SCR Publications.

— (2009) UN Security Council letter dated 26 May 2009, Secretary-General to the President of the Security Council, 1 June 2009, S/2009/281.

Shepler, S. A. (2005) 'Conflicted childhoods: fighting over child soldiers in Sierra Leone', California: University of California.

Sherman, N. (2002) 'NIRP Research for Policy Series 11: Refugee resettlement in Uganda', Amsterdam: Royal Tropical Institute.

Singer, P. W. (2005) *Children at War*, New York: Pantheon Books.

Sisk, T. (1996) *Power Sharing and International Mediation in Ethnic Conflicts*, New York: Carnegie Corporation.

Spear, L. P. (2000) 'The adolescent brain and age-related behavioral manifestations', *Neuroscience & Biobehavioral Reviews*, 24(4): 417–63.

Stahn, C. (2002) 'United Nations peace-building amnesties and alternative forms of justice: a change in practice?', *International Review of the Red Cross*, 845: 191–205.

Steinberg, L. and E. Cauffman (1996) 'Maturity of judgment in adolescence: psychosocial factors in adolescent decision making', *Law and Human Behavior*, 20(3): 249–72.

Steinberg, L. and S. Silverberg (1986) 'The vicissitudes of autonomy in early adolescence', *Child Development*, 57(4): 841–51.

Summerfield, D. (1998) 'The social experience of war and some issues for the humanitarian field', in P. Bracken and C. Petty (eds), *Rethinking the Trauma of War*, New York: Free Association Books.

— (1999) 'A critique of seven assumptions behind psychological trauma programmes in war-affected areas', *Social Science and Medicine*, 48(10): 1449–62.

— (2000) 'Childhood, war, refugeedom and "trauma": three core questions for mental health professionals', *Transcultural Psychiatry*, 37(3): 417–33.

Taleb, N. N. (2007) *The Black Swan: The Impact of the Highly Improbable*, London: Penguin.

Tangri, R. and A. Mwenda (2001) 'Corruption and cronyism in Uganda's privatization in the 1990s', *African Affairs*, 100(398): 117–33.

— (2004) 'Military corruption and Ugandan politics since the late 1990's', *Review of African Political Economy*, 30(95): 539–52.

Taylor, T. (1992) *The Anatomy of the Nuremberg Trials*, New York: Knopf.

Triffterer, O. (1999) *Commentary on the Rome Statute of the International Criminal Court*, Baden-Baden: Nomos Verlagsgesellschaft.

UBOS (Uganda Bureau of Statistics) (2006) 'The informal cross border trade survey report, August 2004 to December 2005', Kampala: UBOS.

Uganda Human Rights Commission (2003) 'Annual Report January 2001–September 2002', Kampala: Ugandan Human Rights Commission.

Uganda National NGO Forum (2005) 'A long way to go: civil society perspectives on the progress and challenges of attaining the millennium development goals in Uganda', Kampala: Uganda National NGO Forum.

Ugandan Ministry of Health (2005) 'Health and mortality survey among internally displaced persons in Gulu, Kitgum and Pader districts, northern Uganda', Kampala: UNICEF, WFP, UNFPA, IRC.

UN Secretary-General (2005) 'Report of the Secretary-General on the protection of civilians in armed conflict'.

UN Security Council (2006) 'Letter dated 5 January 2006 from the Permanent Representative of Canada to the United Nations adressed to the President of the Security Council'.

— (2009) 'Letter dated 26 May 2009 from the Secretary-General addressed to the President of the Security Council', S/2009/281.01-06-09.

UNEP (United Nations Environment Programme) (2007) 'Sudan Post-Conflict Environmental Assessment', Nairobi: UNEP.

UNOCHA (2000) 'Financial tracking service, Uganda', Geneva: UNOCHA.

— (2002) 'Financial tracking service, Uganda', Geneva: UNOCHA.

— (2007) 'Financial tracking service, Uganda', Geneva: UNOCHA.

USAID (2005) 'Ker Kwaro Acholi and the Northern Uganda peace initiative. Report on Acholi youth and chiefs addressing practices of the Acholi culture and reconciliation', New York: USAID.

Van Acker, F. (2003) 'Uganda and the Lord's Resistance Army: the new order no one ordered', Discussion Paper no. 6, Antwerp: Institute of Development Policy and Management, University of Antwerp.

— (2004) 'Uganda and the Lord's Resistance Army: the new order no one ordered', *African Affairs*, 103(412): 335–57.

Veale, A. and A. Stavrou (2003) 'Violence, reconciliation and identity: the reintegration of the Lord's

Resistance Army child abductees in Northern Uganda', Pretoria: Institute for Security Studies.

Venkatesh, S. (2008) *Gangleader for a Day: A rogue sociologist takes to the streets*, New York: Penguin Press.

Vinci, A. (2005) 'The strategic use of fear by the Lord's Resistance Army', *Small Wars and Insurgencies*, 16(3): 360–81.

— (2006) 'Beyond terror and insurgency: the LRA's dirty war in northern Uganda', in George Kassimeris (ed.), *Warrior's Dishonour: Barbarity, Morality and Torture in Modern Warfare*, Aldershot: Ashgate Publishing.

Vinjamuri, L. and A. Boesenecher (2007) 'Accountability and peace agreements: mapping trends from 1980 to 2006', Nuremberg: Centre for Humanitarian Dialogue.

Vlassenroot, K. (forthcoming) 'Conflict and militia formation in Eastern Congo: the role of magico-religious systems of reproduction'.

Von Hirsch, A., A. Bottoms, E. Burney and P.-O. Wikstrom (1999) *Criminal Deterrence and Sentence Severity: An analysis of recent research*. Cambridge: University of Cambridge Institute of Criminology.

Wainaina, B. (2005) http://www.granta.com/Magazine/92/How-to-Write-about-Africa/Page-1.

Welsh, D. (1996) 'Ethnicity in sub-Saharan Africa', *International Affairs*, 72(2): 477–91.

Wessells, M. (2006) *Child Soldiers: From Violence to Protection*, Cambridge, MA: Harvard University Press.

Westin, A. (2000) *Best Practices for Television Journalists*, Arlington, TX: Freedom Forum.

Whitehead, N. L. (2004) 'Introduction: cultures, conflicts, and the poetics of violent practice', in N. L. Whitehead (ed.), *Violence*, Santa Fe, NM/Oxford: School of American Research Press/James Currey.

Williams, P. and M. Scharf (2002) *Peace with Justice? War Crimes and Accountability in the Former Yugoslavia*, Oxford: Rowland & Littlefield.

Winans, E. (1992) 'Hyenas on the border', in C. Nordstrom and J. Martin (eds), *The Paths to Domination, Resistance and Terror*. Berkeley: University of California Press.

Wlodarczyk, N. (2004) 'Witchcraft, war and rationality: the strategic functions of traditional religion in contemporary African warfare', Quebec: ISA Conference.

Wohlgemuth, L. (2002) *The Nordic Countries and Africa, Old and New Relations*, Uppsala: Nordic Africa Institute.

Woodward, P. (1991) 'Uganda and southern Sudan 1986–9: new regimes and peripheral politics', in H. B. Hansen and M. Twaddle (eds), *Changing Uganda: The dilemmas of structural adjustment and revolutionary change*, London/Kampala/Nairobi: James Currey/Fountain Press/Ohio University Press/Heinemann Kenya.

World Bank (1998) 'The World Bank experience with post conflict reconstruction: Uganda case study', Washington, DC: World Bank.

— (1999) 'The challenge of Ugandan reconstruction 1986–98', Washington, DC: World Bank.

— (2000) 'Uganda: post conflict reconstruction', Washington, DC: World Bank.

— (2004) 'Uganda: from conflict to sustained growth and deep reductions in poverty', Washington, DC: World Bank.

— (2005a) 'Republic of Uganda cotton subsector development project (Credit 2609) and agricultural research and training project (Credit 2446)', Washington, DC: World Bank.

— (2005b) 'Uganda policy options for increasing crop productivity and reducing soil nutrient depletion and poverty', Report no. 32971-UG, Washington, DC: World Bank.

— (2006a) 'Uganda beyond recovery: investment and behavior change for growth', Country Economic Memorandum, Washington, DC: World Bank.

— (2006b) 'Civil society and peacebuilding. Potential, limitations and critical factors', Report no. 36445-GLB, Washington, DC: Social Development Department, Sustainable Development Network, World Bank.

— (2007) 'World Development Indicators database, Uganda data profile', Washington, DC: World Bank.

Young, A. (1995) *The Harmony of Illusions. Inventing Post-Traumatic Stress Disorder*, Princeton, NJ: Princeton University Press.

Zartman, W. and S. Touval (2007) 'International mediation', in C. A. Crocker et al. (eds), *Leashing the Dogs of War: Conflict Management in a Divided World*, Washington, DC: US Institute of Peace Press.

Zolo, D. (2004) 'Peace through criminal law?', *Journal of International Criminal Justice*, 2.

Notes on the contributors

Jeannie Annan is the director of research and evaluation at the International Rescue Committee and a visiting scientist at Harvard University's FXB Center for Health and Human Rights. She holds a PhD in counselling psychology from Indiana University at Bloomington and completed post-doctoral fellowships at the NYU School of Medicine and Yale University School of Public Health. Dr Annan's research examines the long-term impacts of war and violence on mental health and relationships, with a particular focus on identifying the individual, family and environmental factors that mitigate the worst effects of violence. She is also engaged in the assessment and evaluation of prevention and response programmes for children, youth and women affected by violence. Dr Annan has worked in northern Uganda since 1999 on mental health programmes and research, and co-directed the Survey of War Affected Youth in northern Uganda.

Ronald R. Atkinson teaches African history and is director of African studies at the University of South Carolina, where he has won numerous teaching awards. He has lived and worked in Kenya, Uganda, Ghana and South Africa. Both his earliest and his current major focus of research and writing is the Acholi region and people in northern Uganda. He is the author of *The Roots of Ethnicity: The Origins of the Acholi of Uganda* (1999), a new edition of which, with an afterword on the last thirty years, will be out in 2010; he co-wrote *Traditional Ways of Coping in Acholi: Cultural Provisions for Reconciliation and Healing from War* (2006); and he is author or co-author of numerous articles on Acholi history and contemporary affairs, including the recently published 'From Uganda to Congo and Beyond: Pursuing the Lord's Resistance Army' (International Peace Institute, December 2009). In addition, for nearly seven years during the political transition from apartheid in South Africa, he assisted in establishing and administering a programme to train black educational leaders, helped to develop and co-edited a multi-volume set of materials for that programme, and wrote numerous articles on the topic.

Christopher Blattman is an assistant professor of political science and economics at Yale University and a fellow at the Center for Global Development, the Financial Access Initiative, Innovations for Poverty Action, and the International Growth Centre. He holds a PhD in economics from the University of California at Berkeley and a master's in public administration and international development from Harvard University. Dr Blattman's research examines the causes and consequences of violence and civil war, post-conflict economic recovery, and youth employment and social stability. He is presently conducting randomized evaluations of post-conflict economic development and conflict resolution programmes in Liberia and northern Uganda. He also studies the long-term impacts of factory labour on poverty and political development, particularly in Ethiopia. Dr Blattman co-founded and directed the Survey of War Affected Youth in northern Uganda. He has also worked in Kenya and southern India.

Adam Branch is assistant professor of political science at San Diego State University. He earned a PhD in political science from Columbia University and his undergraduate degree from Harvard University. His work has examined the politics of Western intervention into internal armed conflict in Africa, particularly in Uganda. Recently, he has focused on the politics and repercussions of the International Criminal Court's intervention into Uganda's civil war. He has published widely in political science and international studies journals and is currently finishing a book on human rights intervention.

Matthew Brubacher currently works as a political affairs officer in the DDRRR (Disarmament, Demobilization, Repatriation, Reinsertion and Reintegration) section of MONUC, the UN Mission in the Congo, where he is responsible for the DDRRR team in the Haut Uele territory, repatriating LRA combatants to their countries of origin as well as assisting in efforts to repatriate other foreign armed groups in the Kivus. From 2004 to 2009, Mr Brubacher worked as an analyst and international cooperation adviser in the International Criminal Court on the LRA investigation, including efforts to arrest the five (now three) LRA members wanted by the ICC. Prior to the ICC, Mr Brubacher worked in the West Bank for three years as a political adviser to the Palestinian Liberation Organization, and has also worked for various human rights organizations.

Sverker Finnström is associate professor of cultural anthropology. Starting in 1997, he has conducted recurrent fieldwork in Acholiland with a focus on young adults living in the immediate shadows of civil war.

Besides his articles, popular and academic, he has authored *Living with Bad Surroundings: War, History, and Everyday Moments in Northern Uganda* (2008), for which he received the 2009 Margaret Mead Award. He divides his time between the Department of Social Anthropology, Stockholm University, where he teaches, and the Hugo Valentin Centre, Uppsala University, where he is a researcher in political violence and genocide studies.

Ronald Iya is the cultural leader for the Madi people of Uganda (Adjumani and Moyo). He participated in peace talks with the LRA five times in 2007 and 2008, and twice had face-to-face talks with Joseph Kony, including Kony's final meeting before Operation Lightning Thunder. He is also chair of the Adjumani land board, and has worked with a wide variety of international aid organizations and research groups.

Gerd Junne holds the chair in international relations at the University of Amsterdam, the Netherlands. After studying political science, law and economics in Berlin and Geneva, he worked at different German universities, and for several UN agencies and Dutch ministries. He is on the board of The Network University (TNU), which offers international online programmes on conflict transformation, and of the International Institute of Communication and Development (IICD).

Ben Mergelsberg has recently graduated from the University of Oxford. He has spent prolonged periods living and researching in displacement camps in northern Uganda, and is currently working as a documentary filmmaker in Berlin.

Andrew Mwenda is a well-known Ugandan journalist with a strong reputation for rigorous reporting. He has been the political editor of the *Monitor*, the leading independent Ugandan newspaper, and presenter of *Andrew Mwenda Live* on the KFM radio station. In 2005, he was among sixteen senior journalists invited by the British government to meet then prime minister Tony Blair to discuss the report of the Commission for Africa. He is a leading sceptic about the usefulness of aid to Africa, and has frequently criticized the policies and practices of President Museveni's government.

Sandrine Perrot is a senior research fellow at the Centre for International Research (CERI) at Sciences-Po (Paris). She holds a PhD in political science (2003) from the Institut d'Etudes Politiques (IEP) of Bordeaux

(Centre d'Etudes d'Afrique Noire – CEAN). She joined CERI after a two-year postdoctoral fellowship at CERIUM (Centre for International Studies at the Université de Montréal). Dr Perrot specializes in Uganda and in armed conflicts and violent phenomena in sub-Saharan Africa. She has worked extensively on northern Uganda and the Lord's Resistance Army. Her current research focuses on militias and paramilitary groups. Her PhD will be published soon under the title *La réversibilité du chaos?: Le processus de reconstruction d'un ordre politique dans l'Ouganda de Yoweri Museveni*. She has written numerous journal articles and contributions to edited volumes. She is also the co-director of Research in Question, a member of the editorial board of *Politique africaine* and *Critique Internationale*, an associate researcher at the Centre d'Etudes des Mondes Africains and a visiting researcher at McGill University (Montreal) and the francophone network on peace operations (Réseau des Opérations de Paix – ROP).

Holly Porter and *Frederick Laker* are doctoral candidates at the London School of Economics and Political Science

Mareike Schomerus is currently an LSE fellow at the Development Studies Institute of the London School of Economics (LSE). Having worked extensively in southern Sudan and northern Uganda, she has published on human security, violent conflict and peace, humanitarian aid and small arms. She has also conducted research projects for UNICEF, Human Rights Watch, the Small Arms Survey, DfID, USAID and Conciliation Resources. Before returning to academia, Mareike trained as a journalist at Columbia University. She worked for many years and in many countries as a broadcaster for ARD, the BBC, Arte and the Discovery Channel, among others, covering a diverse range of stories from the Olympic Games to modern-day slavery.

Simon Simonse is senior adviser at Pax Christi, and has worked on aspects of peace and conciliation in northern Uganda for over a decade. He is also co-editor of *Conflict, Age and Power in North East Africa* (1998) and author of *Kings of Disaster: Dualism, Centralism and the Scapegoat King in Southeastern Sudan* (1992).

Kristof Titeca is a postdoctoral fellow from the Research Foundation – Flanders (FWO), based at the Institute of Policy Development and Management (University of Antwerp). He is interested in issues of conflict, cross-border trade, rebel governance and northern Uganda. His PhD

(Conflict Research Group, Ghent University) dealt with issues of cross-border trade and civil society in north-western Uganda. He has published in journals such as *World Development, Journal of Modern African Studies, Studies in Conflict and Terrorism* and *Politique Africaine*.

Willemijn Verkoren is assistant professor at the Centre for International Conflict Analysis and Management (CICAM) of the Radboud University Nijmegen, the Netherlands. At the University of Amsterdam she obtained master's degrees in history and international relations and a PhD degree in international development studies. Willemijn specializes in conflict analysis; the role of civil society in peace processes; processes of democratization, state-building and development; and the role of knowledge and networking in all of this. Her publications include the books *Postconflict Development: Meeting New Challenges* (2005, co-edited with Gerd Junne) and *The Owl and the Dove: Knowledge Stategies to Improve the Peacebuilding Practice of Local Non-Governmental Organisations* (2008).

Index

abductees: initiation of, 65; remuneration of, 146; rules and regulations for, 63

abduction, 10, 20, 131, 179, 222, 272, 274, 277, 285; duration period of, 142, 147–8; escape from *see* escape from abduction; legitimacy of, 169; nature and causes of, 132–55; of adolescents, 134 (effectiveness of, 144–5; reasons for, 145–6); of children, 10, 15, 18, 19, 69, 75, 79, 116, 118–20, 138, 148, 189, 210, 248, 286; of girls, 13; provision of material incentives, 140, 145; scale and incidence of, 134–9; statistics for, 106, 269, 286

'Aboke girls', abduction of, 13

Abudema, Bok, 182

Acana II, Rwot David, 18, 181, 183, 245, 249, 260

accountability, 219, 235, 243, 251, 258, 263–4; hybrid, dilemmas of, 254–7; tension with peace, 264–6

Acellam, Caesar, 183

Acholi language, 157

Acholi people, 2, 6, 7, 8, 10, 12, 28, 30, 31, 77, 78, 120, 121, 122, 203, 272; crisis of, 25, 26; discourse of cleansing of, 41, 42; displacement of, 283; division of, 4; emergence of petty-bourgeoisie among, 27–8; ethnic favouritism towards, 29; ethnicity of, 32, 34, 36–7, 40; excluded from power, 33, 43; imprisonment of, 14; leaders invited to The Hague, 272; middle class, 44; stereotypes of, 261; traditions of, invention of, 242–61

Acholi Pii camp, killings in, 55

Acholikanzo, Lieutenant, 179

Acholiland, political situation in, 25–44

Addis Ababa agreement (1972), 5

adolescents: as soldiers (availability of, as soldiers, 146–7; remuneration of, 147; retention of, 147–50); given guns, 153; theory of behaviour of, 153 *see also* abduction, of adolescents

Afako, Barney, 248

Africa Command of USA (AFRICOM), 1, 201, 279, 286–7

African Union (AU), Somalia mission, 202

Agency for Cooperation and Research in Development (Acord), 247

Agreement on Accountability and Reconciliation, 243, 251, 258

aid: cutting of, 201; dependence on, 51; foreign, 49, 50, 54, 55; politics of, 45–58; through budget support, 202

aid donors, 16, 187, 190, 194, 201; blaming of, 196; competition between, 197; evolution of, 191–3; impossibility of consensus between, 200; lack of cohesion of, 51, 188; lenient attitudes of, 204; pressure from, 192

AIDS *see* HIV/AIDS

Aimani, Swaib, 179

ajwaka, 8, 9, 66, 69, 161, 168, 254, 260

Akandwanaho, Caleb (Salim Saleh), 218, 233–4

Alit, Santo, 111

Allen, Tim, 36, 77, 95–6, 97

American Psychiatric Association, *Diagnostic and Statistical Manual of Mental Disorders*, 173

amnesty, 15, 16, 39, 83, 141, 227, 235, 243, 250, 258, 259; opposition to, 83–4

Amnesty Act (2002), 13–14

angara fish, 178

Anglo-Egyptian Condominium of the Sudan, 4

fighters 'with open eyes', 172
food, 182; prices of, 283; security issue, 203; supplies of, 181 (aid supplies, 166)
Forces Armées de la République Démocratique du Congo (FARDC), 221
forgiveness, meaning of, 250–1
France, 199
Francis, Owot, 157, 161–2, 164, 165, 167–8, 172
fund-raising for children, 155

gacaca courts, 255
Garamba, 178, 179, 183, 275; LRA base in, 207, 221, 274, 277
Garang di Mabior, John, 114, 208; death of, 5, 208
George, Abonga, 157, 159, 161, 165, 174
Germany, 191
ghost soldiers, 52; salaries of, 48
Gingyera-Pinyewa, A. G. G., 30
gomo tong ritual, 246
Government of Southern Sudan (GoSS), 56–7, 101, 205, 208–14, 229, 239; mediation of Juba talks, 216–17; Peace Secretariat, 198; relations with LRA, 98, 209, 210, 213, 275; secession demand in, 6
grassroots communities, involvement of, in peace negotiations, 224
Green, Matthew, 74
group identity, establishment of, 169
Group of Friends of Northern Uganda, 193
guilt, individual, 263
Gulu, 3, 8, 32, 33, 35, 40, 75, 177, 187, 190, 191, 244, 249, 279, 280, 281; as NGO city, 189; radio station, 15
guns, forbidden to be carried, 72
Gusco, 165

Hawking, Stephen, A Brief History of Time, 108
healthcare, 48, 81–2, 208, 282
heart of darkness cliché, 93, 107
HIV/AIDS, 120; awareness campaigns, 256; fight against, 202; pandemic, 47–8
Holmes, John, 202

Holy Spirit, 165
Holy Spirit Mobile Forces (HSMF), 8, 60, 61, 66, 67, 71, 72, 77, 80, 257
Holy Spirit Movement (HSM), 7–9, 25, 36–8, 42, 49; disintegration of, 37
hotel bills, payment of, 238
human rights, 86
Human Rights Watch, 85, 115, 192
humanitarian assistance: figures for, 189–90; threat of withdrawal of, 58
humanitarian interventions, 43, 55, 56, 198, 279
humanitarian workers, targeting of, 194

Idi Amin, 6, 26, 45, 78, 85; coup by, 29; disarmament under, 33
IKV Pax Christi organization, 101, 218; involvement in Juba peace talks, 223–41; transparency, 237
immunity from prosecution, 264
indoctrination of abductees, effectiveness of, 142–4
inflation, 46, 48, 50
initiation rituals of LRA, 10, 63, 141–2, 168
'interests of justice' criterion, 267–8
internal displacement (IDP) camps, 14–15, 20, 42, 45, 52, 58, 157–8, 170, 219, 221, 235, 249, 251, 269; Camp Phase-Out Guidelines, 282; conditions in, 164, 189; killings in, 55; mortality rates in, 56, 192; protection strategy for, 275; UN report on, 195; visit by Jan Egeland, 187–8 see also Barlonyo camp and Pabbo camp
internally displaced persons (IDPs), 196; growing numbers of, 188; in Sudan, 199; leaving camps, 279; return of, 201
International Alert Kacoke Madit meeting, 245
International Court of Justice (ICJ), 195
International Criminal Court (ICC), 2, 75, 95, 96, 108, 184, 194, 242–4, 249; dismissed as neocolonialist, 259; investigation of LRA, 262–77; Kony's view of, 182; Office of the Prosecutor (OTP), 267–72 (Ugandan investigation team, 270); Pre-Trial

142; spiritual powers of, 70; travel documents provided for, 226; video of meeting with Pax Christi, 230 *see also* Machar, Riek, meets with Kony

Laden, Osama bin, 13
Lakwena, a spirit, 8
Lakwena, Alice *see* Auma, Alice
land, access to, 282–3
Langi people, 6, 7, 28, 30, 37, 249, 251, 256, 272; ethnic favouritism towards, 29 *see also* Lango
Lango, 179, 207 *see also* Langi people
languages, Kony's use of, 125
lineage-based authorities, 27, 28, 36, 38, 43, 44
Liu Institute for Global Issues, 248
loads, carrying of, 151; by children, 153
Local Defence Units (LDUs), 37, 39–40
Lokoya, Severino, 9
Lomo, Zachary, 248
loot and looting, 34, 48, 52, 139, 140, 147, 158, 179, 237; forbidden, 35
Lord's Resistance Army (LRA), 5, 37, 45–58, 257; activity of, during ICC investigation, 272–7; and Joseph Kony, 9–10; and Juba peace talks, 87–8; as Christian fundamentalist, 81, 84, 123, 122; attacks on SPLA, 18; belief system of, 65; command and control in, 139–44; defection of delegation members from, 272–4, 276; fluidity of organization of, 154; holy rules of, 160; ICC investigation of, 262–77; joint force to eliminate, 215; labelled terrorist organization, 14, 58, 83, 190, 206; life within, 162–3; major commanders killed, 274; manifestos of, 76, 78, 83, 84–6, 115 (existence of, denied, 85); media view of, 74–89; moves to Central African Republic, 276; moves to Congo, 274; nature and causes of abduction, 132–55; political utility of, 54; politics of, 81, 82, 133, 154; punishments by commanders, 160; reasons for participation in Juba negotiation, 216; reprisals against civilians, 201; rules and regulations of, 165; seen as chaotic gang, 71;

seen as criminal, 195, 204; seen as religious lunatics, 59; spiritual order of, 12, 59–73; strike against, 1; Sudanese support for, 12, 49, 203, 204, 205–6; symbol of, 104; talks with Betty Bigombe, 272; transition into, 167–9; violence of, 25–44, 49, 70, 78, 188 (analysis of, 169–70; as means of control, 140; roots of, 25–44); war of, exported, 284–8 *see also* International Criminal Court, warrants issued for LRA leaders *and* spirit beliefs and practices of LRA
Lord's Resistance Movement/Army (LRM/A), 84, 87
Lukwiya, Raska, 271; death of, 214
Luwala, Rwot Jimmy, 183
Luwero triangle, 30–1
Lwo speakers, 33, 122, 161

Machar Teny Dhurgon, Riek, 5, 17, 18, 102, 108, 119, 129, 180, 181, 197, 209, 212, 215, 216, 217, 218, 220, 229, 231, 232, 233, 236; gives money to Kony, 212–13; joint communiqué with Joaquim Chissano, 221; meets with Kony, 98, 101, 103–4, 212–13; meets with Kony and Otti, 212–13
Madi Cultural Institution, 177–84
Madi people, 249, 251, 272
magical protection from bullets, 142
Maguru, Ruhinda, 234
Mamdani, Mahmood, 259
Mao, Norbert, 13, 82
Maridi, attack on, 285
Mars, Veronica, 80
Matiep Nhial, Paulino, 209
mato oput reconciliation ritual, 16, 184, 244–9, 257, 259, 260–1
Matsanga, David, 180, 182, 183, 219, 220, 288
Mayi-Mayi groups, 72
Mbabazi, Amama, 212
Médecins Sans Frontières (MSF), 15
medicalization of social problems, 175, 176
military equipment, procurement of, 50, 52
Milosevic, Slobodan, 266
mineral resources, of Acholi, 121